Quality Management for Competitive Advantage in Global Markets

José Manuel Saiz-Álvarez
Universidad Católica de Santiago de Guayaquil, Ecuador & Universidad Autónoma de Manizales, Colombia & CEIEF-Universidad de Santiago de Chile, Chile

Beatriz Olalla-Caballero
Universidad Pontificia de Salamanca, Spain

IGI Global
PUBLISHER of TIMELY KNOWLEDGE

A volume in the Advances in Business Strategy and Competitive Advantage (ABSCA) Book Series

Published in the United States of America by
IGI Global
Business Science Reference (an imprint of IGI Global)
701 E. Chocolate Avenue
Hershey PA, USA 17033
Tel: 717-533-8845
Fax: 717-533-8661
E-mail: cust@igi-global.com
Web site: http://www.igi-global.com

Library of Congress Cataloging-in-Publication Data

Names: Sáiz-Álvarez, José Manuel, editor. | Olalla-Caballero, Beatriz, 1978- editor.
Title: Quality management for competitive advantage in global markets / José Manuel Saiz-Álvarez and Beatriz Olalla-Caballero, editors.
Description: Hershey : Business Science Reference, 2020. | Includes bibliographical references and index. | Summary: "This book discusses the importance of quality practices and global market practices. With research that allows practitioners to improve their understanding of the strategic role of quality in the information and knowledge society, it focuses on describing a global economy formed by networks, organizations, teams, workgroups, information systems, and finally, actors in networked environment"-- Provided by publisher.
Identifiers: LCCN 2020005546 (print) | LCCN 2020005547 (ebook) | ISBN 9781799850366 (hardcover) | ISBN 9781799850373 (ebook)
Subjects: LCSH: Total quality management. | Competition. | International economic relations.
Classification: LCC HD62.15 .H36 2020 (print) | LCC HD62.15 (ebook) | DDC 658.4/013--dc23
LC record available at https://lccn.loc.gov/2020005546
LC ebook record available at https://lccn.loc.gov/2020005547

This book is published in the IGI Global book series Advances in Business Strategy and Competitive Advantage (ABSCA) (ISSN: 2327-3429; eISSN: 2327-3437)

British Cataloguing in Publication Data
A Cataloguing in Publication record for this book is available from the British Library.

Advances in Business Strategy and Competitive Advantage (ABSCA) Book Series

Patricia Ordóñez de Pablos
Universidad de Oviedo, Spain

ISSN:2327-3429
EISSN:2327-3437

Mission

Business entities are constantly seeking new ways through which to gain advantage over their competitors and strengthen their position within the business environment. With competition at an all-time high due to technological advancements allowing for competition on a global scale, firms continue to seek new ways through which to improve and strengthen their business processes, procedures, and profitability.

The **Advances in Business Strategy and Competitive Advantage (ABSCA) Book Series** is a timely series responding to the high demand for state-of-the-art research on how business strategies are created, implemented and re-designed to meet the demands of globalized competitive markets. With a focus on local and global challenges, business opportunities and the needs of society, the **ABSCA** encourages scientific discourse on doing business and managing information technologies for the creation of sustainable competitive advantage.

Coverage

- Innovation Strategy
- Value Chain
- Strategy Performance Management
- Foreign Investment Decision Process
- Joint Ventures
- Entrepreneurship & Innovation
- Differentiation Strategy
- Adaptive Enterprise
- Tacit Knowledge
- Outsourcing

IGI Global is currently accepting manuscripts for publication within this series. To submit a proposal for a volume in this series, please contact our Acquisition Editors at Acquisitions@igi-global.com or visit: http://www.igi-global.com/publish/.

The Advances in Business Strategy and Competitive Advantage (ABSCA) Book Series (ISSN 2327-3429) is published by IGI Global, 701 E. Chocolate Avenue, Hershey, PA 17033-1240, USA, www.igi-global.com. This series is composed of titles available for purchase individually; each title is edited to be contextually exclusive from any other title within the series. For pricing and ordering information please visit http://www.igi-global.com/book-series/advances-business-strategy-competitive-advantage/73672. Postmaster: Send all address changes to above address.

Titles in this Series

For a list of additional titles in this series, please visit: http://www.igi-global.com/book-series/advances-business-strategy-competitive-advantage/73672

Reshaping Entrepreneurship Education With Strategy and Innovation
Ayansola Olatunji Ayandibu (University of Zululand, South Africa)
Business Science Reference • © 2021 • 422pp • H/C (ISBN: 9781799831716) • US $205.00

Emerging Business and Trade Opportunities Between Oceania and Asia
Angus Hooke (Australian Institute of Higher Education, Australia) Hardik Vachharajani (Crown Institute of Higher Education, Australia) Harpreet Kaur (Australian Institute of Higher Education, Australia) and Kevin E. Dow (University of Auckland, New Zealand)
Business Science Reference • © 2021 • 325pp • H/C (ISBN: 9781799841265) • US $195.00

Global Challenges and Strategic Disruptors in Asian Businesses and Economies
Patricia Ordóñez de Pablos (The University of Oviedo, Spain) and Miltiadis D. Lytras (American College of Greece, Greece & Effat University, Saudi Arabia)
Business Science Reference • © 2021 • 358pp • H/C (ISBN: 9781799847878) • US $195.00

Global Business Leadership Development for the Fourth Industrial Revolution
Peter Smith (The Leadership Alliance Inc., Canada) and Tom Cockburn (Center for Dynamic Leadership Models in Global Business, Canada)
Business Science Reference • © 2021 • 425pp • H/C (ISBN: 9781799848615) • US $195.00

Advanced Models and Tools for Effective Decision Making Under Uncertainty and Risk Contexts
Vicente González-Prida (University of Seville, Spain & UNED, Spain) and María Carmen Carnero (University of Castilla-La Mancha, Spain)
Business Science Reference • © 2021 • 423pp • H/C (ISBN: 9781799832461) • US $195.00

Knowledge Management for Corporate Social Responsibility
Gregorio Martín-de Castro (Complutense University of Madrid, Spain) and Jaime González-Masip (Rey Juan Carlos University, Spain)
Business Science Reference • © 2021 • 388pp • H/C (ISBN: 9781799848332) • US $195.00

Applications of Soft Systems Methodology for Organizational Change
Maryam Ebrahimi (Independent Researcher, Germany)
Business Science Reference • © 2021 • 236pp • H/C (ISBN: 9781799845041) • US $195.00

IGI Global
PUBLISHER of TIMELY KNOWLEDGE

701 East Chocolate Avenue, Hershey, PA 17033, USA
Tel: 717-533-8845 x100 • Fax: 717-533-8661
E-Mail: cust@igi-global.com • www.igi-global.com

Table of Contents

Detailed Table of Contents

In today's business environment, global competition, which has gained momentum with the increase of consumers' quality awareness and consequently, their expectations, has led to the rise of quality management practices by companies. Hence, companies, with the aim of satisfying the needs and wants of customers and thereby attaining competitive advantage, see the inclusion of quality management in the managerial process as a necessity, and they develop optimal performance criteria for such management. In this context, researchers have investigated the effects of quality management applications on innovation performance, production performance, marketing performance, and financial performance of the organization. The empirical research conducted in the last 10 years investigating the relationship between quality management practices and firm performance revealed a significant positive relationship between quality management practices and firm performance.

This chapter gives an overview of the importance of the quality as a whole in a company, considering it moves in an environment not only determined by the velocity of change of the technologies but also by the cultural change suffered in recent years. It has been proposed a new framework where new factors have to be analyzed to achieve a company pioneer and leader in the industry. Also, it explains all the benefits of doing it and how it will affect the performance of the staff, in the vision of clients and users, and the financial results of the firm. In conclusion, all these advantages will have a great benefit to society.

Preface

Quality management is crucial for firms to achieve competitive advantage in a globalized business world. By having a greater choice, thanks to ICTs (Information and Communication Technologies), consumers have become more demanding in aspects related to the quality of the products and services they buy, making the business competition even stronger as organizations increase their internationalization process. This greater demand from consumers has accelerated with ICTs because prospective clients have more information at their disposal to make decisions.

But as companies develop, they run the risk of generating X-inefficiencies that create bottlenecks in the organization and reduce the speed of decision-making. Given the high competitiveness that exists in the business world, it is essential to solving problems quickly, as well as to prevent them from remaining in the company for a long time to avoid them from becoming structural. Therefore, to eliminate this problem, it is essential to digitize organizations, public and private, so that information flows quickly to force bottlenecks to disappear because they impede a rapid resolution of issues and problems in the organization.

It is essential in competitive environments to achieve processes based on quality processes certified by international organizations. International businesses are now shifting from the North Atlantic to the Pacific Ocean, which will cause a radical swift in the economies involved. This changing process accelerated with the arrival of smart territories due to the Internet (Palma-Ruiz, Saiz-Alvarez, & Herrero-Crespo, 2019). Defined by high speed (1Gbps), low power necessity, and low latency (1ms or less), for mass IoT (Internet of Things), touch Internet, and robotics, the arrival of 5G, led by China and Europe, will accelerate the communication process around the planet, which will, in turn, influence customers and organizations. So, it is vital to achieving greater corporate transparency in procedures, as well as to achieve high standards of quality.

In this context, quality takes on fundamental importance in organizations, especially in the most internationalized companies and in those organizations competing in purple and red oceans, seas, and lakes. In the business world, blue oceans are challenging to be discovered, and, if they are found, they last for a short time. This is why there are so few brand-new unicorns in today's business world. These firms are defined by having a particular and specialized market niche for mass consumption and are determined, in turn, by quality management.

Quality management directly links to the competitive advantages achieved by firms, as it as a tool to attract stakeholders. Internal and external stakeholders strive for their EBITDA (Earnings before Interest, Taxes, Depreciation, and Amortization) to survive and grow in hostile business environments to increase their corporate reputation for sustainable business growth. Only companies that achieve high levels of quality in their products and services offered to the market will have the possibility of becoming leaders within their industries. Leadership positions that will give the company the necessary financial stability in the long term to increase goodwill. That is why achieving sustainable quality management is one of the different ways to gain competitive advantages other than setting low prices, the existence of captive markets, and location advantages.

The health and economic crisis generated by COVID19 is changing the global geopolitical and economic landscape where competitive advantages linked to technology and quality are playing an increasingly significant role. Especially private organizations are living in a world of economic globalization where large corporations have global strategies and are forced to continually tropicalize their products and services, as the customs and consumption habits of each stakeholder are different in each country. But this process of tropicalization is not so intense in aspects related to quality, as stakeholders assume that quality is maximized regardless of the market where that product, project, or service is sold.

Tropicalization allows companies to maximize their EBITDA by selling their products and services based on the end customer wants. These modifications to products and services must be tiny if firms wish not to incur high costs that lead to financial losses. Therefore, products and services endowed with good quality management avoid wasting resources and guarantee the provision of goods and services to the market in a sustainable way over time.

As a result, the world's captive markets are increasingly smaller, isolated, and more dispersed, as they are small market niches characterized by the use of barter, the minimal purchasing power of their consumers, and by being far away from the main international markets. Given these traits, these captive markets are mainly located in particular regions and nations situated in the African continent.

Achieving proper quality management also affects environmental sustainability positively. As a result, the combination of firms melting private-public collaboration and society accomplishes a circular economy (Saiz-Alvarez, 2020). When a country reaches the circular economy, the level of citizens' well-being increases. As they consume, they pressure companies to meet the sustainability and quality requirements necessary to maintain competitive advantages. The importance of attaining this circular economy is even more crucial in those countries characterized by high polluting emissions, which affects the entire planet.

As a result, the competitive advantages of companies strengthen organizations and accelerate economic growth. An ongoing process is defined by continuous and constant innovation if the organization wishes to achieve, or maintain, leadership positions over time. Although large companies are very different in their organization, and it also happens with decision-making and development strategies in startups, micro-companies, and SMEs, the leading companies head the way for the rest of the organizations due to imitation effect. The imitation effect encourages small organizations to grow and compete in hostile environments, even knowing that their competitive advantages are lower in relative terms than those obtained by leading companies. This business behavior commonly happens in family firms (Saiz-Alvarez & Palma-Ruiz, 2019), in both developing and developed countries.

Consequently, the target audience of this book is made up of researchers, lecturers, professors, practitioners, and anyone interested in these topics. Researchers will find cutting-edge research on the issues analyzed in the chapters that make up the handbook. Lecturers and professors will also find useful this handbook, who can use this book as a reference and reference book in their daily work. Practitioners will be able to get ideas on the topics of interest. Any other reader interested in these topics has at your disposal ideas in these chapters that can be applied to their professional and personal life.

ORGANIZATION OF THE BOOK

The book is divided into two sections. The first section (Chapters 1-6) focuses on different aspects related to quality, while the second section (Chapters 7-13) is devoted to several topics linked to increasing the competitive advantage of firms.

Regarding Section 1, Chapter 1 entitled "The Role of Quality Management in Firm Performance," and written by Dr. Özgür Atılgan, from İstanbul Kültür Üniversitesi (Turkey), affirms that the combination of the business environment, global competition, and consumers' quality awareness has forced firms to introduce quality management practices to satisfy the needs and wants of customers and thereby attaining competitive advantage through innovation. According to this author, the empirical research conducted in the last decade to observe the relationship between quality management practices and firm performance revealed a significant positive relationship between quality management practices and firm performance.

This analysis related to quality continues in Chapter 2, called "Enterprise Quality Perception in a Changing Environment," and written by M.Sc. Montserrat Mata-Fernández, from Universidad de Deusto (Spain) who gives an overview of the importance of the quality in firms due to the combination of technology and cultural change. In this chapter, the author proposes a new framework where new quality-related factors must be analyzed to achieve leadership and how they affect staff performance and financial results on clients and users.

These quality-related issues are complemented in Chapter 3, titled "Quality Management Principles for Entrepreneurial Sustainability," and written by Prof. Neeta Baporikar, from Namibia University of Science and Technology (Namibia) and University of Pune (India), who assures that, although quality definitions have been altered with the transition of time, needs, and demands, its relationship with customer satisfaction is weak. For total quality management (TQM) to be successful, it is needed a transformational preference to produce a substantial advancement culture on quality service for achieving a consistent and sustainable competitive advantage. Adopting an exploratory approach, the author critically examines the underlying principles of quality management for entrepreneurial sustainability.

Quality management can also be analyzed through the application of continuous quality improvement (CQI). In this respect, in Chapter 4, titled "A New Continuous Quality Improvement Vision for a Changing Technological Market," and written by Dr. Beatriz Olalla-Caballero, Universidad Pontificia de Salamanca (Spain), and M.Sc. Montserrat Mata-Fernández, Universidad de Deusto (Spain), the authors propose how the application of a continuous quality improvement (CQI) model is an essential tool for those IT (Information Technology) firms that want to succeed in competitive and disruptive markets. A suitable CQI model or framework can help a firm to follow-up the quality level of products, projects, or services, to carry out actions focused on developing agile, immediate, and disruptive responses to satisfy stakeholders.

Quality is also essential in the primary sector, as shown in Chapter 5, named "Extended Quality Processes in Internationalized Agro-Industrial, Rural Collaborative Economy: Capital Accumulation and the Association of Small Farmers," and written by Dr. Uriel Hitamar Castillo-Nazareno, Prof. Jessica Silvana Matute-Petroche, and Dr. María Teresa Alcívar-Avilés, all from Universidad Católica de Santiago de Guayaquil (Ecuador). These authors affirm that strengthening the primary sector is one of the main challenges of Ecuador to overcome poverty. In this regard, these authors propose a collaborative model endowed with comprehensive quality processes for competing in the global market. To support their proposal, they apply this model in two cooperatives of the Ecuadorian province of Chimborazo.

Based on these elements, this chapter proposes a theoretical and technical cooperative model to achieve efficiency in the internationalization process of the rural sector in Ecuador.

Also, quality has a crucial role in the health services, as shown in Chapter 6, entitled "Health Services Delivery and Satisfaction," and written by Mr. Fatih Altan, from University of Erciyes (Turkey), Dr. Aykut Ekiyor, from University of Ankara Haci Bayram Veli (Turkey), and Prof. Demet Unalan, from University of Erciyes (Turkey). Health services are those remedies applied to ensure health recovery or to be adapted to the environment. The authors conclude that satisfaction is one of the critical determinants of quality in health services, and it is achieved with a good health personnel-patient interaction, trust in a health institution, low fees for the service received, physical facilities of the health institution, and nutrition services.

When firms assure sustainable quality for the products and services offered in the market and entrepreneurship, companies achieve competitive advantages. In this respect, Section 2, based on competitive advantage, deals with different aspects of this topic. In Chapter 7, titled "From Entrepreneurial Intentions to Entrepreneurial Behavior: The Role of Institutional Factors," and written by Dr. Sebastian Aparicio, from Durham University (UK), and Dr. Andreu Turro, Dr. Maria Noguera, and Prof. David Urbano, all from Universitat Autònoma de Barcelona, Catalonia (Spain), these authors affirm that although there is abundant literature on entrepreneurial intentions and entrepreneurial behavior, there is still a gap on those factors enabling the pass from purpose to action. Motivated by this breach, this chapter assesses the extent to which the determinants of entrepreneurial intention also affect subsequent entrepreneurial behavior, using an institutional approach as a theoretical framework and simultaneous equations as a statistical tool. The authors find that opportunity identification, business skills, and entrepreneurs' status foster entrepreneurship.

The next chapter analyzes how competitive advantages can also be achieved easily in a blue ocean, as it is seaside tourism in China. This relationship is examined in Chapter 8, entitled "The Blue Economy and Its Long-Term Competitive Advantage: An Examination of China's Coastal Tourism," and written by Haoming Zhang, Dr. Rob Kim Marjerison, and Dr. Yuxi Zhao, all from Wenzhou-Kean University (China). This chapter seeks to determine whether China's coastal tourism industry can remain competitive in the long run under the blue economy ideology. Current literature claims that when the ocean becomes over-commercialized by the tourism industry, it can potentially lose its advantages to attract tourists. The authors survey both coastal tourists and residents regarding their stakeholders, coastal resources, and tourism service characteristics to conclude that such a threat is not delaying progress, only if quality management is achieved, because seaside tourists and residents have not only overlapping requests but also have interchangeable identities.

Quality management related to competitive advantages is also analyzed in Chapter 9, named "Relationship Between Innovation, Human Capital, Institutions, Entrepreneurship, and Economic Growth: A Comparative Analysis Using FsQCA," and written by Prof. Miguel-Angel Galindo Martín, and Dr. Maria-Soledad Castaño, both from Universidad de Castilla-La Mancha (Spain), and Dr. María Teresa Méndez Picazo, from Universidad Complutense de Madrid (Spain). These authors affirm that innovations, institutions, and human capital are the main variables to foster entrepreneurs the creation of innovative products to make them more competitive in the market. As entrepreneurs develop the legal framework and the social impulse for startups, innovations are generated and assimilated, playing quality management a vital role in this development process.

The next two chapters deal with how brands and online shopping determine competitive advantages. In Chapter 10, titled "The Evaluation of the Service and Its Impact on Brand Value: The Case of Language Schools in Guayaquil," and written by Dr. Danny C. Barbery-Montoya, Universidad Espíritu Santo (Ecuador), Mr. Carlos Bautista-Nuques, Ogilvy-Ecuador, and Mrs. Jeaneth P. Wiesner-Mora, Conecel–Claro, (Ecuador), the authors affirm that service companies have the difficult challenge of measuring their brand value, as it is based on consumer perception and subjectivity. Applying the SERVQUAL and CSI questionnaires in some English language teaching institutes in the city of Guayaquil in Ecuador, this chapter aims to know the elements that provide value to the service company's brand to propose a model for this industry.

Concerning online shopping, Chapter 11, named "Exploring the Impact of Peer Influence on Online Shopping: The Case of Chinese Millennials," and written by Prof. Rob Kim Marjerison and Ms. Yiqi Athena HU, both from Wenzhou-Kean University (China), affirms that the commercialization of social media is no longer optional for businesses, especially online firms, as a significant online presence is crucial for creating awareness of new products or services. The objective of this chapter is to investigate peers' influence on Chinese Millennial consumers' purchase behavior, in aspects such as perceived usefulness, perceived risk, and purchase intention. The authors conclude that perceived usefulness positively affects purchase intention, while perceived risk has a negative influence. This chapter provides suggestions for online retailers to attach importance to Peer Influence when advertising their products.

The competitive advantage of a firm can also be analyzed by using managing tools, such as PESTEL, Porter's five forces, CAM (Competitiveness Analysis Matrix), EFE and EFI Analysis Matrix, SWOT, strategic maps, and BSC (Balanced ScoreCard), as shown in Chapter 12, entitled "Development of an Organizational Management Improvement Plan in SMEs: The Case of CVR Ingeniería del Conocimiento SAS," and written by Dr. Omar Orlando Ovalle-Mora, from E3LABSAS (Colombia), and Dr. Maria del Pilar Ramirez-Salazar, Dr. Carlos Salcedo-Perez, Mrs. Anlly Luz Hinestroza Mosquera, all from Universidad EAN (Colombia). With the help of these tools, these authors analyze the internal and external factors to evaluate opportunities, threats, strengths, and weaknesses in a firm to establish a correlation between causes and effects and determine the current situation of the company to find areas of improvement. As a result, competitive advantage and quality are achieved.

Finally, Chapter 13, titled "Shopping for an English Language Tutor: Factors Affecting Chinese College Student's Selection of English Tutoring Institutions," and written by Mr. Hao Zheng, Dr. Rob Kim Marjerison, and Dr.(c) Oliver R. Keels, all from Wenzhou-Kean University, China, affirm that English is often considered the international language of commerce and, more recently, e-commerce. English is also the predominant language of the Internet, science, and many, the language of higher education. As a result, English tutoring institutions are thriving in the Chinese Mainland recently in a substantial and competitive market. The goal of this chapter is to reveal what are the factors that affect Chinese college students' selection of English tutoring institutions in China to make tutoring institution managers focus on the most important criteria for their prospective customers. Through data analysis, the authors show that price, brand image, service variety, and customer relationships are positively associated with Chinese college students' purchase intention of English tutoring institutions.

In sum, this *Quality Management for Competitive Advantage in Global Markets* is a valuable asset for researchers, academicians, practitioners, and any reader interested in optimizing their quality management to strengthen competitive advantages in firms to maximize EBITDA. We invite the prospective readers of this Handbook of Research to wisely internalize and assimilate all the information written by experts and specialists in their areas of research and knowledge. We hope that these pages will be an outstanding benefit for researchers, academicians, practitioners, and anyone interested in these topics.

José Manuel Saiz-Álvarez
Universidad Católica de Santiago de Guayaquil, Ecuador & Universidad Autónoma de Manizales, Colombia & CEIEF-Universidad de Santiago de Chile, Chile

Beatriz Olalla-Caballero
Universidad Pontificia de Salamanca, Spain

REFERENCES

Palma-Ruiz, M., Saiz-Álvarez, J. M., & Herrero-Crespo, Á. (Eds.). (2020). Smart Territories and Entrepreneurial Ecosystems for Social Innovation and Sustainable Growth. Hershey, PA: Information Science Reference (IGI Global).

Saiz-Álvarez, J. M. (2020). Circular Economy: An Emerging Paradigm – Concept, Principles, and Characteristics. In N. Baporikar (Ed.). Handbook of Research on Entrepreneurship Development and Opportunities in Circular Economy, (pp. 1-20). Hershey, PA: Information Science Reference (IGI Global). ISBN 978-1-7998-5116-5

Saiz-Álvarez, J. M., & Palma-Ruiz, J. M. (Eds.), (2019). Handbook of Research on Entrepreneurial Leadership and Competitive Strategy in Family Business. Hershey, PA: Information Science Reference (IGI Global).

Shahabian, A., Fadai, A., & Peruzzi, T. (2019). Future of Life-Cycle Assessment in a Smart and/or Sustainable World. In Interdisciplinary Approaches to Public Policy and Sustainability, (pp. 177-207). Hershey, PA: Information Science Reference (IGI Global).

Acknowledgment

We sincerely thank the IGI Global team, especially Lindsay Wertman (née Johnston) and Maria Rohde, for their assistance, patience, and determination during the development of this handbook of research.

Thanks are due to the 31 authors of seven countries (China, Colombia, Ecuador, India, Namibia, Spain, and Turkey) and four continents for their excellent contributions.

We want to acknowledge the editorial advisory board and reviewers for their help during the double-blind peer-review process.

To our families, for their encouragement, while preparing this handbook of research.

Finally, we also express gratitude to all authors whose works were rejected by referees for publication. We encourage them to persevere in this fascinating world of research.

Section 1
Quality

Chapter 1
The Role of Quality Management in Firm Performance

Özgür Atılgan
İstanbul Kültür Üniversitesi, Turkey

ABSTRACT

In today's business environment, global competition, which has gained momentum with the increase of consumers' quality awareness and consequently, their expectations, has led to the rise of quality management practices by companies. Hence, companies, with the aim of satisfying the needs and wants of customers and thereby attaining competitive advantage, see the inclusion of quality management in the managerial process as a necessity, and they develop optimal performance criteria for such management. In this context, researchers have investigated the effects of quality management applications on innovation performance, production performance, marketing performance, and financial performance of the organization. The empirical research conducted in the last 10 years investigating the relationship between quality management practices and firm performance revealed a significant positive relationship between quality management practices and firm performance.

INTRODUCTION

In today's business environment, global competition has gained momentum with the increase of consumers' quality awareness and, consequently, their expectations, has led to the rise of quality management practices by companies (Agwu, & Afieroho, 2016). In general, quality is defined as the wants of the customers. Based on this definition, arguably, quality is directly associated with the satisfaction of customer demands, necessities, and expectations (Wu, Ai & Cheng, 2019). As such, it is the customers who determine whether the products or services are of high quality. Hence companies, to satisfy the needs and wants of customers and thereby attaining competitive advantage, see the inclusion of quality management in the managerial process as a necessity, and they develop optimal performance criteria for such management (Thakur, & Workman, 2016).

DOI: 10.4018/978-1-7998-5036-6.ch001

In this context, the most prevalent quality management practices across the world are Total Quality Management, Six Sigma, and Lean Management (Zheng, Phan, & Matsui, 2015). Moreover, the implementation of these systems varies according to the geographical location of the companies. Yet, regardless of which of these quality management practices are preferred by a company, the main reasons for implementing them are improving competitive advantage, generating customer satisfaction, increasing firm profit, and/or maintaining firm sustainability, all of which can enhance the firm performance. Firm performance is defined in terms of the financial and non-financial results obtained after operations (Silvi, Bartolini, Raffoni, & Visani, 2015).

In a broad sense, firm performance evaluates to what extent a company is successful in various business operations, such as the supply chain, production distribution and/or after sales (Ralston, Blackhurst, Cantor, & Crum, 2015). Firms operating under extremely competitive conditions periodically evaluate their performance to determine how far they have achieved their goals and objectives (Ji-fan Ren, Fosso Ramba, Akter, Dubey & Childe, 2017). Therefore, it is of great importance to identify the link between quality management practices and firm performance. In this context, recent literature suggests that quality management practices can positively affect firm performance (Kumar, Maiti, & Gunasekaran, 2018).

The purpose of this chapter is to prove quality management practices to determine how they can help companies to gain competitive advantage and thereby lead to better firm performance. The chapter is composed as follows. First, the methodology of the literature review is explained, and the types and characteristics of total quality management practices are identified. Second, the measures used to evaluate firm performance are described. Finally, the role of quality management practices in increasing firm performance is explained.

METHODOLOGY OF THE LİTERATURE REVİEW

An integrative type of literature review for eliciting comprehensive knowledge of the role of quality management in firm performance was deployed. Specifically, 78 documents from electronic databases, including JSTOR, EBSCOhost, ScienceDirect, Scopus, ProQuest, Springer, and SAGE, that reported quantitative and qualitative study findings on quality management associated with firm performance between 2001 and 2020 were scrutinized. For identifying the relevant studies, the following key terms were utilized: quality, quality management, total quality management practices, Six Sigma, Lean Management, financial performance, and non-financial performance.

Quality

The word "quality" originates from the Latin word "qualis," which means "how something is formed" (Gökdemir, & Ali, 2017). Today, its meaning is associated with superiority and goodness, but there are many perspectives on quality, and a wide variety of definitions have been put forward by various schools (Beckford, 2016). For example, Joseph Juran defined it as fitness for use. Philip B. Crosby, who introduced the concept of "zero error," defined quality as the usage of goods and services according to the customers' needs and convenience (Aft, 2018). The American Quality Association defined it as the characteristics of a product or service that demonstrates the ability to meet a specific need. Alternatively, according to the Japanese Industrial Standards Committee, quality is a production system that economically produces products or services and responds to the demands of the consumer. This definition is influenced by the "Lean management approach," which originated in Japan as a Toyota production philosophy (Kıran, 2016).

Quality Management

Quality management is a holistic approach to achieving and maintaining high-quality outputs, and it gained substantial importance in recent years owing to the globally rising fierce competition (Montgomery, & Borror, 2017). Notably, as national borders have become blurred, new international markets have opened up for global companies, and as a consequence, competition has grown proportionally. International markets for many products and services have now matured, with those offered by different countries or even by different companies have become, basically, identical. Accordingly, the basis of competition has come to rely on the quality of the products and services offered (Garza-Reyes, Rocha-Lona, & Kumar, 2015).

The Aim of Quality Management

The primary purposes of quality management are to increase organizational consistency, improve customer satisfaction, and reduce business process costs. As markets, products, and technologies have become mature, the basis of competitive advantage has increasingly become concentrated on quality. Hence, quality management is considered a fundamental approach for gaining or sustaining competitive advantage, thereby increasing firm performance (Goetsch & Davis, 2014). Nowadays, for many organizations, the only certainty about competition is that it will become even stricter and one feasible way to survive this fierce competition is by implementing quality management. The importance of quality management was also emphasized by the founding father of total quality management practices, Edward Demings. He articulated how there will be two types of companies in the future, those that practice quality management and those that must leave the business world (Anderson, Rungstusanatham, & Schroeder, 1994).

The Brief History and Evolution of Quality Management

With the introduction of mass production in the 20th century, the demand for product quality control significantly increased. In the 1940s and 1950s, organizations' pursuit of competitive advantage by improving product quality and lowering costs led to the increasing importance of quality control techniques in business management. After the Second World War, Japan made significant progress in this regard, which left Western countries far behind. In addition to Japan, some other Far Eastern countries, such as South Korea, Taiwan, and Singapore, made significant advances in quality management. As a result of these efforts, new management techniques, such as Total Quality Management, quality circles, equity circles, supplier partnerships, cellular production, just in time production, and hoshin kanri planning emerged (Fisher, & Nair, 2009). In the 1960s and 1970s, the achievements of Japanese manufacturers changed the emphasis from quality control to quality assurance. With the participation of more business functions in quality management, a more comprehensive implementation of timelines became a necessity. In the 1980s, it was not enough to consider the cost element, and the concept of quality began to come to the fore concerning competition (Dooley, 2000). In the 1990s and 2000s, international competition led to a "total approach" to quality management, which meant every employee in the organization was to participate in product development and the prevention of mistakes, with an added focus on teamwork and the customer (Schroeder, Linderman, & Zhang, 2005).

Quality Management Practices

As aforementioned, the three leading quality management practices that are implemented globally are Total Quality Management, Six Sigma, and Lean Management (Raja Sreedharan, Raju, & Srinivas, 2017). Below, each of these quality management practices is explained in detail.

Total Quality Management

In the early 1930s, the first regular studies on total quality management were carried out by Shewhart, his work being Statistical Quality Control. In a similar vein, Edwards Deming contributed to quality control studies through statistical research. Still, his work did not receive much attention from American companies or the US government. The main reason for this situation is that it was a period in which all products produced could be sold in the USA, even those of dubious quality. The size of the market and the lack of consumer awareness led to the neglect of the quality concept. In 1949, Deming was invited to Japan, a devastated country after World War II, where he delivered lectures on quality management (Ross, 2017). He combined the statistical dimension of this new system and the Far East teachings to form a new management philosophy called Total Quality Management (TQM). This theory emerged during the postwar reconstruction of Japan came to affect the whole world. It refers to a management philosophy that disseminates the understanding of quality throughout the entire organization. Japan's approach became a model taken up by the other countries by the 1980s, i.e., they began to implement TQM management practices.

The philosophy of TQM is based on the leadership of the top management, customer orientation, teamwork, training of the employees, zero error, and continuous improvement. In particular, the success of TQM activities requires the support of the top management team. Under TQM, managers are the trainers, and the players are all employees of the organization. Top-level managers should provide a vision for their companies and a unity of purpose (Dahlgaard-Park, Reyes, & Chen, 2018).

Moreover, the success of the business greatly depends on understanding customer needs. The organizational philosophy underpinning TQM can be explained with the following motto: *"The customer pays our money, not the boss."* With TQM, customers are divided into two groups: internal and external. Regarding the former, each person working in the organization produces a good or service for another employee. Accordingly, each employee (worker-officer) should be aware of the idea that another employee uses each good or service produced by him/herself. As a result of this type of mindset, the quality of a product or a service that reaches the external customers (or end-users) is more likely to be higher (Psomas, Vouzas, Bouranta, & Tasiou, 2017) than when such practice is absent.

According to TQM, the most effective way of solving problems and improving processes is by involving employee participation and teamwork. Full participation requires the questioning of why employees do their job, how they do it, and how they can do it better, with the use of scientific reasoning on these matters. Under the TQM lens, it is asserted that those who know the business function best perform it (Lam, O'Donnell, & Robertson, 2015).

Another principle of TQM is continuous employee training. Employees of all levels should be provided with this on subjects involving TQM activities, and managers should train them personally.

Training, like other processes, is an issue that needs to be monitored, measured, and developed in an ongoing manner. In this context, quality training can be classified in terms of three groups. The first is business knowledge and skills training, including basic quality techniques, problem-solving, communication techniques, statistical methods, and process control techniques. The second group is training in support of attitude change, such as customer service, participatory management, teamwork, process management, and change management. The third group relates to behavior change, covering leadership, self-management, time management, and reporting management (Petrick, 2017).

One essence of TQM is emphasizing zero error or error prevention. It is argued that, with meticulous planning of work, it is possible to prevent the vast majority of errors that may occur in the later stages of the operations. While it is impossible to predict all sources of error, it is possible to be prepared for unpleasant surprises in advance, which is vastly preferable to being entirely unprepared for situations. Hence, under TQM, the concept of an "acceptable error level" is rejected and replaced with the mentality of zero error. The main logic in error prevention is to generate solutions before problems arise, thereby striving to create superiority and perfection (Nanda, 2016).

Continuous improvement or Kaizen means searching for never-ending improvements and developing processes to find better methods of converting inputs into outputs. By improving interconnected processes, a company can be more successful in satisfying the needs and expectations of its customers. Continuous improvements in processes, products, or services will reduce scrappage, reprocessing costs, and waste, leading to higher efficiency, delivery time, and delivery performance, which will eventually improve customer satisfaction (Carnerud, Jaca, & Backström, 2018).

Six Sigma

Total Quality Management is applied in various forms in a range of business processes as a management philosophy and understanding, rather than merely a management technique. One of the main points of this understanding is the "zero error" principle. To achieve this as a criterion of excellence, in other companies, rather than TQM, the "Six Sigma" management technique is pursued. Six Sigma can be defined as the effective use of all employee information and quantitative methods to evaluate and improve its core processes to meet customer needs (Surange, 2015).

The Motorola Company first introduced six Sigma quality management systems in 1981. The company primarily used it to increase customer satisfaction by minimizing the number of errors. The company aimed to increase its productivity to higher sigma levels according to a set of indices and achieve radical organizational change. Later, Six Sigma quality management systems were used by General Electric between 1996 and1999, with the company attaining a $2.2 million profit due to such applications (Akpolat, 2017).

Six Sigma is an enterprise and management strategy aimed at increasing the profitability of enterprises. According to this strategy, the purpose is to decrease error and waste rates in the context of meeting consumer needs and expectations through a holistic process management approach. Six Sigma should involve measuring and analyzing all processes of the business, not just a few functions. That is, all operations within the organization are re-evaluated to generate more profit based on customer satisfaction. The data obtained as a result of these analyses are expressed statistically. The Six Sigma approach aims to achieve near-perfect results statistically, i.e., with a probability of 3.4 errors per million (Muralidharan, 2015). As a result of the Six Sigma, and based on customer satisfaction and the quantitative methods applied together with the process management regularly throughout the organization, error rates can be decreased. Also, stock levels can be lowered, efficiency can be increased, costs can be reduced, customer satisfaction can be enhanced, and profitability can be improved along with a rising market share (Munro, Ramu, & Zrymiak, 2015).

While Six Sigma and TQM are applications for the same purposes, meeting customer needs is somewhat different under the two philosophies. For example, when companies apply TQM to satisfy customer needs, very few enterprises make intensive efforts to understand them. In contrast, Six Sigma has all the necessary tools to meet these needs, and prioritizing reality becomes a reality, rather than a paper exercise, as is often the case with TQM (Tennant, 2017).

Hence, Six Sigma is a more detailed approach than TQM and deals with continuous improvement practices. The numerical data from the former allows for measurement regarding business operations, which is utilized to enhance performance. Thus, a scientific perspective is adopted, rather than the interpretive one of TQM (Furterer, 2016).

Lean Management

After World War II, Taiichi Ohno, who investigated the Ford manufacturing system, applied what he learned to the manufacturing processes at Toyota using a different management approach. As a result of this, the foundations of the Lean Management "philosophy were laid down. Unlike the mass production model of the Ford production system, Ohno came up with lean thinking and managed to achieve the same production capacity as at Ford with just 1,500 workers (at Ford, the same level required 6,000), thus attaining more production and sales per employee. Moreover, the factory was physically reduced, the production line was shortened, and diminished all the resources allocated in the company, including financial ones. By carrying out this work, he brought quality up to the highest level, thereby providing optimum customer satisfaction and business excellence (Bhasin, 2015).

Toyota Motor Company President, Fujio Cho, described the success of the Lean Management philosophy as follows: "What makes Toyota stand out is not a particular element. What is essential is to keep all elements together in a single system and implement them consistently every day." The concept of simplicity under the Lean Management philosophy means minimizing the elements of stock, error, waste, cost, production area, and customer dissatisfaction, i.e., it is focused on getting rid of all the unnecessary elements in the organization. The lean Management philosophy is based on meeting customer expectations on time, using precisely the right amounts of raw materials, tools, equipment, and labor (Agarwal, & Sharma, 2016).

Womack and Jones (2003) classified the basic principles of lean production under five headings in their book "Lean Thought":

1) Value should be determined according to the customer's point of view;
2) The value flow must be determined, and the waste must be eliminated;
3) Continous value flow must be maintained;
4) The pull strategy should be created according to the customer's demand;
5) Continuous improvement must be kept to achieve excellence.

Alternatively, Japanese managers adopted the 5S rule, including the following stages: *Seiri*: Categorization, *Seiton*: Ordering, *Seiketsu*: Standardization, *Seiso*: Cleaning, and *Shitsuke*: Discipline. According to them, Lean Management starts with *Seiri*: Categorization, which refers to determining what is necessary and what is unnecessary and deciding the steps of organizing accordingly. In the classification stage, a quarantine area should be identified, with everything not being used in production or not anticipated as being needed, later on, being labeled in red and moved to this area. This classification aims to keep the materials in the right place.

After eliminating unnecessary things identified in the first stage of categorization, the second stage is ordering. The basic approach here is to create a place for everything, i.e., all elements of production to have a specific location. The stage has a 30-second rule, such that any employee should be able to find, retrieve, and replace something within this timeframe. Some of the issues to be considered during ordering are: making sure that everyone gets everything from the same place and returns it there, everything in the warehouse has an allocated shelf, everyone should know everything by the same name, and tools will be appropriately kept.

Standardization pertains to developing systems and procedures to ensure continuity of the first two stages. The usage of markers, marking of borders with tape and paint, coding, layout plans, information showing the minimum and maximum quantity levels assigned to the products, and documented and displayed cleaning plans are part of the standardization stage. As a result of standardization, it becomes easy to determine whether there is an excess or missing material or equipment (He, & Ngee Goh, 2015).

Cleaning is the fourth stage when a cleaning map is prepared to identify contaminated sources, and cleaning zone workers are appointed. Dust, rubbish, and foreign substances should be removed from the working environment by the chosen people. The purpose is to create a clean space and, thus, minimize inefficiency. All employees should be responsible for daily, weekly, or monthly for cleaning their workspace. All workplaces, worktops, machines, cabinet interiors, exteriors, and undersides should always be kept clean and bright (Swarnakar, & Vinodh, 2016).

Discipline is the last step of 5S and implemented to ensure the uninterrupted continuity of the system. Continuity should be conducted and controlled in parallel with the disciplinary rules. The improvements achieved due to implementing 5S, such as the lower costs and convenience, should be demonstrated to everyone by supporting them through slogans and ongoing communications (Sunder, 2016).

Recent literature suggests that all of the aforementioned quality management practices are related to firm performance. Before elaborating upon this relationship, the meaning of firm performance and its different types are explained below.

Firm Performance

Performance is usually defined as the relationship between the means of production and the resulting production amount. Performance can also be defined as the level of fulfillment of the task, and achieving the goals or objectives set from the beginning, meeting the previously specified standards or criteria. But no matter how it is defined, it can be argued that performance is an evaluation criterion for determining quantitative or qualitative output achieved. The evaluation of the result can be explained as absolute or relative. For example, the amount of product obtained from a person, unit, or department in a company, or the ratio of production to planned production, can be evaluated as performance (Kaplan, & Atkinson, 1998).

Performance is defined as the degree of fulfillment of the firm's purpose or objectives at the end of a specified period. Firm performance is measured to determine the level to which an organization achieves its goals. In the literature, researchers and academicians have described company performance according to different dimensions, such as innovation performance, production performance, marketing performance, or financial performance. Below, each firm performance type will be explained in detail (Vij, & Bedi, 2016).

- *Innovation Performance*

The word innovation is derived from the Latin word "innovare," which means to do something new and different in terms of product or service. Based on this definition, innovation performance in firms refers to evaluate the process of inventions, ideas, conversion of these ideas into products or services, and their presentation to the market. Innovation performance covers the company performance from R&D to product promotion; in other words, from the beginning to the end of the innovation process. For example, in the plaster industry, Saint Gobain's new generation gypsum board called Habito, which can carry a 15kg point load with a standard chipboard screw without a dowel is a product that has increased the competitiveness and market share of the company and thus, its performance (Saunila, 2017). The success of innovation performance is dependent on the new product development rate, the revenues generated by the latest products, the contributions of new products to the profit margin. Innovation performance can be considered one of the most critical performance measures for businesses in today's global world due to its positive effect on competitive advantage (Ritala, Olander, Michailova, & Husted, 2015).

- *Production Performance*

The role of production in supporting business strategy and creating a competitive advantage has been an essential issue in production management literature. In case of an inconsistency between production and business strategies, overall firm performance can be lowered due to diminished competitive advantage. Therefore it is of utmost importance in business to create efficient working systems that are less capital and time-consuming (Salguero, Munoz-Cauqui, Batista, Calvino, Aguayo, & Marcos, 2015). At this point, efficiency is the core element in production performance. The production performance of an organization can only be evaluated by the measurement of operational efficiency that includes time spent in production, production costs, and flexibility, all of which are depicting the degree of fulfilling the predetermined objectives in the production process (Fullerton, & McWatters, 2001). Yet, it should not be forgotten that the purpose of measuring a production performance is to provide value for customers from operational outputs by optimizing the use of material and human resources. Because value creation positively connects with quality, a high production performance also means a higher level of the quality manufacturing process and reducing defections in the whole production process (Topalovic, 2015).

- *Marketing Performance*

Marketing performance is defined as the degree to which a product or service maintains, increases, or improves its market share for a specified time. Marketing metrics are the internal and external measurements obtained from financial or market-related data. Marketing performance criteria can be divided into financial and non-financial, with the former generally being the first to measure such performance. Market share is one of the most used metrics by both academicians and practitioners in this regard since it is considered as the source of cash flow and profitability (Farris, Bendle, Pfeifer, & Reibstein, 2010).

While traditional performance metrics are based on the financial accounting system, since the 1980s, there has been an increasing interest in non-financial measurement tools for evaluating marketing performance. Among these tools are customer satisfaction, channel satisfaction, customer loyalty, economic added value (EVA), brand value, lifelong customer value (LCV), customer value, relationship value, or new product development success. With the change in market structures, businesses have been striving to provide a competitive advantage by using these non-financial performance criteria. It is argued that quality, customer satisfaction, innovation, and other non-financial metrics generally reflect the firm's economic status and growth prospects better than reported revenues (Wongrassamee, Simmons, & Gardiner, 2003).

Especially in the 2000s, the measurement of customer relations gained more importance than product success, with the concept of "make customers not sales" being introduced. According to Achrol and Kotler (1999), one of the most significant changes experienced by marketing is that the marketer has increasingly become the consultant of the customer, instead of being the sales representative. This fact can be considered as the main reason why customer-related factors have become more critical in the evaluation of marketing performance.

Yet despite these developments, there has been no significant change in the details of corporate reporting. Despite substantial literature on brand success measurement, the results are not usually included in the reporting of companies (Arifeen, Hussain, Kazmi, Mubin, Mughal, & Qadri, 2014).

- *Financial Performance*

Financial performance evaluates how much of the organization's predetermined economic targets are achieved and in terms of profit/loss. In short, financial performance shows the extent to which an organization achieves the economic objectives it sets to accomplish (Upton, 1994). Understanding and interpreting the financial position of the enterprise is not only crucial for the users of the financial statements within the organization, but also various stakeholder groups. In particular, the financial position of the business is of paramount importance for stakeholders who aim to invest externally in the industry. However, the massive amounts of data generated by the company's activities and included in the business' financial statements are highly problematic for both managers and investors, being thus tricky for them to assess. Making this information easier to understand and more usable is achieved through financial analysis (Merton, & Bodic, 1995).

The purpose of financial analysis is to examine and evaluate the financial statements of the company. There are three main parts to financial statements: the balance sheet, the income statement, and the net cash flow statement. The primary function of the financial statements is to provide the shareholders and the stakeholders, including creditors, reliable information about the company's current status, and past financial performance. Moreover, it allows for a template to be created for shareholders for financial planning and to specify performance targets to the managers (Brigham, & Houston, 2012).

To measure the financial performance of a company, much financial analysis, such as ratio analysis, comparative tables analysis, percentage analysis (vertical analysis), trend percentage analysis (trend analysis), fund flow, and/or net cash flow analysis, can be utilized. However, financial ratios are the most commonly used indicators for measuring the financial performance of an enterprise. The reason for this is that relations between items in the balance sheet and income statement mean more than the figures seen in the financial statements of the business. The ratio is a simple mathematical expression of the relationship between any two items in the financial statements. Yet, they can give important information about the business management and the financial situation of the company, when they are compared to the previous ratios of the enterprise or the ratios of others in the same sector (Mun, Yuh, & Hanna, 2002).

In ratio analysis, the most common evaluation is comparing the ratios of the companies operating in the same sector with the sector average and their financial performance, accordingly. However, sometimes there are structural differences even between businesses in the same sector. In this case, even if these companies are operating in the same sector, it is not correct to make comparisons between enterprises, as they will exhibit different characteristics. Hence, in the interpretation of the analysis, ratios that give meaningful results appropriate to the purpose at hand should be used. The most commonly used ratio analyses are liquidity ratios, financial structure (leverage) ratios, activity ratios, and profitability ratios (Ross, Westerfield, Jaffe, & Jordan, 2011).

To provide a clear understanding of the relationship between quality management practices and firm performance, qualitative and quantitative studies carried out within the last ten years are reviewed next.

The Role of Quality Management in Firm Performance

In general, researchers have investigated the effects of quality management applications on innovation performance, production performance, marketing performance, and financial performance of the organization. These are important for the competitiveness of the organization and its existence in business life. Despite many articles published on TQM, the vast majority have been focused on the philosophy and methods of quality management practices, with only a tiny amount involving testing the strength of the relationship between quality management and organizational performance. While some researchers have identified high costs and barriers to implementing quality management applications, most have concluded that these applications increase firm performance. Those who have been skeptical about quality management implications on firm performance have pointed to the burdens regarding these practices, such as excessive training costs, disproportionately consuming management time, increased paperwork and formalities, unrealistic loyalty demanded from employees, and extreme results orientation (Kumar et al., 2018). Below in Table 1, the results of some studies conducted in the last ten years about the relationship between total quality management practices and firm performance are summarized.

In this context, Sadıkoğlu & Zehir (2010) investigated the effects of innovation and employee performance on the relationship between TQM practices and firm performance in 373 ISO 9001 certified firms in different industries Marmara region in Turkey. The results of this study elicited that employee performance and innovation performance partially mediate the relationship between TQM practices and firm performance. Kim, Kumar, & Kumar (2012) examined the relationship between TQM practices and innovation performance in ISO 9001 certified 20100 manufacturing and service firms in Canada. The findings revealed that total quality management practices are positively associated with all types of innovation performance, i.e., radical product innovation, incremental product innovation, radical process innovation, incremental process innovation, and administrative innovation. Sadıkoğlu & Olcay (2014) conducted an empirical study on the effects of TQM practices on firm performance in 242 firms located in the Kocaeli-Gebze Organised Industrial Zone in Turkey. The results revealed that such practices significantly positively affect operational performance, inventory management performance, employee performance, innovation performance, marketing performance, and financial performance.

Jımenez-Jımenez, Martinez-Costa, Martinez-Lorente, and Rabeh (2015) conducted a study examining the link between TQM and firm performance in 111 medium-sized Spanish manufacturing companies. They elicited that such practices have a positive effect on innovation performance through increased employee idea exploration. In another study conducted by Kafetzopoulos, Psomas, and Gotzamani (2015), 287 certified Greek manufacturing firms were examined to determine the effect of TQM practices on product performance, operational performance, and business performance. According to the findings of the research, these practices significantly increase product quality and operational performance. The results also revealed that the product quality increases with enhanced operational performance. For this reason, it was suggested that industrial organizations should focus on achieving quality management targets to gain a competitive advantage.

Table 1. Studies covering the relationship between total quality management practices and firm performance

Year	Authors	Sample	Results
2010	Sadıkoğlu, & Zehir	373 ISO 9001 certified firms in Turkey	Employee performance and innovation performance partially mediate the relationship between TQM practices and firm performance
2012	Kim, Kumar, & Kumar	ISO 9001 certified 20100 manufacturing and service firms in Canada	TQM practices are positively associated with all types of innovation performance
2014	Sadıkoğlu, & Olcay	242 firms in Turkey	TQM practices have a positive effect on firm performance
2015	Jımenez-Jımenez, Martinez-Costa, Martinez-Lorente, & Rabeh	111 medium-sized Spanish manufacturing companies	TQM practices have a positive effect on innovation performance through increased employee idea exploration.
2015	Kafetzopoulos, Psomas, & Gotzamani	287 certified Greek manufacturing firms	TQM practices significantly increase product quality and operational performance.
2016	Aba, Badar, & Hayden	ISO 9001 certified 397 US companies	TQM practices are positively associated with production performance
2016	Modgil, & Sharma	254 pharmaceutical companies in India	TQM practices have a positive and significant effect on production performance in terms of product quantity and quality
2017	Bazazo, Alansari, Alquraan, Alzgaybh, & Masadeh	191 hotels in Jordan	TQM practices have a positive impact on marketing orientation through increased market orientation
2018	Iqbal, Huq, & Bhutta	248 Pakistani apparel export firms	TQM practices positively affect marketing performance and financial performance.
2019	Jimoh, Oyewobi, Isa, & Waziri	155 medium & large sized construction companies in Nigeria	TQM practices have a significant effect on production performance, financial performance, customer focus, and quality improvement
2019	Anil, & Satish	260 Indian manufacturing firms.	TQM practices have a significant positive effect on quality growth, operation performance, customer satisfaction, innovation performance, and financial performance

Source: The Author

Aba, Badar, and Hayden (2016) investigated whether TQM systems impacted the financial success of American firms over one year before implementing such practices. The production performances of 397 companies that had received ISO 9001 certification were investigated. The findings of the study showed that there was a significant ten percent improvement in production performance in the year of TQM practices compared to the previous year in terms of production quantity and quality. That is, an important finding obtained from this study is that TQM practices are positively statistically associated with product performance. Modgil & Sharma (2016) investigated the impact of TQM practices on production performance, innovation performance, and technology management in 254 pharmaceutical companies in India. The results indicated that these practices have a positive and significant effect on production performance in terms of product quantity, quality, product innovation, and technology management. The findings also revealed that TQM practices reduce the cost of quality attainment in reduced scrappage and fewer defective products.

Bazazo, Alansari, Alquraan, Alzgaybh & Masadeh (2017) analyzed the effects of TQM practices on marketing and e-marketing performance for 191 hotel employees from different hotels located in Jordan. The findings showed that such practices have a positive impact on marketing orientation through increased market orientation, whereas they have no significant association with e-marketing performance. Iqbal, Huq, and Bhutta (2018) investigated the relationship between TQM practices and organizational performance in 248 Pakistani apparel export firms. The results revealed that such practices positively affect marketing performance, as measured by sales growth, market share growth, sales performance, and financial performance, as measured by return on assets (ROA), return on investment (ROI), and profitability.

Jimoh, Oyewobi, Isa, and Waziri (2019) investigated the relationship between TQM practices and organization performance for 155 medium and large-sized construction companies in Nigeria. The results demonstrated that such practices significantly affect production performance, financial performance, customer focus, and quality improvement. Anil and Satish (2019) explored the effect of total quality management practices and firm performance in 260 Indian manufacturing firms. The findings indicated that these practices have a significant positive impact on quality growth, operation performance, customer satisfaction, innovation performance, and financial performance.

As can be inferred from Table 1, the findings of these studies, TQM practices have a significant positive effect in almost all companies from different parts of the world subject to the investigation. Below in Table 2, the results of studies in the last ten years that analyze the relationship between Six Sigma practices and firm performance are summarized.

Table 2. Studies covering the relationship between Six Sigma practices and firm performance

Year	Authors	Sample	Results
2015	Oliya, Owlia, Shahrokh, & Olfat	5 top managers of Saman Bank in Iran	Six Sigma practices had improved marketing efficiency, increased the number of customers as well as increasing the speed of marketing operations and workflow
2017	Uluskan, Godfrey, & Joines	115 US textile and apparel companies	Six Sigma practices have a significant positive effect on net profit margin, order fulfillment cycle time, full and on-time delivery rate, product quality, and employee performance
2018	Lamine, & Lakhal	91 Tunisian companies across different sectors	Six Sigma practices have a significant positive effect on production performance and financial performance.
2018	Hwang, Lee, & Seo	201 respondents from various companies that were qualified Champions, Master Black Belts, Black Belts, and Green Belts in South Korea	Six Sigma's structured methods are positively related to employees' idea exploration and exploitation and improve firm-level innovation performance.

In this context, Oliya, Owlia, Shahrokh, and Olfat (2015) investigated whether Six Sigma practices deliver improvements in marketing processes in a banking environment. For this purpose, a case study was conducted with five top managers of Saman Bank in Iran, with the findings demonstrating that Six Sigma practices had improved marketing efficiency, increased the number of customers, and increased the speed of marketing operations and workflow. Uluskan, Godfrey, and Joines (2017) conducted an empirical study on the effects of Six Sigma practices on organizational performance in 115 US textile and apparel companies. The findings demonstrated that such practices have a significant positive impact on net profit margin, order fulfillment cycle time, full and on-time delivery rate, product quality and employee performance, and satisfaction and lead to a decline in the defects rate.

Lamine and Lakhal (2018) investigated the effects of Six Sigma practices on production performance and financial performance in 91 Tunisian companies across different sectors. The results of the study inferred that such practices have a significant positive effect on production performance and financial performance. Hwang, Lee, and Seo (2018) studied the relationship between employees' idea exploration and exploitation and Six Sigma practices for 201 respondents from various companies that were qualified Champions, Master Black Belts, Black Belts, and Green Belts. The empirical results of this study indicated that Six Sigma's structured methods are positively related to employees' idea exploration and exploitation and also improve firm-level innovation performance.

As can be inferred from Table 2, the findings of these studies, Six Sigma practices have a significant positive effect in almost all companies from different parts of the world subject to the investigation. Below in Table 3, the results of studies in the last ten years that analyze the relationship between lean management practices and firm performance are summarized.

Table 3. Studies covering the relationship between lean management practices and firm performance

Year	Authors	Sample	Results
2011	Yang, Hong, & Modi	309 international manufacturing firms	Lean management practices improve business performance through increased marketing and financial performance.
2012	Hofer, Eroğlu, & Hofer	229 manufacturing firms in the US A	Lean management practices a positive effect on all financial performance measures, i.e., return on sales (ROS), sales growth, and net sales.
2013	Ghosh	400 manufacturing firms operating in India	Lean management practices increase overall production performance.
2014	Khanchanapong, Prajogo, Sohal, Cooper, Yeung, & Cheng	186 manufacturing plants in Taiwan	Lean management practices have a significant positive effect on production performance measured in quality, lead time, flexibility, and operation cost.
2019	Abdallah, Dahiyat & Matsui	238 international manufacturing companies	Lean management practices are positively related to innovation performance.

Source: The Author

In this context, Yang, Hong, and Modi (2011) explored the relationship between Lean Management practices and business performance outcomes in terms of market and financial performance in 309 international manufacturing firms. The results indicated that these practices improve business performance through increased marketing and financial performance. Hofer, Eroğlu, and Hofer (2012) investigated the relationship between Lean Management and financial performance in 229 manufacturing firms in the USA. They found that such management positively affects all financial performance measures, i.e., return on sales (ROS), sales growth, and net sales. Ghosh (2013) investigated the effects of Lean Management practices on firm performance in 400 manufacturing firms operating in India. The findings of this study indicated that these practices increase the total amount of output and quality and, thus, overall production performance. Khanchanapong, Prajogo, Sohal, Cooper, Yeung, and Cheng (2014) explored the effects of Lean Management practices on the production performance of 186 manufacturing plants in Taiwan. They found that these practices positively affected production performance measured in quality, lead time, flexibility, and operation cost. Abdallah, Dahiyat & Matsui (2019) analyzed the effect of Lean Management practices on innovation performance in 238 international manufacturing companies in eight countries across three sectors. The results of structural equation modeling led to the conclusion that such practices are positively related to innovation performance. They also indicated that Lean Management practices are more associated with incremental innovation rather than the radical form.

As can be inferred from Table 3, the findings of these studies, lean management practices have a significant positive effect in almost all companies from different parts of the world subject to the investigation.

New Trends in Quality Management Practices

In recent years, the focus of quality management practices has shifted from production to service industries. Therefore, we mainly see the implementation of quality management practices related to employee empowerment, corporate culture, process improvement, and leadership. In this framework, all of these implementations concentrate on the human side of quality management practices (Valmohammadi, & Roshanzamir, 2015). The role of human resources in total quality management is to ensure that employees are committed to quality by helping them develop an innovative idea. In order to be successful in quality management practices, companies should operate by combining human resources practices such as employee empowerment with the objectives of quality. At this point, it can be argued that leadership can be an essential element of quality management practices (Jasti, & Kodali, 2015).

It should not be forgotten that the injection of quality management philosophy to an organization is usually dependent on the top management's ability to take the leadership role. In this connection, a democratic leadership style should be adopted to implement and apply the philosophy of total quality management, since democratic leaders try to ensure the maximum participation of each employee in group actions and try to reduce tensions and conflicts, conflicts and resistances within the organization. Generally, the characteristics of the ideal of leaders who promote total quality management practices should have internal and external customer orientation with coaching and mentoring abilities towards employees (Ali, & Khatoon, 2016).

SOLUTIONS AND RECOMMENDATİONS

Despite some researchers being critical of the claimed positive implications of quality management practices due to high costs and barriers of implementation of such applications, as aforementioned, much of the research conducted over the last ten years has revealed that such practices, including all related to TQM, Six Sigma and Lean Management, have a positive effect on company performance. Yet, it should not be forgotten that the success of quality management practices is contingent upon top management leadership and internalizing these practices by the organizational members. In this context, it can be argued that training of the employees may help them to adopt changes that are required by quality management practices.

FUTURE RESEARCH DİRECTİONS

This present chapter has been focused on the systematization of the concepts relating to quality management and firm performance concerning TQM, Six Sigma, and Lean Management. Moreover, production performance, innovation performance, marketing performance, and financial performance have been explained. Finally, the empirical research conducted in the last ten years investigating the relationship between quality management practices and firm performance has been reviewed. From the review of the extant studies, it can be seen that most of the research has involved investigating this relationship in the context of manufacturing firms. Hence, future research would benefit from an empirical investigation into the relationship between quality management practices and firm performance in service sectors. Moreover, future research would also benefit from the inclusion of top management leadership and employee training and/or empowerment as a mediator in the relationship between quality management practices and firm performance.

CONCLUSİON

Globalization has brought about fierce competition among companies, along with an increase in consumers' quality awareness. Consequently, their expectations have grown, which has led to the rise of quality management practices in companies to provide goods and services of higher quality to customers. Based on the definition of quality, it can be argued that this is directly related to the satisfaction of customer demands, requirements, and expectations. Hence, firms have the objective of satisfying the needs and wants of customers and thus, attaining a competitive advantage with better firm performance.

In this regard, the most widely utilized quality management practices worldwide are TQM practices, Six Sigma, and Lean Management. Under TQM, the aim is for zero error or error prevention with meticulous planning work by preventing a large part of the errors that may occur in the later stages of the operations. With Six Sigma, the effective utilization of all employee information is encouraged, with quantitative methods being deployed to assess and improve the organization's basic processes for responding to customer needs. Lean Management, on the other hand, involves concentrating on minimizing the elements of stock, error, waste, cost, production area, customer dissatisfaction, and getting rid of all the unnecessary processes that do not create value for customers. In sum, all of these three quality management practices aim to provide goods or services of a higher quality to customers.

Nonetheless, despite the evident advantages of quality management practices, some researchers remain skeptical about the performance implications of quality management practices due to the difficulties associated with excessive training costs, disproportionately consumption of management time, increased paperwork and formalities, unrealistic loyalty expectations from employees, and extreme results orientation. Overriding these concerns, the results of those empirical studies conducted in various settings in the last ten years display positive performance implications for quality management practices. More specifically, the findings have revealed that there is a positive relationship between quality management practices and innovation performance as well as the financial performance of companies. Given the fact that the vast majority of these studies were conducted on manufacturing firms, practitioners should be careful about the implementation of quality management practices in service-providing sectors. Accordingly, future research necessitates more effort to investigate the effects of such practices on firm performance in service sectors. Also, top management leadership and employee training should be included as mediators when examining the correlation between these two variables. It should also not be forgotten that the success of implementing quality management practices is highly contingent upon the guidance of top management and internalization of these practices by all organization members.

To sum up, it has been elicited that quality management practices, such as Total Quality Management, Six Sigma, and Lean Management, have a positive effect on firm performance in manufacturing firms, in particular, on innovation performance and financial performance. Moreover, it has emerged that top management leadership and the training of organization members are critical enablers in this positive relationship.

REFERENCES

Aba, E. K., Badar, M. A., & Hayden, M. A. (2016). Impact of ISO 9001 certification on firms' financial operating performance. *International Journal of Quality & Reliability Management*, *33*(1), 78–89. doi:10.1108/IJQRM-02-2014-0021

Abdallah, A. B., Dahiyat, S. E., & Matsui, Y. (2019). Lean management and innovation performance: Evidence from international manufacturing companies. *Management Research Review*, *42*(2), 239–262. doi:10.1108/MRR-10-2017-0363

Achrol, R. S., & Kotler, P. (1999). Marketing in the network economy. *Journal of Marketing*, *63*(4_suppl1), 146–163. doi:10.1177/00222429990634s114

Aft, L. S. (2018). *Fundamentals of industrial quality control*. CRC Press.

Agarwal, A., & Sharma, M. K. (2016). Lean management–a step towards a sustainable green supply chain. *Competitiveness Review*, *26*(3), 311–331. doi:10.1108/CR-05-2015-0040

Agwu, E., & Afieroho, E. (2016). Impact of Product Quality Management on the Growth of Small and Medium-Sized Enterprises. *European Journal of Soil Science*, *52*(2), 175–190.

Akpolat, H. (2017). *Six sigma in transactional and service environments*. Routledge. doi:10.4324/9781315243030

Ali, S. I., & Khatoon, S. U. E. B. H. A. (2016). Implementation of total quality management. *International Journal of Emerging Trends in Engineering and Development*, *6*(6), 114–119.

Anderson, J. C., Rungtusanatham, M., & Schroeder, R. G. (1994). A theory of quality management underlying the Deming management method. *Academy of Management Review*, *19*(3), 472–509. doi:10.5465/amr.1994.9412271808

Anil, A. P., & Satish, K. P. (2019). Enhancing customer satisfaction through total quality management practices–an empirical examination. *Total Quality Management & Business Excellence*, *30*(13-14), 1528–1548. doi:10.1080/14783363.2017.1378572

Arifeen, N., Hussain, M., Kazmi, S., Mubin, M., Mughal, S. L., & Qadri, W. (2014). Measuring Business Performance: Comparison of Financial, Non-Financial and Qualitative Indicators. *European Journal of Business and Management*, *6*(4), 38–45.

Bazazo, I., Alansari, I., Alquraan, H., Alzgaybh, Y., & Masa'deh, R. E. (2017). The influence of total quality management, market orientation and e-marketing on hotel performance. *International Journal of Business Administration*, *8*(4), 79. doi:10.5430/ijba.v8n4p79

Beckford, J. (2016). *Quality: a critical introduction*. Routledge. doi:10.4324/9781315644028

Bhasin, S. (2015). *Lean management beyond manufacturing*. Springer. doi:10.1007/978-3-319-17410-5

Brigham, E. F., & Houston, J. F. (2012). *Fundamentals of financial management*. Cengage Learning.

Carnerud, D., Jaca, C., & Bäckström, I. (2018). Kaizen and continuous improvement–trends and patterns over 30 years. *The TQM Journal*, *30*(4), 371–390. doi:10.1108/TQM-03-2018-0037

Dahlgaard-Park, S. M., Reyes, L., & Chen, C. K. (2018). The evolution and convergence of total quality management and management theories. *Total Quality Management & Business Excellence*, *29*(9-10), 1108–1128. doi:10.1080/14783363.2018.1486556

Davidson, J. (1999). Transforming the value of company reports through marketing measurement. *Journal of Marketing Management*, *15*(8), 757–777. doi:10.1362/026725799784772657

Dooley, K. (2000). The paradigms of quality: evolution and revolution in the history of the discipline. *Advances in the Management of Organizational Quality*, *5*(1), 1-28.

Farris, P. W., Bendle, N., Pfeifer, P., & Reibstein, D. (2010). *Marketing metrics: The definitive guide to measuring marketing performance*. Pearson Education.

Fisher, N. I., & Nair, V. N. (2009). Quality management and quality practice: Perspectives on their history and their future. *Applied Stochastic Models in Business and Industry*, *25*(1), 1–28. doi:10.1002/asmb.756

Fullerton, R. R., & McWatters, C. S. (2001). The production performance benefits from JIT implementation. *Journal of Operations Management*, *19*(1), 81–96. doi:10.1016/S0272-6963(00)00051-6

Furterer, S. L. (2016). *Lean Six Sigma in service: applications and case studies*. CRC Press. doi:10.1201/9781420079104

Garza-Reyes, J. A., Rocha-Lona, L., & Kumar, V. (2015). A conceptual framework for the implementation of quality management systems. *Total Quality Management & Business Excellence*, *26*(11-12), 1298–1310. doi:10.1080/14783363.2014.929254

Ghosh, M. (2012). Lean manufacturing performance in Indian manufacturing plants. *Journal of Manufacturing Technology Management*, *24*(1), 113–122. doi:10.1108/17410381311287517

Goetsch, D. L., & Davis, S. B. (2014). *Quality management for organizational excellence*. Pearson.

Gökdemir, K., & Ali, T. (2017). The Examination and Comparison of Recreational Sports Centers With Regard to Quality of Service. *International Journal of Applied Exercise Physiology*, *6*(4), 26–36. doi:10.22631/ijaep.v6i4.195

He, Z., & Ngee Goh, T. (2015). Enhancing the future impact of Six Sigma management. *Quality Technology & Quantitative Management*, *12*(1), 83–92. doi:10.1080/16843703.2015.11673368

Hofer, C., Eroglu, C., & Hofer, A. R. (2012). The effect of lean production on financial performance: The mediating role of inventory leanness. *International Journal of Production Economics*, *138*(2), 242–253. doi:10.1016/j.ijpe.2012.03.025

Hwang, G. H., Lee, K. C., & Seo, Y. W. (2018). How does Six Sigma influence creativity and corporate performance through exploration and exploitation? *Total Quality Management & Business Excellence*, *29*(13-14), 1668–1684. doi:10.1080/14783363.2017.1297199

Iqbal, T., Huq, F., & Bhutta, M. K. S. (2018). Agile manufacturing relationship building with TQM, JIT, and firm performance: An exploratory study in the apparel export industry of Pakistan. *International Journal of Production Economics*, *203*, 24–37. doi:10.1016/j.ijpe.2018.05.033

Jasti, N. V. K., & Kodali, R. (2015). Lean production: Literature review and trends. *International Journal of Production Research*, *53*(3), 867–885. doi:10.1080/00207543.2014.937508

Jiménez-Jiménez, D., Martinez-Costa, M., Martínez-Lorente, A. R., & Rabeh, H. A. D. (2015). Total quality management performance in multinational companies: A learning perspective. *The TQM Journal*, *27*(3), 328–340. doi:10.1108/TQM-01-2014-0002

Jimoh, R., Oyewobi, L., Isa, R., & Waziri, I. (2019). Total quality management practices and organizational performance: The mediating roles of strategies for continuous improvement. *International Journal of Construction Management*, *19*(2), 162–177. doi:10.1080/15623599.2017.1411456

Kafetzopoulos, D. P., Psomas, E. L., & Gotzamani, K. D. (2015). The impact of quality management systems on the performance of manufacturing firms. *International Journal of Quality & Reliability Management*, *32*(4), 381–399. doi:10.1108/IJQRM-11-2013-0186

Kaplan, R. S., & Atkinson, A. A. (1998). *Advanced Management Accounting*. Prentice-Hall.

Khanchanapong, T., Prajogo, D., Sohal, A. S., Cooper, B. K., Yeung, A. C., & Cheng, T. C. E. (2014). The unique and complementary effects of manufacturing technologies and lean practices on manufacturing operational performance. *International Journal of Production Economics*, *153*, 191–203. doi:10.1016/j.ijpe.2014.02.021

Kim, D. Y., Kumar, V., & Kumar, U. (2012). Relationship between quality management practices and innovation. *Journal of Operations Management*, *30*(4), 295–315. doi:10.1016/j.jom.2012.02.003

Kiran, D. R. (2016). *Total quality management: Key concepts and case studies*. Butterworth-Heinemann.

Kumar, P., Maiti, J., & Gunasekaran, A. (2018). Impact of quality management systems on firm performance. *International Journal of Quality & Reliability Management*, *35*(5), 1034–1059. doi:10.1108/IJQRM-02-2017-0030

Lam, M., O'Donnell, M., & Robertson, D. (2015). Achieving employee commitment for continuous improvement initiatives. *International Journal of Operations & Production Management*, *35*(2), 201–215. doi:10.1108/IJOPM-03-2013-0134

Lamine, K., & Lakhal, L. (2018). Impact of TQM/Six Sigma practices on the company's performance: Tunisian context. *International Journal of Quality & Reliability Management*, *35*(9), 1881–1906. doi:10.1108/IJQRM-05-2017-0097

Merton, R. C., & Bodie, Z. (1995). A conceptual framework for analyzing the financial system. *The global financial system: A functional perspective*, 3-31.

Modgil, S., & Sharma, S. (2016). Total productive maintenance, total quality management and operational performance: An empirical study of the Indian pharmaceutical industry. *Journal of Quality in Maintenance Engineering*, *22*(4), 353–377. doi:10.1108/JQME-10-2015-0048

Montgomery, D. C., & Borror, C. M. (2017). Systems for modern quality and business improvement. *Quality Technology & Quantitative Management*, *14*(4), 343–352. doi:10.1080/16843703.2017.1304032

Moon, S. J., Yuh, Y., & Hanna, S. D. (2002). Financial ratio analysis of Korean households. *Family and Consumer Sciences Research Journal*, *30*(4), 496–525. doi:10.1177/1077727X02030004004

Munro, R. A., Ramu, G., & Zrymiak, D. J. (2015). *The certified Six Sigma green belt handbook*. ASQ Quality Press.

Muralidharan, K. (2015). Six Sigma for organizational excellence. *Springer Proceedings of the Institution of Mechanical Engineers, 203*, 43-50.

Nanda, V. (2016). *Quality management system handbook for product development companies*. CRC Press.

Oliya, E., Saleh Owlia, M., Dehdashti Shahrokh, Z., & Olfat, L. (2012). Improving marketing process using Six Sigma techniques (case of Saman Bank). *International Journal of Lean Six Sigma*, *3*(1), 59–73. doi:10.1108/20401461211223731

Petrick, J. (2017). *Total quality in managing human resources*. Routledge. doi:10.1201/9780203735534

Psomas, E., Vouzas, F., Bouranta, N., & Tasiou, M. (2017). Effects of total quality management in local authorities. *International Journal of Quality and Service Sciences*, *9*(1), 41–66. doi:10.1108/IJQSS-04-2016-0035

Raja Sreedharan, V., Raju, R., & Srivatsa Srinivas, S. (2017). A review of the quality evolution in various organisations. *Total Quality Management & Business Excellence*, *28*(3-4), 351–365. doi:10.1080/14783363.2015.1082421

Ralston, P. M., Blackhurst, J., Cantor, D. E., & Crum, M. R. (2015). A structure–conduct–performance perspective of how strategic supply chain integration affects firm performance. *The Journal of Supply Chain Management*, *51*(2), 47–64. doi:10.1111/jscm.12064

Ren, J. (2017). Modelling quality dynamics, business value and firm performance in a big data analytics environment. *International Journal of Production Research*, *55*(17), 5011–5026. doi:10.1080/00207543.2016.1154209

Ritala, P., Olander, H., Michailova, S., & Husted, K. (2015). Knowledge sharing, knowledge leaking and relative innovation performance: An empirical study. *Technovation*, *35*, 22–31. doi:10.1016/j.technovation.2014.07.011

Ross, J. E. (2017). *Total quality management: Text, cases, and readings*. Routledge. doi:10.1201/9780203735466

Ross, S. A., Westerfield, R. W., Jaffe, J. F., & Jordan, B. D. (2011). *Core principles and applications of corporate finance*. McGraw-Hill/Irwin.

Sadikoglu, E., & Olcay, H. (2014). The effects of total quality management practices on performance and the reasons of and the barriers to TQM practices in Turkey. *Advances in Decision Sciences*, *2014*(2), 1–17. doi:10.1155/2014/537605

Sadikoglu, E., & Zehir, C. (2010). Investigating the effects of innovation and employee performance on the relationship between total quality management practices and firm performance: An empirical study of Turkish firms. *International Journal of Production Economics*, *127*(1), 13–26. doi:10.1016/j.ijpe.2010.02.013

Salguero, J., Muñoz-Cauqui, M. C., Batista, M., Calvino, A., Aguayo, F., & Marcos, M. (2015). R&D&I management system in distributed manufacturing systems. *Procedia Engineering*, *132*, 54–61. doi:10.1016/j.proeng.2015.12.479

Saunila, M. (2017). Understanding innovation performance measurement in SMEs. *Measuring Business Excellence*, *21*(1), 1–16. doi:10.1108/MBE-01-2016-0005

Schroeder, R. G., Linderman, K., & Zhang, D. (2005). Evolution of quality: First fifty issues of production and operations management. *Production and Operations Management*, *14*(4), 468–481. doi:10.1111/j.1937-5956.2005.tb00234.x

Silvi, R., Bartolini, M., Raffoni, A., & Visani, F. (2015). The practice of strategic performance measurement systems: Models, drivers and information effectiveness. *International Journal of Productivity and Performance Management*, *64*(2), 194–227. doi:10.1108/IJPPM-01-2014-0010

Sunder, M. V. (2016). Lean Six Sigma project management–a stakeholder management perspective. *The TQM Journal*, *28*(1), 132–150. doi:10.1108/TQM-09-2014-0070

Surange, V. G. (2015). Implementation of Six Sigma to reduce cost of quality: A case study of automobile sector. *Journal of Failure Analysis and Prevention*, *15*(2), 282–294. doi:10.100711668-015-9927-6

Swarnakar, V., & Vinodh, S. (2016). Deploying Lean Six Sigma framework in an automotive component manufacturing organization. *International Journal of Lean Six Sigma*, *7*(3), 267–293. doi:10.1108/IJLSS-06-2015-0023

Tennant, G. (2017). *Six Sigma: SPC and TQM in manufacturing and services*. Routledge. doi:10.4324/9781315243023

Thakur, R., & Workman, L. (2016). Customer portfolio management (CPM) for improved customer relationship management (CRM): Are your customers platinum, gold, silver, or bronze? *Journal of Business Research*, *69*(10), 4095–4102. doi:10.1016/j.jbusres.2016.03.042

Topalović, S. (2015). The implementation of total quality management in order to improve production performance and enhancing the level of customer satisfaction. *Procedia Technology*, *19*, 1016–1022. doi:10.1016/j.protcy.2015.02.145

Uluskan, M., Godfrey, A. B., & Joines, J. A. (2017). Integration of Six Sigma to traditional quality management theory: An empirical study on organisational performance. *Total Quality Management & Business Excellence*, *28*(13-14), 1526–1543. doi:10.1080/14783363.2016.1150173

Upton, D. M. (1994). The management of manufacturing flexibility. *California Management Review*, *36*(2), 72–89. doi:10.2307/41165745

Valmohammadi, C., & Roshanzamir, S. (2015). The guidelines of improvement: Relations among organizational culture, TQM and performance. *International Journal of Production Economics*, *164*, 167–178. doi:10.1016/j.ijpe.2014.12.028

Vij, S., & Bedi, H. S. (2016). Are subjective business performance measures justified? *International Journal of Productivity and Performance Management*, *65*(5), 603–621. doi:10.1108/IJPPM-12-2014-0196

Womack, J. P., & Jones, D. T. (2003). *Lean Thinking: Banish Waste and Create Wealth in Your Corporation*. Free Press.

Wongrassamee, S., Simmons, J. E., & Gardiner, P. D. (2003). Performance measurement tools: The Balanced Scorecard and the EFQM Excellence Model. *Measuring Business Excellence*, *7*(1), 14–29. doi:10.1108/13683040310466690

Wu, H. C., Ai, C. H., & Cheng, C. C. (2019). Experiential quality, experiential psychological states and experiential outcomes in an unmanned convenience store. *Journal of Retailing and Consumer Services*, *51*, 409–420. doi:10.1016/j.jretconser.2019.07.003

Yang, M. G. M., Hong, P., & Modi, S. B. (2011). Impact of lean manufacturing and environmental management on business performance: An empirical study of manufacturing firms. *International Journal of Production Economics*, *129*(2), 251–261. doi:10.1016/j.ijpe.2010.10.017

Zeng, J., Phan, C. A., & Matsui, Y. (2015). The impact of hard and soft quality management on quality and innovation performance: An empirical study. *International Journal of Production Economics*, *162*, 216–226. doi:10.1016/j.ijpe.2014.07.006

KEY TERMS AND DEFINITIONS

5S Rule: It is a strategy used for optimizing business results and formed by *Seiri*: Categorization, *Seiton*: Ordering, *Seiketsu*: Standardization, *Seiso*: Cleaning, and *Shitsuke*: Discipline.

30-Second Rule: It is a rule that forces an employee to find, retrieve, and replace something within this timeframe.

ISO 9001: It is an international standard that specifies requirements for a quality management system in providing quality products and services to meet customers and regulatory requirements.

Kaizen: Also known as Continuous improvement, it consists of searching for never-ending improvements and developing processes to find better methods of converting inputs into outputs.

Lean Management: It is a management method focused on improving business performance through developing capabilities of all of its human resources.

Quality Management: It is a holistic approach to achieving and maintaining high-quality outputs, and it gained substantial importance in recent years owing to the globally rising fierce competition.

Six Sigma: It is the effective use of all employee information and quantitative methods to evaluate and improve its core processes to meet customer needs.

TQM (Total Quality Management): A sort of management based on the leadership of the top management, customer orientation, teamwork, training of the employees, zero error, and continuous improvement.

Chapter 2
Enterprise Quality Perception in a Changing Environment

Montserrat Mata-Fernández
Universidad de Deusto, Spain

ABSTRACT

This chapter gives an overview of the importance of the quality as a whole in a company, considering it moves in an environment not only determined by the velocity of change of the technologies but also by the cultural change suffered in recent years. It has been proposed a new framework where new factors have to be analyzed to achieve a company pioneer and leader in the industry. Also, it explains all the benefits of doing it and how it will affect the performance of the staff, in the vision of clients and users, and the financial results of the firm. In conclusion, all these advantages will have a great benefit to society.

INTRODUCTION

Although quality and value have always been a concern for small or large entrepreneurs, this vision must be checked and updated. Based on IT (Information Technology) quality and its evolution from its origins until now, the business environment is now moving needs to be taken into account. It is an environment disruptive, changing, and hyperconnected where the power of social networks has grown exponentially. The impact and speed of communication are so high that it has made companies invest money and efforts to control as far as possible the effect of social networks.

In this scenario, some of the big, or known, trends adopted or assimilated by most companies must be reviewed to survive. The value of quality is taking on particular relevance since it must be considered from another perspective, the new technologies that require a change. In this chapter, it has been considered some of these technologies or technological advances, such as Big Data, Internet of Things (IoT), or cybersecurity, among others that are now priorities for every company (Blosch, 2019). This quality factor, so relevant here and now, has to be led and commanded by the company's Chief Executive Officer (CEO). However, the collaboration and participation of all the staff are not only necessary but also indispensable, due to they are also part of the social networks, not only from the point of view of employees but also, in some cases, from the point of view of the user or even an influencer.

DOI: 10.4018/978-1-7998-5036-6.ch002

As mentioned previously, the support and follow-up of the leader is essential, but not enough. The disruptive environment has led the company to require the existence of new profiles, among which the profile of a quality management leader stands out, whose weight will increase day by day. Other existing profiles need to be updated because they will have to cover more needs, such as the Chief Learning Officer (CLO), that changes slightly regarding the past, and can have a significant impact in this changing environment (Lackey, 2000).

Leaders' roles related to quality are not limited to products and services. Quality-related leaders increase EBITDA, manage human resources efficiently, and optimize quality management. The rankings made by many consulting groups show the desire of many people to work or be part of a specific company. The vision people have of it is very positive. They will see the company as an excellent place to develop a professional career, to work, they will want to be part of its staff. Usually, they will wish to have products or services offered by such a company, since it is assumed to have the same high quality. People's perception of the company is more relevant now than in the past due to the echo of each comment or review vertiginously spread through social networks.

This chapter proposes a new quality framework, based on the experience of more than fifteen years working on projects carried out by different companies. By analyzing how quality has to be considered in the current environment, significant due deficiencies have been detected in many companies. It has been observed that the focus continues to be placed mainly on products and services, without considering quality weight in the leadership style and in the way of managing the company. Nowadays, more people are looking at the behavior of the company when there is some change in technology, normative, or anything that influences it. Thus, it has been detected the necessity of designing a quality analysis proposal, considering the factors that affect and influence this quality in the current digital ecosystem, so different and changing from recent years.

This proposal is framed in the area of management, leadership in terms of quality, without losing the way the quality gained in products and services, but thinking more about how the company responds and reacts to current events. This is the reason why several Critical Success Factor (CSF) have been enumerated. It is necessary to have them in mind when thinking about how to lead with quality from a high point of view, the point at which the CEO is the responsibility of leading a company where quality is the benchmark in each one of its actions, and what makes them different and better than competitors.

The chapter aims to propose factors to maximize quality in the firm and control projects. As a result, organizations will be leaders in their industries. CEOs' role regarding quality cannot be passive. They must participate and decide what to do for being quality leaders in quality companies. It will also enumerate the advantages of establishing a new quality framework, always considering the current environment and the forecasts of the future regarding technology. All these ideas here proposed, based on the experience and in the study carried out, have to be added to the ones that previously existed in the company.

VISION OF QUALITY AND ITS EVOLUTION

Quality Control (QC) is a concept that has not appeared in recent times. It has always been a human worry, from Neolithic until now, the idea was to offer high-quality products or services. It was not born with the enterprises; the quality concept was already used in the great Giza pyramids. Although in the past, maybe the objective was slightly different, because they thought about how to have products with outstanding durability (something that can be measured, a pivotal point to have in mind when talking about quality). But something started to change as the needs changed. Everyone knew that quality impacted everything that was done, and they realized that lousy quality provoked complaints and dissatisfaction with the results. And even though the evolution of the quality has focused mainly on the product and services, now is time to redirect the look and focus on other aspects, consider and analyze it from a higher position (López, 2016). Quality movement has undergone an evolution from master-apprenticeship to a standardized quality system where all processes and results are measured, documented, and analyzed (Hellman & Liu, 2013).

Doing a quick review and knowing that quality has always been important, the limited route to companies started in the fifties when the consideration of Quality Assurance (QA) appeared as a management strategy for the companies. It was the response to the necessity of being more effective and productive, and consequently, much more successful than his competitors. Probably the competition was not so fierce. However, it began to matter because of the birth of new companies within the same sector. To reach this objective, new methods and improvement quality tools were developed. It has to be highlighted the contribution of Walter A. Shewhart, who demonstrated that with a simple control graph, it was possible to control the variability of the processes being evaluated so far process quality and product quality. This was a significant change due to quality started to be seen as something that affected not only products and services but also other areas and things. Companies are nowadays applying a quality model based on processes (Cubillos, & Rozo, 2009).

Years later, new theories appeared related to it, and they were developed in post-war Japan. Such approaches managed not only to relaunch the Japanese economy but also to facilitate their companies with a high level of competitiveness to position themselves above American companies. Those theories revealed the effectiveness of a more collaboration-oriented organization, participatory, and sharing of ideas. One of these ideas was the key to creating and quality circles start-up (Wood, Hull, & Azumi, 1983). To make this work more accessible, Kaoru Ishikawa collected and grouped several statistical techniques and tools. These tools can be classified into two groups: tools for QC and tools to improve quality.

The first ones are simple tools, applicable, and handy, being used when the information about the problem or situation to be evaluated needs to be available, but it is required to be organized and grouped systematically to be successfully analyzed. These can be mentioned: Pareto chart, cause-and-effect diagram, histogram, check sheet, scatter diagram, flowchart, and statistical process chart (Pavletić, Soković, & Paliska, 2008).

The second ones are tools applied when there is not too much information about the problem, or when there is no data available, for instance, in the design phase of a product. In these cases, the approach is more proactive because it allows us to identify possible mistakes before it happens. These planning and management tools, known as the seven new tools for improving quality, are a complement to the seven classic tools proposed by Ishikawa and previously mentioned. These tools were published by JUSE (Union of Japanese Scientists and Engineers) with the aim that managers could use it in their planning and management tasks. The cited tools are affinity diagram, interrelationship diagram, tree diagram, prioritization matrix, matrix diagram or quality table, process decision diagram chart, and activity network diagram (López, 2016).

All these tools have to be considered, but it cannot be forgotten that one of the basic principles of Ishikawa regarding quality was the one that says that quality starts with education. The clients' and user's quality perception are increasingly being more critical. But he also added that the most crucial point of education and training is that QC is a way to change the quality of the company itself (Inove, 1985).

Anyway, the first common standard for quality management was published in 1987 by the International Organization for Standardization (ISO), providing the guidelines of what any quality management systems should contain (Hellman & Liu, 2013). And it did not take too much time to spread from its industrial origins to non-profit organizations, health care organizations, educational institutions, etc. (Hackman & Wageman, 1995). Nowadays, it can be said that there is no organization from the public or the private sector that does not use the concept of quality to some extent. Although, when it was created, the focus was only on satisfying the client (Jenner, 1995), the key now is to extend this idea to all the company. It is, therefore, unavoidable to adapt all the products, ideas, or objectives to current needs, with the quality as the primary guide.

But previously, it has to be clear the definition of quality and how this definition can be applied nowadays in these disruptive environments. One of the great experts in quality and quality management gave two explanations of it: first, was oriented to the fact of having zero deficiencies, to avoid reworking and consequently reduce the cost, and second, he focused on the customer satisfaction and, therefore, incurred in higher costs (Juran & Godfrey, 1999). Both points of view have to be applied nowadays, where organizations coexist in a hypercompetitive world. They have to face paradoxical challenges, like the one that combines the way of work efficiently today while innovating effectively for tomorrow. Both things have to be managed simultaneously. To manage its, companies have to understand and learn to deal with the dynamics of innovation that underlie both disruptive and sustaining innovations (Paap & Katz, 2004). But trying to know what this concept is precisely, it is necessary to go back to the 90s where disruption was defined as the process whereby a smaller company with little resources can successfully challenge established incumbent business (Christensen, Raynor, & McDonald, 2015). This challenge has to be seen from some of the existing innovations.

INFORMATION TECHNOLOGIES AND QUALITY MANAGEMENT

In a world where globalization has shaped management, and the vertiginous evolution of technologies marks the rhythm, these technological innovations are changing the business world (Hellman & Liu, 2013). If a company does not want to become obsolete and disappear, it needs to be continuously reinventing itself and reviewing the processes to adapt to the changes. Therefore, inaction is not an excellent strategy to follow, no matter the size of the company, its primary goal is to achieve higher competitiveness (Suwandej, 2015). And the increasing competitive struggle makes indispensable the use of new methodologies or different frameworks, as will be seen in this chapter (Topalović, 2015).

Undoubtedly, it is a challenging task for any company to keep continuously updated in technology. Changes are so quick, significant, and sometimes disruptive that considering new technologies has to be done with a high periodicity and with a sound judgment, based on organizational goals and in its capabilities. And in the way of adopting some of these new technologies, it is mandatory to try to meet the organization's ever-changing needs. Still, the problem is that quality usually falls by the wayside (Swanson, 1999). It is a crucial premise that the latest mission of quality management is to add value to the organizations by improving the quality of all the aspects, from applications to the administration of the company. This idea cannot be forgotten because it will determine the success of new adoptions. As it will be detailed in this chapter, it is the responsibility of the leader to elaborate a strategy that covers recent technological trends that maintain or improve the quality.

Quality is a concept that has to be extended to all the fields, covering all future technologies that have appeared. Some technologies are popular and well known, like cloud computing, but new ones have to be considered. Emerging technologies and applications for mobile computing and IoT are changing evolution through other directions (Satyanarayanan, 2017). A new paradigm has appeared and has to be considered, for example:

- **IoT**, it is relevant to highlight that all electronic devices as wearable devices, laptops, cars, sensors, and industrial components are connected via a network and empowered with data analytics that are changing our lives. Many companies and start-ups have embraced the concept of IoT in a lot of areas such as smart cities, traffic, homes, environments, and even intelligent healthcare, among others. IoT is getting better, but there are technical issues that have to be addressed. Anyway, it is indisputable that the data streams generated by IoT devices are high in volume, and it will grow in the future (Sun & Ansari, 2016). So, it is essential to control the quality of this information, being this a responsibility of the company. This will be a task of the department of quality management. New concepts related to IoT have emerged, such as the Internet of Everything (IoE) and the Intelligence of Things.
- **Cybersecurity** has always been critical to some organizations. The idea of being attacked is now a risk for all kinds of organizations. Frequently it appears some news about an attack with negative consequences, at least in reputation. In a world dominated by social networks, this is a stain in the history of the company, sometimes challenging to correct. This is why the quality in all the controls carried out by the cybersecurity department is so significant. Prevent is the key, and to do that, every analysis has to be done with the highest precision and quality. It is essential to prevent and document what has happened and how it was solved to reach this status. Someone outside the department will review the quality of such documentation. They will also check that the cybersecurity team manages the vulnerabilities in the best way.
- **The digital transformation** of this challenge leads companies to remain competitive in their industries, and this is carried out by leaders that formulate and execute strategies that embrace this transformation and drive better operational performance. This is concerned with the changes digital technologies can bring about in a company's business model, what will result in a change may be in the organizational infrastructure, and this requires a shift of cultural mindset and an organizational transformation, which will depend on the degree of maturity of the company. These changes can be seen in the rising demand from clients or users who use the internet regularly. So, the quality of the changes is determinant for the quality of the company, not only for the offered products. For this reason, it is so essential the role of the CEO, as it will be seen in this chapter because the risk of failure when considering relevant elements of digital transformation or disregarding solutions that can be more suitable to the firm depends on him. Every decision related to new technologies must be carried out after a thorough analysis, evaluating pros and cons, without losing sight that the goal is to be positioned as a leader in the sector (Hess, Matt, Benlian, & Wiesböck, 2016).
- **Artificial Intelligence** (AI) is growing at high speed and will be adopted by more and more companies. It will be accompanied by machine learning and deep learning. The relevance of quality in AI is obvious since Marvin Minsky defined AI as the science of making machines do things that would require intelligence if done by men. As far as the orders were adequate and suitable, the results will be optimum (Bolter, 1984). The aim is to imitate the human mind, so every step in

this technology must be considered quality. It can also highlight terms such as adaptive machine learning, edge analytics, transfer learning, generative adversarial networks, or graph analytics.

- **Virtual reality,** the use of virtual reality has extended to many fields and offers the enticing premise of rich sensory experience. It has been applied to several domains, from education to entertainment, being his collaboration especially relevant in medicine. Nowadays is used in surgery, so the quality here is critical and the main point to be considered.
- **Robotic Process Automation**, considering robots, it has to be mentioned in the emerging business of collaborative robots. Robots now are more accessible and capable, thanks to the advances of other technologies as AI, deep learning, etc. Some people start to talk also about the internet of business. The quality in the design of the robot is not only essential but also critical. The use of them is for warehouses and small companies that have studied the benefits of using one, maybe in the same way as drones, a field where it can be seen the offer of Drones as a Service (DaaS) (Brown, 2019).
- **Big Data** is a concept well known. However, the definition is not so clear. It can be said that it is a data set so vastly that it stresses the limits of traditional databases in volume, velocity of searches, veracity of conclusions, and various formats, according to Porche, Wilson, Johnson, Tierney, and Saltzman (2014). The definition itself naturally leads to the idea of quality, firstly in data quality. But deepening a bit, it is decisive to think about the quality of the data treatment. The decisions based on accurate, complete, and timely data will be better and will facilitate the enterprise to achieve his goals. It is a question of having the right data at the right time in the right place to obtain the best result to make a decision or to satisfy client expectations. A lack of complete, accurate, relevant, and time data will impact the development of a sound strategy. The effect of managing low-quality data will be a disaster, so all have to be treated and studied under the quality umbrella. Some of the consequences of managing low-quality data are ineffective decision making, client and employees' dissatisfaction, increased cost, reduction ability to execute one strategy, etc. All this together will contribute to what has been called information ecology (Redman, 1998). Preventing these adverse effects will be easy due to the risks that have been identified so that it can be treated and avoided. Regarding this effect, it is essential to say that sometimes it is fundamental to think more about the cost of poor quality than quality (Davenport & Prusak, 1997).

Its importance was highlighted by Olalla and Mata (2012). They said that it is a good investment for all those companies that want to improve their economic results, a way to achieve better client satisfaction and protection of the companies' brand.

- **Blockchain,** although it has been used mostly by the financial sector, it has already been seen the utility of using it in companies of healthcare, shipping, and transportation. The implications of using records are essential, but what is more important is the quality of those records (Beck, Avital, Rossi, & Thatcher, 2017).

The number of new technologies or ideas is vast and impossible to cover. In this chapter, some of them have been considered. Still, the idea is to have in mind that the company has to be aware of any emerging idea that can affect, positive or negative, on the performance of its activity. Other technologies such as Augmented Reality (AR), biotech, augmented intelligence, emotion AI, biochips, AR Cloud, or edge computing.

ROLES INVOLVED TO GUARANTEE QUALITY

It is essential to identify and satisfy client requirements. Still, it is also necessary to know the level of quality of all the processes and steps the company is developing to achieve this satisfaction. Such satisfaction has to do with emotions, and this emotion cannot be only motivated by clients, but also by employees (López, 2016). So, quality, as part of the result, is also a responsibility of all employees. It has to be inherent to the company and to its way of managing. Also, the leaders' role, involvement, and adaptation to the modern forms of management and new technologies are decisive, being important their capacity to anticipate competitors and their transparency since users and clients coexist in this technological world highly influenced by social networks.

The first role to be considered in the field of quality is the CEO. He has to be involved in every task related to quality. He will have to be part of the quality team, having a set of functions defined and bound. He will have to know how they are going to achieve marked objectives with quality. Consequently, and due times have changed, the leader needs to exercise leadership new and different. Currently, the most typical kind of leadership was autocratic leadership. Nowadays, his role requires a change in the mindset and improving his skills and procedures (Lundberg, & Westerman, 2019).

Having in mind the changes suffered by society, it has been identified some of the main qualities the new leather needs to have:

- Creativity, the CEO is no longer limited to a merely managerial environment. It would be advisable to have a more varied profile, from both soft and hard skills. The power of a creative leader is so high it can relaunch a brand or a company.
- Have initiative, be knowledgeable.
- Intuitive, facilitated with the investigation, experimentation, and data-driven analysis (Lundberg & Westerman, 2019).
- Have a strong leadership to cascade down.
- Confident and decisive, cool-headed in the face of adversity (Viscomi, 2017). His decisions will affect everyone and everything, and he will have to decide in a short period and with innovative solutions (Lipman-Blumen, 2000).
- Goal-oriented and achiever (Viscomi, 2017).

Summarizing, a good leader has to be consistent with the purpose of product and service improvements for the company's survival in his changing and competitive conditions, something studied by Kamcharoen (as cited in Suwandej, 2015), but he has also to have in mind the importance of quality management. Nowadays, he can be considered as a connective leadership as it was defined by (Lipman-Blumen, 2000).

To achieve that degree of leadership excellence, the following tasks regarding quality have to be executed:

- Reconsider how to train and manage his internal innovation teams. There is a clear lack of digital talent, and the solution is not also to give employees some training, assign them a mentor. Still, he will have to think about a strategy to incentivize and empower them to expedite new tasks, especially those highly qualified. Talent has to be retained or recruited because its contribution is invaluable.

- Create a fair workplace, where all feel their participation is necessary and essential, and where there would be fluent communication among members of different teams or departments, and with a strong relationship among members of each unit.
- Have an optimal communication network with all the staff is required to extend it vertically and horizontally within the organization and outward to clients and suppliers (López, 2016; Goolsby, 2018). This channel has always been considered, but not in the same way as nowadays, the effect and the repercussion of social networks is so high now that it deserves a separate treatment. Another point to be considered is the distribution of the information. If it is made in the wrong direction or time, the result will not be expected, and the opposite effect can be achieved (Davenport & Prusak, 1997).
- Create an ecosystem that allows the emergence of good ideas. This fact implies the development of capabilities for exploring and experiment with original and maybe disruptive ideas, have excellent tolerance to failures and work with external partners when required, which is now an already established trend. The leader has to know that collaboration with external innovators can increase revenue considerably. To reach this objective, he will have to lose the fear of exposing ideas at round tables.
- Reserve some money to invest in both the quality department and in all the tasks the company will develop related to quality. This fact implies a commitment from the leader who will have the strategic vision, and who will have to support the best ideas or solutions proposed by quality responsible wholeheartedly (Goolsby, 2018).
- Supervise the control performed by the new department of quality. The responsible will be a member of this department, but with a role of decision, taking part in the most relevant meetings, not only to give his opinion and point of view but also to decide and support the work of this department and to emphasize its importance in the company's strategy.
- Keep updated about emerging technologies as far as possible, the CEO has to get ahead of the competition, and this requires a high level of updating in advanced trends and technologies. The quality in the choice of the equipment in charge of new technologies will determine success in terms of advice on which one the company could address.
- Be compliant with recent regulations; he has to be aware of any change in the compliance and regulatory norms. As new technologies emerge, states find it necessary to regulate some aspects of them. Consequently, companies must be aware of these current rules, adopting all appropriate for the organization.
- Schedule periodic meetings with strategists, financial, quality teams, and primary responsibility to keep updated and prevent possible problems or identify opportunities.

All the mentioned tasks must be oriented towards leadership, to govern the firm's transformation in a changing world without losing quality, neither in the service and products offered, nor in the way of management, being a referent in business management to reach a high level of transparency. The benefits of this transparency will be that users, providers, clients, and even employees will consider the company as an example of good practices and high quality through all the processes and services offered. Even more, all the companies should chase to be transparent to build trust and attract investment. The result will be a capacity to change things and contribute to the growth of the society with which it has to interact.

It can be concluded that if leaders want to have sustainable growth for the company, a fundamental requirement nowadays, they need to create the conditions for the best ideas to get picked up. These conditions imply leveraging talent both inside and outside the company to respond to a competitive, ever-changing environment (Osterwalder, Viki, & Pigneur, 2019). With good quality management, the reputation of the CEO will be improved internally and externally, and consequently, it will report a great benefit to the company (Francis, Huang, Rajgopal, & Zang, 2008). And his behavior will be decisive to create an organizational culture marked by the idea of quality in all his lifecycle, from material products to people and regulations (Whitehurst, 2016).

In the strategy of the leadership, quality has to occupy a privileged place, since it is a vital component of the business strategy, and quality improvement is a strategic variable employed in the highly competitive international business world (Adam, Flores, & Macias 2001, p. 43). Nowadays, where innovations appear continuously is elusive to think about technical changes without enhancing quality (Bourke & Roper, 2017).

But to carry out this task, the CEO will need the help of someone, the quality, and management leader, a role that, if it does not exist, it will have to be created. CEOs will need to have some relevant characteristics to play a quality role. Even though some of them can be like the ones described for a leader, it can be forgotten that their vision is different due is focused only on quality, obviously aligned with the company's objectives. The main attributes he will need to have are the following ones:

- Have a strategic transversal vision.
- Define the mission, vision, and values of the quality management team, always according to the goals of the company.
- Have a sound vision of what is to be a brand of this century.
- Be an artist of influence. He has to be able to create a culture in the company, knowing that this corporate culture has to evolve, so he has to be able to transmit it and to manage that everyone gets involved. To do this, he will have to collaborate with the team of change management to spread that quality idea all around the company. With his example and knowing the mindset of his teams, he will manage to change old behavior patterns or habits. Also, it is necessary to highlight the importance of the corporate culture to help employee involvement and participation in the company's decisions, making transparency a reality (Kpakol, Aborlo, & Amah, 2014).
- In the past, it was seen as a facilitator, but now he has to be more than this. He must have a creative mind to lead employees in quality.
- Have the ability to combine standardization and disruption. Every company has to meet specific standards, this is unquestionable, but with the emerging technologies, a study has to be done to know if it affects the compliance of this standard.
- Being an innovator, he has the responsibility to understand not only business process implications, but also the social impact.

Besides having the qualities described, the quality management leader will have to do some tasks that have been enumerated below:

- He will have to analyze the advanced technologies the company wants or can adopt and the mandatory standards to conclude if it affects or not and how.
- He would try to have good teamwork with a strong relationship among them and with the capability to understand the goal of the company and the importance of the participation of every team member. And he will give each member the independence to establish connections into the qual-

ity community, helping the team to detect points of improvement or weak points that need to be analyzed and solved to improve the quality of every process in the organization.

- He would try to extend the quality concept to all the company through training, talks, and any other kind of communication helped by the change management team.
- He will have to create a quality team considering: the scope of the functions they will have, the structure of the team thinking about the contemporary trends, what will be the focus of the group, the abilities, capabilities, and talent of each member of the team and which role will play each one. This team must be agile. It cannot be a bureaucratic entity. Team responsibilities also include the prioritization of quality issues once identified, the collaboration to create an action plan according to the root cause analysis, the documentation of the solution of the problem, to anticipate and address quality issues. Others will need to be defined with the quality management leader, which will be updated when necessary (Swanson, 1999).
- He will report periodically to the Chief Information Officer (CIO) of all the tasks related to quality, and this recently created team will inform him of quality.
- He would build and sustain an excellent executive network in the company, having the quality of communicating in the best way with the board committee, peers, and other members of all departments (Swanson, 1999).

Another role that will be more and more indispensable is the one known as transformer CLO. This comes from the necessity of organizations being more adaptable, which means changing the goals of corporate learning. CEO and quality management leader will train employees to position the company for success, with the help of the CLO in these aspects: transforming learning methods, balance face-to-face and digital learning, emphasize digital thinking and act as co-creators, among others (Lundberg & Westerman, 2019).

QUALITY ANALYSIS PROPOSAL

QC helps to strengthen the country's economy and ensure a solid economic foundation for the future. Ishikawa presented this, and it has not lost his value, but in a so changing environment like this one, is critic the necessity of having a solid foundation for products and services offered. However, it is also essential for a trustworthy and respectable company model in his field at an international level, which can only be achieved if the management is of high quality (Ishikawa, 1989).

Nowadays, it is necessary to have a strategic look, with an innovator and creative spirit, both the CEO and the enterprise have to be more flexible than in the past. Based on the study of several projects for more than fifteen years in different areas and companies, it can be concluded that the following reasons need to be considered to define a new framework:

- The environment where enterprises are now making the big concern to survive overall lets in second face things as quality. But they have to be aware because emerging companies can engulf the big ones if they do not move quickly. After all, these last ones were born with the peculiarity of continuous change and high quality. All this comes from the rise in competitiveness; the born of start-ups is a threat for more prominent companies where a change takes much more time to be implemented and adopted.

- The change in the regulations, not only derived from globalization like the new General Data Protection Regulation (GDPR) and others more bounded explicitly to a particular field.
- It also has to be considered the importance of Corporate Social Responsibility (CSR) in the Quality Management System (QMS). QMS is a formal system that includes documenting the processes, structure, and responsibilities required to achieve effective quality management (Hellman & Liu, 2013). Firstly, it has to be clarified what it is CSR, to define it, several concepts are used, such as social performance, social responsibility, sustainable, responsible business, etc. Several authors gave their definition as Bowen, Berger, and Luckmann, or Later Wood. Still, in this chapter, it has been considered one of the latest, given by Carroll, who suggested that four kinds of social responsibilities constituted CSR: economic, legal, ethical, and philanthropic (Carroll, 1991). In 2006 even the European Commission defined it. Some years later, in 2010, the ISO released a standard ISO 26000:2010 Guidance on Social Responsibility and defined CSR as a responsibility of an organization. Anyway, it has been proved that due to the implementation of employee-related CSR activities in QMS is a good option not only to minimize the staff rotation but also to reduce organization cost, increase commitment and loyalty. What is more important, it helps to improve the quality of processes and the performance of an organization (Frolova & Lapina, 2014).
- The final client has changed its behaviors and habits betting on companies already engaged in new technologies and agile enough to adopt recent changes in a short time.
- The time to implement new trends has been considerably reduced. In the past, most companies spent a lot of time planning their digital future and thinking about it without taking any action. In contrast, others were more agile and have already positioned themselves advantageously.
- Functions related to quality have to be shared in all the companies. It cannot be separated by department or role. The responsibility of senior management and the support and encouragement from their level to achieve the desired quality is required. Still, CEOs have also to participate and collaborate to create a quality plan, analyzing points like the degree of commitment and involvement of employees and the possible innovations being carried by the company.

Key Aspects of Quality From a High Level

One of the keys to achieving organizational excellence is the combination of focusing on quality at the process level and considering and managing to cover the needs of stakeholders. These facts will contribute to the well-being of society, according to Frolova and Lapina (2014), and this is something that every leader must have in mind. Hence, his compromise is mandatory to achieve excellence in quality management.

In the environment where companies move nowadays, the way the leader manages the organization will have a needed cultural transformation, including new methods, an open collaboration, and a high level of soft skills added to the required hard skills. He will have to be more receptive to clients and users because they are marking the steps in the evolution of products and services (Rusu, 2016). They are demanding better quality, quick response to their necessities, and lower prices, so improving the quality of the organization is essential (Bolatan, Gozlu, Alpkan, & Zaim, 2016).

But the leader has to think also about the future of the company, so he must prevent the emergence of some problems taking prophylactic measures. His attitude has to be always preventive, foreseeing what could happen, and taking the adequate preventions are responsibilities of the CEO. And this is a continuous task to be done so that it can be used the Plan-Do-Check-Act (PDCA) cycle. It will help improve processes, including in every step task related to quality (Rusu, 2016).

Quality is a competitiveness factor, so everything has to be considered under this umbrella. Companies need to prove their quality performance, mostly to survive in a context where there is no chance to fail. The objective is to acquire a high degree of differentiation, decreased costs, improve the brand image, and answer customer's demand avoiding errors and the waste of time (Claver, Tari, & Molina, 2003). As a result, competitiveness has turned into one of the main goals for most organizations (Suwandej, 2015).

But there are other factors to be considered that have been listed below:

- Innovation, each new technology or way of working, needs to have an adequate level of quality, which must be continuously improved to meet the demands of the stakeholders, and therefore cover the new needs of the disrupting environment, generating a social benefit. The process of innovation has to be a key growth driver for the increase in resilience.
- Flexibility, the fast-moving organization this characteristic is relevant because organizations are susceptible to any change in the environment (Lipman-Blumen, 2000). The capacity to adapt to the changes without losing its level of quality will put distance between this company and its competitors.
- Training is essential not only for boosting their knowledge and keeping them updated but also for shaping their behavior in learning all their tasks and incrementing their loyalty to the organization. All training will be done to the right persons in the appropriate moment (Suwandej, 2015), to whom and when are questions to have in mind when thinking about training and mentoring. This task is closely related to knowledge management, defined by Bhatt as a process to facilitate knowledge-related activities such as creation, transformation, and use of knowledge (as cited in Duran, Çetindere, & Şahan, 2014). This fact will improve the decisions of the organization and, therefore, of the business processes, making it possible to reduce costs and delays. It can be said that overall, this will create a knowledge-sharing culture that will depend on the mutual trust and positive individual and group relations (Duran et al., 2014).
- Communication, for facilitating the improvement.
- Measurements and evaluation. According to Ahire and Golhar (1996), the measures of quality performance are reliability, durability, and suitability of product standardization. Several authors have considered the measures considering others, but what is clear for everyone is that one of the technology transfer's reasons is quality control, as Verbano and Venturini (2012) manifested.
- Teamwork, the level of participation of each member will increase facts like the amount of information received, time spent in perceiving this information, understanding of tasks to do, providing all this positive effect on each team member, on the leader of the team, and of the company (Suwandej, 2015).
- Continuous process improvement, the focus now has to be to concentrate on general targets of the enterprise in process improvement, rather than individual practices (Suwandej, 2015). As has been said, the PDCA can be used but adding in every step of quality control.
- Horizontal integration of functions and tasks developed by other departments.
- To understand users or clients, social networks nowadays can be the difference among being on the top or disappear. The relationship between Total Quality Management (TQM) and customer satisfaction is very close (Topalović, 2015). Regarding TQM, it can be said that in the past, it was seen more from the customer perspective. Therefore, nowadays, it is essential to know the

demands of the customers as regards the quality (Suwandej, 2015). It has been demonstrated that the benefits of implementing TQM in terms of customer orientation, the participation of employees, QC, etc. are high for customers, quality culture, and quality procedure (Duran et al., 2014). The concept and significance of the quality culture have been widely studied. It is considered the grouping of all those intangible factors that coexist in a company that sometimes establishes the difference between being a benchmark in the market or not (Harvey, & Stensaker, 2008).

This work related to quality control must be seen as more than mandatory for every company or organization nowadays. It is necessary from the CEO's point of view, which cost will be calculated in the improvement plan and the adaptation process of the firm to the new requirements of the market. It has to be an integrated philosophy that will also improve the competitiveness of the firm and its benefits (Bolatan et al., 2016).

There is no management model applied only for a CEO, maybe because his work always has been considered the task of managing the company, centered on financial and strategic points of view, letting the decisions related to quality to other departments or responsible. Nevertheless, one of the leading CEO's tasks in these disruptive environments is to guarantee the quality as it has been hitherto mentioned, not only of services and products offered by the company, but also and even more critical of managing. The goal is to have high-quality management to improve efficiency, productivity, and quality of everything offered by the company to give a social benefit.

Management models nowadays applied, quality ones as ISO or excellence European Foundation Quality Management (EFQM), are based in some way in the principle cause-effect, being its effect evidence of something that has already happened. The pursued objective by quality varies as the scenery changes, being now more and more competitive. Other models focus on client satisfaction (ISO 9001) or the stakeholders (ISO 9004), being already introduced themes as the CSR, which nowadays is a factor that needs to be deeply studied, even more having in mind this continuously changing world (De Velasco, 2012).

Nowadays, quality management focused on excellence is still in force. Still, it has to be completed or reformulated because it has to cover previous visions delegated to the background. The objective cannot only be to satisfy client expectative, but also to unify them with the personal purpose of each employee. This fact will contribute to having an excellent company not only in the service quality but also in the management quality carried by the high staff. This can only be achieved with the compromise and involvement of the CEO. Everyone has to participate and work on it. Thanks to the support of the leader, the positioning of the company will be better and could stay longer in a complicated environment. Anyway, there would be an available higher period somewhat more remarkable than the other companies to have prepared the new service to offer.

Characteristics of the new Framework

The quality concept will now have a global reach that will include all business activity: operative, support and management, and direction. So, the new quality model thought and designed due to the experience and study carried out in this chapter, has to cover the objectives that are commented below:

- **Develop a more proactive leadership**, as leaders need to be determined, patient, loyal to team, transparent, challenge-taking, goal-oriented, and with a high level of initiative, without losing the perspective of the execution of leadership good aligned with his management (Suwandej, 2015).

- **Involve all the employees** by covering all the activities as part of the value chain. Employees have an impact on the results of the company, and the weight of employees now is more significant due to social networks. It is a proven fact that teamwork if it is carried out with the correct diligence, obtains better results since the contribution of new ideas is stimulated. The concept of continuous improvement is strengthened (Olalla, San José, & Mata, 2012). Evangelization campaigns about quality will be ongoing and should start from the beginning.
- **Have an internal network of connexion between departments**, all joined and in tune to boost efficiency and satisfaction of the client. To do this, it would be necessary to ask for the help of the change management group. They will elaborate on a plan to make them see the importance of the work of everyone, working on empathy and transparency.
- **Increase the transparency level** inside the company to offer a real image of a committed and aware because social and cultural changes are continuously happening. Any enterprise can use this transparency achieved as a bridge for the adaptation of new technology. All the initiatives started have to be communicated to everyone, and the success or failure has to be shared.
- **Adapt to the new economic and social environment**, considering that this may need innovative and revolutionary thinking where clients, users, providers, and products can be regarded as raw material (Rusu, 2016).
- **Provide to the social environment the vision of quality** in every field of it. They are necessary to have transparency proven and strengthened previously. Clients and users are sensitive to what is being published on social networks, so every comment must be considered. The marketing department will work with a quality team to launch the right campaigns and messages.
- **The capability to work with new technologies** will need a thoughtful plan to decide which one can be useful or significant for the company. Several departments, including the quality department, will have to work on it following these steps (Bolatan et al., 2016):
    - **Identify the technological needs (I);** not all the technologies have to be adopted. It will depend on the necessities or in the goal established by the board committee. At this point, it is relevant to make the quality department participate. The new technology was chosen to have to give an added value to the quality of the company.
    - **Share the managed information (S)**. Communication has always been a key to address the objective of transparency and honesty and is the best way to have the commitment and loyalty of employees, customers, and users. It is essential to involve everyone from the start point to let them give an opinion or suggestion. Subsequently, all decisions will be communicated to all departments simultaneously, with the participation of marketing and the team of change management.
    - **Evaluate and select the best technology (E)**. Once the decision of what technology will be adopted, complying with the quality regulations established by it, it has to be evaluated. The evaluation and assessment of the technology will be done for other equipment because it is more technological. Besides, the financial department will have to assess the risks and the viability of adopting it, raising the Return On Investment (ROI).
    - **Adapt and absorb the improved technology (A)**, new technology has to be incorporated into working or the company's portfolio services in a natural way and faster than the competition. This work will be facilitated by the collaboration of the change management team: the sooner it is accepted by everyone, the positive results will be shown, not only internally but also for customers, suppliers, and users.

- ◦ **Optimize the exploitation and utilization of the new technology (O).** Once incorporated, the next logical step is not only to exploit it but also to optimize its utilization. Indeed, customers and users' opinions have to be considered in this changing digital environment so hyperconnected. This task is part of the continuous improvement process and will be done by several departments as marketing who will collect user reviews, IT will make the improvements deemed necessary, and human resources will carry out the appropriate training, for instance.

It has been summarized in Table 1. It has been elaborated based on accumulated experience and the company's department's process of selecting new technology, quantifying their participation as High (H), Moderate (M), or low (L).

Table 1. The relation between steps and departments

ID	Quality Management	Financial/ Accounting	Human Resources	Marketing	IT
I	M	L	L	L	H
S	H	L	M	H	M
E	M	H	L	L	H
A	H	L	M	M	H
O	M	M	M	M	H

Source: the Author

Another point to consider is the fact that nowadays, there is not thought of quality as a way of identifying and detecting mistakes, but as a way of achieving the improvement objectives set and satisfy more and in the best way client requirements, giving an added value (Evans & Lindsay, 2015). This is the idea: the CEO has to reach the quality that his competitors cannot offer.

Advantages of the new Framework

The advantages of this new model of quality control are detailed below:

- **Increase the reliability** of the company, improving the trust that customers and investors have on it. The image will be reevaluated without the participation of the marketing department. The effect of word of mouth is potent, heightened, and bolstered using social networks.
- **Have a company better positioned** in the rankings of the market, because its adaptation to the new technologies would be quicker. The capacity to analyze the best technology to incorporate in a short time will make the company engage more customers because, in a world ruled by immediacy, the first to arrive in the early to win the market, but this will be lost if the offered quality is no good.
- **Have a quality guarantee system.**
- **Increment of the employee productivity** and his compromise with the mission, vision, and values of the company. The staff will be involved with the company's values because they will think

and feel that everything made has a high quality, making them proud of their work due it affects the final product or service.

- **Increase the talent retention** and the recruitment of new talents, being considered as a desirable place to work so that it will result in a call effect for new value recruitments.
- **The creation of a collaboration network** between departments to avoid the silo effect.

To evaluate the quality management of the company, it can be considered the following TQM Success Factors Dimensions (Bolatan et al., 2016; Suwandej, 2015):

- Leadership, the way of leading a company, has changed. Modern leaders need to be: empathetic, innovative, always looking at the big picture, committed to diversity (they have to think about how diversity enhances the culture of the company, helping it to grow), high-risk tolerance, the strong capability to inspire, etc. (Richmond, 2018).
- Strategic planning process. This process will start with defining or reviewing the vision, mission, and values of the company and continuing with the goal in the level of quality and how it is going to be measured.
- Strategic Quality Management (SQM) or Strategic Quality Total Management (SQTM), factors that determine the quality management from the overall performance of a company (Madu & Kuei, 1993).
- Conception quality management. This dimension has been broadly defined throughout the chapter.
- Customer satisfaction. Its value needs to be measured in the satisfaction level and the customers' share of spending in the brand. Improving this share usually represents a greater opportunity than efforts to keep customer loyalty, contemplating that single-brand commitment is very unusual nowadays (Keiningham, Gupta, Aksoy, & Buoye, 2014).
- Communication and any way of engaging with everyone need to have a different treatment. As far as possible, employees have to know what initiatives the company is carrying out.
- Employee loyalty and involvement (incentives, teamwork).
- Innovation, new technologies.
- The quality results in a business environment.
- Knowledge, measurements, and evaluation.

This proposal is not exclusive. Any company can combine it with other methods already used, as the following ones (Adams, 2018):

- Lean thinking, the main idea, in this case, is to avoid and remove waste. Levinson and Rerick (2002) identified seven different types of waste. Three will be considered in this study because it applies directly to quality management: waiting, time in queue, non-value-adding processes, and costs of quality: rework and inspection.
- Model for improvement, using the Plan-Do-Study-Act (PDSA) cycle. All learned in each process will be used for the next one.
- Six Sigma methodology aims to reduce as much as possible defects, cycle time, and improve customer satisfaction, using DMAIC (Define, Measure, Analyze, Improve, Control) (Hellman & Liu, 2013).

- The theory of constraints seeks to identify the rate-limiting step in a system, focusing mainly on removing the bottleneck.

It will be the decision of the company, and it needs to use one of the listed models, but regardless of the chosen one, the new framework has to be adopted to improve the management and the results of the company.

CONCLUSION

After considering the scenario of several companies been analyzed, it has been seen a gap in quality that needs to be covered. Most of them were centered on results, and not so much on how everything is done. This philosophy could be valid in the past, but not now where changes happen so quickly and where companies need to differentiate and stand out for being pioneers or early adopters of new technologies. The company's gear must be a combination of people, costs, and quality, with the help and work of the leader.

Thus, in this chapter, several factors have been taken into account for achieving high-quality, excluding product or service quality in detail. Quality encompasses all the company, and that must start from the highest levels. Its participation is also fundamental throughout all the processes carried out. The presence of the CEO in the quality meetings must be essential since without his support the attractive, and possible repercussion of the quality department will blur and disappear when the problems and day-to-day management engulf him. He will have to participate and decide, so he will have to work closely with the quality management team.

With all the information shown, quality management must be considered in every task developed in a company. To be a market leader and be seen as a model, quality has to govern the firm. To achieve this goal, the firm must be supported by the CEO and the collaboration of all employees. All of them must keep an eye on what happens around to study and anticipate adopting innovation that reports the best benefit.

Quality cannot be achieved without the help of intellectual capital, one of the central values that a company can have today. The search and retention of talent will be among the most significant challenges that the company will face. It is more difficult nowadays to retain an employee than a client, it is a trend that is already being seen, and that will increase in the coming years. Thus, firms, to be considered acceptable, must offer quality in products, services, and management of resources. The adoption of this strategy is critical to stay in a highly competitive market and position itself as the industry leader.

This is the first step to build a framework, and the next step would be to define some good practices to consider increasing benefits, not only for the company but also for society. It is a trend that companies can help with its work to the well-being of the society because the environment nowadays is not local; the scope of action is global. The framework has been built with this premise making it available and useful for any company in all sectors. This study can be completed in the future with the definition of good practices to follow in every process developed in the company.

REFERENCES

Adam, E. E. Jr, Flores, B. E., & Macias, A. (2001). Quality improvement practices and the effect on manufacturing firm performance: Evidence from Mexico and the USA. *International Journal of Production Research, 39*(1), 43–63. doi:10.1080/00207540150208853

Adams, D. (2018). Quality improvement; part 1: Introduction and overview. *BJA Education, 18*(3), 89–94. doi:10.1016/j.bjae.2017.12.002

Ahire, S. L., & Golhar, D. Y. (1996). Quality management in large vs. small firms. *Journal of Small Business Management, 34*(2), 1–11.

Beck, R., Avital, M., Rossi, M., & Thatcher, J. B. (2017). *Blockchain technology in business and information systems research.* Academic Press.

Blosch, M. (2019). *2019 Hype Cycles: 5 Priorities Shape the Further Evolution of Digital Innovation: A Gartner Trend Insight Report.* Gartner.

Bolatan, G. I. S., Gozlu, S., Alpkan, L., & Zaim, S. (2016). The impact of technology transfer performance on total quality management and quality performance. *Procedia: Social and Behavioral Sciences, 235*, 746–755. doi:10.1016/j.sbspro.2016.11.076

Bolter, J. (1984). Artificial Intelligence. *Daedalus, 113*(3), 1–18. www.jstor.org/stable/20024925

Bourke, J., & Roper, S. (2017). Innovation, quality management, and learning: Short-term and longer-term effects. *Research Policy, 46*(8), 1505–1518. doi:10.1016/j.respol.2017.07.005

Brown, A. (2019). The Real Robotics Revolution Arrives as a Service. *Interesting Engineering.* Retrieved from https://interestingengineering.com/

Carroll, A. B. (1991). The pyramid of corporate social responsibility: Toward the moral management of organizational stakeholders. *Business Horizons, 34*(4), 39–48. doi:10.1016/0007-6813(91)90005-G

Christensen, C. M., Raynor, M. E., & McDonald, R. (2015). What is disruptive innovation? *Harvard Business Review, 93*(12), 44–53. PMID:17183796

Claver, E., Tari, J. J., & Molina, J. F. (2003). Critical Factors And Results Of Quality Management: An Empirical Study. *Total Quality Management, 14*(1), 91–118. doi:10.1080/14783360309709

Cubillos Rodríguez, M. C., & Rozo Rodríguez, D. (2009). El concepto de calidad: Historia, evolución e importancia para la competitividad. *Revista de la Universidad de la Salle, 2009*(48), 80–99.

Davenport, T. H., & Prusak, L. (1997). *Information ecology: Mastering the information and knowledge environment.* Oxford University Press on Demand.

De Velasco, J. A. P. F. (2012). *Gestión Por Procesos.* 5a Edicion. ESIC editorial.

Duran, C., Çetindere, A., & Şahan, Ö. (2014). An analysis of the relationship between total quality management practices and knowledge management: The case of Eskişehir. *Procedia: Social and Behavioral Sciences, 109*, 65–77. doi:10.1016/j.sbspro.2013.12.422

Evans, J.R., & Lindsay, W.M. (2015). *Administración y control de la calidad*. Cengage Learning Editors.

Francis, J., Huang, A. H., Rajgopal, S., & Zang, A. Y. (2008). CEO reputation and earnings quality. *Contemporary Accounting Research*, *25*(1), 109–147. doi:10.1506/car.25.1.4

Frolova, I., & Lapina, I. (2014). Corporate social responsibility in the framework of quality management. *Procedia: Social and Behavioral Sciences*, *156*, 178–182. doi:10.1016/j.sbspro.2014.11.166

Goolsby, D. (2018). *Critical Challenges faced by Quality Departments and Recommended Actions*. Quality Magazine.

Hackman, J. R., & Wageman, R. (1995). Total quality management: Empirical, conceptual, and practical issues. *Administrative Science Quarterly*, *40*(2), 309–342. doi:10.2307/2393640

Harvey, L., & Stensaker, B. (2008). Quality culture: Understandings, boundaries, and linkages. *European Journal of Education*, *43*(4), 427–442. doi:10.1111/j.1465-3435.2008.00367.x

Hellman, P., & Liu, Y. (2013). Development of quality management systems: How have disruptive technological innovations in quality management affected organizations? *Quality Innovation Prosperity*, *17*(1), 104–119. doi:10.12776/qip.v17i1.154

Hess, T., Matt, C., Benlian, A., & Wiesböck, F. (2016). Options for formulating a digital transformation strategy. *MIS Quarterly Executive*, *15*(2), 103–119.

Inove, K. (1985). *Education & Training of Industrial Manpower in Japan*. DIANE Publishing.

Ishikawa, K. (1989). *Introducción al Control de Calidad*. Díaz de Santos.

Jenner, M. G. (1995). *Software quality management and ISO 9001: how to make them work for you*. John Wiley & Sons, Inc.

Juran, J., & Godfrey, A. B. (1999). *Quality handbook*. Republished McGraw-Hill.

Keiningham, T., Gupta, S., Aksoy, L., & Buoye, A. (2014). The High Price of Customer Satisfaction. *Harvard Business Review*.

Kpakol, A., & Amah, E. (2014). Re-Engineering Corporate Culture for Organizational Receptivity to Change. *European Journal of Business and Management*, *6*, 167–176.

Lackey, R. M. (2000). *The role of the chief learning officer: Implications for theory and practice*. The University of New Mexico.

Levinson, W. A., & Rerick, R. A. (2002). *Lean Enterprise: A Synergistic Approach to Minimizing Waste*. ASQ Quality Press.

Lipman-Blumen, J. (2000). *Connective Leadership: Managing in a Changing World*. Oxford University Press.

López, P. (2016). *Herramientas para la mejora de la Calidad*. FC Editorial. Fundación Confemetal.

Lundberg, A., & Westerman, G. (2019). The Transformer CLO. *Harvard Business Review*. Retrieved from https://hbr.org/

Madu, C. N., & Kuei, C. H. (1993). Introducing strategic quality management. *Long Range Planning*, *26*(6), 121–131. doi:10.1016/0024-6301(93)90214-Z

Olalla, B., & Mata, M. (2012). *Little Big Data*. ITSMF Service Talk.

Olalla, B., San José, C., & Mata, M. (2012). Factor humano: un elemento clave en la búsqueda de la eficiencia de los proyectos. In *VII Congreso Nacional VISION12*. Madrid: itSMF Spain.

Osterwalder, A., Viki, T., & Pigneur, Y. (2019). Why Your Organization Needs an Innovation Ecosystem. *Harvard Business Review*. Retrieved from https://hbr.org/

Paap, J., & Katz, R. (2004). Anticipating disruptive innovation. *Research Technology Management*, *47*(5), 13–22. doi:10.1080/08956308.2004.11671647

Pavletić, D., Soković, M., & Paliska, M. S. G. (2008, January). Practical application of quality tools. *2nd International Quality Conference*.

Porche, I., Wilson, B., Johnson, E., Tierney, S., & Saltzman, E. (2014). Big Data: Challenges and Opportunities. In Data Flood: Helping the Navy Address the Rising Tide of Sensor Information (pp. 1-6). RAND Corporation.

Redman, T. C. (1998). The impact of poor data quality on the typical enterprise. *Communications of the ACM*, *41*(2), 79–82. doi:10.1145/269012.269025

Richmond, J. (2018). *What Does Modern Leadership Really Mean?* Retrieved from https://www.business.com/articles/leadership-styles-millennials/

Rusu, C. (2016). From quality management to managing quality. *Procedia: Social and Behavioral Sciences*, *221*, 287–293. doi:10.1016/j.sbspro.2016.05.117

Satyanarayanan, M. (2017). The emergence of edge computing. *Computer*, *50*(1), 30–39. doi:10.1109/MC.2017.9

Sun, X., & Ansari, N. (2016). EdgeIoT: Mobile edge computing for the Internet of Things. *IEEE Communications Magazine*, *54*(12), 22–29. doi:10.1109/MCOM.2016.1600492CM

Suwandej, N. (2015). Factors influencing total quality management. *Procedia: Social and Behavioral Sciences*, *197*, 2215–2222. doi:10.1016/j.sbspro.2015.07.361

Swanson, D. L., Esposito, R. A., & Jester, J. (1999). Managing Quality for Information Technology. *Quality Digest*, *19*, 43–45.

Topalović, S. (2015). The implementation of total quality management in order to improve production performance and enhancing the level of customer satisfaction. *Procedia Technology*, *19*, 1016–1022. doi:10.1016/j.protcy.2015.02.145

Verbano, C., & Venturini, K. (2012). Technology transfer in the Italian space industry: Organizational issues and determinants. *Management Research Review*, *35*(3/4), 272–288. doi:10.1108/01409171211210163

Viscomi, C. (2017). *7 New Types of Leadership Models for Innovative Thinkers*. Retrieved from https://alistemarketing.com/blog/types-of-leadership-models/

Whitehurst, J. (2016). Leaders Can Shape Company Culture Through Their Behaviors. *Harvard Business Review.* Retrieved from https://hbr.org/

Wood, R., Hull, F., & Azumi, K. (1983). Evaluating quality circles: *The American application. California Management Review*, *26*(1), 37–53. doi:10.2307/41165049

KEY TERMS AND DEFINITIONS

Connective Leadership: It is when a leader works as a facilitator between team members, helping to work together and to create a collaborative environment.

Disruptive: A change that breaks with previous ideas and conventions, implying a significant shift in enterprises to survive in the new environment.

Influencer: It is a person that uses social networks to give an opinion and who is considered by a sector of the population as a reference to follow.

Intelligence of Things: It is the way to give any machine attributes of human beings, thanks to the AI and connecting all among them.

Internet of Everything: The fact of considering that in the future, almost all devices will be connected, so every machine will have the required technology to be more automatic and, in a certain way, more intelligent.

Mentoring: A way of teaching an employee through the experience of another employee with an extensive professional career and acquired knowledge for his expertise in a diverse group of projects, departments, or companies.

Quality Circle: It consists of a group of employees who periodically dedicate part of their time to find and implement the solutions to problems related to their work.

Resilience: It is the capacity that a company has to face any problem or difficulty and recover from it quickly, minimizing the impacts.

Transformer CLO: They are formed by senior managers that help companies and employees to thrive. They drive the main changes in a company, transforming their learning methods, forgetting old ways of learning.

Chapter 3
Quality Management Principles for Entrepreneurial Sustainability

Neeta Baporikar
https://orcid.org/0000-0003-0676-9913
Namibia University of Science and Technology, Namibia & University of Pune, India

ABSTRACT

Quality definitions have been altered with the transition of time, needs, and demands. But the vitality has more or less been progressed to resolve the issue by compliance to standards approach for customer satisfaction. With management routine getting complicated, attacks to managing quality in operational areas are becoming unmanageable. For TQM to be victorious, all of the elements within the enterprise must be conjointly engaged. While the critical factors are the basis for transformational preference to produce a substantial advancement culture for consistent competitive advantage and be sustainable, basically, the main objective of TQM is to generate an environment in which all the assets are used ingeniously and effectively in order to provide quality service. TQM is a way of managing the efficiency, viscidity, adaptability in general, and in the future would be to ensure entrepreneurial sustainability. Hence adopting an exploratory approach, the aim of this chapter is to critically examine the underlying principles of quality management for entrepreneurial sustainability.

INTRODUCTION

Quality definitions have been altered with the transition of time, modification of customer's needs and demands. But the vitality has more or less been progressed to resolve the issue, compliance to standards for customer satisfaction. With management routine getting complicated, attacks to managing quality in operational areas are becoming unmanageable. Enterprises and entrepreneurs which have victorious outcome with TQM principles have customer and quality integrated into their overall corporate scheme as any enterprise is a system of interconnected units. For TQM to be victorious, all of the elements within the enterprise must be conjointly engaged. Some characteristics of TQM are considered to be fundamental:

DOI: 10.4018/978-1-7998-5036-6.ch003

modification, customer preference, communication, consistent improvement, restorative measures, the enterprise structure of network type in the process or case management, creativity, IT, organizational culture, team, and future orientation. While the critical factors are the basis for transformational preference to produce a substantial advancement culture for consistent competitive advantage and be sustainable. But basically, the main objective of TQM is to generate within the organization an environment in which all the assets are used ingeniously and effectively in order to provide quality service the institution needs to adapt in this fast-paced world. TQM is a way of managing the efficiency, viscidity, adaptability, and aggressiveness of business in general and in future would be to ensure entrepreneurial sustainability.

Determining quality in entrepreneurial sustainability is a monumental exception considering the underlying receiver is us, humans. It is the quality of entrepreneurial sustainability that shapes incessant wealth and safety of both societies and their people. What is really the relevance of learning for the evolution of brilliance and proficiency of a person that will lead to a progressive economy should not be subverting. This has used a powerful scheme for the upgrading of higher entrepreneurial sustainability in almost all countries all over the world. The higher learning system was proven effective in producing remarkable professionals to rule the nation in the future. But then, quality improvement is a constant process. Thus, perception on index rate and execution is necessarily precedent. In order to enhance quality service, entrepreneurial sustainability al institution needs to know the necessities. These necessities, must be understand the essence of the uniqueness. However, people foresee quality variously specify that in order to give verdict to quality, and correspondingly improve quality, it is vital to find out the characteristics of quality. Thus, it is crucial to determine the characteristics of quality for the measurement of the entrepreneurial sustainability process. Hence adopting an analytical approach the aim of this chapter is explore the quality management principles for entrepreneurial sustainability

LITERATURE REVIEW

TQM means handling of all the components of organization principles and procedures, patterns, arrangement, and all those who are affected in any way with the quality of the product or service. The main objective of TQM is to generate within the organization an environment in which all the assets are used ingeniously and effectively in order to provide quality service the institution needs to adapt in this fast paced world. TQM has been acquired as a management epitome by many organizations worldwide. Quality movement started with quality improvement project at manufacturing companies. But afterwards it dispersed to other service organizations including banking, insurance, nonprofit organizations, health care, government and entrepreneurial sustainability al institutions. TQM molds rooted on imparting of prime instructors, more often than not, demands a number of rules such as cooperation, top management leadership, customer focus, employee engagement, consistent advancement tool, trainings, etc. The higher entrepreneurial sustainability sector at both government and institution level has been progressively introducing high quality management systems over the last two decades, the urge for accurate quality measure and security methods has been increased boost swiftly. At the same time, huge funds from governments makes it very crucial for those who handle entrepreneurial sustainability to guarantee that entrepreneurial sustainability provided in schools, entrepreneurs and institutions of learning will be fruitful. Furthermore, some other circumstantial demand called for more competent and exceptional quality of learning where students are more creative and develop originality in thinking rather than copy to develop by cut and paste method (Baporikar, 2019). These consist of developing surroundings in the figure of students; intensifying clash in higher entrepreneurial sustainability institutions, intensive challenges to students, and more adaptable programs for both in undergraduate and graduate level Nevertheless, the entrepreneurial sustainability sector is not completely comfortable with the TQM method. Schools thought that TQM methods are not suitable for them having the fundamental concept of "Customer Satisfaction" they felt uneasy with the thought of them just pleasing their students who are their valuable customers. Alternatively, schools can use the quality method such as the European Foundation for Quality Management (EFQM) excellence model, ISO 9000, Malcolm Baldrige National Quality Award to boost-up the students' performance. Even the most known service quality procedure, SERVQUAL, is also used to calibrate the quality in the entrepreneurial sustainability context. Models and concepts, such as EFQM, Singapore Quality Award (SQA), School Excellence Model (SEM) and Malcolm Baldrige National Quality Award (MBNQA), are widely used to entrepreneurial sustainability al institutions. These posers adopt the methodology of TQM which has been adjusted for the school environment. Most schools and entrepreneurs recognize the welfare of these quality models, and comprehensive research has been done in this area to investigate the school performances in relation to the quality management philosophy. This has led to a substantial deliberation within academic institutions on the essence of such systems to higher entrepreneurial sustainability.

Antagonist aim on concerns about the parameters to academic freedoms, risk unenthusiastic processes that may restrain diversity and the evolution of managerialism, or the bloom of administrative control, when in fact advocates alluded the advantage of potent change management, constant progressive cycles, higher academic standards, increased staff and students' fulfillment and cutting edge planning . This research aims to determine how quality is acknowledged by diverse groups of people, namely the students, parents, faculty members and employers, regarding the effectiveness of TQM in Entrepreneurial sustainability. The perception acquired from the study will configure the benchmarking with TQM methods which will lead to focus the general principles of TQM.

In an ongoing competition for the brightest minds and external funding, the motivation for entrepreneurs to redesign business processes is often to reduce the administrative overhead and improve the services delivered to students, industry partners, faculty and researchers. Entrepreneurs are increasingly working systematically to improve business processes. Entrepreneurs are also increasingly showing interest in the Lean Six Sigma method, which is a structured approach to process improvement. The Lean Six Sigma program was launched in 2011 to systematically improve business process quality in administrative procedures and provide staff members with a platform to initiate process improvements. To disburse the knowledge of Lean Six Sigma within a short timeframe, the yellow belt and green belt training was made available to staff members free of charge via the organizations learning and development department. The Lean Six Sigma method was selected to ensure that team members had the necessary tools and a structured method for changing administrative processes. The program has progressed to the point where approximately 25 percent of the administrative staff has been trained on the method and improvement projects are being executed across the organization. It is believed that the KAUST Lean Six Sigma program is one of the largest Lean Six Sigma programs in higher entrepreneurial sustainability (HE) in terms of trained staff. The purpose of this paper is to support other organizations contemplating a Lean Six Sigma program by providing an overview of the sequence of activities in establishing a Lean Six Sigma program from initiation to maturity and highlighting some of the challenges. This chapter deliberates on the successful implementation of quality management principles for entrepreneurial sustainability.

Understanding Total Quality Management

Definitions of quality has been altered with the transition of time, modification of customer's needs and demands. But the vitality has more or less been progressed to resolve the issue, compliance to standards for customer satisfaction. With management routine getting complicated, attacks to managing quality in operational areas are becoming unmanageable. Institutions which have victorious outcome with TQM principles have customer and quality integrated in their corporate scheme any institution is a system of interconnected units. For TQM to be victorious, all of the elements within the organization must be conjointly engaged. Some characteristics of TQM are considered to be fundamental: modification, customer preference, communication, consistent improvement, restorative measures, the organizational structure of network type in the process or case management, creativity, IT, organizational culture, team and future orientation. While the critical factors form the basis for transformational preference to produce a substantial advancement culture for consistent competitive advantage. But basically, the main objective of TQM is to generate within the organization an environment in which all the assets are used ingeniously and effectively in order to provide quality service the institution needs to adapt in this fast paced world. TQM is a way of managing to amend the efficiency, viscidity, adaptability and aggressiveness of a business in general. As specified by British Standard Institution, TQM is compose of a "management doctrine and company patterns which intent to rein the human and material resources of an organization in the most efficient way to attain the goal of the organization".

Significance of Total Quality Management

In an aggressive environment, organizations are compelled to develop and apply methods within global context. TQM has been distinguished as a management doctrine and a belief that has support many organizations progress towards reaching splendid businesses. TQM aids in making a culture of trust, cooperation, teamwork, quality-mindedness, eagerness for consistent advancement, continuous learning and eventually, a working environment that imparts to a firm's success and existence. TQM is the process of modifying the essential culture of an organization and channeling it towards superior product or service quality. It also focuses on customer satisfaction through a concept of "continuous improvement" that will lead to joyous victory. As a general management TQM is identified as philosophy and a set of instruments which grants an institution to follow an outline of quality and a way for achieving quality, with quality being a consistent development determined by customers' satisfaction with the services they have experience . TQM has been greatly acknowledged and victoriously applied in many small and large organizations, providing them the advantage in international as well as local competence through the creation of high quality products or service to fulfill the customers demand. They also proved that TQM in supply chain is significant to ameliorate key elements such as quality, delivery and lead-time. Besides it also showed that the firms with human resources that concentrate in TQM methods can raise employee satisfaction. The striking improvements in employee satisfaction resulted to a higher level of customer's devotion.

Advantages and Disadvantages of TQM Strategies

According to Kelchner (2008), TQM is a system of constant development that includes all workers from top management down to production line workers. The focal point of the program is to upgrade customer service and lessen waste in business. Quality development team use problem-solving methods and research to be knowledgeable and decrease weaknesses in the company or institution. But of course in every system or program there would always be advantages and disadvantage. In case of TQM strategies it is as below.

Making disruption: To execute TQM system in institutions, there is a need for comprehensive training of employees at all levels. The employee training compose of information in problem solving techniques and the tools to appraise a procedures and verify deficiency such as statistical process control, Pareto diagrams and brainstorming techniques. During the initial training period, productivity can drop. Communication for quality developing teams also takes workers away from their duties, which also lessens productivity. While the development do weaken lead time, eliminate waste and improve productivity, the beginning stages of implementing TQM in an organization can weaken the worker productivity.

Lower creation cost: TQM program eradicate defects and waste, which lessen production costs in a business. As team members assemble to recognize faults and issues are spotted and sorted quicker than when ousting weaknesses in the business, the company continues to enjoy lessen costs and higher profit. Quality development teams can remove defects (zero defects), lessen lead time and verify redundancies in the production process that can significantly add to the profit the company earns.

Employee resistance: TQM demands revision in mindset, character and techniques for exhibiting their jobs. When management does not efficiently convey the team approach of TQM, workers may become doubtful, which leads to employee resistance. When workers resist the program, it can decrease employee confidence and productivity for the business. TQM uses small accumulative developments to progress the business forward. It can take years for a company to adore the advantage of the program.

Employee participation: Once workers figure out their attendance and cooperation in TQM is vital to its victory, self-confidence and productivity increase. Workers become advocates through cooperation on quality improvement teams. Businesses can increase morale further by acknowledging developing teams that make significant improvement in the production procedure to lessen or eliminate waste.

Critical Success Factors

There are numerous substantial matters that capture your concentration in business that it's often difficult to identify the things that really matter for success. What's more, it can be insanely challenging to get everyone in the team driving in the same path and targeting on the true essentials. That's where Critical Success Factors (CSF) comes into the rescue. CSF are the vital areas of exercise that must be carried out well if you are to accomplish the goal, target or aim for your business or project. By being aware of your CSF, you can establish a probable point of attribute to guide you handle and evaluate the progress of your business or project. As a trivial point of reference, CSF assists the team to learn exactly the crucial part of the business or project. In this manner, it aims to motivate the people to execute their own job in the right context and climb up on the same goal. Forster & Rockart (1989), defines CSF as the definite number of areas in which outcome, if they are sufficient, will guarantee a prosperous competitive action for the organization. They are the few important areas where things must head the right way for the business to prosper. If outcome in these areas are not sufficient, the organization's work for the time being will be less than expected. He also derived that CSF are field of activity that should acquire consistent and precise treatment from management. Direct engagement of higher management grants all agreements to be made expeditiously and safeguarding TQM journey. Top managements advocacy is vital to confirm the availability of detailed actions. The activities can be taken to organize the divisional top management and quality policy, provide a quality management structure, captivate a whole staff, publicize information on quality, process management operating quality and systematize the day of quality. The management is dedicated to be constantly mindful of required development. Amidst the obligation that should to be emphasized is to restore and amend key components of the organization, create fundamental development in the organization, formulate a new job specification, settling struggles to be faced, to guarantee the cooperation of members and create an adequate plan to upgrade the administration of an organization. In order to publicize quality strategy across the organization, top management should create an organizational atmosphere that centralizes on constant development. Their dedication advocates the creation of precise and discernible quality values, along with a management system to facilitate all activities of the company towards quality excellence. Critical Success Factors are vigorously associated to the mission and critical goals of business or project. Whereas the mission and goals concentrate on the objectives and what is to be attained, Critical Success Factors eyed on the most essential areas and get to the very center of both what is to be attain and how you will achieve it.

Sustainability Frames

"There is some truth in the criticism that [sustainable development] has come to mean whatever suits the particular advocacy of the individual concerned. This is not surprising. It is difficult to be against 'sustainable development'. It sounds like something we should all approve of, like 'motherhood and apple pie'" (Pearce, Markandya & Barbier, 2013). As put in a nutshell in the introductory quotation, sustainability is that magic word of consensus (Worster, 1993), which has many faces and shapes. The popularity of the notion and underlying concept of sustainability as well as sustainable development in politics, media, economy and science is based on the fact that it has positive connotations and radiates moral legitimacy (Grabe, 2010). For this reason, it seems natural that "confusion about sustainable development arises as people use the same words to mean a wide divergence of views on the goals, routes and the methods of moving towards sustainable development" (Hopwood, Mellor & O'Brien, 2005). Sustainability is therefore considered to be a "fuzzy, controversially interpreted principle", with a plurality of connotations that cannot be homogenized (Brand & Jochum, 2000).

The reasons for engaging in sustainability are usually presented in the literature using three frames that are often looked at independently. Figure 1 shows the frames of sustainability followed by a brief discussion.

Figure 1. Sustainability Frames
Source: Self-Developed

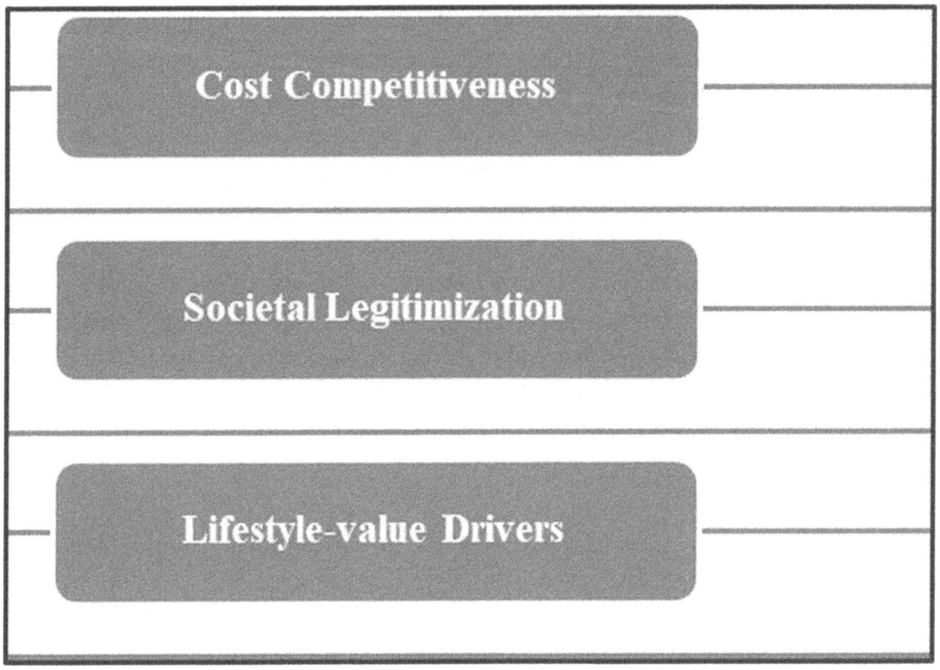

Cost reduction competitiveness that cost competitiveness has been the most referenced frame (Carroll and Shabana, 2010; Revell and Blackburn, 2007). It explains enterprises taking sustainability actions that accrue a direct operational and internal benefit and is related with the traditional resource-based interpretation of the enterprise suggesting that enterprises will undertake sustainability actions that can provide a competitive advantage, based on cost reduction, differentiation or other economic elements. It has a direct association with literature trying to justify the introduction of responsibility in terms of its relationship with financial performance and it has been especially useful to analyze great enterprises' behaviours.

Going beyond purely economic reasons, a second frame (Brønn and Vidaver-Cohen, 2009; Garay and Font, 2012) that has been usually used to understand pro-sustainability motivations can be called societal legitimization, and presents enterprises taking sustainability actions visible or expected by others. In the traditional business case, analyzing big enterprises this has been interpreted through stakeholders' theory but for educational institutions this needed to be interpreted from social capital literature.

Finally, and considering the particular nature of education ownership and management, literature highlights another frame beyond (but still including) the expectation of economic gain and associated with the values and lifestyle of their owners. This third frame (Ateljevic and Doorne, 2000; Shaw and Williams, 2011), that we have called lifestyle-value drivers differs from these first two frames in explaining pro-sustainability behaviours because of personal choices and habit and sometimes is presented in conflict with an exclusive pursuit of economic gain.

Sustainability overall, however, can be explained this way because most enterprises competing in the same market do not see it as a strategic opportunity for competitiveness (Bonilla-Priego et al., 2011). It is possible for successful enterprises to be copied by other more commercial enterprises in a way that would suggest the resource-based view of the enterprise applies to sustainable tourism (Ateljevic and Doorne, 2000).

TOTAL QUALITY MANAGEMENT IN ENTREPRENEURIAL SUSTAINABILITY

Entrepreneurial sustainability plays a vital part in a person's achievement, apart from inborn talent. Entrepreneurial sustainability will mold and guide a person to be what they want to be. Of course, if discussing entrepreneurial sustainability, teachers will play a very important role. Teacher has many responsibilities not only to the students but also to the society. Now in the 21st century, a time when technology is at its peak, entrepreneurial sustainability faced a deep challenge to adopt on fast paced world. Changes in global entrepreneurial sustainability at settings have compelled the institutions of higher learning to revolutionize its activity (Baporikar, 2020b, 2019, 2017).

The aggressive business environment leads the collaborator of the entrepreneurial sustainability al sector to require for more dependable, ingenious, and multi-skilled & knowledgeable work force. These have imposed the higher entrepreneurial sustainability institutions to be more interested on quality entrepreneurial sustainability system, which consists of observations of students, instructors, administrative staff, physical facilities and procedures. The procedures compose of teaching, learning, and administration. While, output consist of examination outcome, employment, profit, and satisfaction, because of an open competition, students are now turning more to customers as well as consumers and anticipate to pay an increasing due of entrepreneurial sustainability cost. This resulted to competition causing generating different programmers for different student groups. The abstract issues consider whether TQM in higher entrepreneurial sustainability should be people or problem adjustments, trouble in presenting the implementation and acceptance of TQM in higher entrepreneurial sustainability institutions, which have not accepted dogma of TQM, group versus single preference towards TQM, and sustaining the range of invention amongst others.

Thus, TQM is a philosophy and system for continuously improving the services and/or products offered to customers. Now that the technologics of transportation and communication have substituted national economic systems with a global economy, nations and businesses that do not implement TQM can become globally non-competitive quickly. This matter towards non-competitiveness can be prevented if societies are trained to become TQM advocates.

Therefore, the possible advantages of TQM in entrepreneurial sustainability at institutions are very clear like:

- TQM will support entrepreneurial sustainability al institutions to create an upgraded service to its customers namely the students and employers.
- The consistent improvement focus of TQM is an essential component for satisfying the accountability essential to entrepreneurial sustainability al reform.
- Executing a no-fear TQM system offers more exciting challenge to students and teacher to empower teamwork and cooperation with one another. In that way, each observation can be utilized to help each other for better advancement

There are three generic approaches to TQM in higher entrepreneurial sustainability. First, there is a customer focus where the ideas of services to student are supported through staff coaching and development, which encouraged student's preference and self-reliance. The second approach is staff focus which pertains to appraise and heighten the share of all members of staff to the potency of an institution's procedure, to the setting of rules and priorities. This implies a blandish management structure and the acceptance of obligation for action determined by working groups. The third approach focuses on service agreement positions and attempt to guarantee compliance to stipulation at sealed access measurable degree of the entrepreneurial sustainability al procedures. Evaluation of assignments by faculty within a period of time is an example implies that customer authorization in entrepreneurial sustainability demands outstanding input from students as well as from business industry that will eventually hire them and this in term will contour entrepreneurial sustainability efficiently and extinguish any shadow of the esoteric academic "ivory tower" that is present in business school coursework (Baporikar, 2017). It was urged that top leadership is the way to any TQM platform and the compelling force behind success and failure. The TQM platform must be accepted and not pushed on the employees. Right communication, proper entrepreneurial sustainability using benchmarking, and explore TQM doctrines and program can raise the success rate.

While Gregory, propose four dimensions of institutional leaderships symbolic, political, managerial and academic in his example of administered leadership for successful change in higher entrepreneurial sustainability institutions. Owen states that "Total and continuous quality development is viewed as a journey which has no real beginning or ending". Thus, it is a constant endeavor for the management to sustain a criterion in the institutions. TQM is a managerial instrument to resolve the issues associated to services as well as tactics in the academic industry and it can conform to the standard the entrepreneurial sustainability industry. The accentuate of quality maintenance in higher entrepreneurial sustainability has increased as the numbers of students are climbing up and at the same rate, their anticipation are getting high, as they have to settle the tuition fee, so they looking forward for a suitable result (Becket & Brookes, 2005). Meanwhile, Ormiston & Seymour (2011) clearly defined the kinds of quality for social entrepreneurial enterprises which can be generally applied to achieve higher entrepreneurial sustainability in institutions.

TQM method is viewed as suave beginning of Quality procedures. The key notes in here is to make sure to have the higher management be committed and so that it will be properly initiated and implemented in the institutions quality policy. Though it demands quality time and effort to train and communicate it with the team members it is truly essential, for the implementation of quality procedures and affiliated measures to be successful. Execution of thorough risk analysis and mitigation while contingency plans are established and everything is well documented. Of course, administering of training plan should be as seamless as possible.

Superior quality management methods guides in reducing struggles of the modification that is being introduced. Therefore, if TQM techniques are well facilitated and thoroughly implemented, while the basic principles and practices are accepted and executed, TQM methods will be a great help to have a successful development in upgrading the quality of entrepreneurial sustainability institutions provide to make their students be more competent and competitive globally to face our fast progressing world.

Lean Six Sigma in Entrepreneurial Sustainability

While lean six sigma originated in manufacturing, the method has proven its merits in transactional environments as well. Some of the first organizations to apply lean six sigma to improve administrative processes where the same manufacturing companies who had successfully applied the method in manufacturing. Over time a number of public sector organizations established noteworthy lean six sigma programs such as the US army city of Fort Wayne. While entrepreneurs have been under pressure to deliver measurable results due to increased reporting demands and increased competition for funding, higher entrepreneurial sustainability institutions have been slow in adopting lean six sigma. From the practitioners' perspective, the reasons for the slow adoption of lean six sigma include the decentralized nature of traditional entrepreneurs and no direct linkage to the core business of research and entrepreneurial sustainability. Entrepreneurs are by any standards complex organizations, consuming significant resources. Being complex organizations, there are thousands of business processes facilitating the primary functions and if those processes are streamlined, then efforts can be focused on the primary functions of research, innovation and entrepreneurial sustainability. According to Antony (2014), there are many HEs which have started with lean to improve process efficiency; such as St Andrews University, Cardiff University, Connecticut State University, MIT and more. He also stated that lean six sigma deployment has appeared in a low number of he institutes so far. This could be due to the view that lean six sigma is only applicable in the manufacturing sector and it is not applicable for the he sector. However, improving the entrepreneurial sustainability system can be done in the same way as any other industry, including academic and non-academic processes. this is evident from the benefits gained in some HEs as reported by Simons (2013) and Antony (2014), including increases in student satisfaction, providing HEs with problem solving templates, changing the institution's culture, identifying and reducing hidden costs, tackling process efficiency problems, establishing measures and so on. On the other hand, according to Antony, Krishan, Cullen & Kumar, 2012), some challenges of lean six sigma deployment in HE are:

1. the application of terminologies, tools and techniques from manufacturing and service organizations to HEs;
2. improving processes in isolation instead of designing them from a system perspective;
3. lack of awareness about customers types and needs; and
4. lack of communication, management commitment, visionary leadership, process
5. thinking, resources (financial, technical and physical)

For successful lean six sigma implementation, it is critical for any HE to understand its readiness level, before starting any deployment. typically the group of decision makers is wider in HE's, compared to commercial organization, hence making stakeholder management, communication and change management essential to the successful completion of projects. When the HE is ready for the deployment, it should customize its lean six sigma roadmap to guide the deployment process. It is also important to select the best projects in order to give the best return to the organization.

Tools Used in LSS

The LSS methodology offers a long list of tools, including but not limited to. Business Process Mapping, VSM, SPC charts, SIPOC, 5S, Voice of the Customer Translation Matrix, Operational Definitions, sigma calculations, FMEA, CTQ's, Gauge R&R, scatter plots, house of quality, Affinity Diagram, 5s, 5 whys, A3 report an error-proofing. Selecting the appropriate tools for analyzing and improving process is critical to the successful completion of the projects. Not all of the individual tools are applied in every single project, and one of the project leader's responsibilities is to select the tools appropriate to the project in hand, with the coaching of the master black belt. Looking beyond the fundamental project tools of organizational diagrams and project charters, the survey shows a bias toward the Lean tools supported by basic data monitoring tools, which can be attributed to the developing experience of the belts as well as the balanced complexity of the projects selected at the start-up of the program, where the selected projects primarily been addressing process defects rather than process optimization. While the Lean tools were frequently applied, it was apriority from the organization that the projects were data-driven, hence the common usage of SPC charts. As the LSS program matures and projects become increasing complex it is expected that the master black belt and black belts will apply more advanced data analysis tools. The application of more advanced tools will be a key to the maturing of the LSS program. If the belts in the program do not build experience through the completion of multiple, increasingly complex projects, there is a risk that the organization will not build the advanced capabilities required to systematically improve complex and data-rich processes. As the skill set develops and the program takes on increasingly complex projects it is expected that more of the advanced tools will be applied where applicable.

Figure 2. Factors Influencing Sustainability
Source: Adopted from Horbach, 2008.

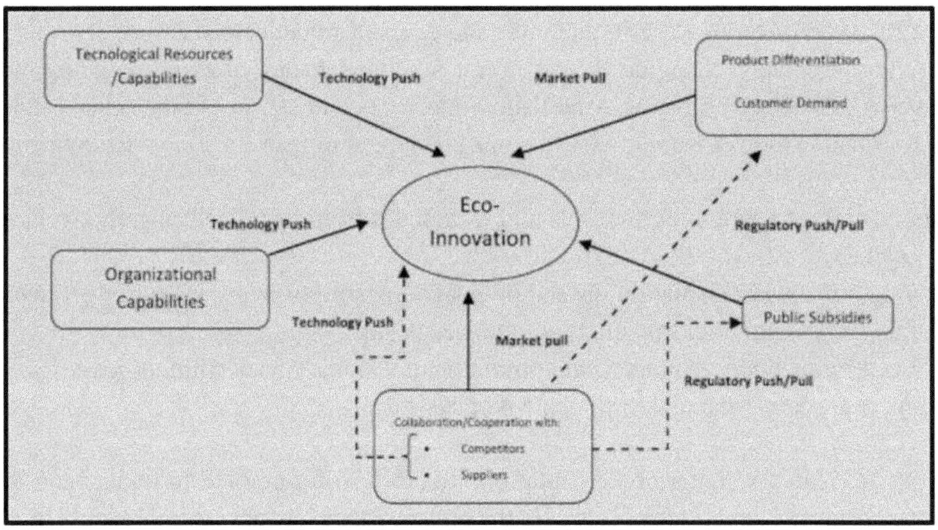

Implications of QM for Entrepreneurial Sustainability

In the era of knowledge economy, innovation and industrial policies are potentially useful tools to spur growth, but the environmental impact will differ depending on the improvements achieved by innovative firms. Environmental sustainability has brought new concerns and pressures to the firm's innovative activity. In this sense, we can distinguish between green innovation and non-green innovation. Green innovation would imply that innovations in products, processes or business models lead the company to higher levels of environmental sustainability (Triguero et al., 2013).

The importance of QM and networks and especially the public policy also plays an important role in the adoption of environmental innovations (Popp et al., 2007). R&D subsidies are necessary to promote the implementation of environmentally beneficial technologies (Kemp, 2000). Effectively, this financial dependence of green innovation to public subsidies has been confirmed by De Marchi (2012), Horbach (2008). Figure 2 shows how various factors influence the sustainability in any organization.

Technology push factors are essential drivers of eco-innovations. Following the strategic management literature, firm-internal conditions (resources) and strategies (capabilities) are the main drivers of innovation. From the resource-based view, the competitive advantage of a firm lies primarily in the use of a bundle of available resources at the firm-level (Rumelt, 1984). Physical, human and financial resources trigger technology push. Corral (2002) also considers that innovation propensity depends on the availability or the lack of resources and capacity to innovate by the firm. In this regard, knowledge resources, human skills and provision and access to finance are essential drivers to green innovation.

Sustainability actions investigated have not shown a direct relationship with performance variables. Further sustainability for any organization or institution can be a fad as they can be seen winning industry awards, collecting sustainability certifications, highlighted in the academic literature, and are used to set government funding and grants (Baporikar, 2018). However, there are more critical issue to propel them by vested interests and reasons for engaging in sustainability, whether they are sufficiently different to other respondents, and how representative they are of the total number of individuals engaging in sustainability actions can be a matter of dispute.

Finally, it is worth reiterating that ethics and sustainability research is a value-laden topic. It is fully expected that some of these pro-sustainability behaviours are the result of over-reporting to create a positive impression; however it is item desirability that will play a stronger influence in self-reporting socially desirable behaviour (Randall & Fernandes, 2013; Ramus & Steger, 2000).

For any constant development effort to be efficient, quality and reliable feedback accumulation is necessary and vital in the assessment procedure of teaching & learning with the result distinctly characterized and evaluated. It includes procedures that ceaselessly accumulate, examine, and pursue on customer information. TQM is one of the most efficient tools in the field of teaching & learning criterion in entrepreneurial sustainability (Baporikar & Sony, 2020a). The dare is to assure each student will gain from the teaching & learning procedure by imparting them adequate time, support, encouragement, resources and chance to acquire and hit the set standard of excellence in entrepreneurial sustainability in a total quality environment. Based on the empirical literature, it demands having the right characteristics and forthcoming with the supreme target of constant endeavor to develop all field of entrusted obligation. The triumph of institutions depends on their management techniques on how to determine, categorize, examine, and succeed to the efficient approach. This study discloses that TQM will provide a superior impact on the institutions objective and produce value in improving the economic value. Although the enforcement of TQM brings comprehensive range of alteration in organization, there are deficiencies of approval of this approach in various organizations. But due to deficient identified reason, many institutions do not support TQM methods into their organization. Nevertheless, some organization and institutions already embraced the advantages of TQM implementation on their organization.

CONCLUSION

Organizations will only understand the full advantage of TQM through successful consolidation of various betterment activities, each of which focuses on the fundamental component of the TQM philosophy. An organization contributes various common attribute or acquires usual elements of management, which let them to recognize the real probability of TQM over a period of time (Baporikar & Sony, 2020a).

Previous studies revealed that organization can improve their management of higher entrepreneurial sustainability by emphasizing values regarding the importance of people, knowledge and continuous improvement. That is also what TQM believes focusing on the right issue to be on the right track to success. TQM convey issue resolution methods and consistent advancement opportunities, it is efficient use to help institution acquire their highest return on investment.

Therefore institution embracing TQM philosophies as a component of their corporate scheme and utilizing any model of Business Excellence for TQM Strategy execution will minimize the cost of its execution and will provide a concrete foundation of necessary increased human function and capabilities, contributive organizational society, best employment of all resources and better procedure. It will alleviate the modification and improvement in an organization given that they will strictly implement TQM methods which will enable them to move towards excellence. The LSS program managed to prove its value to the organization by improving business processes and enabling the university to operate more efficiently. The successful delivery of projects helped individuals and process owners to understand the importance of LSS and also encouraged other process owners to undertake such projects in their respective areas. As a result, the frequency of project requests has increased, at both green belt and black belt levels. Approximately 40 new projects have been initiated this year covering business processes across the university in areas such as IT, Human Resources and Finance. The journey toward structured, data-driven process improvement has not been without challenges. The business process owners often express quite natural impatience for a solution once a problem has been identified. Similarly there will often be a push to rollout systems without having a detailed understanding of the improvements that are sought. The LSS program will remain a cornerstone in providing staff members across the university with the necessary tools, coaching and platform to improve their own business areas, as well as cross-organizational processes. As the program matures, staff members will also be taking on increasingly complex projects which will leverage more advanced statistical tools. To ensure that the process improvements withstand the test of time, cementing the concept of process ownership within the organizations will be critical.

Additionally, and of particular importance, is the continued monitoring of process performance following the completion of any improvement project. Process governance should also be established, including periodic process reviews (Baporikar, 2016). The process owner must take responsibility for measuring and continuously improving process performance. A key component in this will be the identification and monitoring of key performance indicators. From a project delivery perspective, the objective is to reduce the delivery time of a green belt project to between three and six months. This should be possible due to increased knowledge and experience with LSS projects, and also setting it as an objective at the onset of the projects. The program has provided a plethora of benefits, and on a program level, the systematic registration of benefits will be improved by implementing a template for benefits registration inspired by MSP. On a staff level, staff members have benefitted professionally from the training and completion of projects. One of the forthcoming challenges will be to ensure that the belts continue to undertake projects following the completion of their certification. In terms of areas, the target of the program is to further improve the processes in Administration and Finance, as well as to extend its support to the teams within the Academic and Research functions by providing training and support.

REFERENCES

Antony, J. (2014). *Design of experiments for engineers and scientists*. Elsevier.

Antony, J., Krishan, N., Cullen, D., & Kumar, M. (2012). Lean Six Sigma for higher education institutions (HEIs) Challenges, barriers, success factors, tools/techniques. *International Journal of Productivity and Performance Management, 61*(8), 940–948. doi:10.1108/17410401211277165

Ateljevic, I., & Doorne, S. (2000). Staying within the fence': Lifestyle entrepreneurship in tourism. *Journal of Sustainable Tourism, 8*(5), 378–392. doi:10.1080/09669580008667374

Baporikar, N. (2016). Corporate Governance and Value Creation: Indian Experience. *International Journal of Asian Business and Information Management, 7*(2), 51–61. doi:10.4018/IJABIM.2016040104

Baporikar, N. (2017). Imperatives in Leading Institutions of Higher Learning: Focus B-School. *International Journal of Technology and Educational Marketing, 7*(1), 38–51. doi:10.4018/IJTEM.2017010104

Baporikar, N. (2018). *Knowledge Integration Strategies for Entrepreneurship and Sustainability*. IGI Global. doi:10.4018/978-1-5225-5115-7

Baporikar, N. (2019). Preventing Academic Misconduct: Student-Centered Teaching Strategies. In D. Velliaris (Ed.), *Prevention and Detection of Academic Misconduct in Higher Education* (pp. 98–115). IGI Global. doi:10.4018/978-1-5225-7531-3.ch005

Baporikar, N. (2019). Significance and Role of Entrepreneurial University in Emerging Economies. *International Journal of Applied Management Sciences and Engineering, 6*(1), 46–61. doi:10.4018/IJAMSE.2019010104

Baporikar, N. (2020b). Understanding Entrepreneurial University: A Framework for Emerging Economies. In A. Daniel, A. Teixeira, & M. Preto (Eds.), *Examining the Role of Entrepreneurial Universities in Regional Development* (pp. 93–112). IGI Global. doi:10.4018/978-1-7998-0174-0.ch005

Baporikar, N., & Sony, M. (2020a). *Quality Management Principles and Policies in Higher Education*. IGI Global. doi:10.4018/978-1-7998-1017-9

Becket, N., & Brookes, M. (2005). Analysing quality audits in higher education. *Brookes Ejournal of Learning and Teaching, 1*(2), 1-12.

Belin, J., Horbach, J., & Oltra, V. (2011). *Determinants and specificities of eco-innovations–An econometric analysis for the French and German industry based on the Community Innovation Survey* (No. 2011-17). Groupe de Recherche en Economie Théorique et Appliquée.

Bonilla Priego, M. J., Najera, J. J., & Font, X. (2011). Environmental management decision-making in certified hotels. *Journal of Sustainable Tourism, 19*(3), 361–381. doi:10.1080/09669582.2010.530350

Brand, KW, & Jochum, G. (2000). The German Discourse on Sustainable Development. *MPS Texts, 1*, 2000.

Brønn, P. S., & Vidaver-Cohen, D. (2009). Corporate motives for social initiative: Legitimacy, sustainability, or the bottom line? *Journal of Business Ethics, 87*(1), 91–109. doi:10.100710551-008-9795-z

Carroll, A. B., & Shabana, K. M. (2010). The business case for corporate social responsibility: A review of concepts, research and practice. *International Journal of Management Reviews*, *12*(1), 85–105. doi:10.1111/j.1468-2370.2009.00275.x

Corral, C. M. (2003). Sustainable production and consumption systems—cooperation for change: Assessing and simulating the willingness of the firm to adopt/develop cleaner technologies. The case of the In-Bond industry in northern Mexico. *Journal of Cleaner Production*, *11*(4), 411–426. doi:10.1016/S0959-6526(02)00063-X

De Marchi, V. (2012). Environmental innovation and R&D cooperation: Empirical evidence from Spanish manufacturing firms. *Research Policy*, *41*(3), 614–623. doi:10.1016/j.respol.2011.10.002

Forster, N. S., & Rockart, J. F. (1989). *Critical success factors: an annotated bibliography*. Academic Press.

Garay, L., & Font, X. (2012). Doing good to do well? Corporate social responsibility reasons, practices and impacts in small and medium accommodation enterprises. *International Journal of Hospitality Management*, *31*(2), 329–337. doi:10.1016/j.ijhm.2011.04.013

Grave, L. (2010). The "Sustainability Project". The limits of the sustainability concept from a cultural perspective. *Cultura21 eBooks Series on Culture and Sustainability, 1.*

Hopwood, B., Mellor, M., & O'Brien, G. (2005). Sustainable development: Mapping different approaches. *Sustainable Development*, *13*(1), 38–52. doi:10.1002d.244

Horbach, J. (2008). Determinants of environmental innovation—New evidence from German panel data sources. *Research Policy*, *37*(1), 163–173. doi:10.1016/j.respol.2007.08.006

Kelchner, L. (2008). *Theories of Total Quality Management*. Academic Press.

Kemp, R. (2000). Technology and Environmental Policy—Innovation effects of past policies and suggestions for improvement. *Innovation and the Environment*, *1*, 35–61.

Ormiston, J., & Seymour, R. (2011). Understanding value creation in social entrepreneurship: The importance of aligning mission, strategy and impact measurement. *Journal of Social Entrepreneurship*, *2*(2), 125–150. doi:10.1080/19420676.2011.606331

Pearce, D., Markandya, A., & Barbier, E. (2013). *Blueprint 1: for a green economy*. Routledge. doi:10.4324/9781315070223

Popp, D., Hafner, T., & Johnstone, N. (2007). Policy vs. consumer pressure: Innovation and diffusion of alternative bleaching technologies in the pulp industry (No. w13439). National Bureau of Economic Research.

Ramus, C. A., & Steger, U. (2000). The roles of supervisory support behaviors and environmental policy in employee "Ecoinitiatives" at leading-edge European companies. *Academy of Management Journal*, *43*(4), 605–626.

Randall, D. M., & Fernandes, M. F. (2013). The social desirability response bias in ethics research. In *Citation classics from the Journal of Business Ethics* (pp. 173–190). Springer. doi:10.1007/978-94-007-4126-3_9

Revell, A., & Blackburn, R. (2007). The business case for sustainability? An examination of small firms in the UK's construction and restaurant sectors. *Business Strategy and the Environment, 16*(6), 404–420. doi:10.1002/bse.499

Rumelt, R. P., & Lamb, R. (1984). Competitive strategic management. *Toward a Strategic Theory of the Firm, 26*(1), 556-570.

Simons, H. (2013). *Getting to know schools in a democracy: The politics and process of evaluation.* Routledge. doi:10.4324/9780203064528

Triguero, A., Moreno-Mondéjar, L., & Davia, M. A. (2013). Drivers of different types of eco-innovation in European SMEs. *Ecological Economics, 92*, 25–33. doi:10.1016/j.ecolecon.2013.04.009

Williams, A. M., & Shaw, G. (2011). Internationalization and innovation in tourism. *Annals of Tourism Research, 38*(1), 27–51. doi:10.1016/j.annals.2010.09.006

Worster, D. (1993). *The wealth of nature: environmental history and the ecological imagination.* Oxford University Press on Demand.

KEY TERMS AND DEFINITIONS

Critical Success Factor (CSF): The vital areas of exercise that must be carried out well if you are to accomplish the goal, target or aim.

Education: The act or process of imparting or acquiring general knowledge, developing the powers of reasoning and judgment, and generally of preparing oneself or others intellectually for mature life; it also refers to the act or process of imparting or acquiring particular knowledge or skills, as for a profession.

Entrepreneurial: Nature or character or personality to organize and manage any enterprise, usually with considerable initiative and risk.

Principles: Are accepted or professed rule of action or conduct and include a fundamental, primary, or general law or truth from which others are derived. They are guiding sense of the requirements and obligations of right conduct and a determining characteristic of something essential.

Quality: Is an essential or distinctive characteristic, property, or attribute as belonging to or distinguishing a thing with respect to fineness, or grade of excellence.

Sustainability: The ability to be sustained, supported, upheld, or confirmed to support long-term and the quality of not being harmful to the environment or depleting natural resources.

Value: Relative worth, merit, or importance and the worth of something in terms of the amount of other things, for which it can be exchanged; to consider worthy of respect, excellence, usefulness, regard or esteem highly.

Chapter 4
A New Continuous Quality Improvement Vision for a Changing Technological Market

Beatriz Olalla-Caballero
https://orcid.org/0000-0002-1042-2675
Universidad Pontificia de Salamanca, Spain

Montserrat Mata-Fernández
Universidad de Deusto, Spain

ABSTRACT

Continuous quality improvement (CQI) is an essential tool for those information technologies companies (IT) that want to succeed in a competitive and disruptive market, achieving its goals and objectives, obtaining benefits and increasing their market share, or even assuring clients loyalty. Changing the environment and the global economy may affect the purposes of a company and, hence, in the success of the market strategy carried out by the firm. A proper continuous quality improvement model or framework can help a company to follow-up the quality level of products, projects, or services, identifying actions to be developed to be able to have an agile and immediate response among competitors. In this way, a company may be reinforced and may assure its survival in a changing and disruptive environment.

INTRODUCTION

This chapter aims to analyze the importance of quality management nowadays in companies in the Information Technologies (IT) market, underlining how it may help enterprises stay in the market and be strong enough to fight against competition. Quality is a concept that involves cost savings in a company, and thus, there is a need to analyze this perspective of quality regarding see it as a competitive advantage. It is also crucial to carry out an overview of cost savings related to quality management, hierarchy influence, client satisfaction, and quality targets measurement through performance indicators.

DOI: 10.4018/978-1-7998-5036-6.ch004

Some several issues and perspectives should also be considered when talking about quality management in a company. This chapter details these perspectives, their advantages, and other matters related to quality explaining them in detail and trying to identify their importance in an enterprise through a proposed set of Critical Success Factors (CSF) and Key Performance Indicators (KPI). These perspectives are based on the authors' experience in managing IT projects and how to take advantage of them. To detail these results and to define the proposal, a group of 15 IT projects was considered and analyzed. The operation and managing activities of them were taken into account, together with their lessons learned.

First of all, an overview of quality concepts and perspectives, standards, and models are analyzed to identify important factors of them in IT projects to be included in our proposal. The analysis and results of the IT projects considered are gathered, aligned to the factors previously considered and summarized in the chapter, to focus the conclusion and recommendations on getting the advantages of the proposal. But before, it is necessary to start talking about the concept of quality and its origins. It is well known that the importance of quality has passed the time ago from the academic fields to join companies as part of its growth and continuous improvement strategy and is now a vital tool for decision-making by the executive committee. Every company has been adapting to the different quality regulations arising from the needs of the market and society. All of them have been adapting to the various regulations arising from the needs of the market and community. Historically the first focus of quality was the product, then passed to the client and finally focused on all stakeholders (Sánchez, & Castro, 2005). Undoubtedly, quality has been part of the evolutionary process of man since it was something that allowed him to improve his daily activities, and therefore the outcome of them, resulting in an improvement in his quality of life.

But it is at the end of the XIX century, with the arrival of the industrial era, when a significant change took place. Productive chains required a revision of the products, so they adjusted to the required standards. Therefore, quality began to be seen from another perspective. It was then when the quality control departments began to appear in some companies because it was necessary to check and verify the compliance in the requirements in terms of quality. It highlights the design of the American statistician Shewhart of a graph to control the variables of the product to decrease errors and increase productivity, and the design of the Plan-Do-Check-Act (PDCA) cycle, later baptized as the Deming cycle. Deming was an American statistician and engineer that arrived in Japan carrying this cycle and becoming the father of Japanese quality. It was also in this period when the concept of quality management was created by Feigenbaum, who first applied Total Quality Control (TQC) at General Electric and inspired Total Quality Management (TQM), whose importance is reflected in this chapter. These facts, and the contribution of the engineer Juran who highlighted the importance of the management area's commitment to achieving quality, established the foundations and contributed to the explosion of quality in Japan. His trilogy is still in force, and it involves three areas: quality planning, quality improvement, and quality control. It was the consultant Ishikawa who then carried out the consolidation process of the quality (Cubillos, & Rozo, 2009). His contributions to improving quality encompass not only the Fishbone Cause and Effect Diagram (Ishikawa Diagram) but also the implementation of Quality Circles; both are considered in the seven essential quality improvement tools.

Most of the theoretical basis for quality were already defined in the late 1970s, being then when a new stage in the development of quality began. At this stage, the goal was to achieve quality in all departments of the company, from financial to purchasing, requiring the participation of both the Chief Executive Officer (CEO) and the staff to achieve this objective (Cubillos, & Rozo, 2009). The last stage of the development of quality is what is known as continuous improvement, derived from the tough competition that exists between enterprises caused by globalization. Some companies have already implemented quality models based on processes. Organizations need now more than ever to adapt quickly to the needs of each moment because the goal is to achieve a high degree of performance and consequently enjoy a competitive position (Maderuelo, 2002). This necessity of adaptation and the fact that quality is now part of a company's strategy has become the engine of this work.

In this chapter, many perspectives of quality will be described and analyzed from the requirements of a quality management system in a company, always trying to increase client satisfaction. In this chapter, some activities related to quality management will be explained and detailed to understand the weight, charge, and impact in the organization of them. It is imperative to plan all of these activities correctly and assign them to the proper role to be developed successfully.

QUALITY CONCEPT: ADVANTAGES AND BENEFITS IN FIRMS

The current economic situation and globalization have made quality especially relevant, seeing significant results in companies with good quality management. This approach impacts increasing sales, revenue, and return on sales, among others (Hellman, & Liu, 2013), compared to those that do not apply any quality system. For this reason, efforts are focused on designing and implementing a Quality Management System (QMS) that meets customer expectations and increases their satisfaction, and that allows them to position advantageously in a highly competitive and disruptive environment. Accordingly, it is necessary to consider in this system the organizational structure of the company, social factors, and the customer's perception, without forgetting everything that may negatively affect the implementation of the QMS, such as cost, a slowdown on innovation, or delay in making decisions related to what customers demand. This QMS, therefore, is now a strategy of the company to become a reference within its sector for its high quality and its capacity for innovation and adaptation to the new need; the main objective is to improve its services and, consequently, the organization (Saavedra, Avila, & Mendívil, 2020). But to choose and adopt a QMS, it is necessary to carry out a study of the advantages and disadvantages that it may have for the company. This system will become the way to have a suitable TQM.

Bergman and Klefsjö (2010) discuss the importance of quality management to create a sustainable society. Some authors define quality by accelerating change, reducing cost, and protecting reputation (Oakland, 2014). Powell (1995) analyzes TQM as a potential source of sustainable competitive advantage. Besides that, quality is a concept that enables a company to save costs and be competitive in a market and thus, it is crucial to analyze all the costs related to the quality of Information Technologies services, trying to find where and when a company should invest in quality to save costs. If a company has no proactive attitude in quality management, defects, and errors will involve higher costs.

Marsh (2005) considers that there may be four stages related to information quality assurance: audit, clean, prevention, and compliance. Batini, Cappiello, Francalanci, and Maurino (2009) propose three steps in a quality data methodology: state reconstruction, assessment and measurement, and improvement. The second stage (assessment and measurement) involves activities such as data analysis, requirements analysis, identification, and critical areas, process modeling, and measurement of quality. The final stage (improvement) consists of evaluating costs, assignment of process responsibilities, allocation of data responsibilities, identiðcation of the causes of errors, selection of strategies and techniques, design of data improvement solutions, process control, improvement management, and monitoring. There are other perspectives and approaches to quality management, such as those related to other areas or issues in companies, such as information. The increase in the volume of data in companies nowadays and the evolution of MIS (Management Information Systems) are important references to consider the leading role of information in companies. Lee, Strong, Khan, and Wang (2002) explain that it is the leading cause of the increasing awareness and need for high-quality information in organizations. Lee, Strong, Khan, and Wang (2002) analyze this perspective and measure the quality of the information in a company close with the benchmarking of the efforts developed against other companies. This analysis gives some ideas of criteria to be considered when discussing information quality such as accuracy, believability, reputation, objectivity, credibility, consistency, completeness, reliability, correctness, or unambiguity.

Zairi (1997) suggests that several organizations adopt a process-based approach to manage their operations and quality assurance systems such as EN ISO 9000; they are essential but perhaps not enough to provide a culture based on process management in a company. It may also depend on the alignment to corporate goals and adding value to the end customer by every employee in the company. Eppler and Muenzenmayer (2002) explain how to measure the multiple dimensions of information quality in the Internet or intranet context, and identify several criteria that may be measured to have a clear idea of the quality level of information, such as accessibility, consistency, timeliness, conciseness, maintainability, currency, applicability, convenience, speed, comprehensiveness, clarity, accuracy, traceability, security, correctness and interactivity.

There are many benefits after implementing quality projects and programs in companies or after implementing a quality management system in an organization. Psomas, Vouzas, and Kafetzopoulos (2014) suggest several benefits from quality management; some have a direct or indirect impact on quality improvement, employee benefits, and customer satisfaction. Besides that, they explain how quality improvement is also a significant factor that directly influences employee benefits, customer satisfaction, and business performance. Buttle (1997) describes how one of the most important benefits of ISO 9000 certification is profit improvement. The second and third most important benefits are process improvements and marketing benefits (including gaining new customers, keeping existing customers, using the standard as a promotional tool, increasing market share, increasing growth in sales, and improving customer satisfaction). Casadesus, Giménez, and Heras (2001) highlight the following external benefits: better response to customers' requirements, penetration of new markets, improved customer relationships, improvement in customer services, and reduction of customer audits. The internal benefits may be the improvement of the definition and standardization of work procedures, improvement in the description of the responsibilities and obligations of the workers, increased company confidence in their quality, more outstanding commitment to work, and improved guidelines reducing improvisation.

According to Ruzevicius, Adomaitiene, and Sirvidaite (2004), the implementation of quality systems has a strong inñuence on improving the activities developed in the company, production quality, and overall competitiveness. Besides that, some of the benefits that may result after the implementation of a quality system are to ensure the production of uniform quality products, better fullðlment customer needs, to increase the company's competitiveness, and to improve the image and prestige of the company. Creating value in a network economy is an essential factor in promoting competitiveness in a company, according to Olalla and Mata (2016).

Among the benefits of implementing a QMS, the following stand out (Saavedra et al., 2020):

- High capacity for transformation; the fact of considering a large number of factors and involving not only suppliers or customers but also all the staff makes it easy to adapt to the new changes imposed by a competitive and continuously changing market.

- The company is endowed with an innovative system and with a great capacity to adapt to the technological changes required by a society that moves in a globalized and highly disruptive environment.
- High differentiation of responsibilities by deepening into existing processes and empowering employees on the importance of quality.
- Increase in sales derived from more significant customer satisfaction.

Although the benefits are noteworthy, it is necessary also to mention the disadvantages presented by the incorporation of a QMS, as the cost of it; due to this fact, it is required to carry out several certifications, among which the most common is the certification ISO 9001, and the corresponding training of employees. Other negative features to consider are (1) inadequate internal communication when objectives and the transcendence of the QMS are not accurately transferred to the staff; (2) lack of commitment when the team lacks the vision of goals and benefits of this system, and (3) difficult adoption of a QMS into the company. Depending on the area analyzed, it will be more or less profitable and straightforward. The increase in the number of companies with this certification is pronounced, a fact that makes it more challenging to position the company in an advantageous position just by owning it. Therefore, another differentiation is required to take the lead. Sometimes a situation of mere imitation of competition occurs, which has been called mimetic isomorphism, resulting in a market with plenty of homogenous organizations without differentiating characteristics (Saavedra et al., 2020). To avoid this situation, there must be a clear strategy by the CEO based on the quality bulwark.

There is another concept to be considered regarding the quality: Continuous Improvement. It is a fundamental concept that contributes to achieving quality goals and results in a company. Patidar, Soni, and Soni (2016) define the Continuous Improvement Philosophy (CIP) as a potent tool that may help an organization to realize improvements in manufacturing performance, thereby leading organizations successfully nowadays in a competitive market. It has been proved that CIP has excellent results, especially in those issues related to defects, productivity, and costs, also leading to an increase in the commitment of the employees.

The first step to work in continuous improvement is based on the study of periods, introducing factors to be measured, and making it possible to identify and estimate errors. With this information, it can be drawn to a graph that reflects the variation in the chosen values (Zangwill, & Kantor, 1998). Lameijer, Antony, Chakraborty, Does, and Garza-Reyes (2020) identify the effects of organizational motivation and coordination in continuous improvement, showing that there are corporate-level drivers that may affect the organizational context of Process Improvement (PI) projects and their success. There are different constant quality improvement models, such as the Deming cycle or PDCA cycle. It is interesting to highlight some of the analyses used to improve quality management, for instance, the Strengths, Weaknesses, Opportunities, and Threats (SWOT) analysis or the Deming philosophy. There are also several ways to measure the effectiveness of an improvement process: KPIs, metrics, or even a Learning Curve (LC) based upon theory, as Zangwill and Kantor (1998) propose to help in decision-making.

Another of the most critical points to achieve a high-level quality is the performance of companies from their internal audits. To carry out these internal audits, it is an essential requirement to have a professional quality manager, whose competencies have been listed in a framework developed by the Chartered Quality Institute (CQI), and it has been called "The CQI competency framework." Briefly, it can be said that the goal of this framework is centered on strong governance, proper assurance, and a culture of improvement. What is indubitable is that these professional needs require to have a good knowledge of ISO 9001 practices, risk analysis, experience in quality management, and a good bunch of soft skills as leadership, emotional intelligence communication (Ingason, & Jónsdóttir, 2017). Based on the studied projects and the study carried out by Addey (2004), the following trends have been observed in the role of quality managers: they try to prevent more than correct, show their preferences for agile working methods, its focus is on having the best quality processes integrated with the business strategy, they try to provide high-level quality consultancy, persuading all the staff to adopt quality actions being themselves mentors and leaders of this cultural change.

Once the internal audit is completed, and after solving the discovered issues, the company will have to pass other audits. It is critical to have the quality of all processes established. Any CEO has to be aware of the assurance that a quality audit is used directly to be compliant with standards. A quality audit can be defined as the probability that an auditor detects and reports some material misstatements in the audited field (Tran, Khairi, & Laili, 2019). This willingness was defined by DeAngelo (1981) as auditor independence because it has to be avoided any conflict of interest. In any case, to avoid unpleasant or unexpected discoveries, every firm has to work hard in the quality of all his processes, and it is a must to have in mind the relationship between audit quality and earnings management (Mättö, 2019). According to Deis and Giroux (1992), the quality assurance system implementation increases the credibility of clients in the company.

Thus, the audit quality is so important, and it is also remarkable the organization culture due it will impact the effectiveness and, consequently, in the quality of the service or product. Different views have to be considered when discussing audit quality: firm's point of view, audit committees, investors and creditors, regulators, and financial management of the company (Martin, 2013). Anyway, some Audit Quality Indicators (AQI) have to be defined to have quantitative measures that provide other aspects and points of view about how good the audit is. The non-profit corporation published a useful guide: the Public Company Accounting Oversight Board (PCAOB), where AQI's are related to Operational Inputs to the audit process and the audit results.

It is crucial to get the feedback of the client through different surveys that allow us to understand those facts and issues that could be reviewed to improve the quality of service. Several activities might be driven to enhance this service quality, but all must be planned according to its requirements. De Ruyter, Wetzels, and Bloemer (1998) analyze the relationship between service quality and service loyalty through the switching costs (defined as the costs involved in changing from one service provider to another). These authors discover three service loyalty dimensions (preference loyalty, price indifference loyalty, and dissatisfaction response). They found a positive relationship between perceived service quality and preference loyalty and price indifference loyalty. The analysis shows that perceived service quality has an impact on customer preference and the willingness to recommend the service to other clients. This point is significant when making decisions and agreeing on the quality objectives of a company. Pitt, Watson, and Kavan (1995) consider five dimensions to evaluate the quality of service, from the perspective of a customer: tangibles (physical facilities and equipment), reliability (ability to perform the promised service), responsiveness (willingness to help customers), assurance (the ability to inspire trust and confidence) and empathy (caring and individualized attention).

It can be said that quality is all related to the customer and what he wants and expects from the service or product offered and how it is delivered. And the main characteristics of quality have been summed up below (Shawyun, 1998):

- It has to achieve a defined "meet requirements."

- It directs to customer satisfaction, so it must focus on people.
- It must apply to every service or product.
- It has to be supported by the management board, and sometimes it can be associated with a change in the organization's culture.
- It is a continuous process. Improvement never ends.
- It is a profitable long-term investment.
- It is everybody's job in the company.

Marsh (2005) remarks on the importance and consequences of the lack of quality data and information. This issue may also involve high costs for the company. Among these consequences, we may find the following ones:

- It is a cumulative increase in costs due to data reconciliation.
- Risk of using inaccurate data to inform or for decision making.
- Lack of trust and credibility with stakeholders.
- Delays in new system deployment.
- Inability to comply with industry and quality standards.
- Wasted time on internal issues that avoid spending time on market competition and involves poor performance.
- Demoralized teams and staff and a frustrating environment.
- High rotation index.
- Reduced ability to respond will affect customer service and slow growth.
- Bad reputation and damage to the brand.
- The legal responsibilities and complaints.
- Economic penalties and fines.

All of them involve costs for companies, besides the other non-economic effects of each of them. The sooner a company detects failures, the sooner it may implement a solution and save unnecessary costs. When analyzing Costs of Poor Quality (COPQs) against the costs related to implementing quality improvement actions, it is difficult to identify all potential adverse monetary effects resulting from low quality. Eppler and Helfert (2004) determine a list of costs resulting from low-quality data, against cost examples of assuring data quality. Considering some of these COPQs in the quality of services, and adding new ones, we propose the following list (a categorization of these costs has been included):

- Operational costs: excess labor costs, data administration costs, process failure costs, and assessment costs.
- Service delivery costs: costs due to increased time of delivery, costs related to noncompliance with the Service Level Agreements (SLAs).
- Market costs: costs of losing current and potential new customers, costs in terms of lost opportunity, expenses due to a damaged image, lost and missed opportunity costs.
- Financial costs: loss of revenue, warranty costs, claims' costs.
- Legal costs: costs because of lawsuits.

Moreover, the costs related to quality improvement actions are listed and categorized below:

- Operational costs: training costs, operational activities-related costs, management, and administrative costs associated with ensuring quality.
- Prevention costs: failure prevention and assessment or inspection costs, quality process/technology/infrastructure improvement costs, quality audits.
- Warranty costs: certification processes costs.

According to Klefsjö, Wiklund, and Edgeman (2001), Six Sigma programs may involve cost savings of a significant amount of money in many companies, resulting from Six Sigma implementations. Many enterprises have demonstrated that Six Sigma has generated a substantial return of the investment (McClusky, 2000). It is also displayed in Aggogeri and Gentili (2008) that Six Sigma reduces the COPQs. The COPQs (Haug, Zachariassen, & Van Liempd, 2011) are composed of internal failures (scraps and rework), external failures (field failures, complaints, and returned material), appraisal (inspection and audit), and prevention (quality planning and process control). Aggogeri and Gentili (2008) show the relationship between the Six Sigma level and the impact of COPQs on sales, identifying that the COPQs are only 5% of sales in a Six Sigma Project (De Feo and Barnard, 2004). Olalla (2011) analyzes costs related to quality in IT Services and the importance of considering this kind of savings in a company.

We have considered in this study the importance of quality assurance's stage, context, and focus, their benefits from different points of view, and the costs derived from low quality. As a result, we affirm that CEOs' influence, involvement, and compromise are vital for the success of applying any quality measure. CEOs must focus their strategy on efficient quality systems, designing formulas to make the firm more competitive.

QUALITY SYSTEMS, MODELS AND STANDARDS

TQM considers some values, such as (Klefsjö et al., 2001): top management commitment, focus on processes, focus on customers, let everybody be committed, base decisions on fact, and improve continuously. The philosophy of TQM is to pursue continuous improvement, beyond maintaining a quality management system such as that based on ISO series 9000:2000 standards (Michalska and Szewieczek, 2007). According to Ruzevicius, Adomaitiene, and Sirvidaite (2004), a quality system may serve as an instrument to implement TQM in the company.

Klefsjö et al. (2001) consider Six Sigma as a methodology within the framework of TQM. It is also of great value regarding business excellence and measuring that progress. Sometimes, Six Sigma may be integrated to get more benefits and synergies between both of them. It is recommended, according to Arnheiter and Maleyeff (2005), to try to implement both of them together in a company, to achieve absolute perfection and more value than every one of them separately. Six sigma should never be seen as an alternative to TQM, considering that TQM is a management system aimed to improve customer satisfaction with a reduced amount of resources, consisting of values, methodologies, and tools (Klefsjö et al., 2001). Six Sigma is implemented in several companies to increase processes and systems (Aggogeri, & Gentili, 2008). Certainly, Six Sigma is one of the most widespread methodologies to achieve such objectives, having in mind the necessity of work in continuous improvement. It starts and finishes in the client (Antony, & Bhaiji, 2003). There has been an increase in the level of use of this methodology as a lot of companies are in the process of cultural change; in this process, employees are being trained on it, so they will need to learn one of the two main methods used within Six Sigma: the DMAIC (Define, Measure, Analyze, Improve, Control) method or the DMADV (Define, Measure, Analyze, Design, Verify) method.

To reach the status of excellence in quality, companies must work and adopt a quality model; among the three most relevant are these: the Deming Application Prize Model (Deming Prize, 2002), the Malcolm Baldrige Model (NIST, 2002), and the model proposed by the European Foundation for Quality Management (EFQM).

Deming's model uses criteria such as the quality of products and processes, the organization and its operations, education and dissemination, standardization, the organization's policies and objectives, management, future, and quality assurance of functions, systems, and methods.

Baldrige's model uses criteria leadership, strategic planning, process and human resource management, customer and market focus, measurement, analysis, and control of knowledge and results. It is essential to say that from this model, there must be some link between leadership (leadership, planning, and customer focus) and outcomes (staff, processes, and results) (Ibrahim, 2013).

The third major model, the EFQM model, is based on the principles of TQM quality, whose values have been cited before, so it bases on criteria related to each other. As a result, it groups into facilitating agents (leadership, alliances and resources, people, processes, and policy and strategy) and outcomes (results in people, clients, society, and critical results) (Sánchez, & Castro, 2005). In this study, it was verified that of the three mentioned, this is the one most used to achieve excellence in quality. To assess the level of quality using this model, companies have to carry out a study of the initial state. In this respect, Saiz-Alvarez and Olalla (2013) also explain how to create value through EFQM.

Anyway, it is worth noting the expansion and current use of the model of the standards of the International Organization for Standardization ISO 9000, finding in this studio the relevance of ISO 9001, that relates to the quality management system regarding development, production, installation, product or service design. These models provide companies a reference and guidelines to achieve the desired level of excellence in the quality of their services and products and to know the areas of continuous improvement and with its best positioning in the global market (Sánchez, & Castro, 2005). All the companies considered in this study have the ISO 9001 certification. Even more, according to the last ISO (The ISO Survey of Management Systems Standard Certification, 2018), the number of companies with this certificate in Spain is 29,562, which places this country within the top 10 positions in a list of 191 countries. That is why this model is highlighted, where quality management is the set of coordinated activities to direct and control an organization in terms of quality. Among its actions is the establishment of a quality policy, control planning, and improvement. Consequently, its primary goal is to promote continuous improvement and the achievement of customer satisfaction (González, 2004).

To work on quality it also requires the use of some tools. One of the most used tools nowadays in the companies is the so-called Quality Function Deployment (QDF) developed by Yoji Akao in the late 1960s and early 1970s, and it consists in knowing customers' requirements and translating them into service or product specifications (Chan, & Wu, 2002). The main advantage of using this tool is that the probability of success in launching a new product or service is very high, although its implementation may be slower. Undoubtedly, it is a valuable tool because it works proactively, something very demanded nowadays. In the studied companies, it has been seen the use of it. Every day, companies realize the benefits of it from customers who will prioritize their requirements to the organizations because it allows them to benchmark against competitors. From this result, it would be easier for them to optimize those things to bring competitive advantage (Mazur, 2003).

Other tools can be used to increase. A widely used tool is SERVQUAL. It measures the gap among expectations and perceptions of clients based on the study of five dimensions (Tangibles, Reliability, Responsiveness, Assurance, and Empathy) and applies several standardized questions to measure service quality (Parasuraman, Zeithaml, & Berry, 1988). Another tool is Failure Mode Effects Analysis (FMEA), a process that collects all possible information in every process to identify potential failure models to put it in a worksheet or Technology Readiness, and in a Pugh Concept Selection.

There are other methods and methodologies, according to Sokovic, Pavletic, and Pipan (2010):

- PDCA or Deming cycle is the cycle followed by the repeated and continuous nature of continuous improvement.
- RADAR (Results, Approach, Deploy, Assess, and Refine) provides a structured approach to analyze an organizational performance; it is an essential part of a company using the EFQM excellence model.
- DMAIC refers to a data-driven lifecycle approach to Six Sigma projects for improving processes.
- DFSS is a systematic and structured approach to new products or processes design that focuses on problem prevention.

QFD is a quality assurance tool designed to hear the voice of both internal and external customers and follow the development of a product or service (Lee, & Sai On Ko, 2000). As a result, it involves constructing a matrix called the House of Quality (HOQ) that is made of two main parts: the 'Whats' and the 'Hows.'

Another tool is the 5S Methodology (Michalska, & Szewieczek, 2007) that consists of the creation and maintaining of a well-organized, clean, highly effective, and high/quality workplace, based on the following principles: sort, set in order, shine, standardize, and sustain. A lot of advantages appear after having implemented this tool in a company, according to Michalska and Szewieczek (2007).

Lee and Sai On Ko (2000) propose an exciting link between a SWOT analysis and a Balanced Scorecard. First, they suggest implementing of SWOT analysis before implementing a Balanced Scorecard, because the BSC requires to have the company vision and the strategy available before its implementation. According to Amaratunga, Baldry, and Sarshar (2001), the BSC model of Kaplan and Norton is a framework for measuring organizational performance. It may help to deploy strategic direction, communicating expectations, and measuring progress towards agreed objectives.

BPM is a structured approach to analyze and continually improve activities (manufacturing, marketing, communications, and other significant elements of a company's operation). According to Zairi (1997), several phases may involve a process' methodology: organizing for quality, understanding the process, streamlining the process, implementation (and measurements and controls), and continuous improvement. Uhl and Gollenia (2016) analyze Business Transformation Management (BTM) and propose Meta Management to provide a frame for different management disciplines and offer the linkages among the management disciplines, leadership, culture, and communication allows the transformation process to be effective. This fact is essential when developing a critical business transformation, such as an evolution towards a culture that focuses on quality.

Nowadays, and derived from a changing and disruptive situation, a question is how satisfied the client is with the service or product offered by the firm. This fact was named 'attractive quality,' a concept used to explain better the roles that different quality attributes have for clients. Based on those attributes, it is possible to know the satisfaction or dissatisfaction level of clients. Consequently, it would be easier to enhance the relationship with clients than, in general, to fight against adverse effects (Löfgren, & Witell, 2008).

QUALITY KEY INDICATORS AND RATIOS

To enhance the quality and considering the projects studied, it has been seen the necessity to define and use a group of valuable KPIs (also known as business indicators, Key Success Indicators (KSIs), or performance metrics). The importance of KPIs is given by their contribution to help the company to define and measure progress toward established or objective organizational goals, such as Sharifi et al. (2009) comment. It can be seen as an excellent way to control the status of the company, making it possible to focus on the weakness to change what is necessary and manage to have a high level of quality. So, to achieve processes more effective and efficient, a group of KPIs will be defined, whose objective will be to ensure the organization is operating, at least, at the level, the customer is expecting and with an acceptable cost (Marr, 2012). CEOs indeed use these KPIs as decision-makers. So, it is crucial to select the best KPIs for the company to achieve the best quality in the processes or services; this is why Sharifi et al. (2009) advise considering basic strategy concepts such as being proactive, meaningful, readily available, among others. The key is to give the right information at the right moment, not only to provide more details.

Some considerations have to be taken into account to define excellent and useful KPIs, as with Mikušová and Janečková (2010):

- The definition of the indicator has to be transparent and objective, to avoid different readings, so they cannot be defined based on personal judgments.
- The implementation of the indicator has to be quick.
- The indicator has to be as simple as possible.
- The indicator measurement period should be as short as possible; measurement over a very long time could give information not too precise so that it might be useless.
- Every KPI has to be aligned with the company's strategy.
- Each indicator has to have the purpose of improving quality.

The chosen indicators depend on the company and its activities. This is why other authors, such as Sukarma and Lukman (2014), collect more and different indicators: cycle time, labor productivity, employee morale and motivation, capital investment efficiency, space efficiency, or equipment performance efficiency. However, the company needs to identify the high-value high-risk Data Quality (DQ) that supports each KPI defined (Masayna, Koronios, Gao, and Gendron, 2007). Masayna et al. (2007) proposed a model to link KPIs and DQ's establishing a classification based on four categories: KPIs, DQs initiatives, the external environment (for instance, client requirements or regulations), and organizational environment (IT capabilities, strategic goals).

To sum up, it can be said that all the KPIs have to be oriented to improve critical aspects of the company, among which the financial, human factors, and client satisfaction are.

QUALITY MODEL PROPOSAL FOR CONTINUOUS IMPROVEMENT

Some several techniques and methodologies may be applied to help organizations to achieve the quality objectives previously defined. Still, the use and success depend on the company (Sokovic et al., 2010). The socioeconomic environment faced by the firm, organizational culture, business policies, and goals determine business success. Quality programs, improvement projects, methodologies, and tools may also be different inside a company, depending on quality goals and objectives defined for every project or program. Depending on the purpose set by every organization, it is required to find a proper way and a combination of methodologies to achieve business success (Sokovic et al., 2010). Several methods and tools, briefly quoted before, involve different applications, purposes, and uses, as seen with PDCA cycle, DMAIC, RADAR, DFSS (Design for Six Sigma), BPM (Business Process Management), QFD, 5S Methodology, SWOT Analysis, and Balanced Scorecard (BSC).

Although several techniques and methodologies might be implemented to give support and allow a proper Quality Management System, the documental support for that system is not an option. Companies must have such plans to guarantee the efficiency of these quality systems. Hernad and Gaya (2013) propose a Document Management Systems to support ISO 9001:2008 Quality Management Systems, which involves six steps:

1. Definition of document requirements.
2. Evaluation of existing systems.
3. Identification of document management strategies in the organization.
4. Design the Document Management System.
5. Implementation of the Document Management System.
6. Maintenance and continuous improvement of the Document Management System.

Also, and according to Dyason and Kaye (1995), a quality framework should include the three main elements: a driver to have a centered organizational direction, an enabler to ensure useful data collection and quality, and optimum results.

Taking into account all these standards and best practices, we defined a continuous improvement framework to assure quality in IT projects and services, considering the following stages in our 15 IT projects:

1. Identify the sources of this model (all the sources which may involve new corrective or proactive activities to be developed).
2. Record continuous improvement actions to be developed during the following months and the information required to complete these tasks.
3. Establish a procedure to do the follow-up of the continuous improvement activities.
4. Once constructed this model and made the marketing campaign among the people and stakeholders involved in the project/service, start operating with this.
5. Finally, evaluate the effectiveness of the actions considered, discovering if the benefits and goals defined at the beginning had been achieved.

The proposed model considered the information and issues detailed in Table 1 for every stage.

Table 1. Continuous Quality Improvement model proposal

Stage	Issues and information to be considered
Sources identification	● Before implementation: Project and quality management standards review (Risk and Project Management standards). ● Sources considered: risk periodical analysis, new requirements, new agreements, strategic decisions.
Information recording	● Before implementation: Project and quality management standards review (ISO 9001 and ISO 2000). ● Information recorded: record date, type of action, action description, start, and finish date, the status of the action, responsible, and other fields required depending on the project.
Follow-up procedure	● Before implementation: Project and quality management standards review (PDCA). ● Considering: relationship model, periodical meetings, responsibility, and involvement.
Operation	● Synergies among projects, leadership, roles, involvement, and gamification issues. ● Documentation and knowledge management.
Effectiveness measure	● Before implementation: Project and quality management standards review (Six Sigma practices and SWOT). ● Performance indicators, quality indicators, and review of actions developed.

Source: the Authors

In this chapter, and based in the experience and the study of 15 IT projects, we affirm that in the definition of each indicator, it is necessary to detail the following information: name and description of the indicator, purpose, relationship with other indicators (if proceed), the formula used to calculate it (when required), tolerated deviation, frequency, method, and measurement periodicity. Besides that, the following KPIs have been considered for its simplicity and applicability in the studied projects:

- Cost of quality: rated as a percentage of annual revenue.
- The number of service/product deviations and the increase/decrease percentage.
- Effectiveness of internal audits and its process: it will measure the quantity of non-conformity of the audits and the proper reduction.
- The number of improvements or corrections implemented and completed.
- The number of quality complaints due to service quality.

The main reason to define and have a useful framework is to provide an effective and efficient way to make it possible that the continuous improvement philosophy can be put into practice in the best possible way. This continuous improvement has to be seen from a competitive point of view. It is something essential for the survival of the company, and it has to start and finish with the client (Dyason, & Kaye, 1995). By defining this continuous improvement framework, it will be possible to manage the standardization of the processes. This fact will result in an improvement and increase not only employees' productivity but also their motivation and satisfaction, empowering the employees to make them responsible for doing high-level quality works, and in a decrease in costs. The direct consequence will be an improvement in the positioning of the company in the current market (Peris, Álvarez-García, & Rueda-Armengot, 2015), and the possibility of anticipating the competition while maintaining a high level of quality.

Success Factors and Advice From our Analysis

It may be challenging to try to change and transform the culture of a company into a quality-focused culture. Uhl and Gollenia (2016) show the different and iterative stages of the transformation cycle: envision, engage, transform, and optimize. This fact may be applied to any quality project or program, and obviously, it is a change from culture to a quality culture. As a transformation into a quality culture, the following stages are proposed:

- Envision: create the need for the change, remark the benefits of a quality culture, develop a sense of urgency.
- Engage employees: empower and motivate people to act and participate in that change, promote quality actions, and plan activities to make that change (considering values, processes, technology, values, etc.).
- Transform: act and develop all planned actions and make people take part in this project.
- Optimize: listen to every source of optimization, and develop a continuous improvement framework to complete the cycle.

Some points should be considered if a firm wants to develop such a change in its culture, focusing on quality policies and values. Considering it as a business transformation and that every business transformation is different, the success may depend on the complexity related to various stakeholders in a very complex ecosystem. Uhl and Gollenia (2016) propose some of the following guidelines succeed. Procedures considered in our projects:

- Specify the cascade of the overall transformational goals for each management discipline.
- Create commitment across all the stakeholders.
- Assign roles and involve the business transformation manager.
- Implement the transformation lifecycle (envision, engage, transform, and optimize).
- Skillful use of communication.

According to Atkinson (1999), some factors may involve success in any project: time, cost, and quality (called the Iron Triangle). Other criteria might include measuring the success of a project, such as system quality, information quality, information use, users' satisfaction, individual impact, and organizational impact. Kwak and Anbari (2006) suggest some key factors succeed in any quality project or program in a company. These factors are management involvement and organizational commitment, project selection, and management and control skills, encouraging and accepting cultural change, and finally, continuous education or training. Knowledge Management (KM) may help quality management to achieve the established goals in a company and develop all the activities of an enterprise according to a quality standard, process, or procedures (Saiz-Alvarez, & Olalla, 2010). Several kinds of research have studied the advantages of incorporating KM in TQM processes. Today more than ever, this integration becomes essential to maintain the competitive advantage that the company needs to work in a quality environment, where knowledge is considered as a potential source of benefits. For managing knowledge properly to survive in such a changing and disruptive environment, the need to train the staff regarding quality was already highlighted (Zhao, & Bryar, 2001).

Quality management is usually planned in a company to be developed by a group of roles that covers all the activities and responsibilities defined in that company related to quality. But the point of view of each of them may be different due to their hierarchy in the company. The human factor is a crucial factor when talking about the success of projects (Olalla, San José, & Mata, 2012). There are also some skills and attitudes that may help a quality leader to complete all the activities related to quality management successfully, and thus, boost the quality culture throughout the company. A quality leader must involve employees in the global and shared quality vision and goals of the company. That is the way a company may afford any quality project or program, and that is the only way to create a quality focus and culture in the organization. It is imperative to develop a proper collaboration culture in the company that supports the development of an adequate quality focus and the creation of value in products or services, taking into account the efforts of all the employees in the company. For instance, according to Goetsch and Davis (2014), one reason that may cause an unsuccessful quality project is senior management delegation and poor leadership. Added to this conclusion, another issue is explained to help to change this point of view to managers and other employees. Quality leaders provide vision to their teams. They are transparent, give a sense of mission and personal attention to their teams, and promote trust and rationality. Quality leaders avoid conflicts by finding reasonable solutions through evading winners and losers (Uhl, & Gollenia, 2016).

Referring to the quality perspective, we propose the following five critical views of a quality leader, from our experience:

1. Provide vision and mission. Explain what is accepted and what is not.
2. Make employees gain trust in the quality and its benefits.
3. Focus efforts and operate in an easy way and with rationality.
4. Give personal attention to each employee and listen to them, understanding the needs of each of them and helping them to understand the quality culture.
5. Manage conflicts properly, always considering the quality level as the first objective itself.

Every level of management in the hierarchy may have their objectives and goals and may consider that quality has a cost for them or affects the achievement of their objectives. That may be caused because the vision, mission, objectives, and goals of the company are not aligned. But anyway, objectives in the company must be aligned, and strategic goals should influence and drive operational purposes and so on. When a quality culture is installed in the firm, all the quality goals should move into operational goals aligned with them. That means that different levels of goals and objectives are aligned, and they take part in a decreasing and consequent structure from a strategic perspective to an operational perspective.

The set of indicators that were defined and introduced in every project could give a way to measure and do the follow-up of the quality service level of every project considered. The success of these projects was achieved when they were completed. From the varied and large projects studied, the following lessons learned have been obtained:

1. The importance of a quality management system, including processes and procedures, and the proper key performance indicators to measure the level of quality of any service/product.
2. It is crucial to consider those methodologies, frameworks, standards, or best practices in the market that best fit the requirements of the company, project, or service, always trying to align this quality system or model to the strategic goals of the company.

3. The importance of a proper quality culture in the organization involves commitment from the CEO to any other employee.
4. Other issues may help to achieve the goals and objectives, such as Knowledge and Document Management, motivation boosters (gamification techniques), and quality tools explained in previous sections of this chapter.

New quality goals and objectives may be defined at a lower level or operational view by considering a set of goals and objectives related to quality from a strategic standpoint. There is no sense in trying to see every level of goals and objectives as an isolated group of goals but as a part of a more prominent structure that considers all the hierarchical levels in a company. A proper definition and implementation of performance indicators is a crucial issue to achieve the quality targets in the service. It is an essential success factor when talking about quality management in a company. The only way to improve service is to understand the real situation of service through measurement. The conclusion is that if quality goals are considered at a high level of the company, they must also be reflected in a lower level of goals and objectives of the company. Managers must consider and take into account those objectives aligned with the strategy of the organization. That is the big engine that may make quality culture works in the firm.

CONCLUSION

In this chapter, through the study of quality in an IT environment, it has been reviewed the importance of measuring processes and services, contemplating different contexts, and enumerating the possible stages to do it. We have analyzed the most notable quality frameworks and methods and the most valuable KPIs to be applied. With this information, and based on projects and working experience, we propose a quality model, and some KPIs be used in IT projects or services.

This proposed model includes a set of stages to implement a quality system, a guide to understanding all the parts gathering this model, and the information considered to be included in this model. We have proposed some indicators to measure the quality level in the project or service and to follow-up on this quality level and model performance. Finally, a set of success factors and recommendations are gathered to give and assure the final success of these projects or services, together with a list of lessons learned that may be considered in future projects.

Future researches could be developed to complete the analysis detailed in this chapter, considering the relative importance of any of these variables and success-related issues in the final project. Further studies could be conducted trying to introduce different standards and methodologies to configure a new model proposal.

The benefits reflected on the implementation of this quality framework for firms, CEOs, and employees, are expressed in saving costs, improving reputation and customer satisfaction, and the perspective of an entity that provides profitability to the country. It can currently serve as a lever to help to improve the country's economic position. Therefore, it will be a potential source of competitive advantage for both company and the nation. Work environments and markets are in constant change and transformation, making it more necessary to apply a quality framework such as the one proposed, not only to differentiate from the competition but also to optimize both the work and the result of the company that applies it.

Firms need to be transformed anyway. Depending on its characteristics, and it will do it in several stages, but always using quality as a gear lever and axis for continuous improvement. For this, and as it has been seen, it is essential to define the general goals that will guide its development and maintenance in a complex environment where quality is the best way to stay ahead.

REFERENCES

Addey, J. (2004). The modern quality manager. *Total Quality Management & Business Excellence*, *15*(5-6), 879–889. doi:10.1080/14783360410001680314

Aggogeri, F., & Gentili, E. (2008). Six Sigma methodology: An effective tool for quality management. *International Journal of Manufacturing Technology and Management*, *14*(3-4), 289–298. doi:10.1504/IJMTM.2008.017728

Amaratunga, D., Baldry, D., & Sarshar, M. (2001). Process improvement through performance measurement: The balanced scorecard methodology. *Work Study*, *50*(5), 179–189. doi:10.1108/EUM0000000005677

Antony, J., & Bhaiji, M. (2003). *Key ingredients for a successful six sigma program*. Warwick Manufacturing Group School of Engineering, University of Warwick.

Arnheiter, E. D., & Maleyeff, J. (2005). The integration of lean management and Six Sigma. *The TQM Magazine*, *17*(1), 5–18. doi:10.1108/09544780510573020

Atkinson, R. (1999). Project management: Cost, time and quality, two best guesses and a phenomenon, it's time to accept other success criteria. *International Journal of Project Management*, *17*(6), 337–342. doi:10.1016/S0263-7863(98)00069-6

Batini, C., Cappiello, C., Francalanci, C., & Maurino, A. (2009). Methodologies for data quality assessment and improvement. *ACM Computing Surveys*, *41*(3), 16. doi:10.1145/1541880.1541883

Bergman, B., & Klefsjö, B. (2010). *Quality from customer needs to customer satisfaction*. Studentlitteratur AB.

Buttle, F. (1997). ISO 9000: Marketing motivations and benefits. *International Journal of Quality & Reliability Management*, *14*(9), 936–947. doi:10.1108/02656719710186867

Casadesus, M., Giménez, G., & Heras, I. (2001). Benefits of ISO 9000 implementation in the Spanish industry. *European Business Review*, *13*(6), 327–336. doi:10.1108/EUM0000000006195

Chan, L. K., & Wu, M. L. (2002). Quality function deployment: A literature review. *European Journal of Operational Research*, *143*(3), 463–497. doi:10.1016/S0377-2217(02)00178-9

Cubillos Rodríguez, M. C., & Rozo Rodríguez, D. (2009). El concepto de calidad: Historia, evolución e importancia para la competitividad. *Revista de la Universidad de la Salle*, *48*, 80–99.

De Feo, A., & Barnard, W. (2004). *Juran Institute's Six Sigma*. McGraw-Hill.

De Ruyter, K., Wetzels, M., & Bloemer, J. (1998). On the relationship between perceived service quality, service loyalty, and switching costs. *International Journal of Service Industry Management*, *9*(5), 436–453. doi:10.1108/09564239810238848

DeAngelo, L. E. (1981). Auditor size and audit quality. *Journal of Accounting and Economics*, *3*(3), 183–199. doi:10.1016/0165-4101(81)90002-1

Deis, D. R. Jr, & Giroux, G. A. (1992). Determinants of audit quality in the public sector. *The Accounting Review*, 462–479.

Dyason, M. D., & Kaye, M. M. (1995). Achieving a competitive edge through continuous quality improvement. In *Total Quality Management* (pp. 517–520). Springer. doi:10.1007/978-94-011-0539-2_92

Eppler, M., & Helfert, M. (2004, November). A classification and analysis of data quality costs. In *International Conference on Information Quality* (pp. 311-325). Academic Press.

Eppler, M. J., & Muenzenmayer, P. (2002, November). Measuring Information Quality in the Web Context: A Survey of State-of-the-Art Instruments and an Application Methodology. In ICIQ (pp. 187-196). Academic Press.

Goetsch, D. L., & Davis, S. B. (2014). *Quality management for organizational excellence*. Pearson.

González López, I. (2004). Modelos de evaluación de la calidad orientados a la mejora de las instituciones educativas. XXI. *Review of Education*, *6*, 155–169.

Haug, A., Zachariassen, F., & Van Liempd, D. (2011). The costs of poor data quality. *Journal of Industrial Engineering and Management*, *4*(2), 168–193. doi:10.3926/jiem.2011.v4n2.p168-193

Hellman, P., & Liu, Y. (2013). Development of quality management systems: How have disruptive technological innovations in quality management affected organizations? *Quality Innovation Prosperity*, *17*(1), 104–119. doi:10.12776/qip.v17i1.154

Hernad, J. M. C., & Gaya, C. G. (2013). Methodology for implementing document management systems to support ISO 9001: 2008 quality management systems. *Procedia Engineering*, *63*, 29–35. doi:10.1016/j.proeng.2013.08.225

Ibrahim, O. (2013). Total Quality Management (TQM) and continuous improvement, as addressed by researchers. *International Journal of Scientific and Research Publications*, *3*(10), 1–4.

Ingason, H. Þ., & Jónsdóttir, E. R. (2017). The house of competence of the quality manager. *Cogent Business & Management*, *4*(1), 1345050. doi:10.1080/23311975.2017.1345050

Klefsjö, B., Wiklund, H., & Edgeman, R. L. (2001). Six Sigma seen as a methodology for total quality management. *Measuring Business Excellence*, *5*(1), 31–35. doi:10.1108/13683040110385809

Kwak, Y. H., & Anbari, F. T. (2006). Benefits, obstacles, and future of six sigma approach. *Technovation*, *26*(5-6), 708–715. doi:10.1016/j.technovation.2004.10.003

Lameijer, B. A., Antony, J., Chakraborty, A., Does, R. J. M. M., & Garza-Reyes, J. A. (2020). The role of organisational motivation and coordination in continuous improvement implementations: An empirical research of process improvement project success. *Total Quality Management & Business Excellence*, 1–17. doi:10.1080/14783363.2020.1757422

Lee, S. F., & Sai On Ko, A. (2000). Building Balanced Scorecard with SWOT Analysis, and implementing "Sun Tzu's The Art of Business Management Strategies" on QFD Methodology. *Managerial Auditing Journal*, *15*(1/2), 68–76. doi:10.1108/02686900010304669

Lee, Y. W., Strong, D. M., Kahn, B. K., & Wang, R. Y. (2002). AIMQ: A methodology for information quality assessment. *Information & Management*, *40*(2), 133–146. doi:10.1016/S0378-7206(02)00043-5

Löfgren, M., & Witell, L. (2008). Two decades of using Kano's theory of attractive quality: A literature review. *The Quality Management Journal*, *15*(1), 59–75. doi:10.1080/10686967.2008.11918056

Maderuelo Fernández, J. A. (2002). Gestión de la calidad total: El modelo EFQM de excelencia. *Medifam*, *12*(10), 41–54. doi:10.4321/S1131-57682002001000004

Marr, B. (2012). Key Performance Indicators (KPI): The 75 measures every manager needs to know. Pearson UK.

Marsh, R. (2005). Drowning in dirty data? It's time to sink or swim: A four-stage methodology for total data quality management. *Journal of Database Marketing & Customer Strategy Management*, *12*(2), 105–112. doi:10.1057/palgrave.dbm.3240247

Martin, R. D. (2013). Audit quality indicators: Audit practice meets audit research. *Current Issues in Auditing*, *7*(2), A17–A23. doi:10.2308/ciia-50581

Masayna, V., Koronios, A., Gao, J., & Gendron, M. (2007, June). Data quality and KPIs: a link to be established. In *The 2nd World Congress on Engineering Asset Management (EAM) and The 4th International Conference on Condition Monitoring* (pp. 1377-1386). Academic Press.

Mättö, T. (2019). Innovation through the implementation of a quality improvement method. *The TQM Journal*, *31*(6), 987–1002. doi:10.1108/TQM-12-2018-0193

Mazur, G. (2003, May). Voice of the customer (define): QFD to define value. In *Proceedings of the 57th American Quality Congress* (pp. 1-7). Academic Press.

McClusky, R. (2000). The rise, fall, and revival of Six Sigma. *Measuring Business Excellence*, *4*(2), 6–17.

Michalska, J., & Szewieczek, D. (2007). The 5S methodology as a tool for improving the organization. *Journal of Achievements in Materials and Manufacturing Engineering*, *24*(2), 211–214.

Mikušová, M., & Janečková, V. (2010). Developing and implementing successful key performance indicators. *World Academy of Science, Engineering and Technology*, *42*, 969–981.

Oakland, J. S. (2014). *Total quality management and operational excellence: text with cases*. Routledge. doi:10.4324/9781315815725

Olalla, B. (2011). Costes asociados a la Calidad en los Servicios de Tecnologías de la Información. Congreso Académico itSMF España.

Olalla, B., & Mata, M. (2016). Value Creation in a Network Economy. In J. M. Saiz-Alvarez (Ed.), *Handbook of Research on Social Entrepreneurship and Solidarity Economics* (pp. 93–110). IGI Global. doi:10.4018/978-1-5225-0097-1.ch006

Olalla, B., San José, C., & Mata, M. (2012). Factor humano: un elemento clave en la búsqueda de la eficiencia de los proyectos. In *VII Congreso Nacional VISION12*. Madrid: itSMF Spain.

Parasuraman, A., Zeithaml, V. A., & Berry, L. L. (1988). Servqual: A multiple-item scale for measuring consumer perc. *Journal of Retailing*, *64*(1), 12–40.

Patidar, L., Soni, V. K., & Soni, P. K. (2016). Continuous improvement philosophy for manufacturing productivity: A critical review. *Trends in Industrial and Mechanical Engineering*, *30*, 34–45.

Peris-Ortiz, M., Álvarez-García, J., & Rueda-Armengot, C. (Eds.). (2015). Achieving competitive advantage through quality management. Cham, Switzerland: Springer.

Pitt, L. F., Watson, R. T., & Kavan, C. B. (1995). Service quality: A measure of information systems effectiveness. *Management Information Systems Quarterly*, *19*(2), 173–187. doi:10.2307/249687

Powell, T. C. (1995). Total quality management as competitive advantage: A review and empirical study. *Strategic Management Journal*, *16*(1), 15–37. doi:10.1002mj.4250160105

Psomas, E., Vouzas, F., & Kafetzopoulos, D. (2014). Quality management benefits through the "soft" and "hard" aspect of TQM in food companies. *The TQM Journal*, *26*(5), 431–444. doi:10.1108/TQM-02-2013-0017

Ruzevicius, J., Adomaitiene, R., & Sirvidaite, J. (2004). Motivation and efficiency of quality management systems implementation: A study of Lithuanian organizations. *Total Quality Management & Business Excellence*, *15*(2), 173–189. doi:10.1080/1478336032000149018

Saavedra, Y. A. M., Avila, E. O., & Mendívil, B. C. (2020). Una Reflexión Crítica de los Sistemas De Gestión de Calidad: Ventajas y Desventajas. *Revista En-contexto*, *8*(12).

Saiz-Alvarez, J. M., & Olalla, B. (2010). Gestión del conocimiento y sistemas de Calidad en los clusters de empresas familiares. *EAN Journal*, *68*, 70–85.

Saiz-Alvarez, J. M., & Olalla, B. (2013). Modelo EFQM y creación de valor: Una aproximación teórica. *The Anáhuac Journal: Business and Economics*, *13*(1), 31–54.

Sánchez, M. F., & Castro, J. G. (2005). *Calidad total: modelo EFQM de excelencia*. FC Editorial.

Sharifi, M., Ayat, M., Ibrahim, S., & Sahibuddin, S. (2009). The most applicable KPIs of problem management process in organizations. *International Journal of Simulation: Systems. Science & Technology*, *10*(3), 77–83.

Shawyun, T. (1998). Quality Assurance and Strategic Implementation in educational institutions: A Holistic Alliance? *International Journal of Quality & Reliability Management*, *15*(1), 1–15.

Sokovic, M., Pavletic, D., & Pipan, K.K. (2010). Quality improvement methodologies–PDCA cycle, RADAR matrix, DMAIC, and DFSS. *Journal of Achievements in Materials and Manufacturing Engineering*, *43*(1), 476-483.

Sukarma, L., & Azmi, H. (2015). The measures of performance for world-class manufacturing practices: A critical review. *Applied Mechanics and Materials*, *761*, 545–549. doi:10.4028/www.scientific.net/AMM.761.545

Tran, M. D., Khairi, K. F., & Laili, N. H. (2019). A longitudinal study of audit quality differences among independent auditors. *Journal of Economic Development*, *21*(2), 234–246. doi:10.1108/JED-10-2019-0040

Uhl, A., & Gollenia, L. A. (Eds.). (2016). *A handbook of business transformation management methodology*. Routledge. doi:10.4324/9781315570631

Zairi, M. (1997). Business process management: A boundaryless approach to modern competitiveness. *Business Process Management Journal*, *3*(1), 64–80. doi:10.1108/14637159710161585

Zangwill, W. I., & Kantor, P. B. (1998). Toward a theory of continuous improvement and the learning curve. *Management Science*, *44*(7), 910–920. doi:10.1287/mnsc.44.7.910

Zhao, F., & Bryar, P. (2001, April). Integrating knowledge management and total quality: A complementary process. *6th International Conference on ISO, 9000, 17-19.*

KEY TERMS AND DEFINITIONS

Attractive Quality: It is a set of attributes that can take five high levels of benefits if they are met, but have no negative consequences if they are not achieved.

Continuous Improvement: This is how every company has to always do better work through several tasks, such as analyzing and reviewing what is being done.

Globalization: It is the way used to help the understanding and work of everyone, independently regardless of his origin: country, company, culture, etc.

Regulation: It is a group of guidelines, usually documented, to establish the rules to be followed to achieve or have the required level (legal, economic, etc.) to work in a specific environment.

Soft Skills: A set of skills or competencies not based on a degree, and with them, it makes easiest to deal with problems or conflicts in a firm.

Standard: Prototypes, models, or references used to know if what has to be measured is compliant with standard requirements.

Transformational Goals: A set of changes needed to apply to go from current to the desired status with the participation of everyone and supported by the CEO.

Chapter 5
Extended Quality Processes in Internationalized Agro-Industrial. Rural Collaborative Economy:
Capital Accumulation and the Association of Small Farmers

Uriel Hitamar Castillo-Nazareno
Universidad Católica de Santiago de Guayaquil, Ecuador

Jessica Silvana Matute-Petroche
Universidad Católica de Santiago de Guayaquil, Ecuador

María Teresa Alcívar-Avilés
Universidad Católica de Santiago de Guayaquil, Ecuador

ABSTRACT

Exploring agricultural production and derived products is one of the challenges that countries like Ecuador have today. The crises in the agrarian economies could find formulas to be reversed if capital is built and distributed so that accumulation is visible in each of the processes that make up the value chains. One formula proposed is the productive strategic partnership in the collaborative line: the little ones must always go together. A perspective of this collaborative model with comprehensive quality processes is proposed in the global market. To this end, two productive attempts in the province of Chimborazo (Ecuador) are studied. The first one from Alausí canton, and the second production and export criterion already developed, is located in Colta Canton of the same province and is called COPROBICH. Based on these elements, the chapter proposes to incorporate theoretical and technical aspects that will make it possible to achieve greater efficiency in the process of internationalization of these business drives

DOI: 10.4018/978-1-7998-5036-6.ch005

INTRODUCTION

The canton Alausí locates in the south of the province of Chimborazo (Ecuador), 84 km from Riobamba and 2,374 meters above sea level. The canton has eight rural parishes: Alausí, Achupallas, Guasuntos, Huigra, Multitud, Pistishí, Pumallacta, Sevilla, Sibambe, and Tixán (GADPCH, 2016; Instituto Nacional de Estadísticas y Censos, 2010).

In this canton, 75.8% of the population is engaged in agriculture, stockbreeding, forestry, and fishing; 4.8% in wholesale and retail trade; 4.2% in construction activities. These three activities account for 84% of the total, so it suggests that improvements in this area will have a significant impact on the territory (Instituto Nacional de Estadísticas y Censos, 2016).

According to the last 2010 census, the Economically Active Population (EAP) at canton Alausí is 17,158, ranking the fifth place in Chimborazo. Rural population is 14,731 (85.85%) having a greater representation compared to urban one (2,427, 14.15%). Most of the rural population labor in activities related to agriculture, livestock, and forestry.

Today, agricultural producers have problems related to the system of marketing and distribution of their products. They are a determining factor of poverty and affect the social and economic situation of the producers in the canton. Despite this fact, in the Development and Territorial Planning Plan of the Alausí Canton (2015), no centers for the collection of agricultural products have been identified, and, as far as marketing is concerned, only two markets are registered in the cantonal capital: *Municipal* and *Jesus Square*.

The destination of its agricultural production is mainly Guayaquil, the most populated city of Ecuador, and Riobamba, the capital of the province where the canton Alausí is located. Locally, producers sell their products in small fairs situated in various parishes of the canton.

In general, both the Ministry of Agriculture, Livestock, Aquaculture and Fisheries (2016) and GADPCH (2015) affirm that the main problems facing the province are (a) the low level of access to the means of production, such as land, labor, irrigation, credit, and seeds, among others; (b) low value-added to production; (c) an inefficient marketing system; (d) low crop yields; and (e) low and weak level of production planning, which results into a low level of family income.

The Productive Problem in Alausí

From this perspective, it should be stressed that most of the canton's agricultural production is stationary. At a particular time, there is overproduction, but generally, there is a shortage, so production never equals to the market demand. Often, this fact mainly affects farmers who receive prices below production costs (Secretaría Nacional de Planificación y Desarrollo, 2017). A study of market demand is not carried out to plan production and cash balance yields.

Another difficulty is the inefficient transport system to connect rural areas with local markets, which worsens for small agricultural producers to have good marketing management (MAGAP, 2016). We argue for the urgency of finding a feasible solution to facilitate this logic of production and commercialization, a systematic impoverishment for the population that can be observed every time the market is reached. As a result, economic heritage is lost.

According to the GADPCH (2015), the cantonal gross value added (GVA) is 4.23% of the province of Chimborazo; Riobamba (capital of the region) has a GVA of 73.35%. In absolute terms, the GVA of

Alausí is $55,952,000.00, representing a per capita of only $1,272.00 or a monthly income of barely $100, which shows the poverty population.

The Possibility of a Viable Experience: COPROBICH

Having in mind these facts, the firm developed by the Corporation of Producers and Commercializers Bio Taita Chimborazo (COPROBICH) created at the end of 2003 and located in Cajabamba, in the Central Andes of the Chimborazo Province, is essential to review as a model of productive organization that tries to make the territory efficient. This business model could be useful for Alausí if some adjustments and contextualization of productive economic are made.

The corporation groups some 650 indigenous Puruha families from 56 quinoa-producing communities in Chimborazo. It represents associativity that shares the property. This fact is to emphasize decisively because here is its strength to imitate in Alausí. With a processing capacity of about 780 tons per year is an average yield of 1.2 tons per hectare, which allows us to conclude that this is a sector of small farms that make it up. Its production of granolas and quinoa flour mixed with oats, has as final market France, Netherlands, among others (COPROBICH, 2020).

COPROBICH tries to practice the logic of quality extended processes with the idea that families achieve better prices. This perspective can be seen in its mission: To *produce, transform and commercialize high-quality products to meet world standards to satisfy and exceed the demand of its clients, promoting the protection of the environment, contributing to the socio-economic development partners the Province of Chimborazo*. It is made up of community organizations in the province of Chimborazo, making the quinoa producer part of the organization.

However, COPROBICH does not become a fully-fledged company. In practical terms, it only has a quinoa processing plant with acceptable technological elements. Farmers produce raw material and international relations (cooperation) that facilitate the sale. But this is insufficient for the activity since the technical processes of management (feedback and pre-feeding) of brand management for sale and international corporate finance do not exist. This business model tries, based on cooperation, to overcome its inefficiencies that could be summarized: (a) low capacity to generate wealth, (b) high marketing risks, (c) increased production costs and (d) dependence on foreign aid. In short, the generation of new capital is in doubt and therefore plays with the risk of bankruptcy (Enciso et al., 2019).

From this circumstance, the COPROBICH perspective can become a proposal for an efficient organization model of value-added production applicable to other cantons and productive sectors; it can impact commercialization by expanding international markets and wealth distribution. This fact is evident from an analysis of the vital elements involved: (a) it is contained in the culture of the territory, (b) it is based on local production, and (c) the products have markets outside the locality and other countries. However, it requires a substantial strengthening of the structure and criteria of production and marketing. In other words, the model must be perfected (Enciso et al., 2019).

Alausí has production and agricultural vocation while COPROBICH is already a proof of the business organization that is possible to forge, from the partnership, to make this canton explore other opportunities and approaches to build new capital (Ospina et al., 2019).

The Reason for Internationalizing Collaborative Modeling

The organization of production at these levels of competitive precariousness implies a strategic partnership to overcome weaknesses in a highly competitive market (Doleski, 2015). This perspective of integration of productive micro-forces, to play a leading role in a market, approaches the definition of Collaborative Economy by applying the criterion of extended processes, vertical and horizontal linkages (Rodriguez & Perez, 2017). As a consequence of this particular alliance, throughout the organization, with processes extended from the production of the raw material to the placement of the value-added product on the market, the property is distributed in a compensated and equivalent manner (Alba et al., 2020; Alcívar, 2015).

Compensation refers to the fact that the organization must not allow deficits to be generated in any property (Sanchez & Moreno, 2019). Both producers and industrializers and marketers must maintain sufficient aspects of wealth to enable them to increase their assets in such a way that they can repeat the process continuously (Ferrer & Maudes, 2019). At the same time, equivalence refers to the fact that distributed wealth must meet the criteria of time for participation in the processes that make up the business organization (Chávez, Castillo, & Alcivar, 2017).

For example, for a big quinoa producer, the cost must accrue the discount rate, which implies higher waiting time. Additionally, it must be compensated to the extent that the distribution of capital must not make some accumulate more than others in this game of different rates of participation. In other words, the result is global in the company (Plaza-Angulo, 2019).

In that sense, COPROBICH has a central problem: the producers who are part of the company are only assigned the price. This fact involves a reduced and simplified allocation of everything that happens in these value-generating chains in which the company is involved (Martínez, 2019). After checking prices, waiting time and compensation should be evaluated to avoid accumulation in one sector of the chain more than in others. It should be noted that the producer's time is much slower than that of the trader in the final market. Therefore, it cannot happen that a collaborative company (compensated and equivalent) does not consider this determinant phenomenon (Cantalapiedra, 2019).

This deficiency is the criticism and the one that aims to be solved since COPROBICH. It can be readily appreciated that the population of the surroundings has not improved its standard of living. Although all the families participate in this association, the model is not generating the expected results. You can see this with a quick tour and some interviews. But we must not lose sight of the fact that all parties are generating work. However, as always, who is in the first links of the chain has the worst result. This fact is the challenge to be solved.

The Extended Quality Processes in Internationalization

Extended processes can be understood as integrating into a single organizational body of many techniques on which business productivity depends (Craviotti & Soleno-Wilches, 2015). It is a strategic partnership not to sell raw materials, but to transform them into value-added products and sell them to the final consumer. This fact implies, on the one hand, incorporating strategic processes that add up to the supply of raw materials and, on the other hand, the process of selling finished products in markets beyond the national markets (Preciado-Hoyos, 2020). The company is therefore defined by the generator of the product to be processed and its resulting supply logistics. Additionally, this subject *generating the raw material is* associated with and incorporated into the company (Contreras, Paredes, & Turbay, 2017).

Here, compensation and equivalence in the distribution of capital are combined as a central aspect of the organization. When each component of this complex business structure receives wealth distribution, according to the time it absorbs its operation (equivalence) and depending on the systematic losses occurred in the first links of the value chain (compensation), it becomes sustainable and relevant (Bulchand & Melián, 2019; Asimakopulos, 1988).

This compensatory and equivalent logic seeks that the extension is, therefore, to reach from the beginning of the chain to the final consumer, expanding the local market. For that reason, internationalization is inherent in this model. Selling beyond the boundaries set by the nation state is necessary to approach processes that behave on an increasing scale. (Rodríguez, 2019; Craviotti & Palacios, 2013).

However, internationalization does not only refer to the sale of the raw material or the value-added product. This fact has a high complexity since it is about the sale of brands generated from the product you want to place and, from this, it is achieved a positioning in the target market using franchises, joint venture, co-branding, or other models of strategic alliances (Rodríguez, 2019; Ashley & Tuten, 2015). Marketing in the game of brands is fundamental in the proposed business model.

Aspects of Alausí that Contextualize the Feasibility of the COPROBICH Model

The producers of the Tixán parish have the highest agricultural participation in the canton with 30.9%, followed by Achupallas (27.2%), and Sibambe (10.22%), as the central parishes of Alausí. The least represented were Huigra (6.99%), Multitud (5.65%), Guasuntos (4.57%), Pumallacta (2.42%), Sevilla (2.15%), and Pistishí (0.81%). Therefore, it is possible to advance in a project such as the one proposed by COPROBICH (Instituto Nacional de Estadísticas y Censos, 2016)

The Farmers' Organization

83.90% of all agricultural producers in the various parishes of the canton are not members of any farm producer association or organization, due to the lack of economically profitable production organization in the sector; only 16.10% belongs to an organization. The real possibility of the organization depends on the generation of capital and its distribution (Petroche, 2019). The associated population by Parish is shown in Table 1.

Table 1. Associated Population by Parish

Parishes	Organization / Farmers' Association				Total
	Yes	In %	No	In %	
Alausí	9	26.47	25	73.53	34
Tixán	12	10.43	103	89.57	115
Achupallas	24	23.76	77	76.24	101
Guasuntos	4	23.53	13	76.47	17
Huigra	6	23.08	20	76.92	26
Multitud	2	9.52	19	90.48	21
Pistishí	0	0.00	3	100.00	3
Pumallacta	0	0.00	9	100.00	9
Sevilla	0	0.00	8	100.00	8
Sibambe	3	7.89	35	92.11	38
Total	**60**		**312**		**372**

Source: Adapted from Petroche (2019)

As you can see, the data are unambiguous and tragic at this point. Producers above 80% are not organized despite the urgent need to do so. A readily observable motivation and criterion is the collaborative structure of COPROBICH, which represents a model to follow. It ensures a more efficient distribution of the wealth generated in cantons such as Alausí (Table 2).

Table 2. Profit from Major Agricultural Products

Product	Price ($)	Average income	Quantity	Unit	Unit cost ($)	Profit
Potato	9.56	319.45	20	Quintal	15.97	nd
Barley	20.07	347.04	30	Quintal	11.57	nd
Bean	19.80	307.62	1	Saco	307.62	nd
Haba	16.32	266.33	8	Saco	33.29	nd
Wheat	18.74	359.57	20	Quintal	17.98	0.76

Legend: nd (no data) Source: The authors

Taking a 10-year average of the prices, you can record the data in Table 2 by taking a simple difference between the sales price and the production costs, the loss is evident. In this line, it is essential to point out that 36.29% sell their products annually, due to the harvest time of certain products; 30.65% do so biannually; 12.63% do so quarterly; 12.10% four-monthly; 5.11% sell their products weekly; 1.88% fortnightly and 1.34% monthly. We must consider that in marketing, times are drastically reduced. For that reason, it is recorded that approximately 77% sell most of the products to intermediaries, and 23.12% sell to final consumers at food fairs.

Table 3. Key Elements of COPROBICH's Business Model

Elements	Description
Value Proposition	The network of producers is organized in comprehensive quality processes.
Customer Segment	The primary aim is to reach the furthest link where the final consumer is at a national or international level.
Market Opportunity	Space within the market is foreseen by the organization and the economic opportunities in that space.
Revenue model	Describes an efficient organization for obtaining income and generating profit. The main revenue aspects are advertising, subscription model, transaction fee, sales, and farmer ownership criteria.
Key Resources	They are the primary input factors or resources that allow the real implementation of the business model. These elements make it possible to offer a product or service and therefore supply the target markets.
Key Partners	Partners' goals are creating value for the customer through the optional cooperation of suppliers and partners within a network.

Source: Adapted from Laudon and Traver (2014).

Regarding forms of payment, 99.46% of agricultural producers are paid for their raw materials and farming inputs in cash, 0.27% pay by check, and 0.27% use bank transactions (Petroche, 2019). This fact means that in peasant production, buyers pay for their products when they make the purchase. This is a way of verifying that impoverishment is evident: pay in cash and charged on credit.

74.48% deliver products in less than a day, after hours of travel from the place or city where products are sent. 23.43% stated a range between one to three days of delay in delivery, and only 2.1% stated between four to six days.

Business Model Proposal: The Strategic Partnership of Peers

The associativity of agricultural producers is presented as an alternative because producers, having little access to and knowledge about markets and value chains, would find it difficult to carry out the process of selling their products individually and even less able to add value to them. Therefore, it was defined for COPROBICH that the type of business model suitable for industrialization, commercialization, and distribution from the Alausí canton will be B2B2C (Business to Business to Consumer) (Siemieniako, 2018). The first B refers to the association, in which producers and traders of agricultural products intervene; the second B to the web platform will be the means and tool for buying and selling products; and the C to potential clients or consumers at the national and international level.

This fact implies creating a distribution center for the main agricultural products produced in the canton, where they are processed as products for final consumption.

Elements of the COPROBICH Collaborative Business Model

Laudon and Traver (2014) state that among the essential elements for formulating a successful business model are (a) value proposition, (b) revenue model, (c) market opportunity, (d) competitive environment, (e) competitive advantage, (f) market strategy, (g) organizational development, and (h) team management. In the case of COPROBICH, the critical elements identified are presented below.

Table 3 summarizes the importance of the components that allow the company to be structured. If one of them is missing, the model would not be viable in the framework of the analysis carried out.

COPROBICH in Alausí: *the Rural Collaborative Economy*

The rural collaborative economy connects suppliers, manufacturers, vendors, distributors, and consumers, all together. It can be approached as Business to Business to Consumer (B2B2C). The first business (B) is a manufacturer who is a supplier of raw materials. The second business (B) is the transformer of raw material into the final product. It is the seller on the platform, finally (C) is a customer who is the final consumer. B2B2C is the core of the intermediaries linking businesses with consumers. It combines upstream vendors and downstream consumers to achieve effective integration. To some extent, the B2B2C model is a supply chain network (Zhao & Guo, 2012).

B2B2C refers to companies that, while earning revenue directly from the organization's customers, manage the customer experience or the marketing of products and services to intermediaries and even the final consumer (Wiersema, 2013). Therefore, the B2B2C companies for Alausi in the COPROBICH model are marketed simultaneously to both companies and consumers. (Iankova, Davies, Archer-Brown, Marder, & Yau, 2018).

In the context of the business to consumer model, companies can communicate with consumers at a much lower cost than ever before through social networks (Neti, 2011), generating online content quickly and economically to develop brand presence (Ashley & Tuten, 2015).

E-agriculture in the Value Chain: a Complementary Aspect That Adds **Value**

In Table 4, the characteristics of the benefits of the COPROBICH collaborative process are represented in the electronic framework of its marketing and management processes:

Table 4. Characteristics of the Collaborative Process with E-agriculture in COPROBICH

Features	Benefit
Process Transformation	Stakeholders collect, analyze, store, and share agricultural information for their daily decision making.
Investments	The development of e-supported agriculture stimulates investment in ICT infrastructure and human capital.
Efficient Markets	It leads to greater efficiencies in rural markets: lower transaction costs, fewer information asymmetries, better market coordination. It reduces waste at various stages of the value chain, improving the efficiency of the supply chain.
Improved vertical and horizontal links	E-supported agriculture results in the development of relationships based on trust among value chain actors. It can help reduce layers of intermediaries and make transactions fair and transparent, thus improving the trust factor.
Value-added services	It leads to the development of value-added services for rural farmers and other actors in agricultural value chains.

Source: Adapted from FAO (2016).

The efficient organizational capacity required to sustain itself within the value chain successfully involves the use of technology and its strategic components outlined in the table above (Food and Agriculture Organization of the United Nations, 2016)

Collaborative Agricultural Production, Electronic Sales, and the Supply Chain as Part of the Extended Process.

In a COPROBICH model, the Internet is a practical, productive exchange facilitator, so electronic commerce maintains a direct relationship between bidders and demanders (Correa et al., 2016). E-commerce has dramatically reduced the intervals along the supply chains by facilitating the sale of agricultural products directly to consumers, thus maintaining sales revenues. Effective use of e-commerce can lower the prices of farm inputs by further expanding purchasing power. Having higher incomes and lower prices allows for improving the standard of living of rural residents (Asian Development Bank, 2017).

E-commerce supply chain management makes extensive use of ERP (enterprise resource planning) systems by incorporating core management (human resources, finance, materials, production, marketing, and supply). As a result, firms standardize their core business and information processes (Huang, & Jia, 2013). Therefore, COPROBICH can establish an electronic collaboration platform to make its operations fully efficient and increase its market reach (Asian Development Bank, 2017).

At present, many problems in traditional supply chain management have seriously limited the market competitiveness of farmers. For example, in the vertically integrated supply chain management model, the emphasis is on competition, while cooperation is overlooked, like the requirement for information platforms and electronic delivery methods. (Asian Development Bank, 2017).

Rural logistics is a component within the supply chain. Development in the supply chain involves reducing the cost of transporting agricultural products, increasing farmers' incomes, and reducing the gap between urban and rural areas. Therefore, it promotes the construction of rural markets and improves the quality of life of farmers (Asian Development Bank. 2017). This type of logistics consists of three forms: supply of agricultural material, sales of farm products, and rural supplies. It also revolves around the style of production in rural areas. It forms the supply chain system from the purchase of agricultural material to the sale of farm products and access to the daily needs of rural residents (Huang & Jia, 2013).

CONCLUSION

Business organizations with comprehensive quality processes and strategic associativity compensate price disadvantages and make temporary equivalences. This business behavior has been reflected in the COPROBICH model. In perfect complementarity in an economically depressed territory. Alausí is a reality that is repeated incessantly in the productive sectors of raw materials in Ecuador, and for that reason, it contains sufficient aspects to apply the indicated model. The collaborative business perspective offers a great possibility in the creation and distribution of capital, overcoming chronic poverty.

Theoretical and technical aspects linked to extended associative criterion reveals increase efficiency in micro-businesses internationalization. The conceptual precisions made show that COPROVICH is a drive with great potential to become a highly efficient company. It is a sample of what can be done in Ecuador, even in some countries of the region.

A central element is to point out that crossing the borders of the Nation-State with local productions, generated in extended micro-societies, implies a possibility of high discipline in the processes and of effective product promotion that the collaborative business model must solve. The need for brands is fundamental since it captures the sense of business organization and transfers it to the market. The sustainability of the business depends on this, in addition to criteria such as risk control, an efficient collection system, cash flow process times, and information on market innovation situations are vital aspects to be internalized.

Production on a growing scale is immediately present with the organization of this business body that forces to internationalize. Internalization emerges after production has begun in a framework of equivalencies and compensations. This reality will go from being local and precarious to a corporation that sells brands in other countries.

The contribution enhances the competitive capacity that each of the participants makes from their human, natural, and financial resource capacities that are integrated. The company is not a production plant. It is not only the economic and sales processes, nor is it the raw material; it is the whole of everything, including decision making and integral quality control. This associative model promises a significant contribution to the better living in territories, such as Alausí and Colta, in the Central Highlands of Ecuador.

REFERENCES

Alba, Y., & Olarte, S. (2020). *Economía colaborativa: análisis de literatura un enfoque hacia el desarrollo local y sus limitantes en la innovación de América Latina*. Universidad Cooperativa de Colombia.

Alcivar, T. (2015). *La compensación Comercial. Tesis de doctorado en Empresa*. Universidad Antonio de Nebrija.

Ashley, C., & Tuten, T. (2015). Creative strategies in social media marketing: An exploratory study of branded social content and consumer engagement. *Psychology and Marketing*, *33*(1), 15–27. doi:10.1002/mar.20761

Asian Development Bank. (2017). *Promoting Logistics Development in Rural Areas*. Mandaluyong.

Asimakopulos, A. (1988). *Theories of Income Distribution*. Springer Netherlands. doi:10.1007/978-94-009-2661-5

Ayala, E., & Gonzales, S. (2015). *Tecnologías de la Información y la Comunicación*. Universidad Inca Garcilaso de la Vega.

Bulchand, J., & Melián, S. (2019). *Trabajo y plataformas de servicios en la economía colaborativa: una oportunidad para emprendedores*. Academic Press.

Cantalapiedra, B. (2019). Crowdfunding y audiovisual de proximidad. La economía colaborativa como instrumento de desarrollo sectorial. *CIRIEC-España, Revista de Economía Pública. Social y Cooperativa*, *95*, 257–288.

Cárdenas, J., & Vallejo, L. (2016). Agricultura y desarrollo rural en Colombia 2011-2013: Una aproximación. *Apuntes del Cenes*, *35*(62), 87–123. doi:10.19053/22565779.4411

Chandra, D. G., & Malaya, D. B. (April 2011). Role of e-Agriculture in Rural Development in Indian Context. In *Proceedings of 2011 International Conference on Emerging Trends in Networks and Computer Communications (ETNCC)*. The Institution of Engineers. 10.1109/ETNCC.2011.6255913

Chávez, J., Castillo, U., & Alcívar, T. (2017). *La naturaleza del desvalor productivo*. UCSG.

Contreras, J., Paredes, M., & Turbay, S. (2017). Circuitos cortos de comercialización agroecológica en el Ecuador. *Idesia*, *35*(3), 71–80. doi:10.4067/S0718-34292017005000302

Correa, G., Carrillo, V., Corona, A., Cruz, R., Ramírez, Y., & Ramírez, M. (2016). Tecnologías de Información y Comunicación en las Organizaciones. Universidad Nacional Autónoma de México.

Craviotti, C., & Palacios, P. (2013). La diversificación de los mercados como estrategia de la agricultura familiar. *Revista de Economia e Sociologia Rural*, *51*(Suppl. 1), s063–s078. doi:10.1590/S0103-20032013000600004

Craviotti, C., & Soleno Wilches, R. (2015). Circuitos cortos de comercialización agroalimentaria: Un acercamiento desde la agricultura familiar diversificada en Argentina. *Mundo Agrario*, *16*(33), 1–19.

Doleski, O. D. (2015). *Integrated business model: applying the St. Gallen management concept to business models*. Springer Gabler. doi:10.1007/978-3-658-09698-4

Dünhaupt, P. (2013). *Determinants of functional income distribution - Theory and empirical evidence.* Working Paper 18. Berlin, Germany: Global Labour University.

Enciso, M., Mugarra, A., Muñecas, I., & Ruíz, A. (2019). Collaborative Economy vs Platform Economy: The Fairbnb Case and its Inspiring Principles Based on Cooperative Economy. *Boletín de Estudios Económicos*, *74*(227), 259–283.

Ferrer, M., & Maudes, A. (2019). Un futuro para la economía colaborativa y los nuevos modelos de negocio en las plataformas digitales. *Cuadernos Económicos de ICE*, *97*(97), 155–185. doi:10.32796/cice.2019.97.6801

Food and Agriculture Organization (FAO) of the United Nations. (2016). *E-agriculture Strategy Guide*. FAO.

Gobierno Autónomo Descentralizado de la Provincia de Chimborazo. (2015). *Plan de desarrollo y ordenamiento territorial de Chimborazo*. Riobamba.

Gobierno Autónomo Descentralizado de la Provincia de Chimborazo. (2016). *Cantón Alausí*. Riobamba.

Huang, X., Jia, H., & Roiseux Racine, P. (2013). Urban and Rural Logistics and Distribution System Based on Supply and Marketing Cooperatives. *Applied Mechanics and Materials*, *253-255*, 1468–1471. doi:10.4028/www.scientific.net/AMM.253-255.1468

Iankova, S., Davies, I., Archer-Brown, C., Marder, B., & Yau, A. (2018). A comparison of social media marketing between B2B, B2C, and mixed business models. *Industrial Marketing Management*, *81*, 169–179. doi:10.1016/j.indmarman.2018.01.001

Instituto Nacional de Estadísticas y Censos. (2010). *Fascículo provincial Chimborazo*. Author.

Instituto Nacional de Estadísticas y Censos. (2016). *Encuesta de Superficie y Producción Agropecuaria Continua ESPAC 2016.* Quito, Ecuador: Author.

Laudon, K. C., & Traver, C. G. (2014). *E-commerce: business, technology, society* (10th ed.). Pearson.

Malhotra, N. K. (2008). *Investigación de mercados: un enfoque aplicado.* Prentice-Hall Hispanoamericana.

Mangstl, A. (2008). Emerging Issues, Priorities, and Commitments in e-agriculture. *Agricultural Information Worldwide, 1*(1), 5–6.

Martínez Martínez, A. (2019). *El paradigma AIRBNB: cambios estructurales en el sector turístico con relación a la economia colaborativa* (B.Sc. Dissertation). Palma de Mallorca, Spain: Universidad de las Islas Baleares.

Martínez-Polo, J., & Navarro-Beltrá, M. (2020). Estudio bibliométrico sobre reputación digital y economía colaborativa (2004-2017). *Revista de Comunicación de la SEECI, 51*, 83–107. doi:10.15198eeci.2020.51.83-107

Ministerio de Agricultura, Ganadería, Acuacultura, Ganadería, Acuacultura y Pesca (2016). *La política agropecuaria ecuatoriana: hacia el desarrollo territorial rural sostenible: 2015-2025 II Parte.* Quito, Ecuador: Author.

Ministerio de Telecomunicaciones y de la Sociedad de la Información. (2014). *Penetración de Banda Ancha incide directamente en crecimiento del PIB.* Author.

Ministerio de Telecomunicaciones y de la Sociedad de la Información. (2015). Plan Nacional de Telecomunicaciones y Tecnologías de Información del Ecuador 2016-2021. Quito, Ecuador: Author.

Ministerio de Telecomunicaciones y de la Sociedad de la Información. (2017). *MINTEL inauguró los Infocentros de Joyagshí y Alausí.* Author.

Moore, J. N., Hopkins, C. D., & Raymond, M. A. (2013). Utilization of relationship-oriented social Media in the Selling Process: A comparison of consumer (B2C) and industrial (B2B) salespeople. *Journal of Internet Commerce, 12*(1), 48–75. doi:10.1080/15332861.2013.763694

Neti, S. (2011). Social media and its role in marketing. *International Journal of Enterprise Computing and Business Systems, 1*, 1–15.

Ohene-Djan, J. (2008). *Electronic commerce.* University of London.

Olivieri, J. (2010). *Comercialización.* Universidad de Belgrano.

Ospina, L., Cifuentes, D., Gaitán, L., & Londoño-Cardozo, J. (2019). La RSO y la Economía Colaborativa: fundamentos para su análisis | The RSO and the collaborative Economy: foundations for its analysis. *Revista Argentina de Investigación y Negocios, 5*(1), 13–25.

Plaza-Angulo, J. (2019). La nueva organización empresarial: Capitalismo, digitalización y economía colaborativa. *Revista Internacional y Comparada de Relaciones Laborales y Derecho del Empleo, 7*(4), 353–384.

Preciado-Hoyos, A. (2020). Marco propositivo de relaciones entre innovación colaborativa abierta y comunicación estratégica: Aplicación a un grupo de empresas de origen antioqueño. *Palabra Clave (La Plata)*, *23*(2), e2326.

Ricart, J. E. (2009). *Business Model: The Missing Link in Strategic Management*. Universia Business Review.

Rodríguez, D., Cruz, C., & Lam, F. (2009). *Logística para la exportación de productos agrícolas, frescos y procesados*. IICA.

Rodríguez, M. (2019). El impacto y los efectos de la economía colaborativa y de plataformas en el empleo del sector turístico, *RIDETUR. Revista Internacional de Derecho del Turismo*, *3*(1), 3–15. doi:10.21071/ridetur.v3i.12132

Rodríguez, R., & Pérez, M. (2017). Modelos de negocio en la economía colaborativa: Síntesis y sugerencias. *Market Economics and Business Journal.*, *48*(2), 255–274.

Romero, M., & Ribadeneria, T. (2010). El comercio electrónico en Ecuador: Régimen jurídico y comentarios. *Iuris Dictio*, *1*(2), 108–114.

Ruíz, S. (2016). El Sector Agroalimentario y su competitividad a partir de modelos asociativos. *Ingeniería Industrial*, *37*(3), 323–332.

Salo, J. (2017). Social media research in the industrial marketing ðeld: Review of literature and future research directions. *Industrial Marketing Management*, *66*(August), 115–129. doi:10.1016/j.indmarman.2017.07.013

Samuelson, P. A., Nordhaus, W. D., Blanco Huitrón, C., & Doras Quiñones, A. (2010). *Microeconomía con aplicaciones a Latinoamérica*. McGrawHill.

Sánchez, J., & Moreno, Y. (2019). Desarrollo de la economía colaborativa en Ecuador, *Espirales: Revista Multidisciplinaria de Investigación Científica, 3*(29), 1.10.

Secretaría Nacional de Planificación y Desarrollo. (2017). Plan Nacional de Desarrollo 2017-2021. Quito, Ecuador: Author.

Siemieniako, D. (2018). Bibliometric Analysis of Scientific Research on Customer Loyalty in the Business-to-Business Context. *Handel Wewnętrzny*, *5*(376), 13–23.

Sistema Nacional de Información. (2015). *Actualización del Plan de Desarrollo y Ordenamiento Territorial del Cantón Alausí*. Author.

Superintendencia de Control de Poder de Mercado. (2017). Supertienda Ecuador, alternativa para comercializar los productos de la EPS (406). Quito, Ecuador: Author.

Swani, K., Milne, G. R., Brown, B. P., Assaf, A. G., & Donthu, N. (2017). What messages to post? Evaluating the popularity of social media communications in business versus consumer markets. *Industrial Marketing Management*, *62*, 77–87. doi:10.1016/j.indmarman.2016.07.006

Torrent-Sellens, J. (2019). ¿Economía colaborativa o economía de plataforma? Más allá de un debate inacabable. *Harvard Deusto Business Review*, *289*, 58–69.

Van Hoose, D. D. (2011). *E.commerce economics* (2nd ed.). Routledge.

Vergés, J. M. V., Tarrés, C. S., Obra, A. R. del Á., & Meléndez, A. P. (2001). La economía digital y su impacto en la empresa: Bases teóricas y situación en España. *Boletín económico de ICE. Información Comercial Española*, *2705*, 7–24.

Weinhardt, C., & Holtmann, C. (Eds.). (2002). *E-Commerce*. Physica-Verlag. doi:10.1007/978-3-642-57487-0

Wiersema, F. (2013). The B2B agenda: The current state of B2B marketing and a look ahead. *Industrial Marketing Management*, *42*(4), 470–488. doi:10.1016/j.indmarman.2013.02.015

Zhao, L., & Guo, S. (2012). The Value Creation of B2B2C E-Business Mode based on SaaS. *Journal of Electronic Commerce in Organizations*, *10*(3), 1–12. doi:10.4018/jeco.2012070101

KEY TERMS AND DEFINITIONS

Collaborative Economy: It is a sort of economy that allows the confluence of many small and micro businesses in coordination and management, as if it were a single company.

Compensation: Recognition of all participants in the value chain and provides relevant income and wealth. It eliminates losses in the first links of the value chain.

E-Commerce: Dynamics of digital commerce.

Equivalence: It recognizes the time involved in the chain by redistributing risks and provides the corresponding monetary flows. The longer the time, the higher the returns.

Extended Quality Partnership: It involves the business concept as a set of actors according to their role in the chain in two perspectives: their size (micro and small) and their activity (producer, processor, trader, financier).

Internationalize Agro-Industry: It is the capacity to generate competitive agricultural finished products in the foreign market.

Strategic Partnership: It is the unit of small and micro with the idea of taking control of the market.

Supply Chain: Logistics specially designed to keep the processes of strategically associated primary and final producers aligned.

Chapter 6
Health Services Delivery and Satisfaction

Fatih Altan
https://orcid.org/0000-0003-3913-309X
University of Erciyes, Turkey

Aykut Ekiyor
University of Ankara Haci Bayram Veli, Turkey

Demet Unalan
University of Erciyes, Turkey

ABSTRACT

Health services include the services provided to prevent the occurrence of diseases and disabilities, to ensure that the sick and disabled are restored to their former health, and to those who cannot regain their health, to adapt to the environment. As an essential element of the health system, health services appear as an important factor in raising the health level of the society. Reforms in health systems worldwide have been carried out to increase the health level of the community and improve the quality of health services. Satisfaction is one of the critical determinants of quality in health services. It is possible to mention many factors that affect satisfaction in health services. However, in the literature, it is emphasized that health personnel-patient interaction, trust in a health institution, the fee of service received, physical facilities of the health institution, and nutrition services affect satisfaction.

INTRODUCTION

Health is the most important concept for everyone. Prevention of diseases, establishing a healthy environment, and consequently raising the health of the society are among the priorities of all governments. The services provided to meet the health needs of society can be defined as health services. Different institutions can provide these services.

DOI: 10.4018/978-1-7998-5036-6.ch006

The content of the concept of health should be well known before the definition of health services. In ancient times, the idea of health as a balance between a human being and the environment, spirit, and body unity, and the natural source of the disease was the backbone of health perception. In the 5th century BC, Pindar emphasized the physical dimension of health as a "harmonious functioning of the organs," along with the absence of pain and a sense of comfort. Even today, his definition is seen as a prerequisite for comprehensive health and well-being. Plato (429-347 BC), on the other hand, emphasizes that "sturdy head in sturdy body" and emphasizes that people can achieve their health as much as they can adapt to the physical and social environment (Svalastog, Donev, Kristoffersen, & Gajović, 2017).

Health is the concept that everyone is cared about and thought to be too well known to define, but everyone is very variable and complex. The World Health Organization (WHO) in 1948 (Hayran, 2013). According to WHO law of establishment (WHO, 2006);

"Health is a state of complete physical, mental, and social well-being and not merely the absence of disease or infirmity."

Although the definition of WHO has been subject to many criticisms, it has not been changed. Criticism concentrates on the word "complete well-being" in the definition, as this expression causes many people to call it unhealthy (Smith, 2008). In fact, this expression expresses perfection, even ideal. It is challenging to reach this degree (Hayran, 2013). From this definition, it can be said that many factors directly or indirectly influence health.

Blum (1974), by developing an environmental approach to the concept of health, argued that health is affected by four primary factors. The factors affecting health in Blum's holistic health model are explained below (Kavuncubaşı, & Yıldırım, 2018).

- **Environment**: the protection and development of health are directly related to the environment. But generally, health is not a high priority in environmental policies. In fact, the quality of the environment is the most crucial determinant of health. The most critical problem globally is infant deaths and diseases caused by biological agents in the human-environment (water, food, air, soil, etc.). They cause illness, disability, or death of millions of people, usually infants and children (World Health Organization (WHO), 1992). In terms of health, the environment is examined in three main groups: microorganisms, vectors, plants, animals, and nutrients in the biological environment; climate, soil structure, air pollution, air pollution, waste, water resources, and so on, in the physical environment; and the socio-demographic characteristics of people, economic conditions, population mobility, aging, education level, and the social environment including factors such as population growth (Kavuncubaşı, & Yıldırım, 2018).
- **Lifestyle (Behavior):** Lifestyle refers to the daily behavior of individuals in a region, referring to the particular time and space characteristics of the inhabitants and the functions of individuals regarding work, activity, entertainment, and diet. Recently, lifestyle as an essential health factor has been of interest to researchers (Fahud, 2015). According to WHO, 60% of the factors related to individual health and quality of life link to lifestyle (Ziglio, Currie, & Rasmussen, 2004). Lifestyle variables affect health, as diet and body mass index, exercise, sleep, sexual behavior, substance abuse, use of modern technologies, rest, study (academic), and so on. It consists of activities (Fahud, 2015).

- **Heredity**: The genes of an individual effectively create its potential, and its environment is effective when limiting and developing this potential. Gene-dependent properties are also effective in the emergence of various diseases. The biological and organic structure of the individual (hereditary characteristics) affects her susceptibility to the disease and causes the congenital disease to pass (Kavuncubaşı, & Yıldırım, 2018).
- **Health Services:** Among the four essential determinants of health mentioned above is the element with the least impact on health. Health services are provided by environmental service organizations and public-private health institutions (Schulz, & Johnson, 2003).

HEALTH SERVICE

Health services can be expressed as all the services provided to protect and improve health, prevent diseases, treat the patients to the extent possible, prevent disabilities, provide medical and social rehabilitation services to the disabled and provide people with qualified and long life (Kavuncubaşı, 2010; Tengilimoğlu, Işık, & Akbolat, 2015). The technology of individuals and communities is an impressive factor. In this regard, it becomes clear that health services are open to health. Factors such as education, housing, living, living environment, lifestyle, heredity are more effective on the health of individuals and communities, and perhaps more (Black, & Gruen, 2005).

Health expectations of individuals and society vary. In addition to health expectations, such as prevention of diseases, symptoms relief, correction of functional losses, and life prolongation, it is seen that people without any pathological findings (healthy) look to how they feel, feel and improve their social relations. The increase in the demand for aesthetic surgery and the widespread use of lifestyle drugs show that health services have modern expectations and traditional expectations (Greenwald, 2010).

Good service delivery is an essential element of the health system. Service provision is a key input in raising the health status of society, including the social determinants of health. Even if the content and organization of health services vary from country to country, health care delivery needs to incorporate certain features. These features are described below (World Health Organization (WHO), 2019).

- **Comprehensiveness:** It is defined as providing a comprehensive health service appropriate to the needs of the society, including preventive, therapeutic, palliative and rehabilitation services and health promotion activities.
- **Accessibility:** It means providing health care services free of unnecessary costs and without barriers to language, culture, or geography. Organizations providing primary health care (not at private or hospital level) should be close to individuals. These services can be conveniently offered at home, in the community, at work, or in a health facility. Coverage: Service delivery should be designed to cover all people in a defined target population, i.e., all social groups with patients and health
- **Continuity**: It is defined as the organization of service provision in such a way that individuals can benefit from this service continuously.
- **Quality:** Health services should be provided in high quality. Quality service; is an effective, safe, and timely service designed to meet the needs of patients.

- **Person-centeredness:** Services should be organized based on the person, not according to disease or financing. The participation of the target audience in the design and evaluation of services should be ensured.
- **Coordination:** Regional health care networks should be actively coordinated with the type of care, type of service provider, or level of service delivery for both routine and emergency jobs. Coordination should also be ensured with other sectors and partners.
- **Accountability and efficiency:** Health services should be well managed to achieve the essential elements described above with minimum waste resources. Therefore, health managers should be given responsibility for overall performance and results by giving them the necessary authorization to achieve the planned targets. Evaluation should be appropriate for the participation of the target audience and the community.

Health services are examined in three categories in terms of their basic characteristics. These are preventive, therapeutic, and rehabilitative health services (Ateş, 2012). There are also health promotion services. The reason for considering health promotion services in a separate category is the primary responsibility of preventive, curative, and rehabilitative health services. In contrast, the responsibility for health promotion belongs to the individual (Kavuncubaşı, & Yıldırım, 2018).

Preventive Health Services

Preventive health services are formed by health protection and disease prevention. Also, these services are examined in two groups as environmental and personal health services (Ateş, 2012). Preventive health services constitute an essential part of basic health services with services for monitoring and preventing diseases. It plays a vital role in the prevention of chronic diseases and in reducing morbidity and mortality. Preventive health interventions include intervention before or during the first stage of the disease (Rosano, 2018).

Preventive Health Services for the Environment

The primary purpose of these services is to make the environment positive by eliminating the biological, physical, and chemical effects that affect environmental health negatively or by preventing the people from being affected. These services are carried out by engineers, chemists, technicians, and similar professionals trained in this field. In other words, it is carried out with the intensive participation of occupations other than health professionals (Ateş, 2012). Many governments and private organizations implement public health environmental health programs. Environmental health services are listed below (Schulz, & Johnson, 2003).

- Reliable water supply and pollution control
- Disposal of solid wastes
- Control of pests
- Milk and food sanitation
- Control of air pollution
- Control of noise pollution
- Housing and land use

- Work health
- Control of radiological hazards

Preventive Health Services for the Personal

Personal services include the services provided by healthcare workers such as physicians, nurses, or health facilities, and these services are listed below (Schulz, & Johnson, 2003; Kavuncubaşı, & Yıldırım, 2018; Ateş, 2012).

- Immunization
- Nutrition regulation
- Early diagnosis and treatment of diseases
- Mother and child health services
- Drug protection
- Personal hygiene
- Health education
- Family planning
- Fighting habits harmful to health and mental health

Therapeutical Health Services

Treatment services include all services provided to restore the health of people with poor health. The team of other health personnel mainly provides these services under the responsibility of specialist physicians. Treatment services can be categorized as outpatient or inpatient services. Outpatient services are provided in surgeries or clinics. It can also be offered by mobile health teams (Schulz, & Johnson, 2003; Kavuncubaşı, & Yıldırım, 2018).

Treatment services are also categorized as primary, secondary, and tertiary. Primary care is the first part of the patient entering the health system given by family physicians who are general practitioners, pediatricians, or general surgeons. They are usually offered in outpatient treatment centers or practice. Secondary care is usually urgent counseling. Tertiary care refers to sub-branch or categorical referral services provided in regional medical centers such as university hospitals (Schulz, & Johnson, 2003).

Rehabilitation Services

They are the services aimed at restoring physical and mental skills lost by people due to illness or accident (Kavuncubaşı, & Yıldırım, 2018). Numerous studies have shown that patients are better at rehabilitation through a well-organized and multidisciplinary approach (Cifu, & Stewart, 1999; Evans, Connis, Hendricks, & Haselkorn, 1995; Stroke Unit Trialists' Collaboration, 2002).

Rehabilitation services are examined in two categories. These are medical rehabilitation and social rehabilitation (Ateş, 2012).

Medical rehabilitation: These services aim to reduce the physical problems of the patient as much as possible. Correction of posture disorders, use of limb prostheses, hearing, vision, etc. and services required to minimize problems.

Social rehabilitation: It includes the services provided to enable disabled individuals to participate actively in daily life and continue their lives without being dependent on others. Job adaptation training, finding new jobs, or teaching activities can be given as examples of these services (Kavuncubaşı & Yıldırım, 2018; Ateş, 2012).

Health Promotion

Health promotion is defined as a process that allows individuals to increase control over their health. Health education and health policies of governments are very effective on these services. Health promotion services include many activities such as increasing the health literacy level of the individual, creating supportive environments, and strengthening social networks. Health promotion can take place in schools, workplaces, or health institutions. These services aim to redirect health care to contribute to the search for better health (Mittelmark, Kickbusch, Rootman, Scriven, & KeithTones, 2017).

HEALTH SERVICES SATISFACTION

In recent years, consumer satisfaction has become more critical in providing health services and health reforms worldwide. Although there is no universal definition in consumer satisfaction studies, studies focus on quality and type of health service and patient satisfaction. In contrast, some researchers focus on health system satisfaction in a more general dimension (Bleich, Özaltin, & Murray, 2009). Customer satisfaction can be expressed as düzey the level of meeting the demands and needs of customers Thomas (Thomas, 2010). Customer satisfaction is a widely used and essential indicator used to measure quality in health care—satisfaction, timely, effective, and patient-centered quality service delivery. In fact, satisfaction is a representative element, but it is a significant indicator for measuring healthcare workers' success and health care organizations (Prakash, 2010). Customer satisfaction is a strategic necessity in the service sector as it provides many benefits such as re-preference of the satisfied customer and recommending the organization to the acquaintances. In addition, advising the organization to individuals around the individual reduces the cost of customer acquisition (Anderson, & Mittal, 2000). Thanks to satisfied customers, health institutions have shown a positive financial performance (Mittal, & Frennea, 2010).

Recent reforms in health have led health care institutions to find effective ways to meet patients' needs and needs. Changing customer demands, increasing expectations of the product, and service quality force companies to compete globally. Quality has become an essential factor in the choice of product or service. For the future of healthcare organizations, the quality of the product or service offered is considered to be a strategic benefit. Improving the quality organizational performance of health institutions contributes to customer satisfaction and loyalty (Mustafi, Islam, & Islam, 2015).

For a production or service sector, it is possible to define the output as "the result or visible impact of an activity." "Output" for health services by Donebedian: "a change to be attributed to the patient's current and future health status compared to the previous health status." Later, this definition extends to include patient satisfaction, knowledge, and behavior by adding social, psychological, and functional areas of health (Phillips, 2003). The concept of satisfaction, which is one of the primary outcomes of health institutions, is defined as m meeting the demands and expectations of the customers or providing services above these demands and expectations. As can be seen from the definition given, two factors determine satisfaction. The first factor is customer expectations. Customer expectations differ according to age, gender, educational level, sociocultural characteristics, and past experiences in health services and health care facilities. The second factor is the perception of customers about the service they receive. Perceptions are measured based on individuals' opinions or assessments about the services they receive and the service production process (Kavuncubaşı, & Yıldırım, 2018).

Figure 1. Measuring Customer Satisfaction
Source: Kavuncubaşı, & Yıldırım (2018)

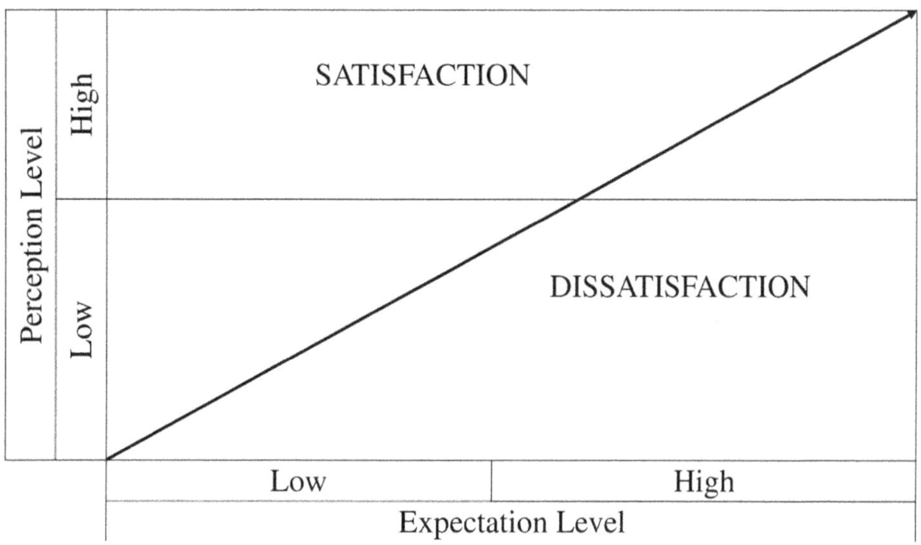

According to Figure 1, when a customer's expectation is met (perception> expectation), that customer will be satisfied with the service he receives. As indicated in Figure 1, the customer in the area above the bold line is the satisfied customer. In contrast, the customer below the line is unsatisfied customers because the expectations are not met.

The concept of customer satisfaction is an essential issue in the service sector and is even more critical in the health sector. The demands and expectations of the patients are changing day by day, and the alternative to purchase the service increases. As a matter of fact, those who demand health care today are more knowledgeable than the past and do not hesitate to choose alternatives if they are not satisfied with the service. Customer satisfaction, therefore, has a key role in strategic superiority and profitability (Ramsaran, 2005).

Added to the structural features of health systems, met quality service concept is evaluated through the relationships established with the patient and the health outcomes that patients will obtain. Most of the research is process-oriented in this quality approach, discussed by Donebedian at three levels: structure, process, and outputs. In other words, patient-physician communication has frequently been the subject of examination to measure quality value. This fact indicates that it focuses on a measurable definition of quality in which a patient-centered process is evaluated (Schuster, McGlynn, & Brook, 1998; Baltaş, 2013). Patient satisfaction in health institutions is attributed to four reasons explained below (Kavuncubaşı, & Yıldırım, 2018).

- **Humanitarian Reasons:** One fundamental right of individuals is to receive the best and highest quality service. People with impaired health have the right to benefit from the health service that gives the best results to individuals. The services to be provided to the patients should be technically and scientifically sufficient and should be provided concerning the personality, values, and attitudes of the patients.
- **Economic Reasons:** Patients are service buyers. Therefore, the conditions they are in are more careful than the customers in different sectors about the service provided to the patients. They will be more severe in determining their preferences and want to be paid for. At the same time, insurance companies attach importance to their members' satisfaction with the service they receive. Customer satisfaction increases the customer and profit potential of the health institution
- **Marketing Reasons:** Health institutions must increase customer/patient satisfaction to increase their market share. Also, patient loyalty is paramount in health institutions, and the satisfaction of the customers from the institution is expressed as an essential factor in ensuring customer loyalty. Many issues come to the forefront of marketing research in health services. Satisfaction surveys are among the critical issues among these issues.
- **Clinical Effectiveness:** It is known that the patient who is satisfied with the service provided shows more positive behaviors during the treatment process. At the same time, satisfied patients follow the recommendations of physicians and other health care professionals. Adherence to the treatment plan significantly determines the effectiveness of the treatment.

CUSTOMER SATISFACTION MEASUREMENT

Organizations generally measure customer satisfaction using questionnaires that include behavioral intentions, attribute-level perceptions, contextual information, and customer background variables. There are many scales in the literature to measure satisfaction. The topics included in the customer satisfaction surveys are described below (Mittal, & Frennea, 2010).

- **Behavioral Intentions:** Behavioral intentions, also called generally "customer loyalty metrics," are often related to the possibility of repurchasing the product or service, the likelihood of recommending it to other people, and the probability of complaining. For example, "What are your chances of choosing the organization in the next six months?", "How intense is the possibility of purchasing products and services from another organization in the future?" and "Do you recommend this organization to your social environment?."
- **Attribute-Level Perceptions:** This measurement tool generally measures customers' perceptions of the performance of various aspects of the product or service. Different questions obtain perceptions of performance at the level of the characteristics. For example, "How do you evaluate the product or service based on your experience?" "Evaluate any aspect of the product or service from 1 to 5 (being 1 very bad, and 5 very good)" and "What is the level of product or service to meet your expectations?".
- **Contextual Information:** Customers may want to evaluate the overall satisfaction level of the organization based on experience or competitors. Customers' requests help the organization to compare its performance with its competitors strategically. Various questions evaluate customer satisfaction in terms of contextual information. For example, "How do you rate your last service

when you compare it with the previous one?" "How do you evaluate the products and services you get from our organization after using competitors' products or services (better or worse than competitors)?".

- **Customer Background Variables:** In addition to demographic data such as gender, age, and income, a satisfaction survey can measure competitor-related variables such as the use of competing products or services.

CONCLUSION: FACTORS AFFECTING CUSTOMER SATISFACTION

Customer satisfaction increases the image of the hospital. This fact means rising market demand for services (Andaleeb, 1988). Satisfied customers are likely to exhibit positive behavior for the long-term success of the healthcare provider. Customers tend to express their intentions positively, such as praising the company and recommending it to others, increasing their purchasing volume (Zeithaml, & Bitner, 2000). To satisfy customers and meet their wishes and expectations, health managers need to know the factors that affect customer satisfaction. Understanding these factors supports managers in improvement activities related to the satisfaction of the services provided (Kavuncubaşı, & Yıldırım, 2018). Socio-demographic characteristics that positively correlate with customer satisfaction in health services include age, education, health status, race, marital status, and social class (Naidu, 2009). However, the relationship between satisfaction and gender, race, marital status, and social class is unknown (Tucker, 2002). Many factors affect customer satisfaction in the literature, and there is no consensus yet. In this context, some of the factors affecting customer satisfaction are: It can be expressed as personnel-patient interaction, nutritional services of the health institution, physical and environmental conditions, bureaucracy, trust, and wage (Kavuncubaşı & Yıldırım, 2018). These factors are described below.

- **Health personnel-patient interaction:** The interaction between the physician and the patient affects satisfaction. There is a clear relationship between medical care and satisfaction. Patients are unlikely to cooperate with the physician if they are not satisfied with the medical service provided (Naidu, 2009). It is emphasized that physicians are the socio-emotional component of health care rather than competence and intelligence. According to the researchers, patients encounter two types of physicians: authoritarian and egalitarian. The authoritarian physician plays the role of an expert and primary decision-maker. The patient who confronts such a physician has great faith in the physician's abilities, foreseeing that the physician will provide definitive treatment. On the other hand, the egalitarian physician plays a role that allows the patient to make doctor's recommendations, discuss alternative treatment methods, and enable the patient to participate in treatment decisions (Ditto, Moore, Hilton, & Kalish, 1995). When evaluating the quality of physicians' service, patients consider behaviors such as being sensitive to listening rather than physician's expertise knowledge, taking sufficient time, courtesy, and respect (Cromarty, 1996). Physician behavior increases patient satisfaction as well as the effectiveness of the service provided. The positive result of the interaction with the physician leads the patient to fully comply with the physician's recommendations and continue the treatment without interruption (Lewis, 1994).
- **Nutrition Services of Health Organization:** Nutritional services are another factor that affects patient satisfaction on hospital services. In a study conducted to determine the factors affecting the satisfaction of patients, nutritional services have been the subject of a wide-ranging assess-

ment in the explanations and evaluations made by patients about hospital services (Carr-Hill, 1992). Nutritional services in the hospital also affect hospital stay and eliminate the thoughts of leaving the hospital (Tomes, & Chee Peng Ng, 1995). A study reveals that patient satisfaction is significantly linked to nutritional services. The satisfaction of nutritional services, satisfaction in food quality (flavor, presentation, freshness and temperature of hot dishes) customization (meal selection, portion size, the flexibility of service), the attitude of staff offering the menu (warmth, attention, and kindness), timely service of food service (allowed to eat) time), the reliability of the food service (punctuality of foodservice) is considered in separate categories (Dubé, Trudeau, & Bélanger, 1994).

- **Physical and Environmental Conditions:** Another critical factor affecting customer satisfaction in health institutions is physical and environmental conditions. Physical and environmental conditions are essential, such as lighting, heat, cleaning, ventilation, noise, easy locating, parking, waiting rooms, and exterior appearance (Kavuncubaşı & Yıldırım, 2018). It has been found that the physical environment in which services are provided affects customer service performance evaluations, including customer satisfaction (Bitner, 1990, 1992; Parasuraman et al., 1985, 1988). A common finding in health literature is that physical facilities are a component of patient health assessments (Woodside et al., 1989). Swan et al. (2003) show that room appearance affects patient perceptions and health satisfaction. Their studies compared the room-changing assessment of patients in terms of quality. The physical environment influences the evaluation of customer service performance and customer satisfaction (Parasuraman, Zeithhaml, & Berry, 1988). Common conclusions in health research are that physical facilities are components of the patient's health assessments (Woodside, Frey, & Daly, 1989). Patient's room affects service perception and satisfaction in terms of physicians and nurses' skills, expertise, and courtesy (answering questions, listening to concerns), food (general satisfaction, receive what was ordered, temperature), general hospital evaluations, intentions to use the hospital again, and hospital recommendation to others (Swan, Richardson, & Hutton, 2003). In this study, patients staying in more attractive rooms of all sizes made more favorable evaluations than patients staying in ordinary rooms.
- **Trust in Health Institutions:** Customers expect it to be both in line with their requirements and sufficient quantities. Informing the patients, feeling that they are in a safe environment, participating in the treatment decisions lead to a sense of trust in them (Kavuncubaşı, & Yıldırım, 2018). Awareness of patient safety has been increasing recently. However, a growing concern has emerged among policymakers, hospital managers, and health professionals about patient safety (Naidu, 2009). Safety concerns may cause patients to stop receiving services from the hospital (Hall, 2005). Also, attention to the privacy of the patients improves the sense of trust in patients (Kavuncubaşı, & Yıldırım, 2018).
- **Healthcare Fee:** Another critical factor affecting customer satisfaction is the cost of the services provided. The issue of wages is particularly essential for those who do not have health insurance. Patients wish to receive quality services at the lowest cost. The increase in hospital costs reduces customer satisfaction (Kavuncubaşı, & Yıldırım, 2018).

REFERENCES

Andaleeb, S. (1988). Determinants of customer satisfaction with hospitals: A managerial model. *International Journal of Health Care Quality Assurance*, *11*(6), 181–187. doi:10.1108/09526869810231541 PMID:10339090

Anderson, E. W., & Mittal, V. (2000). Strengthening the Satisfaction-Profit Chain. *Journal of Service Research*, *3*(2), 107–120. doi:10.1177/109467050032001

Ateş, M. (2012). *Sağlık Hizmetleri ile İlgili Genel Bilgiler. In Sağlık İşletmeciliği*. Beta Yayınclık.

Baltaş, Z. (2013). *Memnuniyet Çalışmaları. In Hastane Yönetimi*. Nobel Tıp Kitabevleri.

Black, N., & Gruen, R. (2005). *Understanding Health Services*. Open University Press.

Bleich, S. N., Özaltin, E., & Murray, C. J. (2009). How does satisfaction with the healthcare system relate to patient experience? *Bulletin of the World Health Organization*, *87*(4), 271–278. doi:10.2471/BLT.07.050401 PMID:19551235

Carr-Hill, R. A. (1992). The measurement of patient satisfaction. *Journal of Public Health Medicine*, *14*(3), 236–249. PMID:1419201

Cifu, D. X., & Stewart, D. G. (1999). Factors affecting functional outcome after stroke: A critical review of rehabilitation interventions. *Archives of Physical Medicine and Rehabilitation*, *80*(5), S-35–S39. doi:10.1016/S0003-9993(99)90101-6 PMID:10326901

Cromarty, I. (1996). What do Patients Think About During Their Consultation? *The British Journal of General Practice*, *46*, 525–528. PMID:8917871

Ditto, P. H., Moore, K. A., Hilton, J. L., & Kalish, J. R. (1995). Beliefs About Physicians: Their Role in Health Care Utilization, Satisfaction, and Compliance. *Basic and Applied Social Psychology*, *17*(1), 23–48. doi:10.120715324834basp1701&2_2

Dubé, L., Trudeau, E., & Bélanger, M. C. (1994). Determining the complexity of patient satisfaction with food services. *Journal of the American Dietetic Association*, *94*(4), 394–401. doi:10.1016/0002-8223(94)90093-0 PMID:8144806

Evans, R. L., Connis, R. T., Hendricks, R. D., & Haselkorn, J. K. (1995). Multidisciplinary rehabilitation versus medical care: A meta-analysis. *Social Science & Medicine*, *40*(12), 1699–1706. doi:10.1016/0277-9536(94)00286-3 PMID:7660183

Fahud, D. D. (2015). Impact of Lifestyle on Health. *Iranian Journal of Public Health*, *44*(11), 1442–1444. PMID:26744700

Greenwald, H. P. (2010). *Health Care in The United States: Organization, Management, and Policy*. Jossey-Bass.

Hall, M. A. (2005). The importance of trust for ethics, law, and public policy. *Cambridge Quarterly of Healthcare Ethics*, *14*(2), 156–197. doi:10.1017/S096318010505019X PMID:15887807

Hayran, O. (2013). *Sağlık ve Hastalık. In Hastane Yönetimi*. Nobel Tıp Kitabevleri.

Kavuncubaşı, Ş., & Yıldırım, S. (2018). Hastane ve Sağlık Kurumları Yönetimi (5. Baskı b.). Ankara, Turkey: Siyasal Kitabevi.

Lewis, J. R. (1994). Patient views on quality care in general practice: A literature review. *Social Science & Medicine*, *39*(5), 655–670. doi:10.1016/0277-9536(94)90022-1 PMID:7973865

Mittal, V., & Frennea, C. (2010). *Customer Satisfaction A Strategic Review and Guidelines for Managers*. The Marketing Science Institute.

Mittelmark, M. B., Kickbusch, I., Rootman, I., Scriven, A., & Tones, K. (2017). *Health Promotion. In International Encyclopedia of Public Health*. Elsevier Inc.

Mustafi, M. A., Islam, M., & Islam, M. J. (2015). Patients' Satisfaction in Healthcare Services: A Comparative Analysis on Public and Private Hospitals in Bangladesh. *Scholar Journal of Business and Social Science*, *1*(1), 14–24.

Naidu, A. (2009). Factors affecting patient satisfaction and healthcare quality. *International Journal of Health Care Quality Assurance*, *22*(4), 366–381. doi:10.1108/09526860910964834 PMID:19725209

Parasuraman, A., Zeithhaml, V. A., & Berry, L. L. (1988). SERVQUAL: A multiple-item scale for measuring consumer perceptions of service quality. *Journal of Retailing*, *64*(1), 12–40.

Phillips, A. (2003). *Healthcare Management Dictionary*. Radcliffe Medical Press.

Prakash, B. (2010). Patient Satisfaction. *Journal of Cutaneous and Aesthetic Surgery*, *3*(3), 151–155. doi:10.4103/0974-2077.74491 PMID:21430827

Ramsaran, R. R. (2005). Identifying Health Care Quality Attributes. *Journal of Health and Human Services Administration*, *27*(4), 428–443. PMID:16318013

Rosano, A. (2018). *Access to Primary Care and Preventative Health Services of Migrants*. Springer. doi:10.1007/978-3-319-73630-3

Saad Andaleeb, S. (1998). Determinants of customer satisfaction with hospitals: A managerial model. *International Journal of Health Care Quality Assurance*, *10*(6), 181–187. doi:10.1108/09526869810231541 PMID:10339090

Schulz, R., & Johnson, A. C. (2003). Management of Hospitals and Health Services: Strategic Issues and Performance. Washington, DC: Academic Press.

Schuster, M. A., McGlynn, E. A., & Brook, R. H. (1998). How good is the quality of health care in the United States? *The Milbank Quarterly*, *76*(4), 517–563. doi:10.1111/1468-0009.00105 PMID:9879302

Smith, R. (2008, July 8). The end of disease and the beginning of health. *Richard Smith: The end of disease and the beginning of health*. Accessed July 22, 2019 https://blogs.bmj.com/bmj/2008/07/08/richard-smith-the-end-of-disease-and-the-beginning-of-health/

Stroke Unit Trialists' Collaboration. (2002). Organised inpatient (stroke unit) care for stroke. *Cochrane Database of Systematic Reviews*, *1*, CD000197. PMID:11869570

Svalastog, A. L., Donev, D., Kristoffersen, N. J., & Gajović, S. (2017). Concepts and definitions of health and health-related values in the knowledge landscapes of the digital society. *Croatian Medical Journal, 58*(6), 431–435. doi:10.3325/cmj.2017.58.431 PMID:29308835

Swan, J. E., Richardson, L. D., & Hutton, J. D. (2003). Do appealing hospital rooms increase patient evaluations of physicians, nurses, and hospital services? *Journal of Management Review, 28*(3), 254–264. PMID:12940347

Tengilimoğlu, D., Işık, O., & Akbolat, M. (2015). *Sağlık İşletmelerinde Yönetim*. Nobel Yayıncılık.

Thomas, R. K. (2010). Marketing Health Services (2nd ed.). Health Administration Press.

Tomes, A. E., & Chee Peng Ng, S. (1995). Service quality in hospital care: The development of an inpatient questionnaire. *International Journal of Health Care Quality Assurance, 8*(3), 25–33. doi:10.1108/09526869510089255 PMID:10143994

Tucker, J. L. (2002). The moderators of patient satisfaction. *Journal of Management in Medicine, 16*(1), 48–66. doi:10.1108/02689230210428625 PMID:12069351

Woodside, A. G., Frey, L. L., & Daly, R. T. (1989). Linking service quality, customer satisfaction. *Journal of Health Care Marketing and Behavior Intention, 9*(4), 5–17. PMID:10304174

World Health Organisation (WHO). (1992). *Our Planet, Our Health: Report of the WHO Commission on Health and Environment*. World Health Organisation.

World Health Organization (WHO). (2006, October). *Constitution of The World Health Organisation.* Accessed July 22, 2019. https://www.who.int/governance/eb/who_constitution_en.pdf

World Health Organization (WHO). (2019). *World Health Organization*. https://www.who.int/healthinfo/systems/WHO_MBHSS_2010_section1_web.pdf

Zeithaml, V., & Bitner, M. (2000). *Services Marketing: Integrating Customer Focus across the Firm.* McGraw-Hill.

Ziglio, E., Currie, C., & Rasmussen, V. B. (2004). The WHO cross-national study of health behavior in school-aged children from 35 countries: Findings from 2001-2002. *The Journal of School Health, 76*, 204–206. PMID:15468523

KEY TERMS AND DEFINITIONS

Customer Loyalty Metrics: They are often related to the possibility of repurchasing the product or service, recommending it to other people, and the probability of complaining.

Health Services: Health services can be expressed as all the services provided to protect and improve health, prevent diseases, treat the patients to the extent possible, prevent disabilities, provide medical and social rehabilitation services to the disabled and provide people with qualified and long life.

Person-Centeredness: It is when services are organized based on the person, not according to disease or financing.

Preventive Health Services: It is when services are formed by health protection and disease prevention.

Primary Care: It is the first part of the patient entering the health system given by family physicians who are general practitioners, pediatricians, or general surgeons. They are usually offered in outpatient treatment centers or practice.

Rehabilitation Services: They are services focused on restoring physical and mental skills lost by people due to illness or accident.

Secondary Care: It is usually urgent counseling.

Tertiary Care: It refers to sub-branch or categorical referral services provided in regional medical centers such as university hospitals.

Section 2
Competitive Advantage

Chapter 7
From Entrepreneurial Intentions to Entrepreneurial Behavior:
The Role of Institutional Factors

Sebastian Aparicio
Durham University, UK

Andreu Turro
Universitat Autònoma de Barcelona, Spain

Maria Noguera
Universitat Autònoma de Barcelona, Spain

David Urbano
https://orcid.org/0000-0001-7600-8656
Universitat Autònoma de Barcelona, Spain

ABSTRACT

Although there is abundant literature on entrepreneurial intentions and entrepreneurial behavior, there is still a lacuna on those factors enabling the pass from intention to action. Motivated by this gap, this study assesses the extent to which the determinants of entrepreneurial intention also have an effect on subsequent entrepreneurial behavior, using an institutional approach as a theoretical framework. With a sample of 2,491 university students from Catalonia (Spanish) through the simultaneous equations, the main findings show that institutions such as opportunity identification, business skills, and entrepreneurs' status encourage students to think of entrepreneurship as a good career choice, which subsequently explains entrepreneurial actions. Theoretical, policy, and practical implications are discussed based on these findings.

DOI: 10.4018/978-1-7998-5036-6.ch007

INTRODUCTION

Entrepreneurship is considered to play a key role in economic growth, innovation, and employment (Urbano & Aparicio, 2016; Wennekers, van Stel, Thurik, & Reynolds, 2005). Such a role is conditioned by different external or environmental factors that encompass policies, regulations, and culture (Bjørnskov & Foss, 2016; Urbano, Aparicio, & Audretsch, 2019). Therefore, in the last three decades, some researchers have focused on studying the factors that might have an influence on the development of entrepreneurial activity (Ireland, Hitt, & Simon, 2003). This implies that entrepreneurship is seen as a process and not as an event (Shane, 2012). From this viewpoint, a significant amount of research has addressed the concept of entrepreneurial intentions (Kautonen, van Gelderen, & Fink, 2015), which are seen as a necessary precursor to performing entrepreneurial behaviors (Liñán & Chen, 2009).

Previous research has shown that situational and personality factors do not predict entrepreneurial activity consistently (Krueger, Reilly, & Carsrud, 2000); hence, the entrepreneurial intention approach has been used. In this regard, since the early 1990s, the number of studies that have applied intention models to explain the decision to start a new business has increased significantly (Liñán & Fayolle, 2015). The underlying idea in these studies is that it is better to predict any planned behavior by observing intentions towards that behavior than to focus on attitudes, beliefs, or demographic measures (Krueger et al., 2000). Overall, intentions have been considered extensively to be the single best predictor of behavior (Ajzen, 1991, 2001; Fishbein, & Ajzen, 1975).

Despite this extensive literature, there are some relevant research gaps. First, very few articles have analyzed the complete "antecedents–entrepreneurial intentions–entrepreneurial action" process empirically. Most researchers have studied this sequence partially (for an exception, see Kautonen et al., 2015). On the one hand, previous studies have examined the role of a wide variety of determinants in entrepreneurial intentions (Verheul et al., 2015). These studies have used different theoretical frameworks and models to explain entrepreneurial intentions, but no specific work has combined different models into a single one (Fayolle & Liñán, 2014). In this regard, Schlaegel and Koenig (2014, pp. 291) pointed out "there has been growing concern about the sometimes inconclusive empirical findings of the relationship between entrepreneurial intention and its determinants."

Second, the study of the intention–behavior link has emerged recently (Gielnik et al., 2014; Goethner, Obschonka, Silbereisen, & Cantner, 2012). The findings have agreed that intentions are a predictor of subsequent action; however, the extent to which intentions can explain a variation in behavior is not clear (Kibler, Kautonen, & Fink, 2014; Van Gelderen, Kautonen, & Fink, 2015). For instance, while Ajzen et al. (2009) found an intention–behavior correlation of 0.90 to 0.96, other authors have reported a less intense relation: Armitage and Conner (2001) found a correlation of 0.47, and Kautonen et al. (2013, 2015) showed that the theory of planned behavior (Ajzen, 1991) accounts for only 31–39% of the variation in startup behavior. Overall, the literature reviews focusing on the entrepreneurial intention area have agreed that most challenges lie in this specific intention–behavior stream of research (Fayolle & Liñán, 2014; Liñán & Fayolle, 2015; Shook, Priem, & McGee, 2003).

Third, the moderating effect of some contextual variables on the relationship between entrepreneurial intentions and their antecedents has rarely been taken into account in previous studies. In fact, the most-cited theoretical models (Ajzen, 1991; Shapero & Sokol, 1982) do not consider this type of effect. This fact is particularly striking as entrepreneurship researchers have highlighted extensively that some environmental conditions moderate key aspects of the entrepreneurship process, such as the ability to identify business opportunities (Short, Ketchen, Combs, & Ireland, 2010) or the acquisition of knowledge

(Knight, & Cavusgil, 2004). In this regard, institutional theory has been used widely in entrepreneurship research to explore the role of environmental and contextual factors (Bruton, Ahlstrom, & Li, 2010; Urbano, 2006). In this theoretical framework, institutions represent the set of rules that articulate and define the interactions between individuals; therefore, they have an effect on several aspects, including entrepreneurship rates and business development (Urbano & Alvarez, 2014).

Taking these explanations into account, the main research question that this study aims to answer is the following: To what extent do the determinants of entrepreneurial intention also have an effect on subsequent entrepreneurial behavior? The study applies a simultaneous equation model to data collected from university students in Catalonia (Spanish) in two different periods of time (2014 and 2016). The results support the simultaneous effect of a set of three different variables (opportunity identification capability, self-assessment of skills, and social prestige associated with entrepreneurial activities) on both entrepreneurial intentions and subsequent entrepreneurial behavior. The results also (partially) support the moderating effect of the institutional context.

These findings contribute to the current literature by providing a broader and more complete perspective of the whole "antecedents–entrepreneurial intentions–entrepreneurial behavior" sequence. Most studies have been limited to analyzing the effect of some determinants on intentions (Kibler et al., 2014), and very few articles have focused on studying the relationship between intention and behavior (Kautonen et al., 2015). In addition, the research contributes to the understanding of this process by introducing the moderating role of the institutional environment, which has rarely been taken into account in these types of studies.

The chapter is structured as follows. In section 2, the main theoretical framework and hypotheses are presented. In section 3, the methodology of the study is detailed. Section 4 presents and discusses the results. Finally, in section 5, the main conclusions of the study are presented, and some limitations and future research lines are suggested.

LITERATURE REVIEW AND HYPOTHESES

The literature has extensively agreed that measuring an individual's intention towards a certain action is the best way to predict that this action will indeed occur (Carsrud & Branback, 2011). In this regard, Shapero and Sokol's (1982) seminal work represents a starting point in the literature on the relationship between intentions and behavior. This approach is known as the entrepreneurial event model (Krueger, 1993; Shapero, 1975; Shapero & Sokol, 1982). It explains that entrepreneurial intentions depend on three main factors: perceived desirability, propensity to act, and perceived feasibility. From this perspective, perceived desirability refers to the extent to which individuals consider the possibility of becoming an entrepreneur to be an attractive option. The propensity to act refers to the extent to which individuals are willing to act towards the exploration and exploitation of entrepreneurial opportunities (Shapero & Sokol, 1982). Finally, perceived feasibility refers to the extent to which individuals consider that they have the skills and capacities required to become an entrepreneur (Schlaegel & Koenig, 2014).

The potential value of the entrepreneurial event model has led to the development of other related models (Bird, 1988). In this regard, the most-cited psychological theory used to explain and forecast individuals' actions is the theory of planned behavior (Ajzen, 1988, 1991), which in turn is based on the theory of reasoned action (Fishbein & Ajzen, 1975). From this perspective, entrepreneurial intentions refer to a state of mind that guides the behavior of people towards the development and execution of new business ideas and concepts (Bird, 1988; Karimi, Biemans, Lans, Chizari, & Mulder, 2016). Therefore, the stronger the intention to perform a certain action, the more likely it is that this behavior will actually take place (Ajzen, 1991). The theory of planned behavior explains that intentions also depend on three different types of antecedents: attitude, subjective norm, and perceived behavioral control. Attitude refers to the degree to which the individual (i.e., the potential entrepreneur) has a favorable or unfavorable evaluation of performing the behavior (i.e., becoming an entrepreneur). Subjective norm refers to the perceived social pressure, meaning the expectations of important referent groups, to perform a specific action (i.e., becoming an entrepreneur). Finally, perceived behavioral control refers to the perceived degree of easiness or difficulty of performing the behavior (i.e., becoming an entrepreneur). In other words, it refers to the extent to which the individual considers that he or she has the capacity to perform the behavior (Ajzen, 2002; Kautonen, Tornikoski, & Kibler, 2011). This concept is analogous to the concept of perceived self-efficacy developed by Bandura (1977).

Overall, the entrepreneurial event model and the theory of planned behavior are considered to share certain assumptions and notions and to overlap partially (Krueger & Brazeal, 1994). They are the two approaches that are the most used to understand the link between intentions and subsequent behavior. Based on them, this study presents a set of four different hypotheses.

Hypotheses Development

Entrepreneurial opportunities can be defined as situations in which new products, services, materials, and organizational methods can be launched onto the market to create greater value (Casson, 1982). Opportunities exist primarily because different agents have different beliefs about the relative value of resources when converted from input into output (Kirzner, 1979; Shane & Venkataraman, 2000). An entrepreneurial opportunity thus invariably involves the development of a new idea that others have overlooked or chosen not to pursue (Alvarez & Busenitz, 2001; Patel, 2019). From this perspective, Kirzner (1979) asserted that the mental representations and interpretations of entrepreneurs do indeed differ because they are driven by entrepreneurial alertness and a distinctive set of perceptual and cognitive processing skills that direct the opportunity identification process.

Identifying and selecting the right opportunities for new businesses are considered to be among the most important abilities of a successful entrepreneur (Stevenson, Roberts, & Grousbeck, 1985); thus, the discovery of entrepreneurial opportunities has appeared as a fundamental aspect of the literature on entrepreneurship in recent years (Ardichvili, Cardozo, & Ray, 2003; Asante & Affum-Osei, 2019; Gaglio & Katz, 2001; Shane & Venkataraman, 2000). The literature has agreed that the development and growth of entrepreneurial initiatives must be preceded not only by having the intention to perform certain behaviors but also by identifying an opportunity. That is, it is believed that opportunities are a necessary first step and condition to develop any type of entrepreneurial activity. For instance, Short et al. (2009, p. 40) stated that "A potential entrepreneur can be immensely creative and hardworking, but without any opportunity to target with these characteristics, entrepreneurial activities cannot take place." Hence, from this perspective, it is considered that, without opportunities, there would be no entrepreneurship at all (Short, Ketchen, Shook, & Ireland, 2009).

For this reason, some researchers have claimed that the most important point in the entrepreneurship field is not to identify people who wish to be entrepreneurs but rather to seek the link between those people and valuable entrepreneurial opportunities (Shane & Venkataraman, 2000; Venkataraman, 1997). Researchers have extensively investigated why some individuals are able to identify and exploit opportunities, and some are not (Cooper & Dunkelberg, 1987). In this regard, most of this literature has proposed that psychological variables, personality traits, and demographic factors have an effect on this capacity (De Carolis & Saparito, 2006). Similarly, other authors, such as DeTienne and Chandler (2007), have shown how creativity and innovation are positively related to the opportunity identification capacity. Based on these explanations, the following hypothesis is posed:

Hypothesis 1: Being able to identify business opportunities increases the likelihood of having an entrepreneurial intention, which in turn has a significant effect on entrepreneurial behavior.

Identifying new business opportunities will depend not only on individuals' knowledge, experience, personal and professional contacts, or educational level but also on their confidence in or self-perception of their own skills and abilities (Gonzalez-Alvarez & Solis-Rodriguez, 2011). In this regard, the concept of self-efficacy has been used in previous studies to explain individuals' "beliefs in their capabilities to mobilize the motivation, cognitive resources, and courses of action needed to exercise control over events in their lives" (Wood & Bandura, 1989, p. 364). Specifically, in the entrepreneurship field, the notion of "entrepreneurial self-efficacy" has been proposed (Bandura, 2006; Szerb & Voros, 2019) and refers to the self-evaluation that people make of the extent to which they possess the required skills to perform a certain task. In addition, it refers to whether they believe that they can rely on these abilities to succeed in their entrepreneurial endeavors (Bandura, 1989, 1997). In other words, the results of actions and outcome expectations are conditioned by how individuals assess their general or more particular task-related abilities (Fishbein & Ajzen, 2011).

Self-perception of skills has been shown to have a key influence on the entrepreneurial spirit, as it positively affects people's entrepreneurial intentions (Sequeira, Mueller, & McGee, 2007; Zhao, Seibert, & Hills, 2005). Individuals will not have entrepreneurial intentions if they do not perceive that it is both possible and desirable to do so (Kundu & Rani, 2007). Moreover, it has been suggested that self-perception of skills could have an impact on subsequent behavior (Rauch & Frese, 2007). Also, it can have an effect on motivation, which is related to the effort that individuals exert in trying to achieve their goals (Wood & Bandura, 1989). This is particularly relevant in the entrepreneurship field, in which decisions are usually taken in an uncertain, changing, and complex environment that can involve financial and professional risks (Baron & Shane, 2007; Boudreaux, Nikolaev, & Klein, 2019). Similarly, previous research has shown that the fact that women have a lower perception of their own skills and abilities (regardless of their real skills) translates into fewer women becoming involved in entrepreneurial initiatives (Noguera, Alvarez, & Urbano, 2013; Wilson, Kickul, & Marlino, 2007). Finally, overconfidence and unrealistically optimistic expectations are reported to be a characteristic of entrepreneurs (Cooper et al., 1988; Szerb & Voros, 2019). Overall, the following hypothesis is posed:

Hypothesis 2: Self-perception of skills increases the likelihood of having entrepreneurial intentions, which in turn have a significant effect on entrepreneurial behavior.

The institutional environment can be categorized into different forms (Urbano, Toledano, & Ribeiro-Soriano, 2011). North (1990) explained that institutions can be formal (i.e., legal regulations) or informal (i.e., cultural values, traditions, or attitudes). From the latter perspective, scholars have long pointed out the importance of socio-cultural factors in the decision to start up new businesses, arguing that entrepreneurship is embedded in a social context (Aldrich & Zimmer, 1986). In this regard, the influence of national culture on individual entrepreneurial behavior has been well established (Hayton, George, & Zahra, 2002), as countries and societies are considered to have collective perceptions and images that lead them to admire entrepreneurial activities to a greater or lesser extent (Busenitz, Gomez, & Spencer, 2000). Culture affects collective and societal mechanisms through joint expectations and preferences. These mechanisms affect how individuals perceive the economic and social probability and attractiveness of developing entrepreneurial activities (Autio, Pathak, & Wennberg, 2013). That is, cultural values define the extent to which certain activities are considered to be socially prestigious or not (Urbano, Audretsch, Aparicio, & Noguera, 2019).

The literature has shown that some factors underlying entrepreneurial behavior are common across cultures (e.g., economic incentives can motivate action in all cultures). However, since culture reinforces specific personal characteristics and penalizes others, these studies have shown how entrepreneurship differs from culture to culture, as some values favor entrepreneurial behavior more than others (Mueller & Thomas, 2001). Shane (1992) demonstrated (following Hofstede's approach) that the national cultural values of individualism and power distance explain the national differences in the rates of inventiveness. Similarly, Wilson et al. (2004) identified significant differences between American ethnic groups in their interest in entrepreneurship. These effects are articulated through a process of social legitimation (Fayolle, Liñán, & Moriano, 2014). Overall, an entrepreneurial culture fosters and supports the continuous search for entrepreneurial opportunities that can be exploited with sustainable competitive advantages (McGrath, McMillan, Yang, & Tsai, 1992). Therefore, the following hypothesis is posed:

Hypothesis 3: Living in an environment in which entrepreneurial activity is perceived as a socially prestigious activity increases the likelihood of having entrepreneurial intentions, which in turn have a significant positive effect on entrepreneurial behavior.

Although research has mostly shown cultural factors to have a direct impact on entrepreneurship, cultural variables in many cases have been theorized and modeled as moderating entrepreneurial outcomes (De Clercq, Danis, & Dakhli, 2010; De Clercq, Lim, & Oh, 2013; Hayton et al., 2002; Wu, Song, & Yang, 2020). Hence, researchers have accepted that social behavior occurs in a specific geographical context that is closely related to the values and beliefs of its population, which affect individuals' processes of perception, interpretation, and behavior (Garcia-Cabrera & Garcia-Soto, 2008). Scholars have argued that, to understand entrepreneurial variations, the social environment in which a firm is created needs to be considered and that "greater attention should be given to the interactions among cultural dimensions and the conception of culture that allows for greater complexity in relation to other characteristics of the environment" (Thornton, Ribeiro-Soriano, & Urbano, 2011, p. 109).

Cultural factors have been a subject of considerable interest in the discipline of entrepreneurship since Aldrich and Zimmer (1986) and Granovetter (1985) discussed the notion of "embeddedness" in economic activity. These authors suggested that entrepreneurship is embedded in a social context and evoked the idea that it is a societal phenomenon rather than a purely economic activity (Steyaert, 2007; Urbano et al., 2011). From this perspective, Kostova and Roth (2002, p. 217) asserted that the institutional environment reflects the "values, beliefs, norms and assumptions about human behavior held by the individuals in a given country." Similarly, the entrepreneurship literature has emphasized that culture can reflect issues such as people's prior experience in starting a new business, knowledge about how to identify good business opportunities, perceived ability to assemble the necessary resources, or confidence in managing and growing a business (Busenitz et al., 2000; Casillas et al., 2015; Riviezzo,

Santos, Liñán, Napolitano, & Fusco, 2019). In this regard, Hayton et al. (2002, p. 33) stated that "Cultural values indicate the degree to which a society considers entrepreneurial behaviors, such as risk-taking and independent thinking, to be desirable." Similarly, Gomez-Haro et al. (2011) explained that one of the reasons for some countries being less entrepreneurial is that innovative activities are socially less prestigious and less appreciated than in other more entrepreneurial countries. In addition, the cultural burden faced by aspiring entrepreneurs is considered to be lower in that information relevant to entrepreneurship is widely distributed (Spencer & Gomez, 2004), and assistance with market research and other business development activities is easily available (Hawkins, 1993). Finally, the following hypothesis is posed:

Hypothesis 4a: Entrepreneurial prestige moderates the relationship between opportunity recognition and both entrepreneurial intentions and behavior such that the relationship is stronger for higher values of entrepreneurial prestige.

Hypothesis 4b: Entrepreneurial prestige moderates the relationship between self-perception of skills and both entrepreneurial intentions and behavior such that the relationship is stronger for higher values of entrepreneurial prestige.

METHODOLOGY

Data and Variables

The study uses a data set containing information from university undergraduate students at two different moments in time (2012–2013 and 2016). Specifically, the first wave of data collection started in September 2012 and continued during the 2012–2013 academic year until February 2013. In almost all cases, the questionnaire was completed in class under the supervision of a professor. Subsequently, an e-mail was sent to all the students taking the course, asking them to fill in the questionnaire if they had not completed it in class. A total of 9 universities located in Catalonia (Spain) participated in the study, specifically the Universitat Autònoma de Barcelona, Universitat de Barcelona, Universitat Pompeu Fabra, Universitat Politècnica de Catalunya, Universitat de Lleida, Universitat de Girona, Universitat Rovira i Virgili, Universitat Oberta de Catalunya, and Fundació Universitària del Bages. The students came from undergraduate programs from different areas and schools: Business, Economics, Business & Law, Law, Labour Relations, Tourism, Hospitality Management, Medicine, Physiotherapy, Nursing, Early Child Education, and Computer Engineering. This approach allowed the study to cover a wide spectrum of universities within Catalonia as well as a wide variety of students. Therefore, this approach ensured that the sample was as representative as possible of the population under study. Overall, a total of 2491 valid observations were collected in the first wave of the study.

The second wave of the study started in April 2016. An e-mail was sent to all the first-wave participants in the study, asking them to fill in a follow-up questionnaire. A second e-mail was sent in May 2016 as a reminder to those individuals who had not completed the follow-up questionnaire. In addition, when the phone number of the first-wave participants was available, phone calls were made asking the participants to respond to the questionnaire over the phone. Overall, a total of 352 observations were collected in the second wave of the study.

Dependent Variables

The study has two different binary dependent variables, *Entrepreneurial Intention,* and *Entrepreneurial Behavior*. Entrepreneurial intention is measured by asking, "Have you ever seriously considered the possibility of becoming a business owner?" In the case of behavior, it was asked, "Have you ever created a new company?" Several previous researchers have used dependent variables that are exactly the same as or very similar to these (see, among others, Torres & Augusto, 2019; Tsai, Chang, & Peng, 2016).

Independent Variables

This study uses three different independent variables: *Opportunity*, *Skills*, and *Status*. These measures are usually used in the entrepreneurship literature, for example, in the Global Entrepreneurship Monitor (GEM) data set. Therefore, they have also been employed in many different studies in the past (see, among others, Autio, Pathak, & Wennberg, 2013; Stuetzer, Obschonka, Brixy, Sternberg, & Cantner, 2014).

Control Variables

In addition, other factors can influence entrepreneurial intentions and subsequent behavior. For this reason, the study controls for demographic characteristics. These types of controls have been used extensively in the past. That is, entrepreneurs behave differently depending on their age (Urbano & Alvarez, 2014), on their income or wealth (Hornsby, Kuratko, Shepherd, & Bott, 2009), or their gender, as men are more likely to start up new businesses than women (Adachi & Hisada, 2017). In addition, this research also controls whether the participants had attended any course in the area of entrepreneurship in the past, as this type of experience tends to increase entrepreneurial intentions (Piperopoulos & Dimov, 2015). Table 1 describes the variables used in the study.

Empirical Strategy and Estimation Methods

As this research is interested in the influence of institutional factors on entrepreneurial intentions, which may lead to entrepreneurial behavior, a set of simultaneous equations is defined, which includes institutions as explanatory variables of the focal elements, intentions in a direct way, and behavior in an indirect manner. This follows similar approaches in entrepreneurship research (cf. Urbano, Turro, & Aparicio, 2019), particularly regarding entrepreneurial intentions (cf. Schmutzler, Andonova, & Diaz-Serrano, 2019). Based on the consensus about the importance of institutions for increasing the probability of an individual wishing to start a new venture (Liñán & Fayolle, 2015), the first equation explains the possible explanatory power of institutional factors in the intentional decision. Thus, the reduced version of equation 1 is as follows:

$$P(EI_i = 1) = f(IF_i, CV_i) \quad (1)$$

where EI_i is the dummy variable that represents the entrepreneurial intentions of individual i. The element IF_i denotes a matrix with institutional factors such as opportunity, skills, and status. Finally, CV_i is the matrix for controls, including gender, income, age, and entrepreneurship course. As entrepreneurship is considered to be a development process, which is affected by different (contextual) variables

(Gnyawali & Fogel, 1994) and the possible sequence may run from the identification of the idea to its evaluation and exploitation (Shane & Venkataram, 2000), different approaches capturing entrepreneurship suggest that intentions are motivational factors to start a new venture (Bosma, 2013; Reynolds, 2007). That is why a second equation is defined, which assesses the influence of entrepreneurial intentions on entrepreneurial behavior. The reduced equation is as follows:

$$P(EB_i = 1) = g(\widehat{EI}_i . CV_i) \tag{2}$$

in which this function g comprises the estimated value of entrepreneurial intentions ($\widehat{EI}_i$. and the same control variables (CV_i) as in equation 1. An entrepreneurial behavior equation is estimated, explaining actions through intentions, while controlling for the same set of relevant demographic characteristics directly related to intentions.

Due to the binary nature of the dependent variables, a combination of logistic regressions and simultaneous equation modeling is used. A binomial logit regression estimates the probability of an event happening by assuming a logistic distribution of the sample (Hoetker, 2007; Wiersema & Bowen, 2009). However, at this point, logit models do not bridge the possible connection between intentions and behavior; hence, a complementary estimation method is required. In this case, the conditional mixed process (CMP) operates within simultaneous equation systems. It has two advantages (Roodman, 2011): first, a recursive multi-stage estimation within a simultaneous equation system; and, second, a complete observation of the right-hand-side endogenous variables.

It has been suggested that the CMP estimates multi-equation, mixed-process models, and the potential hierarchy random effect (Roodman, 2015). It entails different systems of equations, possibly having different dependent variables, so, alternative to linear and continuous (such as OLS) techniques. This technique enables the simultaneous estimation of non-linear models, such as tobit, probit, logit, and ordered probit. The conditional characteristic implies that the same variable could play different roles within the system. That is, a dependent variable in equation 1 could be an independent variable in equation 2. This interplay should have a recursive structure if dependency within a censor is an observed variable, so it needs to be separated into different stages. Based on these characteristics and the empirical structure, the research relies on this method to conduct the analysis.

Table 1. Description of the variables

		Variables description
Dependent variables	Entrepreneurial Intention	Have you ever seriously considered the possibility of becoming a business owner? (Yes/No)
	Entrepreneurial Behavior	Have you ever created a new company? (Yes/No)
Independent variables	Opportunity	In the next six months, there will be good opportunities for starting a business in the area where you live (Yes/No)
	Skills	You have the knowledge, skill, and experience required to start a new business (Yes/No)
	Status	In my country, those successful at starting a new business have a high level of status and respect (Yes/No)
Controls	Gender	Respondents were asked to specify their gender
	Age	Respondents were asked to specify their date of birth
	Income	Approximately, which is the average monthly income at your house? (6 categories)
	Course	Have you ever attended any business creation course? (Yes/No)

RESULTS

Table 2 presents the descriptive statistics and the correlation matrix of the main dependent and independent variables. As can be observed, students in the sample manifest a high level of intentions, as 85.6% would like to start a new company in the near future. This is consistent with the analysis of overoptimism (cf. Brieger, Bäro, Criaco, & Terjesen, 2020; Cieślik, Kaciak, & van Stel, 2018), in which young people see more favorable conditions for seizing available opportunities in the market. Contrary to this result, entrepreneurial behavior among students seems to be very low. However, this is consistent with Urbano et al. (2017), who showed that the probability of becoming an entrepreneur is low for Catalan students across different programs. These authors, in addition, identified certain institutions related to cognitive aspects as explaining such a probability. Comparing this idea with the correlation matrix in Table 2, it was noticed that opportunities, skills, and status are highly correlated with entrepreneurial intentions and behavior. In this regard, the correlation matrix shows relationships that meet the expectations.

Table 2. Correlation matrix

	Mean	Std. Dev.	1	2	3	4	5	6	7	8	9
1. Entrepreneurial intention	0.856	0.259	1								
2. Entrepreneurial behavior	0.120	0.334	0.094***	1							
3. Opportunity	0.369	0.484	0.137***	0.097***	1						
4. Skills	0.417	0.495	0.135***	0.239***	0.112***	1					
5. Status	0.576	0.494	0.106***	-0.005	0.042**	0.001	1				
6. Gender	0.464	0.498	0.116***	0.083***	0.077***	0.111***	-0.048**	1			
7. Age	29.15	8.206	0.065***	0.276***	-0.001	0.320***	-0.085***	0.108***	1		
8. Income	2.785	1.112	0.048**	0.027	0.073***	-0.006	0.081***	0.101***	0.015	1	
9. Course	0.378	0.489	0.095***	0.088***	0.096***	0.225***	-0.009	0.082***	0.099***	0.000	1

*** Significant at $p < 0.01$. Note: Std. Dev. is the standard deviation.

Table 3 displays the estimation results for entrepreneurial intentions and behavior. As this study seeks for further comprehension of the process from intentions to behavior (Krueger et al., 2000) under the influence of institutions, the research defines an empirical strategy that tests the association between institutions and intentions and that between institutions and behavior separately. Afterward, it is explored whether the estimated variable in equation 1 affects behavior in equation 2. Thus, models 1 and 2 in the study regress entrepreneurial intentions on the institutional factors and control variables considering the interaction between opportunities and status as well as between skills and status, respectively. These models are estimated using a logistic regression approach. For model 3, the influence of entrepreneurial intentions on entrepreneurial behavior plus controls is considered. Finally, models 4 and 5 use simultaneous equation modeling (Keshk, Pollins, & Reuveny, 2004), which incorporates entrepreneurial intentions (influenced by institutions) as antecedents of behavior. The specification seems to be strong in terms of the explanatory variables, which is observed through the probability of X^2 equal to zero.

With regard to hypothesis testing, in Hypothesis 1, it is posited that being able to identify business opportunities increases the likelihood of having an entrepreneurial intention, which in turn has a significant effect on entrepreneurial behavior. Based on the results across the models, opportunity recognition is a significant variable when defining a preference for entrepreneurship. These findings are consistent with the extant literature (Ardichvili, Cardozo, & Ray, 2003; Asante & Affum-Osei, 2019), which has suggested that people are equipped with the ability to identify opportunities are more likely to desire entrepreneurial activity as a good career choice. In this case, the variable opportunity oscillates between 0.652 ($p < 0.01$ in Model 1), 0.502 ($p < 0.01$ in Model 2), 0.420 ($p < 0.01$ in Model 4), and 0.320 ($p < 0.01$ in Model 5). Hence, opportunity recognition increases the probability of having entrepreneurial intentions among Catalan university students.

Table 3. Estimation results of the simultaneous equation model

	(1)		(2)		(3)		(4)		(5)	
	Entrepreneurial intention		**Entrepreneurial intention**				**Entrepreneurial intention**		**Entrepreneurial intention**	
	Coef. (Std. error)	**dy/dx**	**Coef. (Std. error)**	**dy/dx**			**Coef. (Std. error)**	**dy/dx**	**Coef. (Std. error)**	**dy/dx**
Opportunity	0.652*** (0.161)	0.652***	0.502*** (0.105)	0.502***			0.427*** (0.093)	0.427***	0.327*** (0.061)	0.327***
Skills	0.932*** (0.112)	0.932***	0.916*** (0.159)	0.916***			0.564*** (0.065)	0.564***	0.582*** (0.092)	0.582***
Status	0.411*** (0.116)	0.411***	0.325** (0.115)	0.325**			0.243*** (0.069)	0.243***	0.197** (0.070)	0.197**
Status x Opportunity	-0.258 (0.211)	-0.259					-0.170 (0.121)	-0.17		
Status x Skills			0.030 (0.212)	0.03					-0.027 (0.122)	-0.027
Gender	0.481*** (0.098)	0.482***	0.481*** (0.098)	0.481***			0.291*** (0.059)	0.291***	0.292*** (0.059)	0.292***
Age	-0.005 (0.007)	-0.005	-0.005 (0.007)	-0.005			-0.004 (0.004)	-0.004	-0.004 (0.004)	-0.004
Income	-0.019 (0.044)	-0.019	-0.020 (0.044)	-0.02			-0.012 (0.027)	-0.012	-0.012 (0.027)	-0.004
Course	0.603*** (0.107)	0.604***	0.606*** (0.106)	0.606***			0.353*** (0.063)	0.353***	0.356*** (0.063)	0.356***
					Entrepreneurial behavior		**Entrepreneurial behavior**		**Entrepreneurial behavior**	
					Coef. (Std. error)	**dy/dx**	**Coef. (Std. error)**		**Coef. (Std. error)**	
Entrepreneurial intention					0.335+ (0.235)	0.008+	1.621*** (0.307)		1.596*** (0.308)	
Gender					0.231 (0.181)	0.005	-0.020 (0.153)		-0.009 (0.154)	
Age					-0.064* (0.025)	-0.001*	-0.052** (0.020)		-0.053** (0.020)	
Income					0.010 (0.076)	0.000	0.019 (0.058)		0.017 (0.059)	
Course					0.475** (0.182)	0.011**	0.104 (0.170)		0.118 (0.170)	
Log likelihood	-1277.17		-1277.92		-103.53		-1375.13		-1376.09	
AIC	2574.35		2575.84		219.05		2782.26		2784.18	
BIC	2631.23		2632.71		253.18		2873.27		2875.19	
Number of observations	2180		2180		2182		2180		2180	
Prob > chi 2	0.000		0.000		0.000		0.000		0.000	

+ p = 0.1, *p<0.05, *p<0.01, *p<0,001

Note: Models 1, 2, and 3 are estimated using logistic regression, whilst models 4 and 5 are the simultaneous equation models

Hypothesis 2 suggested that the self-perception of skills increases the likelihood of having entrepreneurial intentions, which in turn have a significant effect on entrepreneurial behavior. Similar to the previous hypothesis, the results enable us not to reject this statement. In line with other studies (cf. Sequeira, Mueller, & McGee, 2007; Zhao, Seibert, & Hills, 2005), the evidence is provided on the importance of entrepreneurial skills for increasing intentions among students. The estimated models show that self-perceived skills influence the probability of intentions by 0.932% ($p < 0.01$ in Model 1), 0.916% ($p < 0.01$ in Model 2), 0.511% ($p < 0.01$ in Model 4), and 0.553% ($p < 0.01$ in Model 5). Based on these results, it is shown that entrepreneurial skills directly affect entrepreneurial intentions as well as entrepreneurial behavior in an indirect way.

In addition to opportunity recognition and skills, this research assumes that people's perception of entrepreneurship is also important for their intentions and behavior. Hence, Hypothesis 3 suggested that living in an environment in which entrepreneurial activity is perceived as a socially prestigious activity increases the likelihood of having entrepreneurial intentions, which in turn have a significant positive effect on entrepreneurial behavior. Similar to Fayolle, Liñán, and Moriano (2014), this research finds that entrepreneurs' status has strong explanatory power for entrepreneurial intentions. Particularly for this sample of Catalan university students, there is a positive association between these two variables, in which the probability of having intentions increases by 0.411% ($p < 0.01$ in Model 1), 0.325% ($p < 0.01$ in Model 2), 0.228% ($p < 0.01$ in Model 4), and 0.196% ($p < 0.01$ in Model 5) when students consider that there is a well-positioned perception of entrepreneurship as a desirable career. Thereby, the hypothesis cannot be rejected.

As status is an important measure that may capture people's perception of entrepreneurship, this can act as a proxy for a socially support culture (Stephan & Uhlaner, 2010). In this regard, two additional hypotheses were proposed on the possible reinforcement effect of status on the influence of opportunity recognition and entrepreneurial skills on intentions (directly) and behavior (indirectly). Hypothesis 4a posited that entrepreneurial prestige moderates the relationship between opportunity recognition and both entrepreneurial intentions and behavior, such that the relationship is stronger for higher values of entrepreneurial prestige. In parallel, Hypothesis 4b was devoted to understanding whether entrepreneurial prestige moderates the relationship between self-perception of skills and both entrepreneurial intentions and behavior, such that the relationship is stronger for higher values of entrepreneurial prestige. The results do not support such hypotheses, since non-significant associations are found. Perhaps, as Urbano et al. (2017) discussed, university students in Catalonia have lived in a strong environment characterized by high levels of entrepreneurial activity, so the perception of entrepreneurship as a good option in the labor market. However, it has a positive effect on intentions, might result as neutral when influencing other factors related to entrepreneurship (both intentions and behavior). Instead, there is evidence on the importance of appropriate environments that act directly on students' preferences about entrepreneurship. In this regard, Grimaldi and Fernandez (2017) and Urbano et al. (2017) showed that the role of universities in entrepreneurial intentions and innovation outcomes is crucial, as universities provide students with the necessary tools to interpret and behave in the entrepreneurial environment of Catalonia. Apart from Silicon Valley as a region characterized by a solid entrepreneurial environment, Pahnke and Welter (2017) discussed the Mittelstand as a vibrant region where many entrepreneurial activities occur. Regions like these may be characterized by a population with intentions to become entrepreneurs at some point, so the effect on other explanatory factors of entrepreneurship might be marginal.

DISCUSSION

The extant literature about entrepreneurial intentions has grown rapidly from initial discoveries (Krueger, 1993; Shapero & Sokol, 1982). Liñán and Fayolle (2015) showed how different elements had been tested as important determinants to increase the preference for entrepreneurial activity in the near future. Liñán and Fayole's (2015) research suggested that personal factors, such as self-perception of desirability, feasibility, and propensity to act, have been explored widely in entrepreneurship research. In this regard, there is a call for further explorations of other possible factors that may enhance the understanding of why people manifest a preference for entrepreneurship.

Contextual factors come into the analysis of intentions due to their importance to characterize societies' perception of new entrepreneurial activities (Liñán & Chen, 2009). Krueger and Brazeal (1994) suggested that societies can have an entrepreneurial characteristic (or potential) when they create an appropriate environment that motivates people to become entrepreneurs at some point. Accordingly, this creates a sort of loop in which potential entrepreneurs lead to entrepreneurial potential and vice versa. Advances in this line of thought have created initial ideas on the importance of specific institutions related to cognitive dimensions (Aparicio, Urbano, & Stenholm, 2019).

The results could serve to keep building an exhaustive discussion on possible institutional factors that affect intentions and behavior. For example, if a country or region is characterized by having plenty of opportunities and people who identify those opportunities as potential new ventures, then that country or region is expected to grow more than other places (Acs et al., 2009). It is shown that opportunity identification is an element that helps people to think of entrepreneurship as looking for labor market alternatives. As such, Catalonia is a region that matches the knowledge theory of entrepreneurship (Acs et al., 2009) perfectly, as it is characterized by a solid and complex industry that comprises different sectors (food, clothing, cars, financial services, etc.). As Grimaldi and Fernandez (2017) and Urbano et al. (2017) showed, Catalan universities have played a key role in developing capacities to identify those existing opportunities better. In this regard, different activities related to fairs, seminars, conferences, and workshops may enhance the opportunity recognition of people's and industries' needs. For instance, 22@Barcelona is a governmental initiative that seeks to transform a particular space in the city to attract entrepreneurs to collaborate with universities to offer suitable solutions to meet people's demand.

Key alliances with universities create potential entrepreneurs equipped with particular knowledge and skills to live and follow an entrepreneurial process. Within the knowledge spillover theory framework, Audretsch (2014) suggested that, although opportunities might exist in a particular economy, there may a gap related to the necessary knowledge to turn those opportunities into feasible and profitable projects. In this regard, perfect alignment between courses' curricula, universities' activities and programs, and entrepreneurial dynamics should exist. The results show that business skills are an important element that students have when manifesting a preference for entrepreneurship as a good career choice. These findings thereby serve to exemplify the relevance of knowledge to closing a possible gap between existing opportunities and potential entrepreneurs. In addition to this, the results suggest that, if students do not have intentions to undertake entrepreneurial projects, then they have important knowledge to perform and lead other (equally complex) tasks and projects within the companies for which they are working (Aparicio, Urbano, & Stenholm, 2019).

In general, regions like Catalonia may show an entrepreneurial mindset at different levels (Grimaldi & Fernandez, 2017). Precisely, this characteristic is found when students are able to identify good opportunities in the market, and when universities provide enough tools for students to become entrepreneurs.

This entrepreneurial movement is leveraged from society's perception of entrepreneurship. Stephan and Uhlaner (2010) showed how societies support risky activities, such as entrepreneurship. These authors referred to particular mechanisms, for instance, media coverage and entrepreneurial status, that encourage (afraid) people to take risks and become entrepreneurs. The findings also support this idea, as entrepreneurs in Catalonia are considered important and transformational members of the society. On the one hand, this can create role models from whom university students can learn (Nowiński & Haddoud, 2019). On the other hand, this creates a stable environment where people expect entrepreneurship to be a suitable career for their futures as the industrial environment is solid (Stephan & Uhlaner, 2010).

Based on the analysis of these three antecedents of entrepreneurial intentions (i.e., opportunity recognition, entrepreneurial skills, and entrepreneurs' status), it could also be said that entrepreneurial behavior emerges in places where there are good conditions for entrepreneurial intentions (Krueger & Brazeal, 1994; Schillo, Persaud, & Jin, 2016). Particularly, in this case, it is shown that Catalonia offers an appropriate environment for students to move from intentions to practice. Curiously, a major Catalan town's logo contains the phrase *facta non verba* (i.e., facts not words), which might represent this philosophy of moving from ideas and intentions to tangible outcomes and activities.

The current extant literature has focused on the analysis of entrepreneurial intentions (Liñán & Fayolle, 2015), but a few works have tried to explore further the bridge between intentions and behavior (Gielnik et al., 2014; Goethner et al., 2012). This chapter is subscribed to these attempts to explore further the intention–behavior link. Gielnik et al. (2014) and Goethner et al. (2012) explained the importance of intentions for entrepreneurial actions based on personal characteristics. The findings could contribute to the theory by showing that institutions are also important for the early stages of entrepreneurship. Liñán and Fayolle (2015) defined a framework for entrepreneurial intentions in which the context matters. The results extend this view by showing that institutional factors may explain the decision of potential entrepreneurs to create new ventures. In this regard, institutions constitute an environment in which people can freely decide whether entrepreneurship is a good career alternative. If so, new entrepreneurs could enhance the already-solid context by bringing up new ideas based on their capacity to recognize opportunities and their abilities and skills to move entrepreneurial projects forward accurately. If not, then the institutional environment helps them perform tasks in an entrepreneurial way (Aparicio et al., 2019). Another theoretical contribution stemming from the results deals with the idea of dynamism and the role of time (Lévesque & Stephan, 2019). The sample of students was configured by following them in two different periods of time, so it implies that the bridge between intentions and behavior takes time. However, institutions are stable across the two waves, so institutional stability becomes vital for students to maintain their preferences and progress to real actions.

Based on this theoretical discussion, the Catalan Government should keep encouraging entrepreneurial activity at all levels. This implies that not only technological parks (e.g., at universities) and districts (e.g., 22@Barcelona) but also educational programs should be implemented for young students in high schools (García-Rodríguez, Gutiérrez-Taño, & Ruiz-Rosa, 2019) and universities (Urbano et al., 2017). Seminars, fairs, and workshops in educational organizations can be complemented with programs organized by banks or other companies in the financial sector. In this respect, Coad et al. (2016) showed that banks could play an important role not only in providing loans but also in teaching people (particularly entrepreneurs) how to manage financial capital.

Entrepreneurs can also take advantage of these results. For example, this research may serve to identify Catalonia as a good region in which to invest in entrepreneurial projects. The analysis shows that entrepreneurship is a desirable career choice, which encourages other (new and established) companies to bring new knowledge that can later be commercialized by emerging entrepreneurs. Practitioners can also find in Catalonia a good place to live with their families. As the university students in the sample show that universities support entrepreneurial activity, this could mean a strong movement from the educational sector to create shared knowledge about entrepreneurship. For those who already live in Catalonia, they can use the findings to make decisions in terms of the next generations of entrepreneurs as either suppliers or workers. Incoming graduate students tend to be equipped with the necessary knowledge, skills, and tools to advance entrepreneurial projects or behave as entrepreneurs within companies. Either way, this would benefit existing companies as new (tangible and intangible) solutions accompany new entrepreneurs and workers.

CONCLUSION

The main objective of this chapter was to explore the extent to which the determinants of entrepreneurial intentions also have an effect on subsequent entrepreneurial behavior. This study follows Krueger et al. (2000) as the basis for the analysis of institutional factors and entrepreneurial intentions and behavior. Based on this perspective, the results expanded the discussion on traditional elements explaining the desirability to follow an entrepreneurial career to the institutional landscape (North, 1990, 2005). The observation through the institutional lens enabled us to determine whether certain institutional factors, such as opportunity recognition, entrepreneurial skills, and the status of entrepreneurship, play a key role in the development of entrepreneurship (i.e., from intentions to behavior).

Similar to the extant literature (cf. Schillo et al., 2016), this research found that, for example, the capacity to recognize opportunities is crucial for entrepreneurial intentions. This pattern followed the previous suggestions of other theories in entrepreneurship research (cf. Acs et al., 2009). In this case, university students in Catalonia can easily identify opportunities, observing that entrepreneurship is a mechanism to turn those opportunities into real solutions for society. This finding is complemented by the need to have appropriate programs that help students to operationalize those identified opportunities. The results showed that skills increase the probability of a student becoming a potential entrepreneur. This implies that the existing curricula in Catalan universities prepare everyone to face social challenges at the local, national, or international level. However, these institutional factors might not be strong enough in cultures in which entrepreneurship does not have a good reputation. In Catalonia, as observed in the results, there is a good perception of entrepreneurial means, so the Catalan society creates a sort of cultural support for potential entrepreneurs.

In addition to the cultural and institutional factors that are conducive to entrepreneurial intentions, it is observed that there is a bridge between potential entrepreneurs and actual entrepreneurs. This presents Catalonia as a region that moves from words to facts, from ideas to applicable projects. In this case, this research contributes to the literature by extending the idea that institutions matter not only for intentions (Liñán & Fayolle, 2015) but also for behavior. Similar to other studies (cf. Aparicio, Urbano, & Audretsch, 2016; Bjørnskov & Foss, 2016), the findings also expand the idea that institutions affect not only entrepreneurship to reach higher economic growth but also intentions, which are needed to understand entrepreneurial decisions. Governments at the local and regional levels should keep this dynamism not only in the city of Barcelona but also in other regions to create entrepreneurial potential across Catalonia. Thus, people coming from abroad might find a good place for entrepreneurship in Catalonia, and those who already live in this autonomous community can take advantage of the next generations to increase the entrepreneurial orientations and strategies within firms. This will serve to keep improving the context, which is characterized by an entrepreneurial mindset.

Although these analyses and implications can be obtained and discussed thanks to the results, this research has certain limitations. For example, the analysis focused only on university students. Somehow, this can bias the perception of opportunity recognition, skills, and entrepreneurship status. However, other studies in Catalonia and Spain have shown that samples different from students show similar patterns (cf. Noguera et al., 2013). Additionally, students from other countries show similar behaviors regarding the main variables of interest (cf. Liñán, Nabi, & Krueger, 2013). Another limitation comes from the static treatment. Although it is observed that the intentions–behavior link emerges over a certain period of time, other techniques that capture dynamism would help us to understand better the speed of change, as time matters to consolidate any entrepreneurial activity (Lévesque & Stephan, 2019). Based on these limitations, future research could address and overcome important challenges when exploring intentions and behavior.

REFERENCES

Acs, Z. J., Braunerhjelm, P., Audretsch, D. B., & Carlsson, B. (2009). The knowledge spillover theory of entrepreneurship. *Small Business Economics*, *32*(1), 15–30. doi:10.100711187-008-9157-3

Adachi, T., & Hisada, T. (2017). Gender differences in entrepreneurship and intrapreneurship: An empirical analysis. *Small Business Economics*, *48*(3), 447–486. doi:10.100711187-016-9793-y

Ajzen, I. (1988). *Attitudes, personality, and behavior*. Dorsey Press.

Ajzen, I. (1991). The theory of planned behavior. *Organizational Behavior and Human Decision Processes*, *50*(2), 179–211. doi:10.1016/0749-5978(91)90020-T

Ajzen, I. (2001). Nature and operation of attitudes. *Annual Review of Psychology*, *52*(1), 27–58. doi:10.1146/annurev.psych.52.1.27 PMID:11148298

Ajzen, I. (2002). Residual effects of past on later behavior: Habituation and reasoned action perspective. *Personality and Social Psychology Review*, *6*(2), 107–122. doi:10.1207/S15327957PSPR0602_02

Ajzen, I., Czasch, C., & Flood, M. G. (2009). From intentions to behavior: Implementation intention, commitment, and conscientiousness. *Journal of Applied Social Psychology*, *39*(6), 1356–1372. doi:10.1111/j.1559-1816.2009.00485.x

Aldrich, H. E., & Zimmer, C. (1986). Entrepreneurship through social networks. In D. Sexton & R. Smilor (Eds.), *The Art and Science of Entrepreneurship* (pp. 3–23). Ballinger.

Alvarez, S., & Busenitz, L. (2001). The entrepreneurship of resource-based theory. *Journal of Management*, *27*(6), 755–775. doi:10.1177/014920630102700609

Aparicio, S., Urbano, D., & Audretsch, D. (2016). Institutional factors, opportunity entrepreneurship and economic growth: Panel data evidence. *Technological Forecasting and Social Change*, *102*, 45–61. doi:10.1016/j.techfore.2015.04.006

Aparicio, S., Urbano, D., & Stenholm, P. (2019). Institutions in Attracting the Entrepreneurial Potential: A Multilevel Approach. *Academy of Management Proceedings*, *2019*(1), 15408. doi:10.5465/AMBPP.2019.15408abstract

Ardichvili, A., Cardozo, R., & Ray, S. (2003). A theory of entrepreneurial opportunity identification and development. *Journal of Business Venturing*, *18*(1), 105–123. doi:10.1016/S0883-9026(01)00068-4

Armitage, C. J., & Conner, M. (2001). Efficacy of the theory of planned behavior: A meta-analytic review. *British Journal of Social Psychology*, *40*(4), 471–499. doi:10.1348/014466601164939 PMID:11795063

Asante, E. A., & Affum-Osei, E. (2019). Entrepreneurship as a career choice: The impact of locus of control on aspiring entrepreneurs' opportunity recognition. *Journal of Business Research*, *98*, 227–235. doi:10.1016/j.jbusres.2019.02.006

Audretsch, D. B. (2014). From the entrepreneurial university to the university for the entrepreneurial society. *The Journal of Technology Transfer*, *39*(3), 313–321. doi:10.100710961-012-9288-1

Autio, E., Pathak, S., & Wennberg, K. (2013). Consequences of cultural practices for entrepreneurial behaviors. *Journal of International Business Studies*, *44*(4), 334–362. doi:10.1057/jibs.2013.15

Bandura, A. (1977). Self-efficacy: Toward a unifying theory of behavioral change. *Psychological Review*, *84*(2), 191–215. doi:10.1037/0033-295X.84.2.191 PMID:847061

Bandura, A. (1989). Human agency in social-cognitive theory. *The American Psychologist*, *44*(9), 1175–1184. doi:10.1037/0003-066X.44.9.1175 PMID:2782727

Bandura, A. (1997). *Self-efðcacy: The Exercise of Control*. Freeman.

Bandura, A. (2006). Guide for constructing self-efficacy scales. *Self-Efficacy Beliefs of Adolescents*, *5*(1), 307-337.

Baron, R., & Shane, S. (2007). *Entrepreneurship: A Process Perspective*. Cengage Learning.

Bird, B. (1988). Implementing entrepreneurial ideas: The case for intention. *Academy of Management Review*, *13*(3), 442–453. doi:10.5465/amr.1988.4306970

Bjørnskov, C., & Foss, N. J. (2016). Institutions, entrepreneurship, and economic growth: What do we know and what do we still need to know? *The Academy of Management Perspectives*, *30*(3), 292–315. doi:10.5465/amp.2015.0135

Bosma, N. (2013). The Global Entrepreneurship Monitor (GEM) and its impact on entrepreneurship research. *Foundations and Trends in Entrepreneurship*, *9*(2), 143–248. doi:10.1561/0300000033

Boudreaux, C. J., Nikolaev, B. N., & Klein, P. (2019). Socio-cognitive traits and entrepreneurship: The moderating role of economic institutions. *Journal of Business Venturing*, *34*(1), 178–196. doi:10.1016/j.jbusvent.2018.08.003

Brieger, S. A., Bäro, A., Criaco, G., & Terjesen, S. A. (2020). (in press). Entrepreneurs' age, institutions, and social value creation goals: A multi-country study. *Small Business Economics*. Advance online publication. doi:10.100711187-020-00317-z

Bruton, G. D., Ahlstrom, D., & Li, H. L. (2010). Institutional theory and entrepreneurship: Where are we now, and where do we need to move in the future? *Entrepreneurship Theory and Practice*, *34*(3), 421–440. doi:10.1111/j.1540-6520.2010.00390.x

Busenitz, L. W., Gomez, C., & Spencer, J. W. (2000). Country institutional profiles: Unlocking entrepreneurial phenomena. *Academy of Management Journal*, *43*(5), 994–1003.

Carsrud, A., & Brännback, M. (2011). Entrepreneurial motivations: What do we still need to know? *Journal of Small Business Management*, *49*(1), 9–26. doi:10.1111/j.1540-627X.2010.00312.x

Casillas, J. C., Barbero, J. L., & Sapienza, H. J. (2015). Knowledge acquisition, learning, and the initial pace of internationalization. *International Business Review*, *24*(1), 102–114. doi:10.1016/j.ibusrev.2014.06.005

Casson, M. (1982). *The Entrepreneur: An Economic Theory*. Martin Robertson.

Cieślik, J., Kaciak, E., & van Stel, A. (2018). Country-level determinants and consequences of overconfidence in the ambitious entrepreneurship segment. *International Small Business Journal*, *36*(5), 473–499. doi:10.1177/0266242617748201

Coad, A., Frankish, J. S., Roberts, R. G., & Storey, D. J. (2016). Why should banks provide entrepreneurship training seminars? *International Small Business Journal*, *34*(6), 733–759. doi:10.1177/0266242615593138

Cooper, A. C., & Dunkelberg, W. C. (1987). Entrepreneurial Research: Old questions, new answers, and methodological issues. *American Journal of Small Business*, *11*(3), 11–24. doi:10.1177/104225878701100301

Cooper, A. C., Woo, C. Y., & Dunkelberg, W. C. (1988). Entrepreneurs' perceived chances for success. *Journal of Business Venturing*, *3*(2), 97–108. doi:10.1016/0883-9026(88)90020-1

De Carolis, D. M., & Saparito, P. (2006). Social capital, cognition, and entrepreneurial opportunities: A theoretical framework. *Entrepreneurship Theory and Practice*, *30*(1), 41–56. doi:10.1111/j.1540-6520.2006.00109.x

De Clercq, D., Danis, W. M., & Dakhli, M. (2010). The moderating effect of institutional context on the relationship between associational activity and new business activity in emerging economies. *International Business Review*, *19*(1), 85–101. doi:10.1016/j.ibusrev.2009.09.002

De Clercq, D., Lim, D. S., & Oh, C. H. (2013). Individual-Level Resources and New Business Activity: The Contingent Role of Institutional Context. *Entrepreneurship Theory and Practice*, *37*(2), 303–330. doi:10.1111/j.1540-6520.2011.00470.x

DeTienne, D. R., & Chandler, G. N. (2007). The role of gender in opportunity identification. *Entrepreneurship Theory and Practice*, *31*(3), 365–386. doi:10.1111/j.1540-6520.2007.00178.x

Fayolle, A., & Liñán, F. (2014). The future of research on entrepreneurial intentions. *Journal of Business Research*, *67*(5), 663–666. doi:10.1016/j.jbusres.2013.11.024

Fayolle, A., Liñán, F., & Moriano, J. A. (2014). Beyond entrepreneurial intentions: Values and motivations in entrepreneurship. *The International Entrepreneurship and Management Journal*, *10*(4), 679–689. doi:10.100711365-014-0306-7

Fishbein, M., & Ajzen, I. (1975). *Belief, attitude, intention and behavior: An introduction to theory and research*. Addison-Wesley.

Fishbein, M., & Ajzen, I. (2011). *Predicting and changing behavior: The reasoned action approach*. Psychology Press. doi:10.4324/9780203838020

Gaglio, C. M., & Katz, J. A. (2001). The Psychological Basis of Opportunity Identification: Entrepreneurial Alertness. *Small Business Economics*, *16*(2), 95–111. doi:10.1023/A:1011132102464

García-Cabrera, A. M., & García-Soto, M. G. (2008). Cultural differences and entrepreneurial behavior: An intra-country cross-cultural analysis in Cape Verde. *Entrepreneurship and Regional Development*, *20*(5), 451–483. doi:10.1080/08985620801912608

García-Rodríguez, F. J., Gutiérrez-Taño, D., & Ruiz-Rosa, I. (2019). Analysis of the Potential of Entrepreneurship Education in Young Children. *Entrepreneurship Research Journal*, *9*(1), 1–9. doi:10.1515/erj-2017-0064

Gielnik, M. M., Barabas, S., Frese, M., Namatovu-Dawa, R., Scholz, F. A., Metzger, J. R., & Walter, T. (2014). A temporal analysis of how entrepreneurial goal intentions, positive fantasies, and action planning affect starting a new venture and when the effects wear off. *Journal of Business Venturing*, *29*(6), 755–772. doi:10.1016/j.jbusvent.2013.09.002

Gnyawali, D. R., & Fogel, D. S. (1994). Environments for entrepreneurship development: Key dimensions and research implications. *Entrepreneurship Theory and Practice*, *18*(4), 43–62. doi:10.1177/104225879401800403

Goethner, M., Obschonka, M., Silbereisen, R. K., & Cantner, U. (2012). Scientists' transition to academic entrepreneurship: Economic and psychological determinants. *Journal of Economic Psychology*, *33*(3), 628–641. doi:10.1016/j.joep.2011.12.002

Gomez-Haro, S., Aragon-Correa, J. A., & Cordon-Pozo, E. (2011). Differentiating the effects of the institutional environment on corporate entrepreneurship. *Management Decision*, *49*(9-10), 1677–1693. doi:10.1108/00251741111183825

Gonzalez-Alvarez, N., & Solis-Rodriguez, V. (2011). Discovery of entrepreneurial opportunities: A gender perspective. *Industrial Management & Data Systems*, *111*(5-6), 755–775. doi:10.1108/02635571111137296

Granovetter, M. (1985). Economic action and social structure: The problem of embeddedness. *American Journal of Sociology*, *91*(3), 481–510. doi:10.1086/228311

Grimaldi, D., & Fernandez, V. (2017). The alignment of University curricula with the building of a Smart City: A case study from Barcelona. *Technological Forecasting and Social Change*, *123*, 298–306. doi:10.1016/j.techfore.2016.03.011

Hawkins, D. I. (1993). New business entrepreneurship in the Japanese economy. *Journal of Business Venturing*, *8*(2), 137–151. doi:10.1016/0883-9026(93)90016-X

Hayton, J. C., George, G., & Zahra, S. A. (2002). National culture and entrepreneurship: A review of behavioral research. *Entrepreneurship Theory and Practice*, *26*(4), 33–52. doi:10.1177/104225870202600403

Hoetker, G. (2007). The use of logit and probit models in strategic management research: Critical issues. *Strategic Management Journal*, *28*(4), 331–343. doi:10.1002mj.582

Hornsby, J. S., Kuratko, D. F., Shepherd, D. A., & Bott, J. P. (2009). Managers' corporate entrepreneurial actions: Examining perception and position. *Journal of Business Venturing*, *24*(3), 236–247. doi:10.1016/j.jbusvent.2008.03.002

Ireland, R. D., Hitt, M. A., & Simon, D. G. (2003). A model of strategic entrepreneurship: The construct and its dimensions. *Journal of Management*, *29*(6), 963–989. doi:10.1016/S0149-2063(03)00086-2

Karimi, S., Biemans, H. J., Lans, T., Chizari, M., & Mulder, M. (2016). The impact of entrepreneurship education: A study of Iranian students' entrepreneurial intentions and opportunity identification. *Journal of Small Business Management*, *54*(1), 187–209. doi:10.1111/jsbm.12137

Kautonen, T., Tornikoski, E. T., & Kibler, E. (2011). Entrepreneurial intentions in the third age: The impact of perceived age norms. *Small Business Economics*, *37*(2), 219–234. doi:10.100711187-009-9238-y

Kautonen, T., van Gelderen, M., & Fink, M. (2015). Robustness of the Theory of Planned Behavior in Predicting Entrepreneurial Intentions and Actions. *Entrepreneurship Theory and Practice*, *39*(3), 655–674. doi:10.1111/etap.12056

Kautonen, T., Van Gelderen, M., & Tornikoski, E. T. (2013). Predicting entrepreneurial behavior: A test of the theory of planned behavior. *Applied Economics*, *45*(6), 697–707. doi:10.1080/00036846.2011.610750

Keshk, O. M., Pollins, B. M., & Reuveny, R. (2004). Trade still follows the flag: The primacy of politics in a simultaneous model of interdependence and armed conflict. *The Journal of Politics*, *66*(4), 1155–1179. doi:10.1111/j.0022-3816.2004.00294.x

Kibler, E., Kautonen, T., & Fink, M. (2014). Regional social legitimacy of entrepreneurship: Implications for entrepreneurial intention and startup behavior. *Regional Studies*, *48*(6), 995–1015. doi:10.1080/00343404.2013.851373

Kirzner, I. M. (1979). *Perception, Opportunity and Profit*. University of Chicago Press.

Knight, G. A., & Cavusgil, S. T. (2004). Innovation, organizational capabilities, and the born-global firm. *Journal of International Business Studies*, *35*(2), 124–141. doi:10.1057/palgrave.jibs.8400071

Kostova, T., & Roth, K. (2002). Adoption of an organizational practice by subsidiaries of multinational corporations: Institutional and relational effects. *Academy of Management Journal*, *45*(1), 215–233.

Krueger, N. F. (1993). The impact of prior entrepreneurial exposure on perceptions of new venture feasibility and desirability. *Entrepreneurship Theory and Practice*, *18*(1), 5–21. doi:10.1177/104225879301800101

Krueger, N. F. Jr, & Brazeal, D. (1994). Entrepreneurial potential and potential entrepreneurs. *Entrepreneurship Theory and Practice*, *18*(3), 91–104. doi:10.1177/104225879401800307

Krueger, N. F. Jr, Reilly, M. D., & Carsrud, A. L. (2000). Competing models of entrepreneurial intentions. *Journal of Business Venturing*, *15*(5), 411–432. doi:10.1016/S0883-9026(98)00033-0

Kundu, S. C., & Rani, S. (2007). Human resources' self-esteem across gender and categories: A study. *Industrial Management & Data Systems*, *107*(9), 1366–1390. doi:10.1108/02635570710834018

Lévesque, M., & Stephan, U. (2019). (in press). It's Time We Talk About Time in Entrepreneurship. *Entrepreneurship Theory and Practice*. Advance online publication. doi:10.1177/1042258719839711

Liñán, F., & Chen, Y. W. (2009). Development and Cross-Cultural Application of a Specific Instrument to Measure Entrepreneurial Intentions. *Entrepreneurship Theory and Practice*, *33*(3), 593–617. doi:10.1111/j.1540-6520.2009.00318.x

Liñán, F., & Fayolle, A. (2015). A systematic literature review on entrepreneurial intentions: Citation, thematic analyses, and research agenda. *The International Entrepreneurship and Management Journal*, *11*(4), 907–933. doi:10.100711365-015-0356-5

Liñán, F., Nabi, G., & Krueger, N. (2013). British and Spanish entrepreneurial intentions: A comparative study. *Revista de Economía Mundial*, *33*, 73–103.

McGrath, R. G., Macmillan, I. C., Ai-Yuan Yang, E., & Tsai, W. (1992). Does culture endure or is it malleable? *Journal of Business Venturing*, *7*(6), 441–458. doi:10.1016/0883-9026(92)90019-N

Mueller, S. L., & Thomas, A. S. (2000). Culture and entrepreneurial potential: A nine country study of locus of control and innovativeness. *Journal of Business Venturing*, *16*(1), 51–75. doi:10.1016/S0883-9026(99)00039-7

Noguera, M., Alvarez, C., & Urbano, D. (2013). Socio-cultural factors and female entrepreneurship. *The International Entrepreneurship and Management Journal*, *9*(2), 183–197. doi:10.100711365-013-0251-x

North, D. C. (1990). *Institutions, institutional change and economic performance*. Cambridge University Press. doi:10.1017/CBO9780511808678

North, D. C. (2005). *Understanding the process of economic change*. Princeton University Press. doi:10.1515/9781400829484

Nowiński, W., & Haddoud, M. Y. (2019). The role of inspiring role models in enhancing entrepreneurial intention. *Journal of Business Research*, *96*, 183–193. doi:10.1016/j.jbusres.2018.11.005

Pahnke, A., & Welter, F. (2019). The German Mittelstand: Antithesis to Silicon Valley entrepreneurship? *Small Business Economics*, *52*(2), 345–358. doi:10.100711187-018-0095-4

Patel, P. C. (2019). Opportunity related absorptive capacity and entrepreneurial alertness. *The International Entrepreneurship and Management Journal*, *15*(1), 63–73. doi:10.100711365-018-0543-2

Piperopoulos, P., & Dimov, D. (2015). Burst bubbles or builds steam? Entrepreneurship education, entrepreneurial self-efficacy, and entrepreneurial intentions. *Journal of Small Business Management*, *53*(4), 970–985. doi:10.1111/jsbm.12116

Rauch, A., & Frese, M. (2007). Let's put the person back into entrepreneurship research: A meta-analysis on the relationship between business owners' personality traits, business creation, and success. *European Journal of Work and Organizational Psychology*, *16*(4), 353–385. doi:10.1080/13594320701595438

Reynolds, P. D. (2007). New firm creation in the United States a PSED I overview. *Foundations and Trends in Entrepreneurship*, *3*(1), 1–150. doi:10.1561/0300000010

Riviezzo, A., Santos, S. C., Liñán, F., Napolitano, M. R., & Fusco, F. (2019). European universities seeking entrepreneurial paths: The moderating effect of contextual variables on the entrepreneurial orientation-performance relationship. *Technological Forecasting and Social Change*, *141*, 232–248. doi:10.1016/j.techfore.2018.10.011

Roodman, D. (2011). Fitting Fully Observed recursive Mixed-process Models with CMP. *The Stata Journal*, *11*(2), 159–206. doi:10.1177/1536867X1101100202

Schillo, R. S., Persaud, A., & Jin, M. (2016). Entrepreneurial readiness in the context of national systems of entrepreneurship. *Small Business Economics*, *46*(4), 619–637. doi:10.100711187-016-9709-x

Schlaegel, C., & Koenig, M. (2014). Determinants of entrepreneurial intent: A meta-analytic test and integration of competing models. *Entrepreneurship Theory and Practice*, *38*(2), 291–332. doi:10.1111/etap.12087

Schmutzler, J., Andonova, V., & Diaz-Serrano, L. (2019). How context shapes entrepreneurial self-efficacy as a driver of entrepreneurial intentions: A multilevel approach. *Entrepreneurship Theory and Practice*, *43*(5), 880–920. doi:10.1177/1042258717753142

Sequeira, J., Mueller, S. L., & Mcgee, J. E. (2007). The iñuence of social ties and self-efficacy in forming entrepreneurial intentions and motivating nascent behavior. *Journal of Developmental Entrepreneurship*, *12*(3), 275–293. doi:10.1142/S108494670700068X

Shane, S. (1992). Why do some societies invent more than others? *Journal of Business Venturing*, *7*(1), 29–46. doi:10.1016/0883-9026(92)90033-N

Shane, S. (2012). Reflections on the 2010 AMR decade award: Delivering on the promise of entrepreneurship as a field of research. *Academy of Management Review*, *37*(1), 10–20. doi:10.5465/amr.2011.0078

Shane, S., & Venkataraman, S. (2000). The Promise of Entrepreneurship as a Field of Research. *Academy of Management Review*, *25*(1), 217–226. doi:10.5465/amr.2000.2791611

Shapero, A. (1975). The displaced, uncomfortable entrepreneur. *Psychology Today*, *9*, 83–88.

Shapero, A., & Sokol, L. (1982). Social dimensions of entrepreneurship. In C. A. Kent, D. L. Sexton, & K. H. Vesper (Eds.), *Encyclopedia of Entrepreneurship* (pp. 72–90). Prentice-Hall.

Shook, C. L., Priem, R. L., & McGee, J. E. (2003). Venture creation and the enterprising individual: A review and synthesis. *Journal of Management*, *29*(3), 379–399. doi:10.1016/S0149-2063(03)00016-3

Short, J. C., Ketchen, D. J. Jr, Combs, J. G., & Ireland, R. D. (2010). Research methods in entrepreneurship opportunities and challenges. *Organizational Research Methods*, *13*(1), 6–15. doi:10.1177/1094428109342448

Short, J. C., Ketchen, D. J. Jr, Shook, C. L., & Ireland, R. D. (2009). The concept of “opportunity” in entrepreneurship research: Past accomplishments and future challenges. *Journal of Management*, *36*(1), 40–65. doi:10.1177/0149206309342746

Spencer, J. W., & Gomez, C. (2004). The relationship among national institutional structures, economic factors, and domestic entrepreneurial activity: A multi-country study. *Journal of Business Research, 57*(10), 1098–1107. doi:10.1016/S0148-2963(03)00040-7

Stephan, U., & Uhlaner, L. M. (2010). Performance-based vs. socially supportive culture: A cross-national study of descriptive norms and entrepreneurship. *Journal of International Business Studies, 41*(8), 1347–1364. doi:10.1057/jibs.2010.14

Stevenson, H. H., Roberts, M. J., & Grousbeck, H. I. (1985). *New Business Ventures and the Entrepreneur*. Irwin.

Steyaert, C. (2007). Entrepreneuring' as a conceptual attractor? A review of process theories in 20 years of entrepreneurship studies. *Entrepreneurship and Regional Development, 19*(6), 453–477. doi:10.1080/08985620701671759

Stuetzer, M., Obschonka, M., Brixy, U., Sternberg, R., & Cantner, U. (2014). Regional characteristics, opportunity perception and entrepreneurial activities. *Small Business Economics, 42*(2), 221–244. doi:10.100711187-013-9488-6

Szerb, L., & Vörös, Z. (2019). The changing form of overconfidence and its effect on growth expectations at the early stages of startups. *Small Business Economics*. Advance online publication. doi:10.100711187-019-00297-9

Thornton, P. H., Ribeiro-Soriano, D., & Urbano, D. (2011). Socio-cultural factors and entrepreneurial activity: An overview. *International Small Business Journal, 29*(2), 105–118. doi:10.1177/0266242610391930

Torres, P., & Augusto, M. (2019). Cultural configurations and entrepreneurial realisation. *International Journal of Entrepreneurial Behaviour & Research, 25*(1), 112–128. doi:10.1108/IJEBR-12-2017-0525

Tsai, K. H., Chang, H. C., & Peng, C. Y. (2016). Refining the linkage between perceived capability and entrepreneurial intention: Roles of perceived opportunity, fear of failure, and gender. *The International Entrepreneurship and Management Journal, 12*(4), 1127–1145. doi:10.100711365-016-0383-x

Urbano, D. (2006). *New business creation in Catalonia: Support measures and attitudes towards entrepreneurship*. CIDEM.

Urbano, D., & Alvarez, C. (2014). Institutional dimensions and entrepreneurial activity: An international study. *Small Business Economics, 42*(4), 703–716. doi:10.100711187-013-9523-7

Urbano, D., & Aparicio, S. (2016). Entrepreneurship capital types and economic growth: International evidence. *Technological Forecasting and Social Change, 102*, 34–44. doi:10.1016/j.techfore.2015.02.018

Urbano, D., Aparicio, S., & Audretsch, D. (2019). Twenty-five years of research on institutions, entrepreneurship, and economic growth: What has been learned? *Small Business Economics, 53*(1), 21–49. doi:10.100711187-018-0038-0

Urbano, D., Aparicio, S., Guerrero, M., Noguera, M., & Torrent-Sellens, J. (2017). Institutional determinants of student employer entrepreneurs at Catalan universities. *Technological Forecasting and Social Change, 123*, 271–282. doi:10.1016/j.techfore.2016.06.021

Urbano, D., Audretsch, D., Aparicio, S., & Noguera, M. (2019). (in press). Does entrepreneurial activity matter for economic growth in developing countries? The role of the institutional environment. *The International Entrepreneurship and Management Journal*. Advance online publication. doi:10.100711365-019-00621-5

Urbano, D., Toledano, N., & Ribeiro-Soriano, D. (2011). Socio-cultural factors and transnational entrepreneurship: A multiple case study in Spain. *International Small Business Journal*, *29*(2), 119–134. doi:10.1177/0266242610391934

Urbano, D., Turro, A., & Aparicio, S. (2019). (in press). Innovation through R&D activities in the European context: Antecedents and consequences. *The Journal of Technology Transfer*. Advance online publication. doi:10.100710961-019-09752-x

Van Gelderen, M., Kautonen, T., & Fink, M. (2015). From entrepreneurial intentions to actions: Self-control and action-related doubt, fear, and aversion. *Journal of Business Venturing*, *30*(5), 655–673. doi:10.1016/j.jbusvent.2015.01.003

Venkataraman, S. (1997). The distinctive domain of entrepreneurship research: an editor's perspective. In J. Katz & R. Brockhaus (Eds.), *Advances in Entrepreneurship* (Vol. 3, pp. 119–138). Firm Emergence, and Growth.

Verheul, I., Block, J., Burmeister-Lamp, K., Thurik, R., Tiemeier, H., & Turturea, R. (2015). ADHD-like behavior and entrepreneurial intentions. *Small Business Economics*, *45*(1), 85–101. doi:10.100711187-015-9642-4

Wennekers, S., van Stel, A., Thurik, R., & Reynolds, P. (2005). Nascent entrepreneurship and the level of economic development. *Small Business Economics*, *24*(3), 293–309. doi:10.100711187-005-1994-8

Wiersema, M. F., & Bowen, H. P. (2009). The use of limited dependent variable techniques in strategy research: Issues and methods. *Strategic Management Journal*, *30*(6), 679–692. doi:10.1002mj.758

Wilson, F., Kickul, J., & Marlino, D. (2007). Gender, entrepreneurial self-efficacy, and entrepreneurial career intentions: Implications for entrepreneurship education. *Entrepreneurship Theory and Practice*, *31*(3), 387–406. doi:10.1111/j.1540-6520.2007.00179.x

Wilson, F., Marlino, D., & Kickul, J. (2004). Our entrepreneurial future: Examining the diverse attitudes and motivations of teens across gender and ethnic identity. *Journal of Developmental Entrepreneurship*, *9*(3), 177–197.

Wood, R., & Bandura, A. (1989). Social cognitive theory of organizational management. *Academy of Management Review*, *14*(3), 361–384. doi:10.5465/amr.1989.4279067

Zhao, H., Seibert, S. E., & Hills, G. E. (2005). The mediating role of self-efficacy in the development of entrepreneurial intentions. *The Journal of Applied Psychology*, *90*(6), 1265–1272. doi:10.1037/0021-9010.90.6.1265 PMID:16316279

KEY TERMS AND DEFINITIONS

Binomial Logit Regression: Econometric technique focused on estimating the probability of an event happening by assuming a logistic distribution of the sample.

CMP: Acronym of conditional mixed process, it consists of a statistical technique used jointly with simultaneous equation systems and defined by having two advantages: a recursive multi-stage estimation within a simultaneous equation system and a comprehensive observation of the endogenous variables.

Embeddedness: It is the dependence of a phenomenon on its environment.

Entrepreneurial Opportunity: This situation occurs when new products, services, and organizational methods can be launched into the market to create value.

Hofstede's Cultural Dimensions Theory: It is a framework defined to understand cultural differences and attitudes on business across countries.

Perceived Desirability: It denotes the extent to which individuals consider an option to become entrepreneurs.

Perceived Feasibility: It refers to how individuals consider they have the skills and capacities to become entrepreneurs.

Propensity to Act: It defines how individuals are willing to explore and carry out entrepreneurial opportunities.

Chapter 8
The Blue Economy and Its Long-Term Competitive Advantage:
An Examination of China's Coastal Tourism

Haoming Zhang
Wenzhou-Kean University, China

Rob Kim Marjerison
https://orcid.org/0000-0003-1181-8695
Wenzhou-Kean University, China

Yuxi Zhao
Wenzhou-Kean University, China

ABSTRACT

This chapter seeks to determine whether China's coastal tourism industry can remain competitive in the long run under the blue economy ideology. Current literature claims that when the ocean becomes over-commercialized by the tourism industry, it can potentially lose its pristine amenities, which tourists are attracted to in the first place. By surveying both coastal tourists and residents regarding their stakeholders, coastal resources, and tourism service characteristics, this chapter concludes that such a threat is not impeding progress because coastal tourists and residents have not only overlapping desires but also have interchangeable identities. By conducting tourism service quality management, China's coastal regions have the potential to satisfy both tourists and residents' needs simultaneously by taking advantage of the blue economy transition.

DOI: 10.4018/978-1-7998-5036-6.ch008

INTRODUCTION

The phrase blue economy has become more commonly used in the past decades (Garland, Axon, Graziano, Morrissey, & Heidkamp, 2019). The ocean is a priceless heritage of human beings (Pardo, 1984). The amenity value of the ocean has traditionally been regarded as something outside of the economic scope. It was only since the post-productivist era that it has been commercialized and incorporated into the tourism industry (Garland et al., 2019). With China gradually losing its comparative advantage in manufacturing, many Chinese entrepreneurs have begun to divert their investments to ocean-based tourism with hopes of obtaining more sustainable growth.

Can the ocean tourism-based blue economy create sustainable profit as these Chinese entrepreneurs anticipate? Bari (2017) believes so because the blue economy differs from the traditional marine economy. It aims to achieve long-term sustainability by exploring the ocean in a more technology-based, connotative, and environmentally friendly way (Liu, 2014). In other words, if entrepreneurial innovations can make sure that the ocean's amenity value always outweighs its productive value, and if a more economic profit can be created from conserving the ocean resources rather than destroying them, no one would have the incentive to deviate from the path of sustainable growth. As a result, the blue economy can be thought of as an economic development model that creates maximum profit from marine resources in the long run (Bari, 2017).

However, not everyone is this optimistic. Butler (1980) believes that even if the coastal natural resources could be sustainable, the tourism industry is unable to. This is because the tourism industry is not only rooted in the natural coastal heritage but, more importantly, is also rooted in the social heritage of these coasts. The essence of tourism services is not selling the ocean's natural amenities but selling the "rural idyll" coastal lifestyle to city dwellers. From this perspective, "the tourism destination areas carry with them the potential seeds of their own destruction, as they allow themselves to become more commercialized and lose their qualities which originally attracted tourists." (Butler, 1980, p. 6).

There is an element of truth in both optimistic and pessimistic views. Whether the optimistic or pessimistic results occur largely depends on which aspects of the socio-natural amenity of the ocean is commercialized to serve different type of tourists by providing certain recreational services. As a result, the following three components of the issue are of great importance (Figure 1):

1. The characteristics of the stakeholders, including both the tourists and the local residents
2. The characteristics of the coastal resources
3. The characteristics of the tourism services provided

The objective of this chapter is to use the quality management's lens to explore the possibility of maintaining long-term competitive advantages in China's coastal tourism industry. This chapter is organized as follows: first, the literature review synthesizes current literature regarding the aforementioned aspects. Second, this chapter describes the objectives and methodology applied in empirical research. Third, it summarizes the results and consequently draws conclusions and identifies future topics of research.

Figure 1. Three aspects of characteristics associated with the success of the blue economy

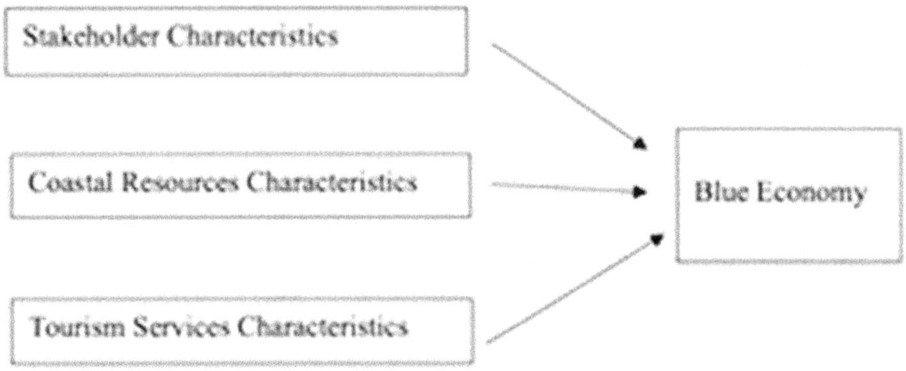

LITERATURE REVIEW

The Characteristics of the Stakeholders

Butler (1980) divides the development of local tourism into five stages: development stage, consolidation stage, stagnation stage, decline stage, and rejuvenation stage (if applicable). Commercialization begins in the development stage, although it may not be welcomed alike by the local population. A local resident's discontent typically occurs in the consolidation stage. This local resident's accessibility to natural amenities is typically limited in the stagnation stage following the exploitation of natural resources. At this point, the commercialization process of tourism comes to a turning point: on the one hand, the destination image has been commercialized to the maximum extent to satisfy the tourists' needs; on the other hand, the destination image has gradually lost its "natural capital" since the original natural, built, and social attractions have gradually been superseded by "commercialized facilities." As a result, the decline stage could potentially approach. If this tourist destination wants to rejuvenate, it can either be turned into a larger attraction or take advantage of previously untapped coastal resources.

Does Butler's (1980) model apply to the Chinese coastal tourism industry? Butler's (1980) model depends on three underlying assumptions:

1. Tourism services are created to give priority to tourists with higher consumption willingness than those with lower consumption willingness.
2. Tourism services are created in a way that gives priority to tourists from the outside rather than to residents who were born in the coastal region.
3. The duality between tourists' consumption-oriented needs and the local residents' traditional means of living cannot be mitigated.

In Chinese coastal regions, however, these three assumptions may or may not be valid. Coastal areas of China have gone through mass urbanization in the past few decades. Due to China's planned economy and land ownership legacy, coastal fishermen are generally given a large sum of money when their status turns to urban residents under the Chinese hukou system[1]. It is not uncommon that a person who used to be a poor rural fisherman has now invested his monetary compensation received during urbanization into coastal tourism development and can now visit the seashore as a tourist for the first time. As a result, the three roles in Butler's model: the local fisherman, tourism investors, and tourists may likely be the same person considering the Hukou system. This unique socio-economic background in China makes tourism service quality management more complicated.

The Characteristics of the Coastal Resources

With its long coastline combined with the largest population in the world, China has great potential to transit to the blue economy (Liu, Heilig, Chen, & Heino, 2007). From the supply side, China is one of the largest oceanic countries in the world (Gu, & Wong, 2008) with 26 major coastal cities. Some of these coastal cities, such as Shanghai, Guangzhou, and Shenzhen have already been major global cities since the industrial age. From the demand side, the number of middle-class Chinese citizens who have both money and time to visit coastal towns as tourists has increased tremendously.

According to Ma (2019), from March 2017 to February 2018, there were about 1.06 billion tourists who visited the Chinese coastal cities. Their destinations covered nine provinces and more than 50 coastal cities, creating enormous amounts of regional wealth. The majority of the tourists chose to visit cities located along the southern Chinese coastline, such as Sanya and Guangdong. There is an obvious seasonal preference with summer and winter visitors being much more common than spring and late autumn visitors.

The Characteristics of the Tourism Services Provided

The blue economy attracts entrepreneurs from other industries to take advantage of this new business opportunity during the amenity transition stage (Cortes-Jimenez, 2008). Schumpeter (1968) points out that entrepreneurs are "creative destructors," causing a continual disturbance to the equilibrium of the market by setting new standards and shifting the preferences of their customers. In the tourism industry, this creative destruction is represented by the reshaping of natural and cultural heritage to create innovative products and services for tourists (Hjalager, 2010). Smith (1994) claims that the key elements of the tourism industry include physical plant (natural and social resources), service (the physical plant requires service to make it marketable), hospitality (the attitude or style with which the service is performed), freedom of choice (tourists' choice combinations), and involvement (not only tourists' physical involvement but emotional engagement as well). Additionally, entrepreneurs' activities consist of four stages: primary inputs (resources, such as trees), intermediate inputs (facilities, such as a park), intermediate outputs (services, such as guide services), and the final outputs (experiences, such as relaxation). What happens during tourism's entrepreneurial creative destruction innovations process is explained as follows:

1. The "physical plants" as "primary inputs" are turned into "intermediate inputs" through investing in technologies (such as building tourism infrastructure) and marketing strategies (such as destination branding).
2. "Service" and "hospitality" are added as "intermediate inputs" and are processed into the "intermediate outputs."
3. When "primary inputs" are turned into "intermediate inputs," the coastal community's traditional natural and social resources are "destroyed."

4. When "service" and "hospitality" are added, a new social relation is "created" by "destroying" the old one.

Following this logic, blue economy entrepreneurs are both "creative" in terms of investing in new technologies and marketing strategies, yet "destructive" in the way that they alter the socio-environmental fabrics of the coastal community.

In addition to creative destruction, tourism entrepreneurs also face "co-opetition" in their tourism service provisions (Nalebuff, & Brandenburger, 2002). On the one hand, tourism entrepreneurs compete with each other by continuously coming up with innovative coastal services (Wahab & Cooper, 2014) such as swimming, boating, fishing, diving, surfing, sandboarding, sail boating, four-wheel driving, walking, camping, horse-riding, and sightseeing (Priskin, 2003). On the other hand, since tourism products are a package, and a tourist may not be able to purchase a twilight trek tour without obtaining a secured hotel room that day (Sundbo, Orfila-Sintes, & Sorensen, 2007), tourism firms must collaborate to come up with new tourism service packages (Hjalager, 2010). This "co-opetition" characteristic determines the types of services provided in the coastal region, also determining the competitive advantages of China's blue economy in general.

OBJECTIVE AND METHODOLOGY

The authors obtained literature from the characteristics of the stakeholders, coastal resources, and tourism services, and this shows three distinct aspects of the complexity of the tourism service quality management. Can China's tourism industry evade Butler (1980)'s warning and enjoy sustainable growth in the long run? The answer largely depends on how tourism services balance the interests of different stakeholder groups. This chapter aims to use China's empirical data to answer the following three research questions:

1. Do tourists with higher consumption intentions and lower consumption intentions have the same desire for the coastal regions?
2. Do external tourists and local residents have the same desire for the coastal regions?
3. Do tourists, either with higher or lower consumption intentions, and either with other coastal or inland residency, desire to migrate to the tourist destination and become residents?

A survey questionnaire with 14 multiple-choice questions (with sub-questions) is designed to collect information about stakeholders, coastal resources, and tourism services characteristics. The majority of questions are formatted as a 5-point Likert scale with fill-in-the-bubble style questions (Table 1). This 5-point Likert scale helps respondents explain their thoughts more conveniently and comprehensively (Joshi, Kale, Chandel, & Pal, 2015).

Table 1. 5-point Likert scale with fill-in-the-bubble style questions

Very not Likely	Not Likely	Normal	Likely	Very Likely
o	o	o	o	o

Survey Questions Related to Stakeholder Characteristics

The first eight questions and the last question are related to stakeholder characteristics. Question one to four are demographic questions asking respondents about their gender, age, occupation, and income. Since respondents are selected from a homogenous demographic group, the purpose of these questions is to test this homogeneity.

Question five, six, seven, eight, and fourteen ask stakeholders whether they live or work in the coastal region, how often they visit the coastal area, and how high their consumption willingness is. These questions reflect the stakeholder's identity and connection with the coastal region. All the respondents are tourists, but some of them are also local residents. Different degrees of their relationship to the territory can be used as the criteria that separate the stakeholders into the following three groups:

1. Tourists who are coastal residents.
2. Tourists who are non-coastal residents but want to migrate to the coastal regions.
3. Tourists who are non-coastal residents and do not want to migrate to the coastal regions

Because local residents can be marginalized during the amenity transition, this may be key to understanding the tourism industry's long-term sustainability potential. These questions are essential in distinguishing tourists among different interest groups.

Survey Questions Related to Coastal Resources Characteristics

Question nine and ten are related to coastal resources. Question nine asks respondents when they travel to coastal regions for tourism purposes. Five choices, including "1 = very not likely", "2 = not likely", "3 = normal", "4 = likely", and "5 = very likely," are provided to measure the tourists' seasonal preference. The following five seasonal periods are asked:

- Spring (April-May)
- Early summer (May-July)
- Summer (July-August)
- Autumn (August-October)
- Winter (October-April)

Generally speaking, people prefer to visit coastal areas during the summer. However, in the Chinese scenario, because there are two week-long holidays of National Day and Chinese New Year, people prefer to visit in the fall and winter. Some tourists likely prefer to see the coastal regions during fall and winter to enjoy the time convenience and off-season discounts. This question indirectly reflects tourists' attitudes towards the ocean. Whether they would like to pay more in exchange for the best ocean amenities, or they would want to sacrifice some ocean amenities in exchange for convenience or lower costs.

Question ten asks respondents which coastal region they would like to visit more. Five choices including "1 = very not likely", "2 = not likely", "3 = normal", "4 = likely", and "5 = very likely" are provided to all four Chinese coastal regions:

- East China Sea
- South China Sea
- Huang Hai
- Bohai

China's long continental coast provides a wide selection for tourists. Because most respondents are located in southern China, the East China Sea is the closet, the South China Sea is a little bit farther away, but Bohai in the northern part of China is the farthest. One interesting phenomenon to note is that respondents living in southern China travel long distances to coastal tourism sites in northern China. One potential explanation for this is that although the ocean as a natural resource is the same, different cultural amenities attract these tourists.

Survey Questions Related to Tourism Service Characteristics

Question eleven to thirteen are related to the tourism services provided. Question eleven asks the respondents about their preferred time span to visit in a single trip. The choices provided include

- No more than 24 hours
- 1 to 2 days
- 3 to 7 days
- More than 7 days

The duration of their stay is an important indicator of what tourists want to get out of the trip because they can only understand the coastal community in-depth, given sufficient time immersed in the local culture.

Question twelve is about accommodation services purchased in the coastal regions, including the following options:

- Homestay
- Hotel
- Purchased home in the coastal region
- Stay with friends or family
- Resorts

These accommodation options reflect tourists' preferences and attitudes toward the coastal regions. Respondents choosing "homestay" or "stay with friends or family" reveal their social connections to the coastal area. By selecting "a purchased home in the coastal region," respondents show their love or attachment to the coastal region. By choosing "hotel" or "resorts," a respondent reflects their external identity to the coastal area.

Question thirteen asks respondents the recreation services they purchase in the coastal regions. Five choices including "1 = very not likely", "2 = not likely", "3 = normal", "4 = likely", and "5 = very likely" are provided to ask about the following eight recreational activities:

- Real estate investment
- Ship traveling
- Sail boating/Surfing
- Swimming
- Diving
- Fishing
- Sightseeing
- Beach Sports

These recreational activities can be found in almost every Chinese coastal region. The demand for these recreational activities is of great importance to tourism service providers.

RESULTS

A total of 201 usable survey responses were collected. The majority of the survey respondents are from Zhejiang Province, located in southern China. There are also a few survey respondents who are from foreign countries such as the U.S and Australia.

Regarding stakeholder characteristics, the majority of survey respondents are college students ranging from 18 to 25 years of age. Some university faculty members and business professionals also participated in the survey. The demographics of the survey respondents are shown in Table 2 and Figure 2.

Table 2. Survey respondent's gender and age distribution

Age Groups	Female	Percentage	Male	Percentage
<18	4	2.0%	5	2.5%
18-25	59	29.4%	61	30.3%
26-30	16	8.0%	22	10.9%
31-40	13	6.5%	8	4.0%
41-50	6	3.0%	5	2.5%
>50	1	0.5%	1	0.5%

Regarding coastal resources characteristics, tables 2 and 3 show how respondents rank their preference (1 = very not likely, 2 = not likely, 3 = normal, 4 = likely, 5 = very likely) to coastal regions visits according to timing and location. Respondents are more likely to see coastal areas in the summer (May to August) (Table 3) and more likely to visit coastal regions closer to their current residential locations

Figure 2. Survey respondent's occupation distribution

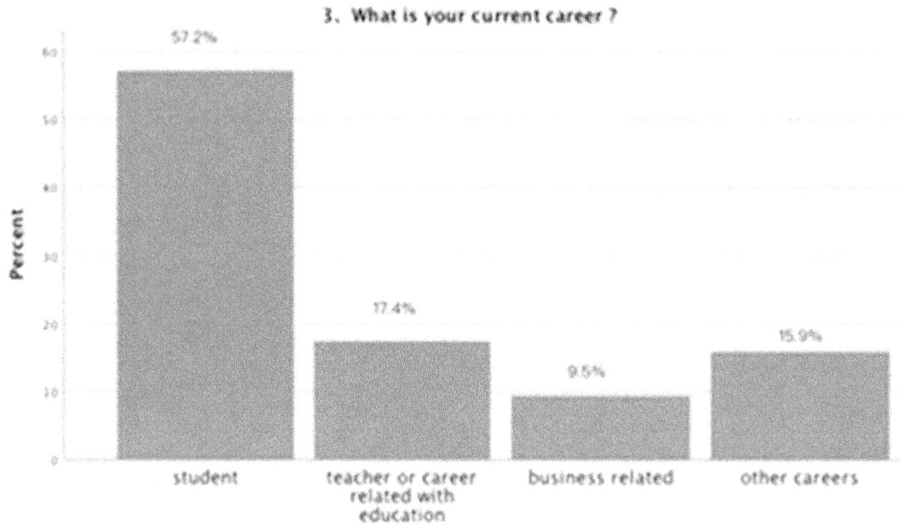

(the East China Sea and Huanghai) (Table 4). This shows that respondents want to enjoy the natural amenities of the ocean at its peak season at the closest location in general.

Table 3. Coastal visit preferences by timing

	Tourism Season				Non-tourism Season
	Spring (April-May)	Early Summer (May-July)	Late Summer (July-August)	Fall (August-October)	Winter (October-April)
Mean	3.23	3.55	3.79	3.35	2.91
Median	3	4	4	4	3

Table 4. Coastal visit preferences by location

	Bohai	Huanghai	East China Sea	South China Sea
Mean	3.08	3.57	3.83	3.18
Median	3	4	4	3

Regarding tourism service characteristics, the vast majority (87.1%) of respondents would like to spend their vacations in coastal regions for 1–7 days (Figure 3).

Figure 3. Survey respondent's vacation length distribution

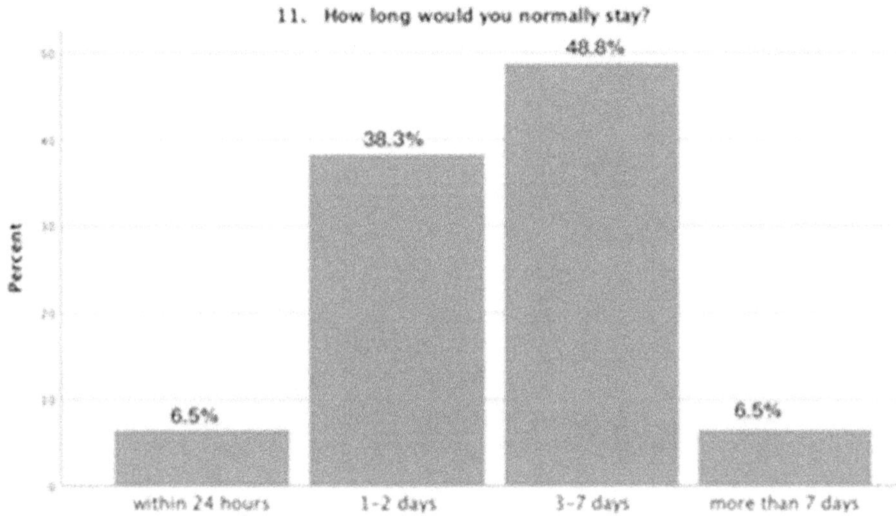

For accommodations, about one third (32.3%) of them chose homestay, about another one third (31.8%) chose hotel, and the rest (35.8%) chose other accommodation option such as staying in their own vacation home, staying with friends, or family, or staying in a resort (Figure 4). For the activities conducted in the coastal region (Table 5), three things are found: first, the most popular ranked recreational activities are sightseeing (mean 3.98), swimming (mean 3.72), and beach sports (mean 3.71). Second, for the other ocean recreational activities, according to Chinese culture, the "high end" recreational activities such as sail boating/surfing are liked the most (mean 3.54); the "middle class" recreational activities such as ship travel (mean: 3.54) and diving (mean: 3.33) are also relatively popular; and the "grass-root" recreational activities such as fishing are relatively unpopular (mean: 3.30). This cultural understanding is deeply rooted in the recent urbanization in China. Some tourists, especially those who used to reside in the coastal rural communities, may have just abandoned fishing as an occupation years ago. Third, real estate investment is ranked the least popular (mean: 2.64). This is understandable because not everyone can afford a vacation home. Empirical findings concerning recreational activity choices agree with cultural preferences in China.

Figure 4. Survey respondent's accommodation choice distribution

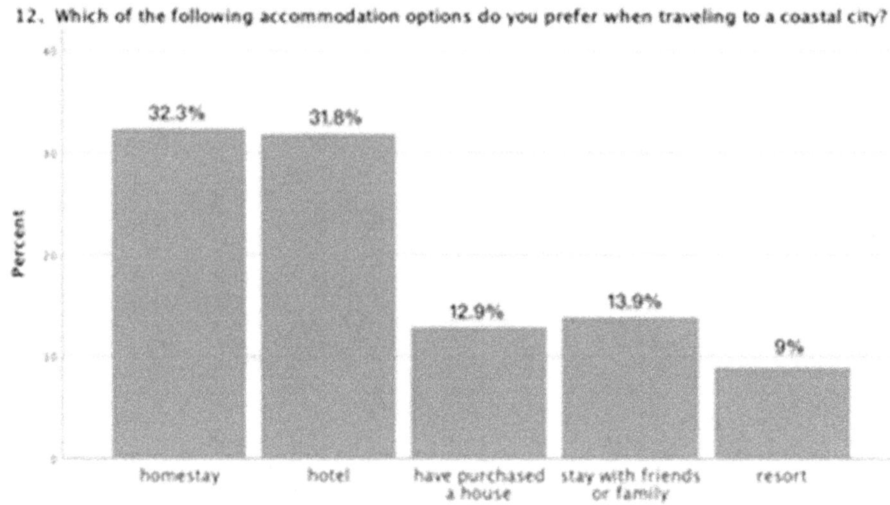

Table 5. Survey respondent's recreational activity choice distribution

	Real estate investment	Ship traveling	Sail boating / surfing	Swimming
Mean	2.64	3.37	3.54	3.72
Median	3	3	4	4
	Diving	Fishing	Sightseeing	Beach sports
Mean	3.33	3.30	3.98	3.71
Median	4	3	4	4

In summary, the exploratory findings from stakeholder, coastal resources, and tourism service characteristics show that younger generations living in southern China generally like to visit coastal regions that are closer to their homes during the summer tourism peak season. They spend around one week per trip on average, choosing to reside in a hotel or homestay for accommodation. They enjoy beach activities such as sightseeing, swimming, and beach sports the most. Still, they also prefer more "high-end" coastal activities such as boating or surfing based on Chinese cultural understandings.

Do Tourists with Higher Consumption Intentions and Lower Consumption Intentions Have the Same Desire for the Coastal Regions?

According to question fourteen, "how much do you think that your consumption in coastal cities can promote the development of a coastal economy?", respondents who have chosen "Strongly Agree" (34%, n=68) and respondents who have not selected "Strongly Agree" (67%, n=133) are divided into two groups, and their answers are compared. Because respondents purchase different tourism services during different time spans at various locations, subjective judgment is used as an approximation.

Table 6. Coastal tourism timing preference differences between tourists with different consumption intentions

	Tourism Season				**Non-tourism Season**
	Spring (April-May)	**Early Summer (May-July)**	**Late Summer (July-August)**	**Autumn (August-October)**	**Winter (October-April)**
Mean of "high expenditure" Group	3.4	3.91	4.07	3.47	2.78
Mean of "low expenditure" Group	3.15	3.36	3.64	3.29	2.97
Chi-square p value	0.003	<0.001	0.017	0.002	<0.001

Table 7. Coastal tourism location preference differences between tourists with different consumption intentions

	Bohai	**Huanghai**	**East China Sea**	**South China Sea**
Mean of "high expenditure" Group	3.28	3.37	3.50	3.79
Mean of "low expenditure" Group	2.98	3.08	3.71	3.84
Chi-square p-value	<0.001	<0.001	0.211	0.938

Comparing stakeholder characteristics, tourists from the two expenditure groups have no significant difference in age, gender, and occupations. More importantly, tourists who "strongly agree" that their consumption contributes to the local economy have no significant difference in their monthly household income. This applies to the other expenditure group as well. This satisfies our assumption that the two comparing samples of tourists come from similar socio-economic backgrounds.

Comparing coastal resource characteristics, these two groups have shown significant differences in coastal resource usage in terms of timing and location. In terms of timing (Table 6), tourists in the higher expenditure group are significantly more likely to visit coastal regions during peak tourism season (which spans from late spring to early autumn), but considerably less likely to see coastal areas during the non-tourism season (winter). This reveals an interesting fact that although both tourist groups prefer summer, which is the best season to enjoy the ocean, tourists in the "low expenditure" groups are more likely to take advantage of the off-season discount by visiting the seashore during the winter. In terms of location (Table 7), another exciting and related result is found. Since the vast majority of survey respondents live in southern China, the South China Sea is not very far away. It is a tropical ocean where tourists can enjoy almost all summer recreational activities year-round.

Interestingly, some tourists who prefer to visit the South China Sea also like to see the coastal regions in the winter ($p<0.001$)(Table 8). Moreover, these tourists are more likely to identify themselves in the low expenditure group. It is possible that these tourists deliberately arrange this to take advantage of the two of the week-long national holidays in the fall and winter and to enjoy the off-season prices of coastal tourism at the same time.

Comparing tourism service characteristics, these two groups have also shown significant differences in terms of which accommodations or recreational services are purchased and how long. To be specific, three differences are revealed by this comparison. First, tourists from higher and lower expenditure groups spend their vacation holidays in the coastal region for a significantly different period of time (p=0.016). The majority (70.6%) of tourists from the higher expenditure group spend 3–7 days or more in the coastal region per trip. In comparison, the majority (52.7%) of tourists from the lower expenditure group spend less than two days in the coastal region per trip (table 7). The second difference comes from the tourist activities performed by tourists in the two groups. For all the eight activities including (1) real estate, (2) ship traveling, (3) sailboating/surfing, (4) swimming, (5) diving, (6) fishing, (7) sightseeing, and (8) beach sports, tourists from the higher expenditure group have a higher participation possibility (Table 8) than the lower expenditure group. The third difference (p=0.041) presents itself through the tourists' accommodation preferences in the resort category. Resort refers to a one-stop commercial establishment that provides both food, drink, lodging, sports, entertainment, and so on. The resort is not a popular choice of accommodations for both groups; however, tourists in the higher expenditure group have significantly higher preferences for such a relatively luxurious accommodation option (Table 9).

Table 8. Coastal tourism length of stay preference differences between tourists with different consumption intentions

	No more than 24 hours	1 to 2 days	3 to 7 days	More than 7 days
Mean of "high expenditure" Group	6%	23%	62%	9%
Mean of "low expenditure" Group	7%	46%	42%	5%

Table 9. Differences in coastal tourism accommodation preference between tourists with different consumption intentions

	Real estate investment	Ship traveling	Sail boating / surfing	Swimming
Mean of "high expenditure" Group	2.65	3.53	3.78	4.12
Mean of "low expenditure" Group	2.62	3.29	3.42	3.52
Chi-square p value	0.018	<0.001	0.006	<0.001
	Diving	Fishing	Sightseeing	Beach sports
Mean of "high expenditure" Group	3.57	3.53	4.21	4.00
Mean of "low expenditure" Group	3.21	3.19	3.86	3.56
Chi-square p-value	0.001	0.003	<0.001	<0.001

In summary, empirical data suggest that tourists with higher consumption intentions and lower consumption intentions differ in that the latter group visit coastal tourism sites during the off-season, spend less vacation time, and purchases less recreational activities. Such differences are more of a consumer choice's issue, and not a social marginalization and exclusion issue, as Butler (1980) claims.

Do External Tourists and Local Residents Have the Same Desire for the Coastal Regions?

Social marginalization and exclusion are not found among tourists themselves, but how about between external tourists and local residents? To test whether Butler (1980)'s concerns apply to Chinese coastal tourism regions or not, according to question five, "are you working/living in a coastal city?," respondents who have chosen "Yes" (41%, n=83) and respondents who chose "No" (59%, n=118) are divided into two groups for comparison.

Comparing stakeholder characteristics, the resident and non-resident groups show no significant differences in demographic variables, including age, gender, occupation, and household incomes. Generally speaking, people who live in China's coastal regions usually have higher incomes. Due to the sampling procedure and size, no such difference is found. This again ensures that these two groups are assumed to have a homogeneous socio-economic background.

Comparing coastal resources characteristics, significant differences are found among the resident and the non-resident groups regarding their usage of coastal resources—both in terms of timing and location (Table 10). First, concerning the timing, when asked whether they would like to visit the coastal regions as a tourist during the fall, 13% of the respondents in the resident group chose "1 = very not likely" and "2 = not likely." In comparison, 29% of the respondents in the non-resident group chose "1 = very not likely" and "2 = not likely. Meanwhile, 59% of the respondents in the resident group chose "4 = likely" and "5 = very likely," while 47% of the respondents in the non-resident group chose "4 = likely" and "5 = very likely". When asked whether they would like to visit the coastal regions as a tourist during the winter, 28% of the respondents in the resident group chose "1 = very not likely" and "2 = not likely." In comparison, 43% of the respondents in the non-resident group chose "1 = very not likely" and "2 = not likely". 46% of the respondents in the resident group chose "4 = likely" and "5 = very likely," while 24% of the respondents in the non-resident group chose "4 = likely" and "5 = very likely". This shows that coastal region residents are more likely to visit the beach and use tourism services during both the fall season (p=0.024) and the winter seasons (p=0.008). This is understandable because, for residents, coastal regions are regarded as part of their community, which they would like to explore even during the off-seasons. Second, in terms of location, a significantly larger percentage of respondents in the non-resident group are willing to visit Bohai— the coastal region that is the furthest away from the respondents' current location (Table 9). Specifically, 31% of the respondents in the resident group chose "1 = very not likely" and "2 = not likely," while 22% of the respondents in the non-resident group chose "1 = very not likely" and "2 = not likely". Meanwhile, 26% of the respondents in the resident group chose "4 = likely" and "5 = very likely," while 36% of the respondents in the non-resident group chose "4 = likely" and "5 = very likely." This shows that the residents are less likely (p=0.034) to travel long distances to vacation in a region like their own home communities.

Table 10. Coastal tourism timing preference differences between tourists and residents

	Timing		Location
	Autumn (August-October)	Winter (October-April)	Bohai
Mean of the resident Group	3.58	3.22	2.86
Mean of the Non-resident Group	3.19	2.69	3.24
Chi-square p-value	0.024	0.008	0.034

Comparing tourism service characteristics, two groups have significant differences in both their recreational activities and accommodation options chosen in three different categories (Table 11). Altogether, real estate investment (p = 0.036), as well as sail boating/surfing (p = 0.013), and fishing (p = 0.035) are found to have a significant difference. It is interesting to find that although respondents in the resident group are more likely to participate in real estate investment and luxury leisure activities such as sail boating or surfing, they are less likely to perform traditional activities that used to be a means of livelihood such as fishing. This fact is because, in China, a vacation home or a yacht is a symbol of luxury, while fishing is regarded as a survival job necessary to put food on the table in most coastal villages. Considering that rapid urbanization has occurred over the last few decades, this is not difficult to understand. Because of the onerous nature of fishing as a job, it would be difficult for a person who has just left fishing professionally to purchase such a task as a leisure activity during his/her vacation. Second, in terms of accommodation, 14% of the respondents from the resident group have chosen resort as their preferred way of accommodation, which is significantly (p=0.022) higher than the non-resident group's percentage of 5%. This provides a one-stop commercial establishment that has most of the features that a tourist desires and would probably give residents more feelings that they are "on vacation," which makes them feel they are doing something different than their daily routines.

Table 11. Coastal tourism recreation and accommodation preference differences between tourists and residents

	Recreation			Accommodation
	Real estate investment	Sail boating /surfing	Fishing	Resort
Mean of the resident group	2.82	3.63	3.20	0.14
Mean of the non-resident group	2.52	3.48	3.37	0.05
Chi-square p-value	0.036	0.013	0.035	0.022

In summary, residents are more likely to choose coastal regions nearby even during the off-season but are unwilling to travel long distances to visit northern coastal regions in China. Also, despite having a similar annual household income compared to their non-resident peers, residents are more likely to make real estate investment, more likely to spend money on luxury services such as resorts or sail boating, but unlikely to pursue traditional livelihood activities such as fishing.

This finding agrees with Butler (1980)'s assertion that activities pursued during a coastal tourist's visit are tightly connected to culture, but differs from Butler (1980)'s prediction because by having similar socio-economic backgrounds, local residents are more likely to have a higher consumption willingness to purchase luxury recreational activates (such as sail boating) and participate in real estate investment, and at the same time wish to deviate from their traditional means of livelihood (such as fishing).

Do Tourists, Either With Higher or Lower Consumption Intentions, and Either With Other Coastal or Inland Residency, Desire to Migrate to Tourist Destinations and Become Residents?

The analysis in the previous two sections shows that contrary to (Butler, 1980)'s modeling, both local residents and tourists with higher or lower consumption intentions generally welcome the blue economy transition. In fact, according to the respondents for question eleven, "are you willing to migrate to a coastal city?" almost half of the tourists (46.3%) are likely to migrate to the coastal region and become coastal region residents (Figure 5).

Figure 5. Survey respondent's willingness to migrate to a coastal city

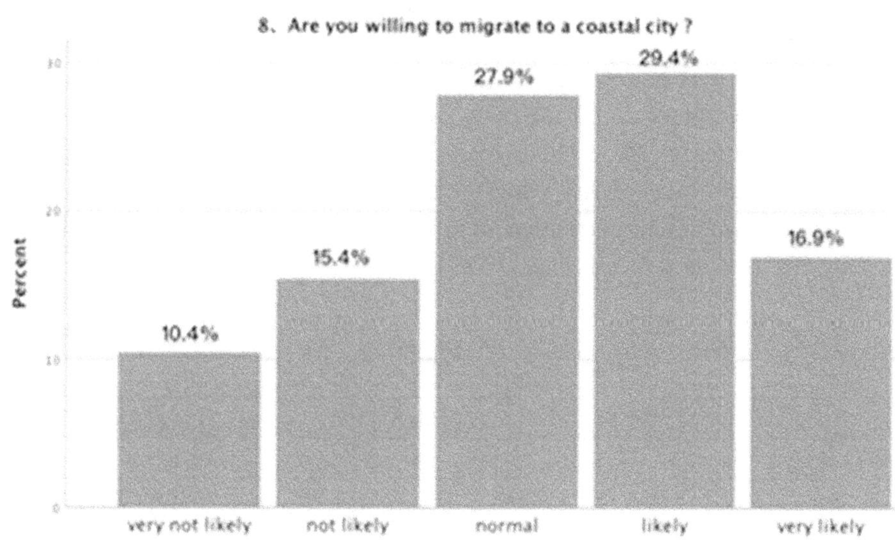

There is a significant difference between both the higher expenditure group and the lower expenditure group (p<0.001), as well as the resident group versus the non-resident group (p=0.032).

First, tourists from the higher expenditure group have an average willingness of 3.62, while tourists from the lower expenditure group only have an average willingness of 2.90. Table 11 shows the percentage of respondents choosing "1 = very not likely", "2 = not likely", "3 = normal", "4 = likely" and "5 = very likely". Data show respondents from the higher expenditure group clearly know their preferences because their choices are more located at the extreme, with 13.2% of respondents choosing "1 = very not likely" and 35.4% of respondents choosing "5 = very likely". For tourists from the lower expenditure group, their preferences are more blurred in the middle, with only 9% of respondents choosing "1 = very not likely" and 7.5% of respondents choosing "5 = very likely". This seems to be a unity of opposites: on the one hand, there is a socially constructed boundary between the identity of "tourists" and "residents." For people who are willing to spend money in the coastal regions, not everyone would like to move here and purchase a home. On the other hand, the identity of "tourists" and "residents" are interchangeable in that the vast majority of tourists (57.4%) have a willingness to migrate to the coastal city (Table 12).

Table 12. Willingness to migrate to a coastal city: differences between tourists with opposing consumption intentions

	Very not likely	Not likely	Normal	Likely	Very likely
Mean of "high expenditure" group	13.2%	4.4%	25.0%	22.1%	35.3%
Mean of "low expenditure" group	9%	21.1%	29.3%	33.1%	7.5%

Second, a significant difference (p=0.032) has also been found between the resident group and the non-resident group concerning their willingness to live in the coastal city (Table 13). Being born in a coastal town does not mean there is a desire to live in a seaside city. 16.8% of the respondents in the resident group have chosen "1 = very not likely" and "2 = not likely". Comparing to 32.2% of the non-residents who are either "1 = very not likely" or "2 = not likely", the data indicate that current living status in the coastal regions reinforces the ideology that the coastal areas are a good location choose as home. Similarly, when comparing the percentage of respondents selecting "4 = likely" and "5 = very likely", the resident's response rate is 57.8% while the non-resident's responsive rate is 38.2%. This result also strengthens the conclusion that respondents currently living in coastal regions are more likely to regard the coastal areas as a place to live.

Table 13. Willingness to migrate to a coastal city: differences between tourists and residents

	Very not likely	Not likely	Normal	Likely	Very likely
Mean of the resident group	8.4%	8.4%	25.3%	33.7%	24.1%
Mean of the non-resident group	11.9%	20.3%	29.7%	26.3%	11.9%

In summary, almost half of the tourists reveal that they are likely to migrate to the coastal region for permanent residency. This rate is significantly higher for current coastal residents, meaning that their preference for living near the coast is higher than the general population. Meanwhile, although some tourists with higher propensities to consume are thinking of moving to coastal communities for a living, there are still others who would prefer to think of coastal regions as only areas to visit occasionally as tourists.

CONCLUSION

This chapter uses empirical survey data to explore the feasibility of China's coastal tourism industry remaining competitive in the long run under the blue economy ideology. Whether "the tourism destination areas carry with them the potential seeds of their own destruction, as they allow themselves to become more commercialized and lose their qualities which originally attracted tourists," as Butler (1980) predicts, largely depends on the tourism service quality management. Butler (1980)'s model relies on three underlying assumptions:

1. Tourism services are created to give priority to tourists with a higher consumption willingness than to tourists with a lower consumption willingness.
2. Tourism services are created to give priority to tourists from the outside rather than to residents born in the coastal region.
3. The duality between the tourists' consumption-oriented needs and the local residents' traditional means of living cannot be mitigated.

The empirical finding after surveying 201 respondents from the southern part of China regarding the characteristics of the stakeholders, coastal resources, and services provision suggests that none of those three assumptions are valid according to the sample data. On the contrary, coastal residents are, in fact, more likely to purchase luxury recreational activities and accommodations, as well as invest in real estate. They are more loyal to their coastal community in that they do not mind visiting their local beach during the fall and winter off-season, and are less likely to see other coastal regions which are further away from where they live. When comparing the respondents among tourists, respondents with lower consumption willingness have shorter trips, purchase less recreational activities, or arrange their travels during the off-season to taking advantage of the discount price. There is no sign of marginalization and exclusion mentioned by Butler (1980). The empirical finding also suggests that the identity of tourists and permanent residents are interchangeable because almost half of the tourists are likely to migrate to the coastal region and become permanent residents.

Although empirical findings do not support Butler (1980)'s prediction, this doesn't mean Butler (1980)'s warnings do not apply to China at all. First, this chapter is based on a small sample size in Zhejiang, and the respondents are mainly young college students. As a result, the conclusion cannot be generalized to a larger scale. Second, due to the purpose of the research design, respondents are intentionally selected from respondents coming from a similar socio-economic background. As a result, the conclusion only reflects individuals' personal consumption preferences and is not associated with their social class. Despite such limitations, this research points out that under this Chinese scenario, due to the relatively large amount of money contributed to coastal dwellers during the recent urbanization, Chinese tourism service quality management may have unique characteristics worth exploring for researchers in the future.

REFERENCES

Bari, A. (2017). Our Oceans and the Blue Economy: Opportunities and Challenges. *Procedia Engineering Procedia Engineering*, *194*, 5–11. doi:10.1016/j.proeng.2017.08.109

Butler, R. W. (1980). The concept of a tourist area cycle of evolution: Implications for management of resources. *The Canadian Geographer. Geographe Canadien, 24*(1), 5–12. doi:10.1111/j.1541-0064.1980.tb00970.x

Cortes-Jimenez, I. (2008). Which type of tourism matters to regional economic growth? The cases of Spain and Italy. *International Journal of Tourism Research, 10*(2), 127–139. doi:10.1002/jtr.646

Garland, M., Axon, S., Graziano, M., Morrissey, J., & Heidkamp, C. P. (2019). The blue economy: Identifying geographic concepts and sensitivities. *GEC3. Geography Compass, 13*(7). Advance online publication. doi:10.1111/gec3.12445

Gu, M., & Wong, P. P. (2008). Coastal zone management focusing on coastal tourism in a transitional period of China. *Ocean & Coastal Management Ocean & Coastal Management, 51*(1), 1–24. doi:10.1016/j.ocecoaman.2007.05.008

Hjalager, A.-M. (2010). A review of innovation research in tourism. *Tourism Management, 48*(1), 1–12. doi:10.1016/j.tourman.2009.08.012

Joshi, A., Kale, S., Chandel, S., & Pal, D. (2015). Likert scale: Explored and explained. *British Journal of Applied Science and Technology, 7*(4), 396–403. doi:10.9734/BJAST/2015/14975

Liu, S. (2014). *From the Marine Economy to Blue Economy*. Retrieved from https://wenku.baidu.com/view/4ef9de21767f5acfa0c7cd5a.html

Liu, S., Heilig, G. K., Chen, J., & Heino, M. (2007). Interactions between economic growth and environmental quality in Shenzhen, China's first special economic zone. *Ecological Economics, 62*(3-4), 559–570. doi:10.1016/j.ecolecon.2006.07.020

Ma, Y. (2019). *2018 China Coastal Tourism Passenger Flow Big Data Report*. Retrieved from https://www.3mbang.com/p-1021774.html

Nalebuff, B., & Brandenburger, A. (2002). *Co-opetition*. Academic Press.

Pardo, A. (1984). *Third-world Lecture 1984-Ocean Space and Mankind*. Carfax.

Priskin, J. (2003). Tourist perceptions of degradation caused by coastal nature-based recreation. *Environmental Management, 32*(2), 189–204. doi:10.100700267-002-2916-z

Schumpeter, J. A. (1968). *The theory of economic development: An inquiry into profits, capital, credit, interest, and the business cycle*. Harvard Univ. Pr.

Smith, S. L. (1994). The tourism product. *Annals of Tourism Research, 21*(3), 582–595. doi:10.1016/0160-7383(94)90121-X

Sundbo, J., Orfila-Sintes, F., & Sorensen, F. (2007). The innovative behaviour of tourism firms. Comparative studies of Denmark and Spain. *Research Policy Research Policy, 36*(1), 88–106. doi:10.1016/j.respol.2006.08.004

Wahab, S., & Cooper, C. (2014). *Tourism in the age of globalisation*. Routledge.

KEY TERMS AND DEFINITIONS

Blue Economy: Using ocean resources sustainably to ensure economic, environmental, and social growth.

Coastal Tourism: They are recreational activities services hosted in the coastal zone.

Competitive Advantage: A position that enables a firm to provide goods and services superior to its customer's other choices.

Entrepreneurs: Innovators who bring new problem-solving ideas into use.

Quality Management: Ensure the quality of the product or service is consistent over long periods.

Sustainability: Meeting the needs of the present without compromising the ability of the future.

Sustainable Business Strategy: A business strategy that positively impacts both the environment and society.

ENDNOTE

1 Hukou is a system of household registration used in mainland China to distinguish rural dwellers and urban dwellers.

APPENDIX – SURVEY QUESTIONNAIRE

1. What is your Gender?
   ϒ Male
   ϒ Female
2. What is your age group?
   ϒ <18 ϒ18~25 ϒ26~30 ϒ31~40 ϒ41~50 ϒ51~60 ϒ>60
3. What is your current career?
   ϒ Student
   ϒ Teacher or career related with education
   ϒ Business related
   ϒ Other careers
4. What is your/your family`s monthly income?
   ϒ <5,000¥
   ϒ 5,000~10,000 ¥
   ϒ 10,000~ 20,000¥
   ϒ 20,000¥~ 50,000¥
   ϒ >50,000¥
5. Are you working/living in a coastal city?
   ϒ Yes
   ϒ No
6. How many times have you traveled to a coastal city during the year? (Includes trips you took in the city where you live/work)
   ϒ 0
   ϒ 1~2
   ϒ 3~5
   ϒ Five times or more
7. How many times have you traveled to a coastal city during the year?
   ϒ 0
   ϒ 1~2
   ϒ 3~5
   ϒ Five times or more
8. Are you willing to migrate to a coastal city?

Table 14.

	Very not likely	Not Likely	Normal	Likely	Very Likely
Migrate to Coastal City	○	○	○	○	○

9. How likely are you to travel coastal cities during the year?

Table 15.

	Very not likely	Not Likely	Normal	Likely	Very Likely
Spring (April-May)	○	○	○	○	○
Early Summer (May-July)	○	○	○	○	○
Late Summer (July-August)	○	○	○	○	○
Fall (August-October)	○	○	○	○	○
Winter (October-April)	○	○	○	○	○

10. How much would you like to visit each of the following areas?

Table 16.

	Very not likely	Not Likely	Normal	Likely	Very Likely
Bohai (Dalian, Qinhuangdao, Tianjin)	○	○	○	○	○
East China Sea (Ningbo, Taipei, Wenzhou)	○	○	○	○	○
South China Sea (Sanya, Guangzhou, Xiamen)	○	○	○	○	○
Huang Hai (Qingdao, Lianyungang)	○	○	○	○	○

11. How long would you normally stay?
ϒ no more than 24 hours

ϒ 1 to 2 days
ϒ 3 to 7 days
ϒ more than 7 days

12. Which of the following accommodation options do you prefer when traveling to a coastal city?
ϒ Homestay
ϒ Hotel
ϒ Purchased home in a coastal city
ϒ Stay with friends or family
ϒ Resort

13. How likely are you to engage in each of the following coastal recreational activities?

Table 17.

	Very not likely	Not Likely	Normal	Likely	Very Likely
Real estate investment	○	○	○	○	○
Ship traveling	○	○	○	○	○
Sail boating/surfing	○	○	○	○	○
Swimming	○	○	○	○	○
Diving	○	○	○	○	○
Fishing	○	○	○	○	○
Sightseeing	○	○	○	○	○
Beach sports	○	○	○	○	○

14. How much do you think your consumption in coastal cities can promote the development of the coastal economy?

ϒ Strongly Disagree ϒ Disagree ϒ Neutral ϒ Agree ϒ Strongly Agree

Chapter 9
Relationship Between Innovation, Human Capital, Institutions, Entrepreneurship, and Economic Growth:
A Comparative Analysis Using FsQCA

Miguel-Angel Galindo Martín
Universidad de Castilla-La Mancha, Spain

María-Soledad Castaño
Universidad de Castilla-La Mancha, Spain

María Teresa Méndez Picazo
https://orcid.org/0000-0002-3045-0980
Universidad Complutense de Madrid, Spain

ABSTRACT

There is important literature that analyzes the relationship between entrepreneurship and economic growth. But it is also essential to consider the variables that influence entrepreneurship. In this sense, innovations, institutions, and human capital would be the main variables to consider, as they allow the entrepreneur to create new products, make them more competitive, or access new markets. At the same time, entrepreneurs establish the legal framework and the social climate to develop its activity, so innovations are generated and assimilated. But it is also essential to consider the degree of development and economic growth that countries present.

DOI: 10.4018/978-1-7998-5036-6.ch009

INTRODUCTION

In recent decades, economic growth has been considered as one of the essential objectives of the economic policy due to its beneficial effects on employment and social welfare. Consequently, there is an extensive literature dedicated to determining the variables that favor its increase, fiscal variables, technology, institutions, etc., that could be included in the economic policy measures designed to achieve this objective.

One of the variables that have been given significant attention in recent years is entrepreneurship. According to Schumpeter (1911, 1950), entrepreneurs create new industries and introduce substantial structural changes in the economy, stimulating economic activity, favoring economic growth, job creation, and, ultimately, more generous social welfare. Due to this circumstance, an extensive literature has emerged in which the relationship between entrepreneurship and economic growth is analyzed (for example, Acs et al., 2012, 2018; Alpkan et al., 2010; Audretsch, 2005; Audretsch and Keilbach, 2004a,b; Audretsch and Fritsch, 2003; Galindo and Méndez, 2014; Méndez-Picazo et al., 2012; Castaño, Méndez, & Galindo, 2016).

However, it is also necessary to take into account other factors that could influence entrepreneurial activity. Two can be mainly considered. First, innovations must be considered. Thanks to innovations, entrepreneurs can enter new markets and make their products more competitive. And second, there must be adequate institutions that defend property rights and generate an appropriate social and legal framework for entrepreneurs to develop their activity. Without that proper legal framework, they will be reluctant to allocate their resources towards new investments and may seek other locations that they consider more appropriate in this regard. Related to all this, it is also necessary for an adequate social climate that favors business activity and enhances new technologies and their acceptance and assimilation. In the latter area, human capital would be a factor to consider.

Therefore, it is convenient to analyze the relationship between all these variables when designing appropriate measures to promote economic growth. Focusing attention, for example, on the role of innovations without taking into account the behavior of institutions, especially if these are not adequate, would mean that the measures would not have the desired effect or would have a lesser influence than expected on economic growth.

But, on the other hand, it must be taken into account that the structural situation of the countries would also be a condition to be considered because the structural circumstances of the economies could affect the results obtained. For this reason, the degree of development and growth of the countries play an essential role in the analysis because they will influence the motivations of the entrepreneurs when developing their activity. Depending on the existing economic situation, especially when there are high levels of unemployment or a particular economic stagnation, entrepreneurship by necessity is higher, considering that it is usually reduced when these adverse situations are mitigated or disappear. Therefore, it is crucial to carry out the study taking into account the position of the countries. For these reasons, the countries sample will be divided into two groups: the nations of group A includes innovation-driven economies characterized by presenting high values of the motivational index, and the countries of the Group B that are described, on the contrary, by efficiency-driven economies that show low values of the motivational index.

The main objective of this paper is to analyze the relationship between innovation, institutions, human capital, entrepreneurship on economic growth, considering different types of entrepreneurship and countries. In this sense, two kinds of entrepreneurship motivation have been considered: by necessity and opportunity, and two groups of countries will be created, a group of countries where entrepreneurship predominates opportunity motivations, and another group which predominates the necessity motivations. To classify the countries, the ratio (opportunity motivations/necessity motivations) will be used.

Section 2 includes the theoretical aspects related to the relationships between the variables considered. Section 3 will focus on performing the empirical analysis FsQCA method, in the case of 33 countries. This study aims to identify the necessary and/or sufficient conditions that explain the differences in opportunity and necessity entrepreneurship by groups of countries. An empirical analysis using the fsQCA model is developed to identify causal configurations in several steps: (1) identification of all possible causal configurations, (2) analyzing the distribution of cases according to such structures, (3) detection of sufficient systems according to a consistency criterion, and (4) reduction of sufficient configurations by applying counterfactual analysis. Section 4 will expose the essential results achieved. And finally, section 5 will include the main conclusions.

INNOVATION AND INSTITUTIONS EFFECTS ON ENTREPRENEURSHIP AND ECONOMIC GROWTH

Policymakers have been considering economic growth as one of the essential objectives in designing the economic policy. This fact is essentially due to the beneficial effects on economic well-being, resulting from the greater employment generated by economic growth and the possibility of improving income distribution, thanks to the higher number of resources developed.

In this sense, several studies have been developed to determine the variables that can benefit the generation of economic growth to design the strategy to follow to achieve this objective. From this perspective, several variables have been considered, and one of them is entrepreneurship.

But it is necessary to take into account, according to Rodrick (2005), that it is not enough to generate or stimulate that economic growth, but that it is also necessary to try to maintain it. This means, among other issues, that we must contemplate different relationships and feedback effects affecting both economic growth and the variables that influence it. As a result, we consider at least two types of actions: those that stimulate economic growth and those they maintain over time (Nissan, Galindo, & Méndez, 2011, p. 312-313).

The first group of actions tries to determine the different variables that stimulate economic growth. In a situation in which the economy has low levels of activity, it is necessary to design measures to reverse the situation, creating greater social well-being. In this sense, there is a vast literature that shows the positive relationship between entrepreneurship and economic growth (see, for example, Alpkan et al. 2010; Audretsch, & Keilbach, 2004a,b; Audretsch, 2005; Méndez-Picazo et al. 2012; Acs et al. 2012; Galindo, & Méndez, 2014). Thanks to the activity of entrepreneurs, a more significant amount of products are generated, increasing the employment rate. A higher number of employees would increase demand, which leads to more remarkable economic growth. Within the concept of entrepreneurship, the entrepreneurial opportunity is contemplated in the analysis.

This fact implies that a social and economic environment must be generated to facilitate the investment process and entrepreneurs to create a business activity or develop the existing one. In this sense, there are several variables to consider: tax policy, human capital, and innovation. In the latter case, according to Schumpeter (1911, 1950), entrepreneurship would play an essential role since it will be responsible for introducing that innovation in the production process, for being more competitive, leading to a process of destruction. For this reason, innovation is usually considered essential for entrepreneurial activity and that, thanks to innovation, entrepreneurs can continue to develop their activity (Drucker, 1998). But, it is also necessary to consider the existing feedback effects between entrepreneurship and innovation, since, although entrepreneurs introduce innovations to gain competitiveness in the developed activity, such innovation also stimulates that other entrepreneurs improve innovations to be more competitive.

The second group of actions consists in sustaining the economic growth generated over time. The first group of actions must be complemented with this second group of variables. The reason for this necessity is because if the appropriate economic policies are not adopted, or the economy continues its path without introducing the right stimuli, economic growth can be negatively affected to return to lower levels of economic well-being. This fact implies, among other issues, that there must have adequate institutions to favor not only the introduction of the appropriate measures but also to improve the activity of the markets that allow economic shocks to be tackled (Acemoglu et al., 2001). In this area, the main variables to consider are the rule of law; property rights are effectively enforced and enshrined in the Basic Law, business freedom, and trade freedom. These variables establish the appropriate environment for employers to create a new activity or develop the existing one with the positive effects on employment and finally on economic well-being.

From this perspective, we verify a relationship between entrepreneurship, institutions, innovations, and economic growth. Traditionally, literature has analyzed these relationships separately, but not in a common way, as intended to be carried out in this chapter.

Regarding the relationship between entrepreneurship and innovation, it should be noted that it has been the object of great attention in the specialized literature. Schumpeter (1911, 1950) is one of the economists that have focused the attention on this relationship. Schumpeter considers that the entrepreneur is the essential agent when it comes to introducing innovations in the production process to improve the product he was making, introducing a new product, or improving the productive organization. The essential consequence of this behavior is twofold. First, it implies the creation of new industries that, in turn, will suppose the appearance of important structural changes in the economy (Baregheh et al., 2009). And second, innovation is inherent in entrepreneurial activity (Drucker, 1998) because thanks to it, many entrepreneurs can develop their activity and be competitive. From this perspective, the entrepreneurial activity promoted by the innovative process produces a feedback effect as entrepreneurs innovate, and thanks to these innovations, many entrepreneurs are encouraged to carry out their activity (De Cleyn, & Braet, 2012; Zortea-Johnston et al., 2012).

Some authors have also contemplated the effects that innovation would have on economic growth. From a modern perspective, companies can take advantage of the advantages and opportunities offered by the globalization that economies have experienced through innovation. Entrepreneurs can access the new markets provided by the globalization process through new products or more competitive products. And this is achieved essentially through innovation. That is why the recent economic growth literature contemplates aspects related to the technological diffusion and catch-up process (Galindo, & Mendez, 2013). In this relationship, the role played by entrepreneurs must be considered because they will be responsible for introducing innovations in the production process. And in this area, the importance of the risk that arises when they introduce new technology in the company must also be considered, since they have to specify the positive and negative effects of such action (Autio et al., 2014). For this reason, it can be considered that innovations have a direct and indirect impact, through entrepreneurs, on economic growth.

In addition to innovations, institutions are another variable that has been considered as economic growth-promoting. Institutions generate and introduce the incentives and restrictions that economic agents have to face when carrying carried out their activity (Acemoglu et al., 2005, Lim et al., 2016; Bosma et al., 2018; Dilli et al., 2018)). And the decisions adopted by economic agents will have effects on economic growth. For this reason, institutions are considered to play an essential role in promoting economic growth through the distribution of resources (Elert, & Henrekson, 2017; Alam et al., 2019).

The protection that institutions provide to entrepreneurs is important because thanks to this factor, they will be interested in investing their capital and developing their activity. Without such protection, they will stop investing their resources in the country. They will move them to other places that they consider safer for their interests, with the corresponding negative effect on the welfare of the country in which they do not invest. For this reason, in the specialized literature, the relationship between institutions and economic growth has been analyzed (see among others, Justesen, & Kurrild-Klitgaard, 2013; Sirowy, & Inkeles, 1990; Przeworski, & Limongi, 1993) and the relationship between institutions, entrepreneurship and economic growth (for example, Acs et al., 2018; Bosma et al., 2018; Urbano et al., 2019; Galindo et al., 2019).

Finally, it must be considered two conditions for that institutions to affect economic growth and entrepreneurship mentioned above positively. First, they must enforce property rights in society. Second, institutions must reduce or eliminate actions exercised by certain pressure groups to harm property rights and ensure a high level of equal opportunities for economic agents. So, most individuals can participate in productive economic activities (Acemoglu, 2003, 27). In this sense, human capital would play an essential role in providing that possibility.

An adequate human capital not only favors the creation of an appropriate social climate from the Schumpeterian perspective, which favors the appearance of entrepreneurial activity but also facilitates the introduction and development of innovations, making production processes more competitive. As indicated, there is a need for an adequate social climate to facilitate the introduction of innovations. In such a variable, Schumpeter includes the reaction of the social group to the entrepreneurial activity, including the innovation process. He considers the existence of legal or political impediments, culture and could be included the rule of law and the role of institutions. On the other hand, Schumpeter states that it would be possible to find some social opposition to the innovation process, and the entrepreneurs would be in difficulty in finding the necessary cooperation. This resistance was more relevant in the beginnings of capitalism; however, it is still effective nowadays (Schumpeter 1911, p. 87). As indicated above, we must also consider the role that human capital plays in this process, since the better training of economic agents will facilitate not only the introduction and creation of innovations but also their acceptance and assimilation.

Therefore, these variables, innovations, institutions, entrepreneurship, and human capital, will have a direct and indirect effect on economic growth (Simón-Moya et al., 2014; Boudreaux et al., 2019; Galindo et al., 2019). For this reason, it is convenient to analyze the effects on growth in a grouped way and not individually or separately as is usually done. This means introducing all the variables at once into the analysis.

Empirical Analysis

The empirical analysis will be carried out for 33 countries using the average values of each indicator to the period 2014-2016. The nations of the sample show different levels of growth and development. To carry out the study, the countries will be classified in two broad groups considering the following GEM classification based on the phases set out by the World Economic Forum (Kelley et al., 2012, p.14):

- Factor-driven economies are the least developed. They are dominated by subsistence agriculture and extraction businesses, with a heavy reliance on (unskilled) labor and natural resources.
- Efficiency-driven economies are increasingly competitive, with more-efficient production processes and increased product quality.
- Innovation-driven economies are the most developed. In this phase, businesses are more knowledge-intensive, and the service sector expands.

According to this approach, two groups have been considered. Group A includes Australia, Belgium, Canada, Denmark, Finland, France, Germany, Ireland, Italy, Japan, Luxembourg, Netherlands, Norway, Spain, Sweden, Switzerland, United Kingdom, United States, and is characterized by predominance the opportunity. It means that these countries present high values of the motivational index, and they can be considered as innovation-driven economies

Group B includes Argentina, Brazil, Bulgaria, Chile, Colombia, Croatia, Ecuador, Indonesia, Latvia, Mexico, Panama, Peru, Poland, Slovak Republic, Uruguay. In this case, the need predominates; that is, these countries show low values of the motivational index and can be considered as efficiency-driven economies.

In order to test the hypothesis, the fsQCA method is used in each group of countries considering the existent relations among the different variables to be analyzed, that is, innovation, institutions, entrepreneurship, and economic growth.

Method and Data

The fsQCA method is a program that uses combinatorial logic, fuzzy set theory, and Boolean minimization to work out what combinations of characteristics may be necessary or sufficient to produce an outcome (Kent, 2005). The fsQCA is a diversity-oriented approach that proposes different alternative paths to understand the construction of a result and small samples (10 to 50 cases) (Kent 2005; Henik 2015; Kraus et al., 2017).

fsQCA allows identifying causal configurations in several steps (Ragin, 1987; Berg-Schlosser et al., 2009): (1) identification of all possible causal configurations, (2) analyzing the distribution of cases according to such configurations, (3) detection of sufficient configurations according to a consistency criterion, and (4) reduction of sufficient configurations by applying counterfactuals analysis. Obviously, if the condition or the combination of them is sufficient, this does not mean that it will be necessary to generate a certain outcome.

Also, fsQCA requires transforming variables into sets calibrated via three meaningful thresholds: full membership, full non-membership, and the cross-over point defined by "the point of maximum ambiguity in the assessment of whether a case is more in or out of a set" (Ragin, 2008, p. 30). Based on these qualitative thresholds, variable raw scores can become set measures using the direct method of calibration. Calibration draws on theoretical and substantive knowledge of the context (Fiss, 2007). This analysis employs the direct estimation method based on descriptive statistics and economic literature. Thus, the indicators of Table 1 become fuzzy variables expressing the degree of membership, where value 1 represents full membership, and value 0 illustrates full non-membership.

The qualitative analysis uses fsQCA 3.0 software, taking as the dependent variable or outcome economic growth (fs_gdrate) in the first equation, and opportunity entrepreneurship (fs_opp) in the second equation. Afterward, the study proceeds to calculate the truth table to identify sufficient causal configurations. The "truth table" allows selecting one of the characteristics as the "outcome," explaining two or more membership scores or "conditions" that may potentially be necessary or sufficient for the outcome to happen. The truth table now treats each case as a combination of the characteristics selected (or "configuration" in fsQCA terminology) (Kent and Olsen, 2008, p. 3). Additionally, the truth table calculates all the possible 2^k combinations of potential causal conditions (where k is the number of causal conditions); the truth table records the number of cases with that configuration and whether or not the outcome happened.

However, this method requires the identification of the different causal configurations with positive cases and removal of those causal configurations that are theoretically possible but do not respond to real cases collected in the study sample (Ragin, 2006).

After selecting causal configurations that depend on the distribution of the cases in the sample, the study chooses a threshold for the level of consistency, 0.8, according to Ragin's (2008) approach.

The calculation of the truth table offers three alternative results: complex, parsimonious, and intermediate solution. The complex solution does not simplify sufficient configurations and therefore is the solution that provides the most details. The parsimonious solution performs the maximum simplification possible based on the consideration that all counterfactual leads to the outcome of interest. Finally, the intermediate solution assumes that only some of the possible causal configurations that do not collect actual cases have led to the results analyzed in Ragin and Sonnet (2005). Ragin (2008) recommends the use of the intermediate due to this is usually the most interpretable. Additionally, to calculate the truth table, the analysis uses the Quine-McCluskey algorithm.

Model Settings

In order to analyze the previous relationships, it is necessary to start by specifying the motivations that economic agents have to develop entrepreneurship activity. In this sense, according to GEM (Kelley et al., 2012, p.13), we would have three types of motives. First, the so-called "entrepreneurship by activity" refers to the net use of a business opportunity. Second, "entrepreneurship by opportunity," which is the one that arises when there are no opportunities to find work, and therefore, in the absence of alternatives, the possibility of creating your own business is contemplated. This motivation usually occurs when there is a high level of unemployment and economic stagnation. Individuals faced with the possibility of remaining unemployed seek other alternatives that allow them to obtain resources, essentially creating their own business. Unlike the previous one, this reason means that when there are greater economic activity and more employment opportunities, these entrepreneurs disappear and enter the labor market. And finally, "entrepreneurship for other motives," which includes situations not contemplated in the previous two. Considering the two first motives, the "motivational index" is elaborated. This index is a ratio between entrepreneurship by opportunity and entrepreneurship by necessity, so the greater the value of the index, the greater the motivation to undertake by opportunity (GEM, 2017).

In order to transform conventional variables into fuzzy variables, it is necessary to calibrate them: calibrating the variables is the process of expressing a degree of membership in the sets and implies the use of three thresholds or breakpoints. In our study, we have followed the Ragin percentile rank method (2008). According to Ragin (2008, p.17), the values of an interval scale variable must be specified that correspond to three qualitative breakpoints that structure a fuzzy set: the threshold for full membership (fuzzy score = 0.95), the threshold for full nonmembership (fuzzy score = 0.05), and the cross-over point (fuzzy score = 0.5). These three benchmarks are used to transform the original ratio or interval-scale values into fuzzy membership scores. So, in table 1, the symbol "fs_" appears that indicates that this variable has been calibrated.

Besides, FsQCA allows us to calculate the shared effect of variables that, through the command "fuzzyand," therefore, the variable "fs_inst" shared of part of sets of the three sub-indices that appear in Table 1. Thus, three sub-items of the Economic Freedom Index "PR" (Property rights), "BR" Business freedom, and "TF" Trade Freedom index, and we have calculated their joint effect by creating the "fs_inst" variable using the "fuzzyand" command.

Considering the first two entrepreneurship motives, two equations are established to be estimated by the fsQCA method. The first equation is related to economic growth and the second to entrepreneurship by opportunity. Specifically, the equations would be established as follows:

Equation 1: Yfs_ = f(EOfs_, ENfs_, INRDfs_, INNfs_, HKfs_, INSTfs_)

Equation 1 refers to economic growth (YFs) that will depend on the first two entrepreneurship motivations, by opportunity (EOfs) and by necessity (Enfs), on the innovations represented by the INRDfs and INNfs variables, human capital (HKfs), and the institutions (INSTfs). As noted above, all the variables considered would have a positive effect on economic growth.

Equation 2: EOfs_ = f(Yfs_, HKfs_, INSTfs_, INRDfs_)

Equation 2 refers to entrepreneurship by opportunity that would be positively related to economic growth (Yfs), human capital (HFfs), institutions (INSfs), and innovations (INRDfs).

The definitions and characteristics of the variables are shown in Table 1

RESULTS AND DISCUSSION

Tables 2 and 3 show the results that attempt to answer the research questions raised above. These tables include measures of coverage and consistency for each solution term and the solution as a whole. Consistency (with sufficiency) measures the degree to which solution terms and the solution are subsets of the outcome. Coverage measures how much outcome is covered (or explained) by each solution term and by the total solution (Ragin, 2008).

Besides, solution coverage and solution consistency refer to the whole model. Instead, Consistency and raw coverage refer to each causal configuration. Woodside (2013) stresses the importance of achieving high consistency over high coverage.

In Table 2, the intermediate solution shows three sufficient configurations to group A and five to group B. The consistency is higher of 0.7 in all causal configuration, which indicates that the model collects most of the cases studied.

Table 1. Variables definitions

Variable	Definition
Economic Growth	**Yfs_[1]:** GDP Growth Rate (World Bank, 2019)
Entrepreneurship	**Opportunity entrepreneurship EOfs_:** Opportunity-driven (% of TEA) (GEM, 2019) **Necessity entrepreneurship ENfs_:** Necessity-driven (% of TEA) (GEM, 2019)
Innovation	**INRDfs_:** Gloss domestic expenditures on research and development (R&D), expressed as a percent of GDP. They include capital and current spending on the four main sectors: Business enterprise, Government, Higher education, and Private non-profit. R&D covers basic research, applied research, and experimental development (World Bank, 2019).
	INNfs_: Product is new to all or some customers, and few/no businesses offer the same product (GEM, 2019)
Human Capital	**HKfs_:** General government expenditure on education (current, capital, and transfers) is expressed as a percentage of total general government expenditure. It includes expenditure funded by transfers from international sources to the government. The general government usually refers to local, regional, and central governments (World Bank, 2019).
Institutions fs_inst=fuzzyand (fs_pr,fs_bf, fs_tf)	**INSTfs_:** **PR:** Property rights are effectively enforced and enshrined in the Basic Law. Commercial and company laws uphold the sanctity of contracts (Heritage Foundation, 2019). **BF:** Business freedom is well protected within an efficient regulatory framework. Transparency encourages entrepreneurship, and the overall environment is conducive to the start-up of businesses (Heritage Foundation, 2019). **TF:** Trade Freedom allows knowing the openness of the country due to there are fewer restrictions on international trade (Heritage Foundation, 2019).

Table 2. The outcome of Equation 1

	Raw Coverage	Unique Coverage	Consistency
Group A			
INSTfz * EOfs * INRDfs	0.579492	0.219191	0.933333
EOfs * ENfs * INRDfs * INNfs	0.304798	0.049859	0.917847
HKfs * INSTfz *~ ENfs * INRDfs * INNfs	0.366886	0.087488	0.904872
Solution coverage	0.716839		
Solution consistency	0.874857		
Group B			
HKfs * ENfs * EOfs	0.544715	0.213705	0.919608
INRDfs * ENfs * EOfs	0.317073	0.025552	0.886364
INRDfs * ENfs * INNfs	0.370499	0.117305	0.866848
ENfs * EOfs * INNfs	0.351916	-0.000000	0.865714
INRDfs * EOfs * INSTfz	0.329849	0.059233	0.982699
Solution coverage	0.806040		
Solution consistency	0.853629		

Source: The Authors

Considering the results by groups of countries, we see that the prevailing causal configuration is "INSTfs * EOfs * INRDfs" with raw coverage of 0.57 and a consistency of 0.93. That means that the quality of institutions, entrepreneurship by opportunity, and expenses in R & D would be a necessary condition to enhance economic growth. Also, group A shows two different causal configurations, with very high consistency, but raw coverage is somewhat more elevated than 0.3. One of them, "EOfs * ENfs * INRDfs* INNfs," indicates the combination of any of the two types of entrepreneurship, plus R&D spending and entrepreneurial innovation, leads to higher economic growth. The other possibility, "HKfs * INSTfs * ~ ENfs * INRDfs * INNfs, "shows that the expenses in human capital, the quality of institutions, innovation, and the absence of entrepreneurship by necessity would enhance economic growth.

In the case of group B, the possible causal configurations are more diverse than in group A. One of them appears human capital in other innovation, but in all of them arises the two types of entrepreneurship motivations. This fact is because entrepreneurship by necessity is very high in this group of countries and, therefore, is determinant for economic growth. However, it has a lower effect than entrepreneurship by opportunity (Wennerkers et al., 2005). By contrast, the last of the causal configurations is quite similar to group A. Still, if the case analysis is considered, Eastern European countries would show this causal configuration with greater than 0.5 membership in term "INRDfs * EOfs * INSTfs." That is, in the case of Eastern European countries, the quality of institutions, innovation, and opportunity would generate economic growth as well as in group A.

Table 3. The outcome of Equation 2

	Raw Coverage	Unique Coverage	Consistency
	Group A		
INSTfz *Yfs	0.561233	0.075771	0.797247
INRDfs * INSTfz * HKfs	0.481938	0.088811	0.714099
~ INRDfs * Yfs	0.380617	0.120705	0.850394
Solution coverage:	0.690749		
Solution consistency	0.726599		
Solution coverage	0.690749		
Solution consistency: 0.726599			
Group B			
Yfs * HKfs	0.644172	0.384049	0.922671
INRDfs * HKfs	0.284663	0.024540	0.760656
INSTfz * Yfs* INRDfs	0.348466	0.109202	0.904459
Solution coverage	0.777914		
Solution consistency	0.812820		

Table 3 shows the causal configurations that promote opportunity entrepreneurship, where the causal configurations of economic growth are determinants of entrepreneurship by opportunity. In particular, "INSTfs * Yfs" represents the largest number of cases in group A. The causal configuration "INRDfs * INSTfs * HKfs" shows the conjunction between innovation, the quality of institutions, and human capital. And, finally, the causal configurations "~ INRDfs * Yfs" represent a group of countries with fewer cases, where GDPpc growth causes entrepreneurship by opportunity, and these countries have low R&D expenses. However, it should be noted that raw coverage and unique coverage have low values.

In group B, observe that the causal configuration to which more cases correspond is "Yfs * HKfs" with raw coverage of 0.64 and consistency 0.92. Thus, as in group A, economic growth determines entrepreneurship by opportunity. Finally, the configuration "INSTfs * Yfs * INRDfs" is the only one in which the quality of the institutions appear and, precisely, if we analyze the cases with greater than 0.5 membership in causal configuration corresponds to Eastern European countries.

CONCLUSION

Policymakers have considered economic growth as one of the crucial objectives of economic policy. For this reason, several studies have been carried out to determine the variables that can influence this objective. Among them, entrepreneurship is the variable that has received the most attention in recent decades. But it is also essential to specify the factors that can affect entrepreneurship. In this sense, innovations and institutions are two variables to be considered. On the other hand, the structural situation of the countries analyzed must also be taken into account, since the variables may have different importance at the time of the economic challenge, depending on the level of development.

Taking all this into account, empirical analysis has been developed for 33 countries that show different levels of growth and development. To carry out the study, nations have been classified into two broad groups taking into account the GEM classification (Kelley et al., 2012, p.14): factor-based economies and efficiency-based economies.

From the empirical analysis, the following conclusions can be drawn. In group A, economic growth would be explained in most cases by the quality of the institutions, entrepreneurship by opportunity, and R&D investment. Likewise, another path followed by the countries belonging to group A would be to contemplate both types of entrepreneurship, invest in R&D, and product innovation. On the other hand, in group B the factors that determine growth would be human capital, entrepreneurship by opportunity, and entrepreneurship by necessity. Also, although the number of cases would be smaller, it is observed that there are countries of group B that are betting on investing in R&D and product innovation. However, it is noteworthy that in almost all group B cause configurations, both types of entrepreneurship appear; that is, entrepreneurship by necessity is more critical in Group B countries than in Group A countries.

On the other hand, from the analysis of equation 2, there are feedback effects between growth and entrepreneurship by opportunity, since GDPpc growth to appear causal configurations of the two groups of countries. However, the rest of the factors change according to the group considered. In group A, together with economic growth, the quality of the institutions would appear as a determining factor, and in group B, there would be human capital. On the other hand, R&D investment and human capital are also decisive for entrepreneurship by opportunity in countries in both groups of countries. Still, in group A, more countries would have opted for this strategy than group B.

This analysis could be improved, including more qualitative variables, mainly income distribution, as an explanatory variable of the social climate and having a larger sample of countries. This can be done as the available statistical information will be improved.

REFERENCES

Acemoglu, D. (2003). Root Causes. A historical approach to assessing the role of institutions in economic development. *Finance & Development*, *40*(2), 27–30.

Acemoglu, D., Johnson, S., & Robinson, J. A. (2001). The colonial origins of comparative development: An empirical investigation. *The American Economic Review*, *91*(5), 1369–1401. doi:10.1257/aer.91.5.1369

Acemoglu, D., Johnson, S., & Robinson, J. A. (2005). Institutions as a fundamental cause of long-run growth. In P. Aghion & S. Durlauf (Eds.), *Handbook of Economic Growth* (pp. 385–472). Elsevier.

Acs, Z. J., Audretsch, D. B., Braunerhjelm, P., & Carlsson, B. (2012). Growth and entrepreneurship. *Small Business Economics*, *39*(2), 289–300. doi:10.100711187-010-9307-2

Acs, Z. J., Estrin, S., Mickiewicz, T., & Szerb, L. (2018). Entrepreneurship, institutional economics, and economic growth: An ecosystem perspective. *Small Business Economics*, *51*(2), 501–514. doi:10.100711187-018-0013-9

Alam, A., Uddin, M., & Yazdifar, H. (2019). Institutional determinants of R&D investment: Evidence from emerging markets. *Technological Forecasting and Social Change*, *138*(1), 34–44. doi:10.1016/j.techfore.2018.08.007

Alpkan, L., Bulut, C., Gundy, G., Ulusoy, G., & Kilic, K. (2010). Organizational support for intrapreneurship and its interaction with human capital to enhance innovative performance. *Management Decision*, *48*(5), 732–755. doi:10.1108/00251741011043902

Audretsch, D., & Fritsch, M. (2003). Linking entrepreneurship to growth: The case of West Germany. *Industry and Innovation*, *10*(1), 65–73. doi:10.1080/1366271032000068104

Audretsch, D. B. (2005). The knowledge spillover theory of entrepreneurship and economic growth. In G. T. Vinig & R. C. W. Van Der Voort (Eds.), *The Emergence of Entrepreneurial Economics* (pp. 37–54). Emerald Group Publishing. doi:10.1016/S0737-1071(05)09003-7

Audretsch, D. B., & Keilbach, M. (2004a). Does entrepreneurship capital matter? *Entrepreneurship Theory and Practice*, *2*(5), 419–429. doi:10.1111/j.1540-6520.2004.00055.x

Audretsch, D. B., & Keilbach, M. (2004b). Entrepreneurship capital and economic performance. *Regional Studies*, *38*(8), 949–959. doi:10.1080/0034340042000280956

Autio, E., Kenney, M., Mustar, P., Siegel, D., & Wright, M. (2014). Entrepreneurial innovation: The importance of context. *Research Policy*, *43*(7), 1097–1108. doi:10.1016/j.respol.2014.01.015

Baregheh, A., Rowley, J., & Sambrook, S. (2009). Towards a multidisciplinary definition of innovation. *Management Decision*, *47*(8), 1323–1339. doi:10.1108/00251740910984578

Berg-Schlosser, D., De Meur, G., Rihoux, B., & Ragin, C. C. (2009). Qualitative comparative analysis (QCA) as an approach. *Configurational comparative methods: Qualitative comparative analysis (QCA) and related techniques*, 1-18.

Bosma, N., Content, J., Sanders, M., & Stam, E. (2018). Institutions, entrepreneurship, and economic growth in Europe. *Small Business Economics, 51*(2), 483–499. doi:10.100711187-018-0012-x

Boudreaux, C. J., Nikolaev, B. N., & Klein, P. (2019). Socio-cognitive traits and entrepreneurship: The moderating role of economic institutions. *Journal of Business Venturing, 34*(1), 178–196. doi:10.1016/j.jbusvent.2018.08.003

Castaño, M. S., Méndez, M. T., & Galindo, M. A. (2016). Innovation, internationalization, and business-growth expectations among entrepreneurs in the services sector. *Journal of Business Research, 69*(5), 1690–1695. doi:10.1016/j.jbusres.2015.10.039

De Cleyn, S. H., & Braet, J. (2012). Do board composition and investor type influence innovativeness in SMEs? *The International Entrepreneurship and Management Journal, 8*(3), 285–308. doi:10.100711365-010-0168-6

Dilli, S., Elert, N., & Herrmann, A. M. (2018). Varieties of entrepreneurship: Exploring the institutional foundations of different entrepreneurship types through 'Varieties-of-Capitalism' arguments. *Small Business Economics, 51*(2), 293–320. doi:10.100711187-018-0002-z

Drucker, P. F. (1998). The discipline of innovation. *Harvard Business Review, 76*(6), 149–157. PMID:10187245

Elert, N., & Henrekson, M. (2017). Entrepreneurship and institutions: A bidirectional relationship. *Foundations and Trends in Entrepreneurship, 13*(3), 191–263. doi:10.1561/0300000073

Fiss, P. C. (2007). A set-theoretic approach to organizational configurations. *Academy of Management Review, 32*(4), 1180–1198. doi:10.5465/amr.2007.26586092

Galindo, M. A., & Méndez, M. T. (2014). Entrepreneurship, economic growth, and innovation: Are feedback effects at work? *Journal of Business Research, 67*(5), 825–829. doi:10.1016/j.jbusres.2013.11.052

Galindo, M. A., & Méndez-Picazo, M. T. (2013). Innovation, entrepreneurship and economic growth. *Management Decision, 51*(3), 501–514. doi:10.1108/00251741311309625

Galindo-Martín, M. A., Méndez-Picazo, M. T., & Castaño-Martinez, M. S. (2019). The role of innovation and institutions in entrepreneurship and economic growth in two groups of countries. *International Journal of Entrepreneurial Behaviour & Research, 26*(3), 485–502. doi:10.1108/IJEBR-06-2019-0336

Global Entrepreneurship Monitor Project (GEM). (2019). *APS-Global data 2014-2016*. https://www.gemconsortium.org/data/sets

Henik, E. (2015). Understanding whistle-blowing: A set-theoretic approach. *Journal of Business Research, 68*(2), 442–450. doi:10.1016/j.jbusres.2014.06.004

Heritage Foundation. (2019). *Index of economic freedom*. Available at www.heritage.org/index/

Justesen, M. K., & Kurrild-Klitgaard, P. (2013). Institutional interactions and economic growth: The joint effects of property rights, veto players and democratic capital. *Public Choice, 157*(3-4), 449–474. doi:10.100711127-013-0143-1

Kelley, D. J., Singer, S., & Herrington, M. (2012). *Global Entrepreneurship Monitor 2011 Global Report*. Global Entrepreneurship Research Association and London Business School.

Kent, R., & Olsen, W. (2008). *Using fsQCA a brief guide and workshop for fuzzy-set qualitative comparative analysis*. Available at: http://www.cmist.manchester.ac.uk/medialibrary/archive-publications/working-papers/2008/2008-10-teaching-paper-fsqca.pdf

Kent, R. A. (2005). Cases as configurations: Using combinatorial and fuzzy logic to analyze marketing data. *International Journal of Market Research*, *47*(2), 205–228. doi:10.1177/147078530504700202

Kraus, S., Ribeiro-Soriano, D., & Schüssler, M. (2018). Fuzzy-set qualitative comparative analysis (fsQCA) in entrepreneurship and innovation research–the rise of a method. *The International Entrepreneurship and Management Journal*, *14*(1), 15–33. doi:10.100711365-017-0461-8

Lim, D. S. K., Oh, C. H., & De Clercq, D. (2016). Engagement in entrepreneurship in emerging economies: Interactive effects of individual-level factors and institutional conditions. *International Business Review*, *25*(4), 933–945. doi:10.1016/j.ibusrev.2015.12.001

Méndez-Picazo, M. T., Galindo-Martín, M. A., & Ribeiro-Soriano, D. (2012). Governance, entrepreneurship and economic growth. *Entrepreneurship and Regional Development*, *24*(9-10), 865–877. doi:10.1080/08985626.2012.742323

Nissan, E., Galindo Martín, M. A., & Méndez Picazo, M. T. (2011). Relationship between organizations, institutions, entrepreneurship and economic growth process. *The International Entrepreneurship and Management Journal*, *7*(3), 311–324. doi:10.100711365-011-0191-2

Przeworski, A., & Limongi, F. (1993). Political regimes and economic growth. *The Journal of Economic Perspectives*, *7*(3), 51–69. doi:10.1257/jep.7.3.51

Ragin, C. C. (1987). *The comparative method: Moving beyond qualitative and quantitative methods*. University of California.

Ragin, C. C. (2006). Set relations in social research: Evaluating their consistency and coverage. *Political Analysis*, *14*(3), 291–310. doi:10.1093/pan/mpj019

Ragin, C. C. (2008). *User's guide to fuzzy-set/qualitative comparative analysis*. Available at: http://www.u.arizona.edu/~cragin/fsQCA/download/fsQCAManual.pdf

Ragin, C. C., & Sonnett, J. (2005). Between complexity and parsimony: Limited diversity, counterfactual cases, and comparative analysis. In *Vergleichen in der Politikwissenschaft* (pp. 180–197). VS Verlag für Sozialwissenschaften. doi:10.1007/978-3-322-80441-9_9

Rodrik, D. (2005). Growth strategies. In P. Aghion & S. Durlauf (Eds.), *Handbook of Economic Growth* (Vol. 1, pp. 967–1014). Elsevier.

Schumpeter, J. A. (1911). *The Theory of Economic Development: An Inquiry into Profits, Capital, Credit, Interest and Business Cycle*. Harvard University Press.

Schumpeter, J. A. (1950). *Capitalism, Socialism, and Democracy*. Harper & Brother Publishers.

Simón-Moya, V., Revuelto-Taboada, L., & Guerrero, R. F. (2014). Institutional and economic drivers of entrepreneurship: An international perspective. *Journal of Business Research, 67*(5), 715–721. doi:10.1016/j.jbusres.2013.11.033

Sirowy, L., & Inkeles, A. (1990). The effects of democracy on economic growth and inequality: A review. *Studies in Comparative International Development, 25*(1), 126–157. doi:10.1007/BF02716908

Urbano, D., Aparicio, S., & Audretsch, D. (2019). Twenty-five years of research on institutions, entrepreneurship, and economic growth: What has been learned? *Small Business Economics, 53*(1), 21–49. doi:10.100711187-018-0038-0

Wennekers, S., Van Wennekers, A., Thurik, R., & Reynolds, P. (2005). Nascent entrepreneurship and the level of economic development. *Small Business Economics, 24*(3), 293–309. doi:10.100711187-005-1994-8

Woodside, A. G. (2013). Moving beyond multiple regression analysis to algorithms: Calling for adoption of a paradigm shift from symmetric to asymmetric thinking in data analysis and crafting theory. *Journal of Business Research, 66*(4), 463–472. doi:10.1016/j.jbusres.2012.12.021

World Bank. (2019). *World development indicators*. Available at http://datatopics.worldbank.org/world-development-indicators/

Zortea-Johnston, E., Darroch, J., & Matear, S. (2012). Business orientations and innovation in small and medium-sized enterprises. *The International Entrepreneurship and Management Journal, 8*(2), 145–164. doi:10.100711365-011-0170-7

KEY TERMS AND DEFINITIONS

Efficiency-Driven Economies: Countries are increasingly competitive, with more-efficient production processes and increased product quality. At this level of development, economies are characterized by higher education and training, goods market efficiency, labor market efficiency, financial market sophistication, technological readiness, and higher market size.

FsQCA: The qualitative comparative analysis of fuzzy sets (fsQCA) is a methodology to obtain causal configurations from data from specific cases. This method attempts to search for logical connections between combinations of causal conditions and a result, the result being paths that describe how combinations of causal conditions would cause the expected result.

Innovation-Driven Economies: Countries are the most developed. In this phase, businesses are more knowledge-intensive, and the service sector expands. The main difference is that these economies are based on knowledge and innovations activities.

Institutions: Are formed by the set of norms and agreements given to actors, organizations, and people to regulate their economic, social, and political relations. Institutions can be formal and informal.

Motivational Index: This index measures the relationship between opportunity entrepreneurship and necessity entrepreneurship, where the higher the score on the index, the greater the opportunity motivation.

Necessity Entrepreneurship: Entrepreneurs that start-up the need to create one's own employment in response to the lack of other job alternatives.

Opportunity Entrepreneurship: Entrepreneur that start-up to net exploitation of a business opportunity.

ENDNOTE

1 "fs_" indicates that this variable has been calibrated.

Chapter 10
The Evaluation of the Service and Its Impact on Brand Value:
The Case of Language Schools in Guayaquil

Danny C. Barbery-Montoya
https://orcid.org/0000-0002-6005-4997
Universidad Espíritu Santo, Ecuador

Carlos Bautista-Nuques
Ogilvy Ecuador, Ecuador

Jeaneth P. Wiesner-Mora
Conecel, Claro Ecuador, Ecuador

ABSTRACT

For service companies, one of the most difficult challenges to measure is brand value, considering the subjectivity of the service, given by consumer perception. In this way, the objective of this chapter is to know the elements that provide value to the service company's brand. To carry out the study, the authors deepen the concepts of service and brand considering the SERVQUAL and CSI questionnaires, which allow them to obtain indexes of measurement of the quality of services and brand valuation and apply them in the English language teaching institutes in Guayaquil (Ecuador). The results show that five high-importance schools have valuation elements that build their brand with characteristics that differentiate them, but also with others that resemble them. Understanding each of the brands and variables, they propose an initial model that allows analyzing this industry in which elements relevant to the consumer are observed.

DOI: 10.4018/978-1-7998-5036-6.ch010

INTRODUCTION

The Real Academia Española defines a service as the action of a person to satisfy some social need, not leading to produce any material well. To put it simply, a service is the action of one person towards another in developing any work (Tigani, 2006). From the economic field, service is established as an economic activity that creates value and provides an intangible benefit to the customer at a specific time and place, resulting in acquiring a desired product or service (Lovelock, Patterson, & Wirtz, 2004). Thus, the customer-focused service establishes two crucial characteristics: contact with the customer and the customer-based relationship (Duque-Oliva, 2005). Its concept is based on the fact that organizations achieve their objectives effectively and efficiently through identifying and understanding clients' needs (Duque-Oliva & Diosa-Gómez, 2014). In other words, how clients meet their needs, so it could be understood that the service is the sum of processes of activities and efforts of organizations to meet the needs of their customers, in an intangible way.

On the other hand, the term quality has evolved according to the time. In the beginning, it was defined towards the product and the industry. Later it focused on the improvement of certain client conditions; and then to satisfy the needs and expectations of the client. For this reason, quality is defined from two approaches: objective and subjective quality. The first one focuses directly on the producer and refers to the inner vision of quality, in terms of production and supply. The second one focuses on marketing with an external vision, where the needs, wishes, and expectations that the client has about a product or service, which are the absolute judges in terms of quality (Vazques, Roríguez, & Díaz, 1996).

In this way, the quality of service is a form of attitude dealing with performance in terms of customer service. For this reason, the quality is evaluated by clients, making a comparison of what he receives to what he wants and expects to receive. Both are experiential associations focused on perceived attention and are not necessarily a natural response of the product or service (Ghobadian, Speller, & Matthew, 1994). For this reason, it is essential to recognize the client's perception to develop a correct judgment of the value of the experience obtained in the care. It must be understood that this attitude is not a linear process, but is mediated between the interaction of the individual with the society where it is immersed. With all this, we understand that to define the quality of service, it must be referred to the perceived quality of the client, which is subjective and greater concerning the physical element produced. For that same reason, it cannot be measured as a tangible product, but by comparing an expected and perceived service, giving results obtained from the differentiation that the consumer perceives between their expectations and the results obtained (Duque-Oliva & Diosa-Gómez, 2014).

With the perception of the quality of service, companies must assess how important the perception of their brand is since it is one of their most important assets. Their perception and valuation allow us to provide substantial advantages and create a unique business personality in the market (Buil, Martínez & De Chernatony, 2010). Still, today modern markets have radically changed their perspective on making a brand have the value and the desired acceptance in the minds of its customers (Steenkamp & de Jong, 2010). For that same reason, every company or organization must make measurements that generate sustainable marketing strategies focused on constructing brands' value (Kotler & Keller, 2012). For many years, there has been an extensive discussion of the different methods used to value a brand. In the last decade, two fundamental approaches emerged (Simon & Sullivan, 1993): (a) the macro approach, to focus on valuing the brand as an asset of the company, and (b) the micro approach, to value brands based on consumer preferences in more specific products. Whether measuring the brand value through financial techniques or measuring them through their relationship with the marketing models, the two will always have different approaches and results, in which the first measures the value of the brand for the company and the second the value it has for consumers (Kamakura & Russell, 1993). In the case of macro methods, most are viewed from a financial point of view and pose different accounting problems, which do not allow a real approach to the value that consumers build in their choices and preferences of products or services. From the marketing-oriented approach, on the one hand, they pose how difficult it is to translate the results into quantitative values. On the other, it only focuses on the brand's value as one of its components without considering the influence caused by the interaction between all the elements that integrate the value of the brand (Gómez cited by Ramos, 2002). The financial methods are more used for their ease of application. Still, the marketing methods are the most appropriate to determine the strategic management of a brand, taking into account that the financial valuation is insufficient, given that the information it would provide is limited to contemplate the perspective of the consumer, offering short-term results. A method that focuses on marketing will allow us to obtain a brand value considered by the client (Ramos, 2002).

Considering the concepts of service quality and brand value mentioned above, we ask ourselves a research question. What are the elements that generate value for a service brand? Thus, the objective of the chapter focuses on demonstrating brand valuation variables taking as an example, the English language teaching services industry in Ecuador. We have chosen this industry, given its importance in the development and growth of economies, since it influences areas related to industries, commercial activities, and even in international interests (Bonilla & Rojas, 2012). Also, English has become an essential tool for education in the country (América-Economía, 2018); its preponderant role as a second language in Ecuador makes it the international language for technology and commerce (D'Andrea, Garré, & Rodríguez, 2012).

For this reason, in Guayaquil, there are many institutions and schools of bilingual education that offer their training services at all ages. At different times, they did not need a registration or a guarantee from the Ministry of Education for its operation. These schools have been built over the years through their trajectory. According to the Universe newspaper, founded 60 years ago, its brands are perceived by the media as educational entities with strength due to their age.

BACKGROUND

Quality of Service

Quality is defined as the property or set of properties inherent in something, which allow its value to be judged. This description first establishes the characteristics or properties, and second, the ability to determine the value of something through them. Duque-Oliva (2005) mentions that there are other definitions in that the quality is related to the characteristics of the products, which are based on the needs of the customer and, for that reason, provide satisfaction since this is implicit in all the elements that make up a consumer need: product, work, service, information, process, people, system, the company, objectives, among others. Quality can also be seen as "what the customer gets from a service and what they are willing to pay" (Drucker, 1990 cited by Sánchez, 2006, p. 41). Sánchez (2006) mentions that for this reason within a company, three crucial elements involved in terms of quality of service are identified: agents, relationships, and the environment. First, it focuses on the inspection and statistical control derived from the internal production approach, headed by the standardized efficiency. Second, it is an external vision, which determines a measure through the fulfillment of needs, desires, and clients' expectations. Third, it comprises customs, behaviors, and beliefs, determining the quality level of products and services consumers wish to receive. Therefore, quality deserves a different conceptualization, being more than a tangible element.

Unlike the products, which can be measured objectively, the quality of the services is somewhat fleeting, existential at the moment, which determines an experience linked to the context of that moment, which can be positive or negative and that makes it more challenging to measure (Parasuraman, Zeithaml & Berry, 1988). Thus, the quality of a service depends very much on comparing the expected service concerning the perceived one, the customer satisfaction judgments being the results of the perceived difference between the expectation and the perception of the results.

Quality of Service Dimension

Druker (1990), cited by Sánchez (2006), establishes five dimensions to carry out a quality evaluation more focused on the satisfaction obtained in the client that defines them as shown in Table 1.

Table 1. Dimension of quality of service

Dimensions	Description
Reliability	The Company can provide a service in a reliable, safe, and careful manner. It also determined the level of professional knowledge of the organization, that is, to provide a service correctly and effectively from the beginning.
Security	It is the level of trust that the customer has towards the company that they can solve any problem related to their product or service. Security implies credibility, integrity, reliability, and honesty.
Response Capacity	It is the attitude to help customers, response times, response fulfillment.
Empathy	It is the disposition on the part of the company before the city and the personalized attention. It is not only about courtesy, but in-depth knowledge of clients and their characteristics.
Tangible Elements	They are the appearance of physical facilities, equipment, employees, and printed materials.

Source: Drucker (1990) cited by Sánchez (2006)

Value in Service Quality

Identify, create, and deliver value to the consumer are currently identified as critical traits in business management (Sirdeshmukh, Singh, & Sabol, 2002). Companies will achieve competitive advantages by implementing strategies focused on the value within the quality of service. The perceived value in services has been considered a new approach in this area. The perceived value constitutes a fundamental pillar in the quality of service, not only because it satisfies the needs of the consumer, but also allows the construction of a long-term relationship, loyalty in their relationship and allowing the customer to be retained for longer. This value link can be classified as a loyalty behavior by the consumer and the company. Kotler and Keller (2012) affirm that all the companies that have as a primary focus to the clients are better positioned in the market, allowing them to establish strategies that provide long-term benefits. The management of maintaining a relationship with the client does not mean ignoring the competition and its plans but staying close to the people who make up its target audience, generating strategies different from the needs of its customers. Whiteley and Hessan (1996) mention that all companies that focus on the needs of customers allow adding value to their internal processes resulting in more significant opportunities for economic growth and recall by the client, creating brand recommendation through word of mouth.

On the other hand, Ralston, cited by Guadarrama and Rosales (2015), mentions that in his model (Satisfaction-Use-Recommendation), he emphasizes the importance of satisfying the client and points out that a satisfied customer repeats his purchase and attracts many more customers. The loyalty of a brand influences a positive attitude of repeated purchase by the customer, but also affects dissatisfaction since the effects of a bad recommendation can be measured by the level of dissatisfaction on the part of the customer: if it is high, There is the disagreement, and there will be a high consequence of negative recommendation, but when it is low, the consumer will not usually complain and accept the experience. Maxham Iii (2001) affirms that any failure is an inconvenience that must be resolved immediately. For this reason, companies attend all complaints from their clients, transforming the needs of the clients, and correcting them. This strategy positively impacts companies creating profitability, thus avoiding harmful recommendations. Complaints by customers should be considered an opportunity for improvement and loyalty for companies because when a customer complains, he/she is showing interest in the company.

Service Quality Evaluation Model (SERVQUAL)

In the 1980s, there was a need to understand how the quality of service influenced the consumer; for that reason, it was necessary to create an efficient measuring instrument, which is why one of the first and most recognized model in the area, called SERVQUAL Model, is developed. This proposal was developed in several stages by the American School of Marketing (Parasuraman, Zeithaml & Berry, 1988), which began with a qualitative study, with interviews with people and managers of service companies: retail banking, cards of credit, securities brokers, and equipment maintenance repair, resulting in a conceptual model of service quality, based on *the gaps* or *gap theory*, The Gaps Models of Service Quality (Mauri, Minazzi, & Muccio, 2013), that talks about the differences between expectations and consumer perception about the service received. The model relates four elements that form expectations: 1) Word of mouth communication, 2) Personal needs of the consumer, 3) Previous expectations, and 4) External communication of the company, which are sized to assess the quality of service. Parasuraman et al. (1988) receive support in a quantitative investigation, simplifying the 5-dimensional model: a) Empathy, b) Reliability, c) Security, d) Responsiveness, e) Tangible elements. Based on these five dimensions, the SERVQUAL multidimensional model is designed, which raises 22 questions from the point of view of consumer expectations, and the same number of items on the perception of the service received, evaluated on a seven-point Likert scale conforming thus the instrument with 44 items. Thus, when the expectations are exceeded by the consumer, the service can be classified as exceptional quality; However, if it fails to meet consumer expectations, the service is rated as deficient. Currently, the SERVQUAL model has been used to measure the level of satisfaction in various areas of studies such as health, supermarkets, education, hotels, telecommunications, among others. Its importance lies in the fact that this model allows us to understand consumer satisfaction with the services received, determining the difference between expectations and perception focused on a specific service.

Brand Value

Businesses should assess how vital their brand perception is since it is one of the most critical assets within a company; its perception and valuation allow substantial advantages and create a unique business personality (Buil et al., 2010). But today, modern markets have radically changed their perspective of how to make a brand have the desired value and acceptance in the minds of its customers (Steenkamp & de Jong, 2010). For that same reason, every company or organization must make measurements that generate sustainable marketing strategies focused on constructing the value of its brands (Kotler & Keller, 2012 cited by Forero & Duque, 2014). The value of the brand is seen as a multidimensional judgment model that focuses on the relationship between the consumer and what he knows about it, which is why two measurement approaches are established, the tangible and intangible. The first is the cost of the brand or so-called price premium, which gives the brand the ability to charge consumers higher prices or, from another point of view, the willingness of consumers to pay higher values for a specific brand compared to similar ones (Tasci, 2016). The second is about the mind of the consumer (Leone et al., 2006), which states that for some products, the intangible value is greater than the value of the company that chairs it; For this reason, the power of a brand lies in the mind of the consumer who experiences, learns and feels the brand over time. Value's brand is considered as "added value," as it is the quality given to a product for the ability to be in the thought, words, and actions of consumers. This value can be active and passive, strongly linked to the brand, its name, symbol, product, which determines the perception, preference, and behavior of consumers (Buil et al., 2010).

Research studies have shown that brands, when creating an identity with consumers, cause repeated purchases (also called repurchases), being positive actions for brand creation as a consequence of word of mouth (Stokburger-Sauer, Ratneshwar, & Sen, 2012). This fact allows companies to have a greater chance of setting their prices in the local market to create purchase loyalty in their customers, even in those who are reluctant to exchange for others. Product criticism is minimal, and this repurchase action is based on impulse (Haumann, Quaiser, Wieseke, & Rese, 2014).

In this way, the brand value refers to how it receives relevant recognition from the consumer and associates it favorably at the time of purchase choice. The brand generates genuine value when perceived in a differentiable, unique, and attractive way from the rest of the rival brands. When the brand value is generated, better benefits can be expected for the company that owns the brand, generating greater customer loyalty by increasing the value offer (Keller, 2013). Increasingly, they emphasize the need to change the transactional vision of a company to an idea where the consumer and brand relationship is the primary strategy at the forefront of its brands (Davvetas & Diamantopoulos, 2018) where firms invest significant resources in building the relationship between brand and consumer. Thompson, Rindleisch, and Arsel (2006) also agree that brand value is defined by the relationship of the consumer and their personal identification, which is tangible and intangible, whose utility is derived from its ability to meet particular specific consumer needs, giving the brand a value purchasing that can be defined by economic terms in the market concerning its competition. However, currently, this vision is challenged with new concepts, which not only see products or services as elements of easy replacement; Today, the public sees the product more than mere possession. The consumer theory approaches affirm that brands are in the center of the market and have cultural values linked to consumers' experience (Sichtmann, Davvetas, & Diamantopoulos, 2018). Also, Richins (1994) argues that products are extensions of their own and are part of consumers' identities. For example, during the life of a person, people buy products and brands endowed with sentimental values (gifts, photo albums, and family heirlooms), high-value goods (houses, properties, vehicles, appliances, entertainment objects for sports, and musical instruments), and items related to personal appearance (clothing, jewelry, and perfumes). Consumers can also mention objects that represent personal achievements linked to the past, and aesthetic items: paintings, antiques, among others. This fact leads to defining that the value of a brand is related to an intimate relationship between the person who consumes them and their brand relationship in the consumer's situation or lifestyle, instead of associating it with an inert and worthless purchasing possession (Fournier, 1998).

Brand Personality

Brand personality is defined as values and cultural beliefs that consumers mentally add to a product, based on the central axis of the environment where he lives and relates (Sung & Tinkham, 2005) since a Brand relationship is very similar to the relationship between people. In the beginning, a brand has no emotional value. Still, as the consumer uses it in their daily lives, it becomes essential in such a way that the brand name becomes a powerful representation symbol that the person keeps in their minds (Saavedra, Colmenares & Pirela, 2007). According to Aaker (1997), the personality of a brand includes positive and negative traits in human nature when it consumes them, such as feelings and concern. Since the nineties, brands began to be studied as elements that cause emotions, defining them as elements possessing an emotional dimension in the mind of the consumer. To understand this, we must understand the buying behavior of the consumer when selecting a product or service, as the set of logical steps that the person performs progressively, with a minimum of usual change of decision, to reach the action or final purchase decision. There are several brand models; however, the following phases have been established as coincident: the awakening, identifying or recognizing the consumer craves; the formulation and implementation of the purchase choice; and the evaluation of the consequences (Coca-Carasila, 2010). The studies also coincide that the purchase decision depends a lot on internal or external factors, whether emotions, environment, time, purchasing value, among others, which influence the moment of purchase of a product or service (Khan, 2006).

Thus, Schiffman and Kanuk (cited by Coca-Carasila, 2010) synthesize four models of consumer behaviors:

From the economic: the purchase is the rational use that the person makes at the time of deciding what product or service he will need. This action is known as "economic man" since the person investigates other product proposals before purchasing.

From the passive point of view: the person makes their purchase impulsively and irrationally. Their behavior is submissive and emotionally high compared to the advertising campaigns promoting the company and its products.

The cognitive point of view: the person seeks to solve their problems, which analyzes and evaluates the information of a product or service to make a correct purchase decision.

The emotional or impulsive point of view: the person gives less importance to the information, giving more priority to the mood and their feelings by carrying out the buying action that is performed irrationally.

Emotions a high impact axis as a unique factor that influences consumer purchasing decisions; This is emotional intelligence, a way of interacting with the world with emotions in mind, including skills such as impulse control, self-awareness, motivation, enthusiasm, empathy, and mental agility, among others (Goleman, 2007). Thus, emotions are a crucial factor in life, but this factor is very complicated to be analyzed. Still, there is no doubt that emotions play an essential role in making decisions to make a purchase. In this way, this theory is not very evident in everyday purchases, since they do not mark a definite and clear emotional state because it is a routine process. However, it is much more precise and more evident in complex purchases. Rational or emotional decision-making is needed, which is why it is a factor of high involvement. Therefore, companies understood that by incorporating the brand as intangible asset value, they would strengthen their finances (García, 2000), even allowing them to grow, carrying out operations of the merger of companies or the sale and transfer of the brand itself in a franchised manner. Kapferer (cited by Ramos, 2002) mentions that knowing how to do and communicating the value of the brand is often difficult to understand since brand management is created in a time range valued in the processes that the company develops so that the brand gets its value. Brand valuation methods should be concerned with establishing a valuation measure, even when a brand is sold to another company to continue maintaining the same value in other hands (Ramos, 2002).

Brand Value Measurement

For many years now, there has been a comprehensive discussion of the different methods proposed to value a brand. Whether measuring brand value through financial techniques or measuring them through their relationship with marketing models, the two will always have different approaches and results. The first measures the value of the brand for the company and the second the value it has for consumers m. In the case of macro methods, most are viewed from a financial point of view and pose different accounting problems, which do not allow a real approach to the value that consumers build in their choices and preferences of products or services. From the marketing-oriented approach, on the one hand, they pose how difficult it is to translate the results into quantitative values. On the other, it only focuses on the value of the brand as one of its components without considering the influence caused by the interaction between all the elements that integrate the brand's value (Gómez cited by Ramos, 2002). The financial methods are more used for their ease of application. Still, the marketing methods are the most appropriate to determine the strategic management of a brand, since the financial valuation is insufficient since the information it would provide is limited by not contemplating the consumer perspective, offering short-term results (Ramos, 2002).

Dimensions to Measure Brand Value

In recent years, people have been creating a society where the basis of their actions is given to the increase in consumption, whose meaning is that people have easier access to new goods and services. Although it is correct at all times, there have been behaviors concerning consumption. Today, society imposes what should be consumed, since having the ability to choose between one or more products, the consumer today chooses what to wear or to eat, where to study, among others. Aaker (cited by Ramos, 2002) proposes ten dimensions that will serve as a basis to reflect the value of the brand asset, which are based on the four most important components: loyalty, perceived quality, association, and name recognition, and an additional one that is the behavior of the brand, as shown in table 2.

Table 2. Dimension to measure the brand value

Dimensions	Description
Higher price or overprice	What the client is willing to pay for a brand
Client's Satisfaction and fidelity	It is the client's loyalty for the brand
Quality	It is the way the customer reacts to the degree of quality perceived by a brand
Leadership/Popularity	It is the way the customer perceives how innovative a brand is independent of its quality
Usage Value	How generating value and functional benefit is the brand for the consumer
Personality	It is a symbolic and emotional benefit from the brand; how interesting it is perceived and the clarity with which the image of the brand user is given
Brand Recognition	Brand presence in the mind of the consumer (recognition, assisted recall, top of mind, and mastery of the brand)
Organization	It is the perception of the company with which the brand is associated
Market Share	It is the performance that a brand has in the market with its sales volume. Assuming a positive correlation between brand value and sales
Price index and distribution	It is the quoted value of a brand in the market both by investors and shareholders

Source: Aaker cited by Ramos, 2002

The Consumer Style Index model - CSI

The decision-making style is a fascinating segment of research and should be studied carefully. For this reason, a model called Consumer Style Inventory (CSI) developed by Sproles and Kendall (1986) and cited by Mokhlis (2009) was developed, which provides a potentially useful instrument to help companies examine the styles of taking consumer decisions. According to Sproles and Kendall (1986), the identification of decision-making styles among consumers helps to build an outline of an individual consumer-style and establishes profiles to allow consumers to be taught on specific characteristics of products and services useful for decision-making and financial management. Over time, the CSI model has been improving its structure, and therefore, a more consistent scale has been developed; Ungaretti (2013) proposes eleven dimensions that highlight consumer decision-making styles (Table 3).

Table 3. Consumer decision-making styles dimensions

Dimensions	Description
Conscious consumer, high-quality perfectionist	They look for the best quality of products and give great importance to their purchases, which make them carefully and very systematically
Conscientious brand and price consumer is equal to the quality	It focuses on the purchase of recognized and expensive brands; the price reflects the quality of the product
Novelty consumer and fashion awareness	It focuses on keeping up to date on all the trends that fashion marks
Recreational and hedonistic consumer	Making a purchase is very pleasant and entertaining
Consumer conscious price and value for money	The style of consumption is to find the lowest prices concerning products or services and seeks to assert your money
Impulsive and careless consumer	He does not seek to plan his purchases because he is not interested in understanding how much he spends and neither in making a good purchase
Consumer confused over the choice	The consumer always has significant difficulties for purchasing a product, due to the high number of products and services in the market
Consumer consents to ecology	The style of the consumer is to be responsible for the environment. It implies an ethical consumption against the environment and the society with which it is surrounded
Health-conscious consumer	The consumer is aware of what he acquires, seeks to know and inform himself about the consequences that a product can have on his body and his health through a conscious consumption
Purchase intent	Prefer a product or service brand over other existing products

Source: Ungaretti, 2013

THE PERCEPTION OF ENGLISH LANGUAGE TEACHING INSTITUTES IN GUAYAQUIL

Ecuador has a low level of English compared to other countries, according to a study conducted by Education First, ranked 35th in 63 countries; however, there is an upward trend in teaching this language in this country (El Universo, 2015). Many young people seek to learn this language in other countries such as Australia, England, Scotland, or Canada (El Universo, 2013), given that learning takes place not only within a classroom but also in activities outside it, where they also keep learning (Beltrán, 2017). Additionally, another existing problem is the marked difference between public and private teaching institutions, where gaps can be seen in the language knowledge transfer system (Mejia, 2016).

So it is that there are particular institutes of language teaching that are looking for a space in the market (El Universo, 2019), which has been projecting its supply growth since 2014 (El Comercio, 2014). Given the Ecuadorian context, it has been considered the brand study of the leading private institutes that teach this language in Guayaquil. This city is the most important seaport of Ecuador and, with a high level of commerce, is considered the capital Commercial of Ecuador (Ekos, 2018). Under this environment, a study was carried out to understand the relationship of assessment between brand perception and the quality of service of the English teaching institutes in the District of Guayaquil, so it was necessary to gather the information that allows us evidence both their coincidences and their differences.

Table 4. Service variables that stand out in each of the brands of English Teaching Institutes in Guayaquil

	Dimension	Benedict		CEN		KOE		Multibilingüe		Wall Street	
SERVQUAL	*Tangibles Elements*	**Publicity Elements**	**1,12**	**Publicity Elements**	**1,05**	Infrastructure	1,05	**Publicity Elements**	**1,30**	**Publicity Elements**	**1,08**
	Reliability	Compliance	1,04	Solution interest	1,04	**Effective compliance**	**1,10**	Solution interest	1,04	Effective compliance	1,02
	Response Capacity	Effective response	1,03	Interest in service	1,04	Professional Assistance/ Care and services	1,04	Interest in service	1,04	Effective response	1,04
	Security	Trust Generation	1,04	**Employee Knowledge**	**1,05**	Kindness	1,07	**Knowledge or employees**	**1,30**	**Trust Generation**	**1,08**
	Empathy	Client Knowledge	1,05	Convenient Hours	1,04	Client Knowledge	1,03	Cordial Attention	1,02	Client Knowledge	1,02
CSI	*Perfectionism*	Buying preference	1,39	**Buying preference**	**1,26**	Brand Interest	1,17	**Buying preference**	**1,30**	**Buying preference**	**1,47**
	Brand Awareness	Brand Choice	1,10	Brand Publicity	1,01	Brand Choice / Product Place	1,03	Brand Choice	1,08	Brand recognition	1,17
	Novelty awareness	Trends Interest	1,09	Trends Interest	1,05	Variety of products	1,13	Trends Interest	1,10	Trends Interest	1,08
	Creative consumer	Optimize time	1,18	Acción de compra	1,07	Optimize time	1,10	Optimize time	1,06	Optimize time	1,09
	Creative consumer	Lower price	1,14	Lower price	1,04	Lower price	1,10	Lower price	1,07	Lower price	1,04
	Impulsive consumer	Purchase Desire	1,17	Purchase Desire	1,07	Purchase Planning	1,02	Impulse purchase	1,13	Impulse purchase	1,18
	Consumer Confused Over-Choice	The difficulty of purchase choice	1,04	The difficulty of purchase choice	1,01	Choice to buy	1,06	Choice to buy	1,01	Brand Information	1,03
	Regular consumer	**Brand Change**	**1,43**	Brand Change	1,20	**Brand Change**	**1,24**	Brand Change	1.23	Brand Change	1,05
	Environmental awareness	Ecological brands preference	1,04	Ecological brand preference	1,02	Ecological brand preference	1,04	Ecological brand preference	1,03	Ecological brand preference	1,00
	Health awareness	Interest in health care	1,03	Interest in health	1,01	Interest in health	1,04	Interest in health care	1,04	Conscious consumer / Health interest	1,02
	Purchase intent	Interest in environmental care	1,02	Interest in organic brands	1,02	Buy organic brands	1,02	Buy organic brands	1,04	Buy organic brands	1,03

Source: The Authors

An analytical, descriptive, and correlational research of the cross-sectional, non-experimental type that allows knowing the characteristics and profiles of the clients through surveys was carried out to see the perception of the client in terms of brand preference and quality of service. For the investigation, two questionnaires were made according to the CSI research models for brand value and SERVQUAL for services. The study was chosen as the population composed of people between 20 and 44 years of age, with a high socioeconomic level (A), medium-high (B), and typical medium (C +) who have studied in a language school English. The sample size was 384 people according to the profile, considering 95% confidence and 5% error. A weighted stratified sample was prepared, where the population was divided into different social strata, considering proportionally, people living within the District of Guayaquil.

For the result analysis, it was considered as a starting point to compare SERVQUAL and CSI models, the variables that make up each dimension, and their respective average. For each brand of the English teaching institute, an average of points for each variable was obtained to know the average and deviation. As a result, the most relevant elements that a mark has on its dimensions are being understood. In this way, the highlighted variables of each dimension were obtained, and a map of the strengths of each dimension was created by the brand evaluated.

The results obtained determined five brands as the most recognized in the market of Guayaquil: Bénédict, CEN, KOE, Multibilingüe, and Wall Street. The most relevant values in each brand dimension are defined in Table 1, and the outstanding elements in each model are highlighted, that is, in SERVQUAL and CSI (Table 4).

Similarly, in Figure 1, the outstanding attributes in each of the dimensions and classified by the brand are presented graphically, separating these results as service valuation (SERVQUAL) and brand valuation (CSI).

Figure 1. Predominant variables for each brand of English Teaching Institutes in Guayaquil
Source: The Authors

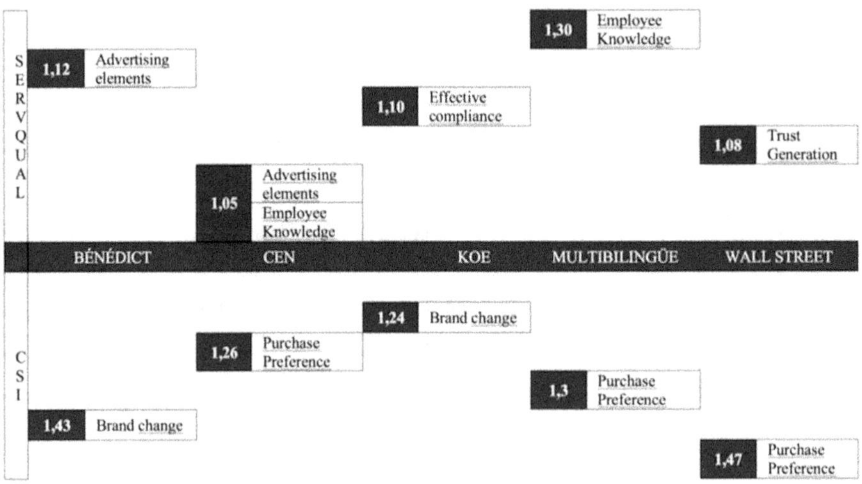

After identifying the results of the variables highlighted by each brand, the contingency tables corresponding to each model were prepared, where the service and brand attributes' dependence was measured with the names of the English Schools. To verify this dependence, we worked with chi-square tests and tests of association of V-Cramer and contingency coefficient. With this, it was determined that the variable with the best association in quality of services of the Bénédict brand is advertising elements with a C = 0.400 as a contingency coefficient, indicating that one of the fundamental pillars of this institution is its communication. On the other hand, it was determined that not all variables have a dependence on the brand, since there are values whose $p > 0.05$ such as the cases of the variables: *Time fulfillment, Professional Assistance, Attention and service, Generation of trust, Friendliness, personalized service, cordial attention and customer knowledge (yellow color in table 5).* This fact is not intended to indicate that the industry, in general, does not present these attributes. Instead, it would be understood that these are not the characteristics or characteristics of a particular brand. On the contrary, the details that show dependence explains how brands are dependent on them.

Table 5. Chi-square test to measure the dependence between English School brands and service variables

Chi-square tests						
Variables		Chi-square	df	Asymptotic significance (bilateral)	V Cramer	Contingency Coefficient
1	Equipment and technology	49,019	30	0,016	0,159	0,335
2	Attractive facilities	69,763	30	0,000	0,190	0,390
3	Employee Knowledge	68,572	30	0,000	0,188	0,388
4	Advertising elements	73,742	30	0,000	0,195	0,400
5	Compliance	50,604	30	0,011	0,162	0,340
6	Solution interest	61,819	30	0,001	0,179	0,371
7	Effective compliance	49,425	30	0,014	0,160	0,336
8	Time fulfillment	41,747	30	0,075	0,147	0,312
9	Fault handling	45,992	30	0,031	0,154	0,326
10	Professional assistance	38,665	30	0,133	0,141	0,301
11	Effective response	53,678	30	0,005	0,166	0,349
12	Attention and service	42,652	30	0,063	0,148	0,315
13	Interest in service	43,610	30	0,052	0,150	0,318
14	Trust generation	34,922	30	0,245	0,134	0,287
15	Real and complete information	54,472	30	0,004	0,168	0,351
16	Friendliness	35,608	30	0,221	0,135	0,290
17	Employee Knowledge	51,139	30	0,009	0,162	0,341
18	Personalized service	37,617	30	0,160	0,139	0,297
19	Convenient hours	50,937	30	0,010	0,162	0,341
20	Cordial attention	38,740	30	0,132	0,141	0,301
21	Interest in the client	44,185	30	0,046	0,151	0,320
22	Customer knowledge	33,429	30	0,304	0,131	0,282

Source: The Authors

Within the brand assessment, it was possible to detect that the dependence between the brands and the attributes of the dimensions measured through the CSI model is limited, showing only 11 of the 49 attributes with a low association relationship. Thus, attributes that show a $p < 0,05$ are: *Purchase preference, Purchase time, Value for money, Purchase planning, Purchase impulse, Brand choice decision, Brand change, Choice of ecological brands, Interest in health, Purchase ecological brands, Interest in ecological brands (blue color in table 6).* These attributes are defined as a differential in consumer perception and are the ones that give value to the brands studied.

Table 6. Chi-square test to measure the dependence between English School brands and brand assessment variables

Chi-square tests						
	Variables	Chi-squared	df	Asymptotic significance (bilateral)	V Cramer	Contingency Coefficient
1	High quality	13,608	20	0,850	0,094	0,184
2	Convenience	19,795	20	0,471	0,113	0,220
3	Quality preference	14,099	20	0,825	0,095	0,187
4	Quality choice	25,267	20	0,191	0,128	0,247
5	Brand interest	15,944	20	0,720	0,101	0,199
6	Quality standards	22,214	20	0,329	0,120	0,233
7	Purchase Preference	31,574	20	0,048	0,143	0,274
8	Product quality	24,966	20	0,203	0,127	0,246
9	Brand recognition	25,146	20	0,196	0,127	0,247
10	Brand choice	26,440	20	0,152	0,131	0,253
11	Quality vs. price	25,835	20	0,171	0,129	0,250
12	Product square	26,276	20	0,157	0,130	0,252
13	Recognition for sale	17,340	20	0,631	0,106	0,207
14	Brand advertising	29,097	20	0,086	0,137	0,264
15	Brand preference	21,883	20	0,347	0,119	0,231
16	Trend	24,276	20	0,231	0,125	0,243
17	Brand Importance	27,465	20	0,123	0,133	0,257
18	Variety of products	17,868	20	0,596	0,107	0,210
19	Interest in trends	21,166	20	0,387	0,117	0,227
20	Purchase Action	23,821	20	0,250	0,124	0,241
21	Purchase sentiment	18,793	20	0,535	0,110	0,215
22	Optimize time	26,518	20	0,149	0,131	0,253
23	Shopping experience	16,358	20	0,694	0,103	0,201
24	Purchase time	34,463	20	0,023	0,149	0,286
25	Offer prices	28,807	20	0,092	0,136	0,263
26	Lower price	15,675	20	0,737	0,100	0,197
27	Value for money	45,005	20	0,001	0,170	0,322
28	Purchase planning	33,821	20	0,027	0,148	0,283
29	Purchase impulse	31,613	20	0,048	0,143	0,274
30	Wish to purchase	22,037	20	0,339	0,119	0,232
31	Purchase awareness	22,099	20	0,335	0,119	0,232
32	Budget	23,428	20	0,268	0,123	0,239
33	Buying options	19,547	20	0,487	0,112	0,219
34	Difficulty of purchase choice	23,195	20	0,279	0,122	0,238
35	Brand Choice Decision	32,024	20	0,043	0,144	0,276
36	Brand Information	30,810	20	0,058	0,141	0,271
37	Shopping habits	18,878	20	0,530	0,110	0,215
38	Brand loyalty	27,858	20	0,113	0,134	0,259
39	Store Loyalty	20,785	20	0,410	0,116	0,225
40	Brand change	43,402	20	0,002	0,167	0,317
41	Environmental interest	27,282	20	0,128	0,133	0,256
42	Ecological brand preferences	19,039	20	0,519	0,111	0,216
43	Choice of ecological brands	29,820	20	0,073	0,139	0,267
44	Interest in health care	24,676	20	0,214	0,126	0,245
45	Conscious consumer	23,517	20	0,264	0,123	0,239
46	Interest in health	32,628	20	0,037	0,145	0,279
47	Purchase ecological brands	31,545	20	0,048	0,143	0,274
48	Interest in ecological brands	36,695	20	0,013	0,154	0,294
49	Interest in environmental care	21,985	20	0,341	0,119	0,232

Source: The Authors

After performing the data analysis, it is possible to identify more clearly how the consumer perceives each of the brands, detecting in each one which is the most outstanding variable, which allows a clearer vision of its differential characteristics.

Therefore, for the Bénédict brand, the most outstanding variables are ***Advertising elements*** and ***Brand change***. This brand has an attractive communication for the consumer. It quickly reaches undefined consumers who are persuaded either by the tone or form of the advertising content and the means of transmitting them, which can be traditional (radio, tv), modern (outdoor, magazines, experiential), or digital (social media, smart devices). This public is easily influenced since it chooses to change or vary its brand choice, so they can be impulsive people, trendsetter, or fashions; while considering that this is a few faithful target groups precisely because of its willingness to change the brand.

For the CEN brand, the value that stands out, in the same way, is ***Advertising elements***, while incorporating new values such as ***Employee knowledge*** and ***Purchase preference***. Like Bénédict, CEN's client is attracted to his communication; However, the brand differs by the service or differential benefit it offers. CEN's public is inclined towards a differential element, while Bénédict is prone to be more impulsive. CEN consumers are interested in choosing a service that stands out above the others. They value the knowledge of the employees and, therefore, the brand is reflected as a reliable, safe, and high-level brand of know-how.

KOE stands out in its ***Effective compliance*** and ***Brand change***. In this case, consumers consider that this brand fulfills what it promises by seeking its effectiveness, rather than its added value; however, it tends to change brands easily, making the KOE brand vulnerable in terms of fidelity.

Multibilingüe shows as dominant variables, ***Employee knowledge,*** and ***Purchase preference***. Therefore, the public is more rational and requires knowing the alternatives of a product or service to choose the most appropriate one. It can be evidenced that the client thinks, within the comparisons he makes with the other brands, that it provides quality services with trained employees and with high levels of response, which becomes its added value.

The last brand is Wall Street, identifying values such as ***Trust generation*** and ***Purchase preference;*** what shows a behavior generated by bonds of trust, honesty, and security that the brand projects and based on experience. These elements are strengthened to be the added value that generates your preference to buy.

In general, Chi-square tests show that marks are not dependent on all SERVQUAL variables. The Quality-price ratio in the CSI model with a contingency coefficient of 0.322 and *Advertising elements* with a contingency coefficient of 0.400 in SERVQUAL have the best association, and they are the most valued attributes by consumers. As they are statistically significant ($p < 0.05$), it shows that these variables are highly dependent on the marks. It implies that the public seeks to obtain high-quality services at comfortable prices, and being persuaded by advertising at the time of their choice.

Analyzing the quality of service, it can be evidenced that the proximity of dependence in the variables, *Attractive installations*, *Knowledge of employees*, and *Advertising elements*, are of great importance for the consumer. Brands generate a competitive advantage reflected in the association consumers do with the concepts they have in memory. On the other hand, the variable *Generation of trust* has the least dependence on brands since a customer to create trust with the company must have some experience for some time, to create a positive or negative criterion of the same.

Additionally, there is a high dependence on the change of brands variable, which shows that in this sector, consumers, despite choosing a brand with differentiating attributes, do not decide to change to another brand, even if the new brand of their choice has *Other features*. It is also identified that the variables of high quality and quality preference have no dependence on the brands studied, stating that the association with value for money is essential for the public.

Figure 2. SERVQUAL + CSI brand valuation model and proposed marketing actions according to the results
Source: The Authors

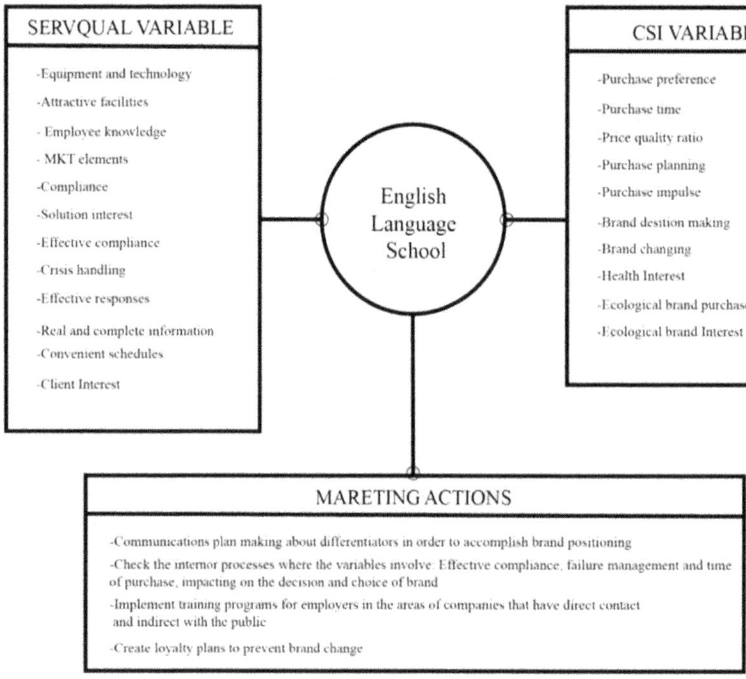

SOLUTIONS AND RECOMMENDATIONS

English schools in Ecuador must develop action plans that strengthen their most prominent attributes, guiding the purchase decision of current and future consumers by creating concrete messages that show the value of the brand. Internal processes that involve variables such as effective compliance, fault handling, and purchase times that reflect a significant influence on the perception and image that consumers have of brands must be reviewed.

Another action to include for the construction of brands is to connect them with the variables: Employee knowledge, Real and complete information, Effective response. For this, it is necessary to implement training programs for all areas that maintain direct and indirect contact with current and potential clients, which leads to the creation of long-term loyalty plans to prevent and make subsequent decisions on the change of brand by the public.

In this way, Figure 2 connects the SERVQUAL and CSI variables that have excelled in the industry, along with marketing actions, focused on the creation of services.

CONCLUSION AND FUTURE RESEARCH DIRECTIONS

The present investigation shows a system of valuation of service marks using the SERVQUAL and SCI models to determine the variables that predominate in the perception of value. Within the industry of English teaching institutes, various elements of the service are appreciated, ranging from equipment and technologies to the interest of the staff and their compliance to provide solutions to the client. Similarly, several elements of brands are dispersed in different brands, ranging from their differentiating characteristics to impulse buying. However, brands have different meanings according to their service perception and assessment related to the tastes and preferences of consumers.

We believe that the study is not accurate. Still, it generates an approach to understanding the variables of the service and the brand, which can be used for companies to apply to measure their value. For companies, the union of the SERVQUAL and CSI models can be the first step to measure the brand perception of the service they offer and monitor if there are changes in time in the value of their brand.

We emphasize the need to study in greater depth the perception of the consumer and what are the elements that do not cause loyalty with existing brands, despite having all the optimal factors in building a brand. We believe that the study should not only be in knowing the attributes of the brand but in understanding the consumer's process for purchase, contemplating it from the perception of communication. It is also essential to investigate what are the elements that the consumer establishes as standards of models between price-quality to develop a purchase decision.

REFERENCES

Aaker, J. L. (1997). Dimensions of Brand Personality. *Journal of Marketing*, *3*(3), 347–355. doi:10.1177/002224379703400304

América-Economía. (2018, July). *Tres razones por las que el idioma inglés es fundamental para el ámbito laboral*. Retrieved from https://mba.americaeconomia.com/articulos/notas/3-razones-por-las-que-el-idioma-ingles-es-fundamental-para-el-ambito-laboral

Beltrán, M. (2017). El Aprendizaje del Idioma Inglés como Lengua Extranjera. *Boletin Virtual*, *6*(4), 91–98. doi:10.36260/rbr.v6i4.227

Bonilla, A., & Rojas, R. (2012). El aprendizaje de lenguas extranjeras como herramienta para el desarrollo humano. *Congreso Iberoamericano de Lenguas En La Educacion y En La Cultura*, 11.

Buil, I., Martínez, E., & De Chernatony, L. (2010). Medición del valor de marca desde un enfoque formativo. In Cuadernos de Gestion (Vol. 10). doi:10.5295/cdg.100204ib

Coca-Carasila, A. M. (2010). Neuromarketing: Las Emociones Y El Comportamiento De Compra. *Perspectivas*, (25), 9–24. http://2011.www.redalyc.org/articulo.oa?id=425942454003

D'Andrea, M., Garré, A., & Rodríguez, M. (2012). Una Lengua extranjera, ¿sólo una herramienta para la comunicación? *Invenio: Revista de Investigación Académica*, *15*(28), 11–17.

Davvetas, V., & Diamantopoulos, A. (2018). "Should I Have Bought the Other One?" Experiencing Regret in Global Versus Local Brand Purchase Decisions. *Journal of International Marketing*, *26*(2), 1–21. doi:10.1509/jim.17.0040

Duque-Oliva. (2005). Revisión del concepto de calidad del servicio y sus modelos de medicioón. *Revista Innovar, 15*(25), 64–80. Retrieved from https://www.redalyc.org/articulo.oa?id=81802505

Duque Oliva, E. J., & Gómez, Y. D. (2014). Evolución conceptual de los modelos de medición de la percepción de calidad del servicio: Una mirada desde la educación superior. *Suma de Negocios*, *5*(12), 180–191. doi:10.1016/S2215-910X(14)70040-0

Ekos. (2018, August). *Guayaquil, capital comercial del Ecuador*. Retrieved from https://www.ekosnegocios.com/articulo/guayaquil-capital-comercial-del-ecuador

El Comercio. (2014, March 27). *Las academias privadas amplían la oferta de clases de inglés*. Retrieved from https://www.elcomercio.com/tendencias/academias-privadas-amplian-oferta-de.html

El Universo. (2013, October 6). *Estudiar idiomas en otro país, opción para jóvenes*. Retrieved from https://www.eluniverso.com/vida-estilo/2013/10/06/nota/1542306/estudiar-idiomas-otro-pais-opcion-jovenes

El Universo. (2015, February 11). *Ecuador tiene "nivel bajo de inglés", según informe de Education First*. Retrieved from https://www.eluniverso.com/noticias/2015/02/11/nota/4547176/ecuador-tiene-nivel-bajo-ingles-segun-informe-education-first

El Universo. (2019, March 26). *Inglés, cuando un idioma cambia vidas*. Retrieved from https://www.eluniverso.com/guayaquil/2019/03/26/nota/7252358/ingles

Forero, M., & Duque, E. (2014). Evolución y caracterización de los modelos de Brand Equity. *Suma de Negocios*, *5*(12), 158–168. doi:10.1016/S2215-910X(14)70038-2

Fournier, S. (1998). Consumers and Their Brands: Developing Relationship Theory in Consumer Research. *Chicago Journals, Journal of Consumer Research Inc.*, *24*(4), 343–353. doi:10.1086/209515

García, M. J. (2000). La valoración financiera de las marcas: Una revisión de los principales métodos utilizados. *Investigaciones Europeas de Dirección y Economía de la Empresa*, *6*(1), 31–52.

Ghobadian, A., Speller, S., & Matthew, J. (1994). Service Quality: Concepts and Models. *International Journal of Quality & Reliability Management*, *11*(9), 43–66. doi:10.1108/02656719410074297

Goleman, D. (2007). La Práctica de la Inteligencia Emocional. Editorial Kairós. S.A, Ed.

Guadarrama, E. G., & Rosales, E. M. (2015). Marketing relacional: Valor, satisfacción, lealtad y retención del cliente. In Ciencia y Sociedad (Vol. 40). doi:10.1017/CBO9781107415324.004

Haumann, T., Quaiser, B., Wieseke, J., & Rese, M. (2014). Footprints in the Sands of Time: A Comparative Analysis of the Effectiveness of Customer Satisfaction and Customer–Company Identification over Time. *Journal of Marketing*, *78*(6), 78–102. doi:10.1509/jm.13.0509

Kamakura, W. A., & Russell, G. J. (1993). Measuring brand value with scanner data. *International Journal of Research in Marketing*, *10*(1), 9–22. doi:10.1016/0167-8116(93)90030-3

Keller, K. L. (2013). *Strategic Brand Management Building, Measuring, and Managing Brand Equity*. Pearson; doi:10.2307/1252315

Khan, M. (2006). Consumer Behaviour and Advertising Management. New Age International Publishers.

Kotler, P., & Keller, K. L. (2012). *Dirección de Marketing*. Pearson; doi:10.1017/CBO9781107415324.004

Leone, R. P., Rao, V. R., Keller, K. L., Luo, A. M., McAlister, L., & Srivastava, R. (2006). Linking brand equity to customer equity. *Journal of Service Research*, *9*(2), 125–138. doi:10.1177/1094670506293563

Lovelock, C., Patterson, P., & Wirtz, J. (2004). Services Marketing. Edinburgh Business School.

Mauri, A. G., Minazzi, R., & Muccio, S. (2013). A Review of Literature on the Gaps Model on Service Quality: A 3-Decades Period: 1985–2013. *International Business Research*, *6*(12). Advance online publication. doi:10.5539/ibr.v6n12p134

Maxham Iii, J. G. (2001). Service recovery's influence on consumer satisfaction, positive word-of-mouth, and purchase intentions. *Journal of Business Research*, *54*(1), 11–24. doi:10.1016/S0148-2963(00)00114-4

Mejia, A. (2016). *La evaluación del idioma inglés en el Ecuador*. Retrieved from http://repositorio.uasb.edu.ec/bitstream/10644/5457/1/T2168-MINE-Mejia-La evaluacion.pdf

Mokhlis, S. (2009). An Investigation of Consumer Decision-Making Styles of Young-Adults in Malaysia. *International Journal of Business and Management*, *4*(4), 140–148. doi:10.5539/ijbm.v4n4p140

Parasuraman, A., Zeithaml, V. A., & Berry, L. L. (1988). SERVQUAL: A Multiple-Item Scale for Measuring Consumer Perceptions of Service Quality. *Journal of Retailing*, *64*(1), 12–40. doi:10.1016/S0148-2963(99)00084-3

Ramos, V. (2002). Modelos multidimensionales para la medición del valor de marca. *Investigaciones Europeas de Dirección y Economía de la Empresa*, *8*(3), 13–44.

Richins, M. L. (1994). Valuing Things: The Public and Private Meanings of Possessions. *The Journal of Consumer Research*, *21*(3), 504–521. doi:10.1086/209414

Saavedra, J. L., Colmenares, O., & Pirela, J. L. (2007). Correlación entre dimensiones de personalidad de marca y la marca emocional. Estudio en Cadena de Farmacias. *Revista de Ciencias Sociales*, *10*(2), 9–20. doi:10.1111/j.1532-5415.2012.04166.x

Sánchez, A. (2006). Peter Drucker, innovador maestro de la administración de empresas. *Cuadernos Latinoamericanos de Administración*, *2*(2), 69–89. doi:10.1039/C1DT11184A

Sichtmann, C., Davvetas, V., & Diamantopoulos, A. (2018, October 16). The relational value of perceived brand globalness and localness. *Journal of Business Research*. Advance online publication. doi:10.1016/j.jbusres.2018.10.025

Simon, C. J., & Sullivan, M. W. (1993). The Measurement and Determinants of Brand Equity: A Financial Approach. *Marketing Science*, *12*(1), 28–52. doi:10.1287/mksc.12.1.28

Sirdeshmukh, D., Singh, J., & Sabol, B. (2002). Consumer Trust, Value, and Loyalty in Relational Exchanges. *Journal of Marketing*, *66*(1), 15–37. doi:10.1509/jmkg.66.1.15.18449

Sproles, G. B., & Kendall, E. (1986). A methodology for profiling consumers' decision-making. *A Methodology for Profiling Consumers'. Decision-Making Styles*, *2*(20), 267–279.

Steenkamp, J.-B. E. M., & de Jong, M. G. (2010). A Global Investigation into the Constellation of Consumer Attitudes Toward Global and Local Products. *Journal of Marketing*, *74*(6), 18–40. doi:10.1509/jmkg.74.6.18

Stokburger-Sauer, N., Ratneshwar, S., & Sen, S. (2012). Drivers of consumer-brand identification. *International Journal of Research in Marketing*, *29*(4), 406–418. doi:10.1016/j.ijresmar.2012.06.001

Sung, Y., & Tinkham, S. F. (2005). Brand personality structures in the United States and Korea: Common and culture-specific factors. *Journal of Consumer Psychology*, *15*(4), 334–350. doi:10.120715327663jcp1504_8

Tasci, A. D. A. (2016). Consumer Value and Brand Value: Rivals or Allies in Consumer-Based Brand Equity? *Tourism Analysis*, *21*(5), 481–496. doi:10.3727/108354216X14653218477561

Thompson, C. J., Rindleisch, A., & Arsel, Z. (2006). Emotional branding and the strategic value of the Doppelganger brand image. *Journal of Marketing*, *70*(1), 50–64. doi:10.1509/jmkg.70.1.050.qxd

Tigani, D. (2006). Excelencia Excelencia en Servicio. Liderazgo 21.

Ungaretti, J. (2013). Adaptación del Consumer Style Inventory (CSI) al contexto argentino. *Revista de Investigación En Psicología Social*, *1*(1), 25–34.

Vazques, R., Roríguez, I., & Díaz, A. (1996). Estructura multimensional de la calidad de servicio en cadenas ve supermercdos: desarrollo y validación de la escala CALSUPER. In *Documentos de trabajo (Universidad de Oviedo. Facultad de Ciencias Económicas)* (Vol. 119). Retrieved from https://www.ncbi.nlm.nih.gov/pubmed/17295951

Whiteley, R., & Hessan, D. (1996). *Customer centred growth: Five strategies for building competitive advantage*. Academic Press.

KEY TERMS AND DEFINITIONS

Brand Personality: Everything that can be represented as the values and cultural beliefs that the consumer mentally adds to a product.

Brand Value: The brand value refers to how it receives a relevant recognition from the consumer and associates it favorably at the time of purchase choice. The value of the brand can be understood as the differential effect of brand awareness in response to a product or service.

CSI (Customer Style Index): It provides a potentially useful instrument to help companies examine the styles of taking consumer decisions understanding some dimensions, and creating consumer profiles.

Dimensions: They are variables included in the CSI and SERVQUAL. These variables help build brand and service profiles based on consumer perception.

Perception: It is how the brain detects the environment through the senses forming criteria about its reality.

Quality Measure: They are ways to measure the perception of quality from the perspective of the consumer.

SERVQUAL (Service Quality Index): It is a model of quality measurement that considers five dimensions.

Chapter 11
Exploring the Impact of Peer Influence on Online Shopping:
The Case of Chinese Millennials

Rob Kim Marjerison
https://orcid.org/0000-0003-1181-8695
Wenzhou-Kean University, China

Yiqi Athena Hu
Wenzhou-Kean University, China

ABSTRACT

Commercialization of social media is no longer optional for businesses, especially online businesses. An effective online presence is crucial for creating awareness of new products or services and triggering activity. The objective of this chapter is to investigate peers' influence on Chinese millennial consumers' purchase behavior. To be specific, this study examines the relationship between peers' purchase histories and consumers' purchase decisions among Chinese millennials. Specifically, this study explores whether and to what extent peers' purchase histories affect consumers' purchase perception, such as perceived usefulness, perceived risk, and purchase intention. Analysis of online surveys shows how peer influence affects Chinese millennial's purchase intention and decision in online shopping. Furthermore, perceived usefulness positively also affects purchase intention, while perceived risk has a negative influence. This chapter provides suggestions for online retailers to attach importance to peer influence when advertising their products.

INTRODUCTION

The Millennial generation are generally considered to be those who were born in 1980's and 1990's (Ng, Schweitzer, & Lyons, 2010). The Millennial generation is a massive market which due to their high level of adoption and tech proficiency can be very powerful in changing the economic landscape of the internet (Sullivan, & Heitmeyer, 2008). Having been the first generation to grow up with computers in

DOI: 10.4018/978-1-7998-5036-6.ch011

their homes, Millennials are proving to be a large commercial demographic, especially when it comes to online shopping (Acheampong, Zhiwen, Abubakar, Antwi, & Akomeah, 2016a). Millennials were much more likely to have their own technology devices than any generations before and can utilize more widely of technologies in these devices (Keith, & Simmers, 2013). Millennials enthusiasm and familiarity with the internet and devices make them be the essential group of online shopping. Hence, millennials generation online buyers are a significant group of customers for online sellers to target.

According to Acheampong (2016b), factors such as external environment, vendor, service, product characteristics, website design and ease of use, as well as materials and methods can all contribute to consumers' online purchase behavior. Park, Sharman, and Rao (2015) and others have found that website design affect customers' decision making and perceived level of enjoyment, including visual aids and aesthetics, information organization (He, & Mykytyn, 2007).

Related research also found that along with the exponential increase in online business transactions, the integrated and "one-click" online payment system has become an indispensable feature because vendors and creditors realize its growing importance as a foundation to improve their information infrastructure and to achieve operating efficiency However, due to different characteristics among customers and Web-systems, both sides' perspectives and technology factors could cause a significant level of variation in customers' acceptance of online payment methods (Aghdaie, Piraman, & Fathi, 2011).

This research involved 148 subjects who completed an online survey. Their responses were examined to identify the impact of a series of possible decision factors including perceived risk, perceived benefits, vendor's system features, and customers' characteristics on the intention to use an online payment system. Some significant associations are observed and their implications are discussed.

Major players in online commerce in China, such as Taobao, Wangyi Koala and Jing Dong all have similar recommender systems on their web pages. Taobao provides recommendations by showing products related to those for which consumers have previously searched. According to consumers' search and browse histories, Taobao recommends products that consumers would most likely be interested in. Also, Taobao, like other online shopping platforms gives recommendations from previous consumers. Every product shopping page shows the sales volume in one month and previous consumers' comments about the product (Fan, & Jarinto, 2018; Kwahk, & Kim, 2017).

Currently, the recommender system of online shopping websites provides recommendations mostly based on customer interests and purchased items (Linden, Smith, & York, 2003), and does not consider the peer influence of their neighbors, though peers influence is one of the factors that affect consumers' purchase decision in online shopping (Hsin Chang, & Wen Chen, 2008; Hirt, & Limayem, 2000).

Owing to the growth of competition in online commerce, businesses decision makers realize that it is important to better understand the customer and through that understanding, design and update their websites to better meet the customers' expectations (Duyne, Landay, & Hong, 2002).

Therefore, this study aims to investigate peer influence on online shopping. To be specific, this study examines the relationship between a peer influence and a consumer's purchase decision among Chinese millennials generation. Moreover, this research aims at determine whether peer influence has an effect on consumer perceptions of perceived usefulness and perceived risk, and whether perceived usefulness and perceived risk have influences on purchasing intention.

LITERATURE REVIEW

Scholars have studied the many factors that affect consumers' purchase intentions in online shopping in order to promote sales and customer satisfaction (Jiang, Hoegg, Dahl, & Chattopadhyay, 2009). Salespersons utilize purchase intention to predict sales. Thus, purchase intention is crucial for measuring customers purchase willingness. Peer influence is a factor that affect consumers' purchase intention and decision (Hsin Chang, & Wen Chen, 2008a). Therefore, peer influence and purchase intention have relationship that is worthy of further investigation.

Peer Influence

The power of peer influence is well researched and there is little dissention among the findings. Peer influence is one of the factors that affect consumers' purchase decision in online shopping (Hsin Chang, & Wen Chen, 2008a); Hirt, & Limayem, 2000). According to Zhu, Wang, Wang, and Wan (2016), owing to increasing ease of communication and online interaction, peer influence among online friends is increasing. Mangleburg, Doney, and Bristol (2004) have found that consumption communication among peers can promote purchase behavior specifically among teens.

Perceived Usefulness

Perceived usefulness is regarded as whether using the product or service will increase the performance of the user or not (Davis, 1989). The perceived usefulness of online shopping usually lies on the technology efficiency and the personal service to consumers (Kim, & Song, 2010). Hernández et al. (2008) found that perceived usefulness is an important influence in the decision to engage in online shopping in Spain while (Aghdaie, Piraman, & Fathi (2011) claimed that perceived usefulness is not significant to in the decision to engage in online purchase behavior in Iran. Implying that there are other factors involved. There is general nevertheless consensus that perceived usefulness has been shown to have significant effect on consumers' online purchase intention (Bigne-Alcaniz, Ruiz-Mafé, Aldás-Manzano, & Sanz-Blas, 2008; Kim, & Song, 2010; Xie, Zhu, Lu, & Xu, 2011).

Perceived Risk

Perceived risk is related to purchase intention and behavior. It has been found that perceived risk is a decisive factor for consumers considering whether to shop online or not (Doolin, Dillon, Thompson, & Corner, 2005; Perea, & Monsuwé, Dellaert, & de Ruyter, 2004). Further, perceived risk is highly likely to increasing online shopping environment instability (Ying Li, & Huang, 2009).

Purchase Intention

Purchase intention is the willingness of a consumer to buy a certain product or service and is typically related to consumers' actual purchase decision. Marketing managers routinely use purchase intentions to predict sales. In this study, purchase intention is an important measurement to know consumers' willingness and probability of buying the product.

Previous research has suggested that the shopping experience provides consumers with a combination of utilitarian and hedonic benefit (Jones, Reynolds, & Arnold, 2006). Others have found that purchase intention is positively related to both price and product information (Chang & Wildt, 1994). There are many factors influence purchase intention, such as perceived enjoyment, perceived risk, perceived value and ethical self-efficacy (Huang, Phau, & Lin, 2010; Lim, Osman, Salahuddin, Romle, & Abdullah, 2016). How and to what extent Peer Pressure is one of them is worthy of further exploration.

STATEMENT OF HYPOTHESIS

Research Question (RQ): How does Peer Influence affect Chinese millennials' purchasing intention and decision-making in online shopping?

Peer Influence

Previous studies have shown that peers can influence people's purchasing behaviors. Hsin Chang and Wen Chen (2008b) claimed that Peer Influence is one of the factors that most affect consumers' purchase decision in online shopping. And specifically in Hong Kong, Chan (2006) and Lee (2010a) reported that more than half of Hong Kong adolescents would ask for their peers' suggestion when purchasing of unfamiliar products and that peer influence has the highest impact affect Hong Kong adolescents green purchasing behavior respectively (Lee, 2010b).

Regarding the above discussion, it is reasonable to expect then, that when peers purchasing history is present, it will influence a person's perceived enjoyment in online shopping?

H1: When a peer's purchasing history is present, Chinese millennials will have a higher purchase intention.

Perceived Usefulness

Various studies have found that perceived usefulness is related to people's purchase intention. (Kim & Song, 2010) found out that perceived usefulness of online shopping relates a lot with consumers' technology efficiency and the personal service. In addition, perceived usefulness positively influences consumers attitudes toward online airlines ticketing Renny, Guritno, & Siringoringo, (2013). In summary, perceived usefulness significantly affects people's online shopping activity (Cho, & Sagynov, 2015; Ramayah, & Ignatius, 2005).

Regarding the above discussion, it is reasonable to expect that, when peers' purchasing history is present, it will influence a person's perceived enjoyment in online shopping.

H2: When peers' purchasing history is present, Chinese millennials will receive higher perceived usefulness and higher perceived usefulness resulting in higher purchase intention.

Perceived Risk

Li and Huang (2010) reported that perceived risk significantly contributes to perceived instability of the online shopping environment. Others have found that that reducing the perceived risk in e-commerce is likely to promote consumers' purchasing behavior and online sales (Chen & Barnes, 2007; Corbitt, Thanasankit, & Yi, 2003; Masoud, 2013).

Considering the above discussion, it is reasonable to expect that, when peers' purchasing history is present, it will influence a person's perceived enjoyment in online shopping.

H3: When peers' purchasing history is present, Chinese millennials will receive lower perceived risk and lower perceived risk will cause higher purchase intention.

METHODOLOGY

Instrumentation Design (Qualitative Method)

Due to the relative lack of depth in the literature regarding of studies on the Peer Influence on online shopping in China, it was necessary to formulate part of the survey as original questions. This was done by means of a series of brief interviews with a sample of twenty college students. Based on the frequency of their responses, the final three questions for the online survey were developed.

Instrumentation Design (Quantitative Method)

In order to investigate peer influence's effect on consumers' purchasing decisions, an online survey was be conducted by Wenjuanxing (问卷星), a Chinese online survey application which is integrated with WeChat, the most popular social media platform in China (Zhou, Hentschel, & Kumar, 2017). The online survey was offered via Chinese college students' groups on WeChat. Respondents voluntarily participated in the survey. This study adopted an online survey because online surveys can target unique populations, save time for researchers, and save money as using the electronic form (Wright, 2005; Wright, Filatotchev, Hoskisson, & Peng, 2005). The survey contained questions concerning perceived usefulness, perceived risk and purchase intention measured by a 5-point Likert scale with closed-end questions (Joshi, Kale, Chandel, & Pal, 2015).

Two hundred Chinese college students participated in the survey, 47.5% of them males and 52.5% females. The age ranges from 18-22 included 79.5% of the respondents.

A fictitious photo of a pillow was presented before participants to measure perceived usefulness, perceived risk and purchase intention parts. The photo consisted of two parts. The left part is a normal product description page with the images of the pillow, price and some information. On the right, there was a text or message box showing "Your peers also bought this product". Respondents were asked to imagine they are planning to purchase a dining table on Taobao.

The questionnaire consists of four parts and 16 item measurements, some of which were developed from previous studies. Part One was designed to segment participants by demographic information because the target demographic of this study is millennials. Part Two aims to measure perceived usefulness. There are five items for measuring perceived usefulness. Items such as "I think it's useful to buy this product because the goods delivered may help me fall asleep faster" was adapted from Ramayah, & Ignatius, (2005). Part Three is concerned with perceived risk and contains four items. These items include "I believe that purchasing this product are risky because the products delivered may fail to meet my expectations." These items were adapted from Corbitt et al., (2003). Purchase intention was assessed with three items, for instance, "I intend to purchase this product in the future," which was adapted from Chen and Barns (Chen, & Barnes, 2007).

Survey Questions on Perceived Usefulness

Five options were presented as possible responses for the questions regarding perceived usefulness. (Prendergast, Ho, & Phau, 2002)

1. I think it's useful to buy this product because the goods delivered may promote my comparison shopping
2. I think it's useful to buy this product because the goods delivered may help me fall asleep faster
3. I think it's useful to buy this product because the goods delivered may promote my sleep quality
4. I think it's useful to buy this product because the goods delivered maybe beneficial to my health (e.g. Neck health)
5. I think it's useful to buy this product because the goods delivered may help me increase interaction with peers

Survey Question on Perceived Risk

Four alternatives were provided to measure the factor of Perceived Risk:

1. I think it's risky to buy this product because the goods delivered may not meet my expectations
2. I think it's risky to buy this product because it may bring me economic loss
3. I think it's risky to buy this product because it may waste my time
4. I think it's risky to buy this product because it may lead to other people's low opinion of me

Survey Question on Purchase Intention

Three questions regarding purchase intention were based on the frequency of repeated responses in the Pilot Study.

1. The possibility that I will buy this product
2. I will buy this product in the future
3. I will recommend this product to others

THEORETICAL FRAMEWORK

The theoretical framework for this study is shown in Figure 1

Figure 1. Theoretical Framework

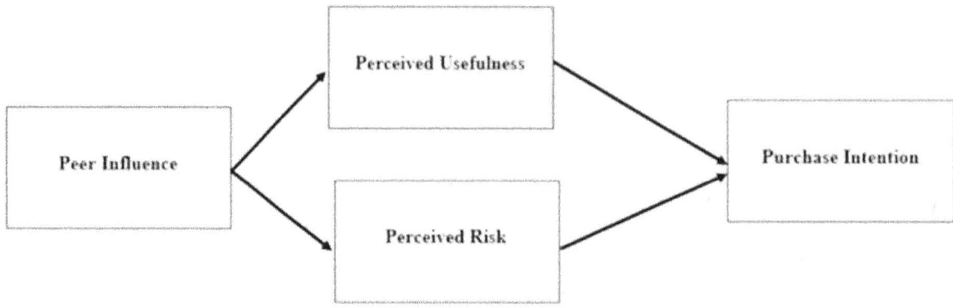

ANALYSIS / RESULTS

Reliability Analysis

This study conducted a reliability test using SPSS software. Reliability testing is designed to measure the consistency of the measurements (Bruton, Conway, & Holgate, 2000). The data was subjected to Cronbach Alpha to test internal consistency, it was found that all the Cronbach alpha number are greater than 0.7, as shown in Table 1. Therefore, these items are quite reliable in the study.

Purchase Intention Profile Analysis

Table 1. Reliability

Items	Cronbach's Alpha
Perceived usefulness	0.852
Perceived risk	0.810
Purchase intention	0.838

Source: The Authors

This study aims to measure the extent to which possible consumers will buy a product online when peers' purchasing history is present. Specifically, of Chinese millennial consumers on Taobao. When Chinese millennial consumers have reported that they are willing or planning to buy the product, it means that their purchase intention is high.

In Hypothesis 1, we assumed that when a peer's purchasing history is present, Chinese millennials will have a higher purchase intention, which means more likely to buy the product than not buy it. To test H1, a frequency and percentage table, Table 2, has been generated. In Table 2, we can conclude that more than one-third of the participants are willing to buy this product when the peer's purchase history is present. Meanwhile, 45.27% of participants chose "very possible" or "possible" to buy the product now. which exceeds the total percentage (37.32%) of "Not very possible" or "Impossible" to buy the product now. This means that people have the purchase intention to buy this product rather than not buy it when the peer's purchase history is present. Moreover, 39.8% participants are likely to buy this product in the future. The possibility to buy this product now and in the future reveals participants' purchase intention for this product. Hence, the result shows that when a peer's purchase history is shown, Chinese millennials will have high purchase intention to buy the product. H1 is supported.

Table 2. Purchase Intention Profile

Hypothesis	Items	Levels	Frequency	Percentage
H1	The possibility that I will buy this product now	Very possible	19	9.45%
		Possible	**72**	**35.82%**
		Indifferent	35	17.41%
		Not very possible	57	28.36%
		Impossible	18	8.96%
	The possibility that I will buy this product in the future	Very possible	14	6.97%
		Possible	**80**	**39.80%**
		Indifferent	21	10.45%
		Not very possible	77	38.31%
		Impossible	9	4.48%
	I will recommend this product to others	Very possible	13	6.47%
		Possible	47	23.38%
		Indifferent	32	15.92%
		Not very possible	**86**	**42.79%**
		Impossible	23	11.40%

Source: The Authors

Factor Analysis

In this study, there were three significant factors: perceived usefulness, perceived risk and purchase intention. A Factor Analysis is conducted by using SPSS computer software. According to Samuels (Samuels, 2017), Factor Analysis analyses the validity of the relationship between the variances of the individual item and the variances of those variances between items. A factorability which is 0.3 should be suppressed (Samuels, 2017).

First, the factorability of 5 items which are related with perceived usefulness were measured. All of these items were correlated with each other at levels exceeding 0.3, which reveals factorability among them. Secondly, 4 items about perceived risk were having at least 0.4 of factorability which also shows correlation among each other. Last, 3 items related to purchase intention were having great factorability which all of them were greater than 0.7. From what has been recounted above, Factor Analysis is suitable for all the items factors above.

Table 3. Factor Analysis, Extraction Method: Maximum Likelihood

	Factor 1	Factor 2	Factor 3
PU1	0.688		
PU2	0.725		
PU3	0.877		
PU4	0.793		
PU5	0.628		
PR1		0.683	
PR2		0.856	
PR3		0.826	
PR4		0.548	
PI1			0.834
PI2			0.701
PI3			0.858

Source: The Authors

Correlation Analysis

In order to more deeply explore the relationships between these three factors; perceived usefulness, perceived risk and purchase intention, the study conducted a Correlation Analysis with the support of Factor Analysis.

As indicated in Table 4, perceived usefulness has positive correlation (0.669) with purchase intention, which means that perceived usefulness has a positive influence to purchase intention. Meanwhile, perceived risk is negatively related with purchase intention since the Pearson Correlation of them is -0.216. This indicates that perceived risk has a negative impact on purchase intention.

Table 4. Correlation Analysis

Items	Measurements	Perceived Usefulness	Perceived Risk	Purchase Intention
Perceived Usefulness	Pearson Correlation	1	-.301**	.669**
	Sig.(2-tailed)		.000	.000
	N	201	201	201
Perceived Risk	Pearson Correlation	-.301**	1	-.216**
	Sig (2-tailed)	.000		.002
	N	201	201	201
Purchase Intention	Pearson Correlation	.669**	-.216**	1
	Sig (2-tailed)	.000	.002	
	N	201	201	201

** Correlation is significant at the 0.01 level (2-tailed).
Source: The Authors

Regression Analysis

The study then explores the relationship between purchase intention, perceived usefulness and perceived risk among Chinese millennial consumers on Taobao. SPSS computer software was used to conduct Regression Analysis. Table 5 is the result for Regression Analysis (Linden et al, 2003).

Table 5. Summary of Regression Analysis

Hypothesis	Items	Standardized Coefficients Beta	t	Result
H2	PU-PI	0.669	12.682	Supported
H3	PR-PI	-0.216	-0.318	Supported

*** $p<0.01$. PU: Perceived usefulness; PR: Perceived Risk; PI: Purchase Intention
Source: The Authors

For Hypothesis 2, it was proposed that when peers' purchasing history is present, Chinese millennials will receive higher perceived usefulness and higher perceived usefulness which will results in higher purchase intention. Table 5 together with Table 4 (Correlation Analysis) indicated that perceived usefulness has a significant positive influence on purchase intention since the standardized coefficient beta for PU-PI is 0.669 which is positive. Hence, Chinese millennial consumers are more willing to buy a product when they perceived high usefulness of the product based upon their peers' purchase histories present. Consequently, H2 is supported.

For Hypothesis 3, it was proposed that when peers' purchasing history is present, Chinese millennials will receive lower perceived risk and lower perceived risk will result in higher purchase intention. Table 5 together with Table 4 (correlation Analysis) suggested that perceived risk does have significant negative influence on purchase intention since the standardized coefficient beta for PR-PI is -0.318 which is negative. So that Chinese millennial consumers are less likely to buy a product when they perceived high risk of the product when their peers' purchase histories present. Thus, H3 is supported.

CONCLUSION AND PRACTICAL IMPLICATIONS

The result of the study indicated that Peer Influence does have a significant impact on Chinese millennial consumers' online shopping behavior. This finding is not surprising as previous studies have shown that Peer Influence has positive influence on people's purchase behavior. To be specific, Martin and Bush (2000) founds that peers affect teenagers purchase and where do they purchase as well. Previous research has also found out that the influence of peers on purchase intention is significant and is being more strongly and positively related to publicly consumed goods than the privately consumed goods (Makgosa, & Mohube, 2007). Based on the findings of this study, marketers can relate Peer Influence with Chinese millennial consumers' purchase behavior. If the peer's purchase history is present on the recommendation system, Chinese millennial consumers would gain more perceived usefulness and less perceived risk, which in turn will increase their purchase intention for the product. Marketers could display more information of Chinese millennial consumers' peers which can trigger consumers purchase intention. When consumers have more intention, they will consequently purchase more.

Moreover, perceived usefulness and perceived risk have significant influence on purchase intention. Perceived usefulness positively influences Chinese millennials purchase intention in online shopping. On the contrary, perceived risk has negative influence on Chinese millennials purchase intention in online shopping.

This study utilized a product (pillow) selling page of Taobao and combined Peer Influence into Taobao's recommendation system. Thus, the conclusion can beneficial to Taobao's recommendation system. Knowing more about the reliance of Chinese millennials on their peers' purchase histories and the extent to which is increases their purchase intention it would benefit inline platforms such as Taobao as well as online merchants to increase peer reviews and feedback when displaying the products reviewed by their peers. In order to prompt the efficiency and usefulness of the system, the Taobao recommendation system should include peers' purchase histories, especially for the Chinese millennial consumers. In addition, this study is also helpful to online sellers. When displaying the products, online sellers can have the Chinese millennial consumers peers' purchase histories on display. Consumers' purchase intention can be promoted in this way. Besides, since perceived usefulness positively affect purchase intention, online sellers can focus on placing more emphasis and communicating more usefulness of the product, such as including positive emotions descriptions and images "that depict products with people in emotional and dynamic settings" (Hassanein, & Head, 2007). Nevertheless, online sellers should reduce the perceived risk on when displaying their products on websites, which include reduce privacy and security concerns (Nepomuceno, Laroche, & Richard, 2014). Reducing the perceived risk for consumers can promote their purchase intention. In turn. Increase sales.

LIMITATIONS AND FUTURE RESEARCH

This study has limitations. Firstly, most of the participants are from south or east part of China (i.e. Zhejiang Province, Guangdong Province & Jiangsu Province). Hence, they may not accurately represent the entire population of Chinese millennial consumers. Future studies could have a wider and more diverse demographic sample characteristics. Second, most of the participants in the study are born in late-1990s; therefore, the age group is not evenly distributed, and those participants may not represent the population of millennial consumers. Future studies can explore a more varied age group even with the demographic of millennial consumers. Finally, this study focused on Chinese millennial consumers. However, Peer Influence, perceived enjoyment and perceived risk affect not only purchase intention of millennial consumers in China but also other nationalities. There is similar research on millennial consumers of other cultures. Future study could be conducted from a cross-cultural perspective, comparing how Peer Influence affects millennial consumers' purchase intention between different nationalities and cultures.

REFERENCES

Acheampong, P., Zhiwen, L., Abubakar, R., Antwi, H. A., & Akomeah, M. O. (2016a). Stimulants of Online Shopping Behaviour among Chinese Millenials in China. *International Journal of Academic Research in Business and Social Sciences*, *6*(5), 331–349. doi:10.6007/IJARBSS/v6-i5/2152

Acheampong, P., Zhiwen, L., Abubakar, R., Antwi, H. A., & Akomeah, M. O. (2016b). Stimulants of Online Shopping Behaviour among Chinese Millenials in China. *International Journal of Academic Research in Business and Social Sciences*, *6*(5), 331–349. doi:10.6007/IJARBSS/v6-i5/2152

Aghdaie, S. F. A., Piraman, A., & Fathi, S. (2011). An analysis of factors affecting the consumer's attitude of trust and their impact on internet purchasing behavior. *International Journal of Business and Social Science*, *2*(23).

Bigne-Alcaniz, E., Ruiz-Mafé, C., Aldás-Manzano, J., & Sanz-Blas, S. (2008). Influence of online shopping information dependency and innovativeness on internet shopping adoption. *Online Information Review*, *32*(5), 648–667. doi:10.1108/14684520810914025

Bruton, A., Conway, J. H., & Holgate, S. T. (2000). Reliability: What is it, and how is it measured? *Physiotherapy*, *86*(2), 94–99. doi:10.1016/S0031-9406(05)61211-4

Chan, K. (2006). *Advertising and Hong Kong Society*. Chinese University Press.

Chang, T.-Z., & Wildt, A. R. (1994). Price, product information, and purchase intention: An empirical study. *Journal of the Academy of Marketing Science*, *22*(1), 16–27. doi:10.1177/0092070394221002

Chen, Y.-H., & Barnes, S. (2007). Initial trust and online buyer behaviour. *Industrial Management & Data Systems*, *107*(1), 21–36. Advance online publication. doi:10.1108/02635570710719034

Cho, Y. C., & Sagynov, E. (2015). Exploring Factors That Affect Usefulness, Ease Of Use, Trust, And Purchase Intention In The Online Environment. *International Journal of Management & Information Systems*, *19*(1), 21–36. doi:10.19030/ijmis.v19i1.9086

Corbitt, B., Thanasankit, T., & Yi, H. (2003). Trust and E-commerce: A study of consumer perceptions. *Electronic Commerce Research and Applications*, *2*(3), 203–215. doi:10.1016/S1567-4223(03)00024-3

Davis, F. D. (1989). Perceived usefulness, perceived ease of use, and user acceptance of information technology. *Management Information Systems Quarterly*, *13*(3), 319–340. doi:10.2307/249008

Doolin, B., Dillon, S., Thompson, F., & Corner, J. L. (2005). Perceived Risk, the Internet Shopping Experience and Online Purchasing Behavior: A New Zealand Perspective. *Journal of Global Information Management*, *13*(2), 66–88. doi:10.4018/jgim.2005040104

Duyne, D. K. V., Landay, J., & Hong, J. I. (2002). *The design of sites: Patterns, principles, and processes for crafting a customer-centered Web experience*. Addison-Wesley Longman Publishing Co., Inc.

Fan, Z., & Jarinto, K. (2018). Taobao, the marketing problem and recommendations for improving customer satisfaction. *RMUTT Global Business Accounting and Finance Review, 2*(1). Retrieved from http://www.profile.rmutt.ac.th/index.php/gbafr/article/view/1102

Hassanein, K., & Head, M. (2007). Manipulating perceived social presence through the web interface and its impact on attitude towards online shopping. *International Journal of Human-Computer Studies*, *65*(8), 689–708. doi:10.1016/j.ijhcs.2006.11.018

He, F., & Mykytyn, P. (2007). Decision Factors for the Adoption of an Online Payment System by Customers. *International Journal of E-Business Research*, *3*(4), 1–32. doi:10.4018/jebr.2007100101

Hernández, B., Jiménez, J., & José Martín, M. (2011). Age, gender and income: Do they really moderate online shopping behaviour? *Online Information Review*, *35*(1), 113–133. doi:10.1108/14684521111113614

Hernandez, M. D., Wang, Y. J., Minor, M. S., & Liu, Q. (2008). Effects of superstitious beliefs on consumer novelty seeking and independent judgment making: Evidence from China. *Journal of Consumer Behaviour: An International Research Review*, *7*(6), 424–435. doi:10.1002/cb.261

Hirt, S., & Limayem, M. (2000). Integrating three theoretical perspectives to explain internet-based technology usage by university students: A qualitative study. *ICIS 2000 Proceedings*, 47.

Hsin Chang, H., & Wen Chen, S. (2008a). The impact of online store environment cues on purchase intention: Trust and perceived risk as a mediator. *Online Information Review*, *32*(6), 818–841. doi:10.1108/14684520810923953

Hsin Chang, H., & Wen Chen, S. (2008b). The impact of online store environment cues on purchase intention: Trust and perceived risk as a mediator. *Online Information Review*, *32*(6), 818–841. doi:10.1108/14684520810923953

Huang, Y., Phau, I., & Lin, C. (2010). Consumer animosity, economic hardship, and normative influence: How do they affect consumers' purchase intention? *European Journal of Marketing*, *44*(7/8), 909–937. doi:10.1108/03090561011047463

Jiang, L., Hoegg, J., Dahl, D. W., & Chattopadhyay, A. (2009). The persuasive role of incidental similarity on attitudes and purchase intentions in a sales context. *The Journal of Consumer Research*, *36*(5), 778–791. doi:10.1086/605364

Jones, M. A., Reynolds, K. E., & Arnold, M. J. (2006). Hedonic and utilitarian shopping value: Investigating differential effects on retail outcomes. *Journal of Business Research*, *59*(9), 974–981. doi:10.1016/j.jbusres.2006.03.006

Joshi, A., Kale, S., Chandel, S., & Pal, D. (2015). Likert Scale: Explored and Explained. *British Journal of Applied Science and Technology*, *7*(4), 396–403. doi:10.9734/BJAST/2015/14975

Keith, N. K., & Simmers, C. S. (2013). Adapting the marketing educational environment for multicultural millennials: The Chinese experience. *Academy of Educational Leadership Journal*, *17*(3), 83.

Kim, H., & Song, J. (2010). The quality of word-of-mouth in the online shopping mall. *Journal of Research in Interactive Marketing*, *4*(4), 376–390. Advance online publication. doi:10.1108/17505931011092844

Kwahk, K.-Y., & Kim, B. (2017). Effects of social media on consumers' purchase decisions: Evidence from Taobao. *Service Business*, *11*(4), 803–829. doi:10.100711628-016-0331-4

Lee, K. (2010). The Green Purchase Behavior of Hong Kong Young Consumers: The Role of Peer Influence, Local Environmental Involvement, and Concrete Environmental Knowledge. *Journal of International Consumer Marketing*, *23*(1), 21–44. doi:10.1080/08961530.2011.524575

Li, Y., & Huang, J. (2009). Applying theory of perceived risk and technology acceptance model in the online shopping channel. *World Academy of Science, Engineering and Technology*, *53*(1), 919–925.

Li, Y-H., & Huang, J. (n.d.). *Applying Theory of Perceived Risk and Technology Acceptance Model in the Online Shopping Channel*. Academic Press.

Lim, Y. J., Osman, A., Salahuddin, S. N., Romle, A. R., & Abdullah, S. (2016). Factors Influencing Online Shopping Behavior: The Mediating Role of Purchase Intention. *Procedia Economics and Finance*, *35*, 401–410. doi:10.1016/S2212-5671(16)00050-2

Linden, G., Smith, B., & York, J. (2003). Amazon.com Recommendations: Item-to-Item Collaborative Filtering. *IEEE Internet Computing; Los Alamitos*, *7*(1), 76–80. doi:10.1109/MIC.2003.1167344

Makgosa, R., & Mohube, K. (2007). *Peer influence on young adults' products purchase decisions*. Academic Press.

Mangleburg, T. F., Doney, P. M., & Bristol, T. (2004). Shopping with friends and teens' susceptibility to peer influence. *Journal of Retailing*, *80*(2), 101–116. doi:10.1016/j.jretai.2004.04.005

Martin, C. A., & Bush, A. J. (2000). Do role models influence teenagers' purchase intentions and behavior? *Journal of Consumer Marketing*, *17*(5), 441–453. Advance online publication. doi:10.1108/07363760010341081

Masoud, E. Y. (2013). The Effect of Perceived Risk on Online Shopping in Jordan. *European Journal of Business and Management*, 13.

Nepomuceno, M. V., Laroche, M., & Richard, M.-O. (2014). How to reduce perceived risk when buying online: The interactions between intangibility, product knowledge, brand familiarity, privacy and security concerns. *Journal of Retailing and Consumer Services*, *21*(4), 619–629. doi:10.1016/j.jretconser.2013.11.006

Ng, E. S. W., Schweitzer, L., & Lyons, S. T. (2010). New Generation, Great Expectations: A Field Study of the Millennial Generation. *Journal of Business and Psychology*, *25*(2), 281–292. doi:10.100710869-010-9159-4

Park, I., Sharman, R., & Rao, H. R. (2015). Disaster Experience and Hospital Information Systems: An Examination of Perceived Information Assurance, Risk, Resilience, and HIS Usefulness. *Management Information Systems Quarterly*, *39*(2), 317–344. doi:10.25300/MISQ/2015/39.2.03

Perea y Monsuwé, T., Dellaert, B. G. C., & de Ruyter, K. (2004). What drives consumers to shop online? A literature review. *International Journal of Service Industry Management*, *15*(1), 102–121. doi:10.1108/09564230410523358

Prendergast, G., Ho, B., & Phau, I. (2002). A Hong Kong view of offensive advertising. *Journal of Marketing Communications*, *8*(3), 165–177. doi:10.1080/13527260210147342

Ramayah, T., & Ignatius, J. (2005). Impact of perceived usefulness, perceived ease of use and perceived enjoyment on intention to shop online. *ICFAI Journal of Systems Management*, *3*(3), 36–51.

Renny, G., Guritno, S., & Siringoringo, H. (2013). Perceived Usefulness, Ease of Use, and Attitude Towards Online Shopping Usefulness Towards Online Airlines Ticket Purchase. *Procedia: Social and Behavioral Sciences*, *81*, 212–216. doi:10.1016/j.sbspro.2013.06.415

Samuels. (2017). *Advice on exploratory factor analysis*. Academic Press.

Sullivan, P., & Heitmeyer, J. (2008). Looking at Gen Y shopping preferences and intentions: Exploring the role of experience and apparel involvement. *International Journal of Consumer Studies*, *32*(3), 285–295. doi:10.1111/j.1470-6431.2008.00680.x

Wright, F., Filatotchev, I., Hoskisson, R. E., & Peng, M. W. (2005). Strategy research in emerging economies: Challenging the conventional wisdom. *Journal of Management Studies*, *42*(1), 1–33. doi:10.1111/j.1467-6486.2005.00487.x

Wright. (2005). Researching Internet-based populations: Advantages and disadvantages of online survey research, online questionnaire authoring software packages, and web survey services. *Journal of Computer-Mediated Communication, 10*(3).

Xie, G., Zhu, J., Lu, Q., & Xu, S. (2011). Influencing factors of consumer intention towards web group buying. *2011 IEEE International Conference on Industrial Engineering and Engineering Management*, 1397–1401. 10.1109/IEEM.2011.6118146

Zhou, R., Hentschel, J., & Kumar, N. (2017). *Goodbye text, hello emoji: Mobile communication on wechat in China*. ACM. doi:10.1145/3025453.3025800

Zhu, Z., Wang, J., Wang, X., & Wan, X. (2016, August 9). *Exploring factors of users peer-influence behavior in social media on purchase intention: Evidence from QQ*. Retrieved November 16, 2019, from Computers in Human Behavior website: https://eurekamag.com/research/064/849/064849121.php

Chapter 12
Development of an Organizational Management Improvement Plan in SMEs:
The Case of CVR Ingeniería del Conocimiento S.A.S.

Omar Orlando Ovalle-Mora
https://orcid.org/0000-0003-0407-4755
E3LABSAS, Colombia

Maria del Pilar Ramirez-Salazar
https://orcid.org/0000-0002-9462-0897
Universidad EAN, Colombia

Carlos Salcedo-Perez
https://orcid.org/0000-0002-4433-5537
Universidad EAN, Colombia

Anlly Luz Hinestroza Mosquera
Universidad EAN, Colombia

ABSTRACT

SMEs must carry out an analysis of the micro and macro environment that is necessary to counteract threats. Then internal and external factors must be identified to evaluate opportunities, threats, strengths, and weaknesses to establish a correlation between causes and effects, to determine the current situation of the enterprise, and to find areas of improvement. The information analysis is performed using tools applied and tailored to the development of this model, such as PESTEL and Porter's five forces, CAM (competitiveness analysis matrix), EFE and EFI analysis matrix, SWOT analysis, strategic maps, and the balanced scorecard.

DOI: 10.4018/978-1-7998-5036-6.ch012

INTRODUCTION

According to Law 905 issued in 2004, MSMEs (micro, small and medium enterprises), including family firms, is the entrepreneurial bases of Colombia. They operate in any economic activity, whether entrepreneurial, agricultural, livestock, manufacturing, trade, services, urban or rural, and performed by a person or legal entity (Congreso de la Republica de Colombia, 2004). Micro enterprises employ 50.3% of jobs in Colombia, and small and medium firms employ 30.5%; however, their survival is threatened by the lack of a sound strategic organizational management (Garcia, 2017). Some SMEs operate under the myth that organizational management concerns only big corporations, not acknowledging the added value that this strategy can offer to smaller organizations (Cámara de Comercio de Medellin, 2015).

Adequate management and clear guidelines for strategic management will allow the firm to have a better knowledge about its situation to find new opportunities, identify threats, define market strategies, and be prepared for changes. As a result, it will improve resource management and will measure and evaluate the immediate and/or future impact of making strategic decisions for strengthening growth and development. It is crucial to consider that entrepreneurial activities require high levels of competitiveness based on the process' efficacy, efficiency, and effectiveness nowadays.

This chapter presents a process to develop a plan for improving organizational management in a small Colombian firm. The objective of the chapter is to show the main characteristics of this process, tools, and methods included, to maximize business results and strategies proposed to improve the situation encountered by the firm. It is expected that this chapter can provide managers and researchers with the knowledge necessary to perform similar processes in other firms with similar size and organizational characteristics.

DESCRIPTION OF THE PROBLEM IN THE FIRM SELECTED

CVR Ingeniería del Conocimiento SAS was founded in 2011. It has over five years of experience developing comprehensive solutions for the agriculture and livestock industry by applying knowledge management, following commercial strategies, and linking with other businesses. Its staff varies in number depending on its operational needs; on average, they employ 12 professionals, outsourcing any additional required personnel. CVR had a profit margin of 8.82% (2018), 9.09% (2017), and 6.25% (2016), not considering financial neither tax expenses.

It comprises four business lines: i) training; ii) consulting; iii) alliances; and iv) marketing and communications. Regardless of its experience in the market, the management team considers that the enterprise has difficulties regarding its management model, resource optimization, the lack of tools to define clear objectives, and lack of control, measuring, and follow up of its processes. Therefore, research aimed at identifying the enterprise´s current situation to develop a management improvement plan to boost its growth and development. Management and operating processes are not transparent. There is a lack of organizational planning, expenses control, and forecast verification. The cash flow is affected since financial statements show a high operating cost, which has a notorious effect on the final performance. The previous factors show the need to have appropriate consulting to propose a management model to improve organizational performance, serving as a model for other SMEs.

A BRIEF OF STRATEGY IN FIRMS

Change in the world is happening at a faster pace and as Kotler (1999) stated, enterprises must be aware of globalization, technology, and economic deregulation. Organizations need leaders to guide them to achieve their objectives. Then, strategic management becomes a must, so managers can make the right decisions based on analyzing the environment, markets, new technologies, social trends, consumer preferences, trade, and political agreements. As a result, firms are more competitive and adapt to changes quicker than their competitors (Kotler, & Keller 2006).

The Marketing Science Institute (MSI)(2006) determines the following priorities in marketing management by analyzing surveys answered by its members: [1] the analysis of quantitative models to understand causality, levels, and influence in a complex world; [2] evaluation of the organizational environment; [3] the ability to change processes by making the right decisions; [4] knowledge of data mining, new methods and tools necessary for the job position, and [5] innovation, design, and strategy for this time of disruption. Richardson (2018) identified the following competencies as those most relevant for a marketing manager: [1] Technical competencies: formulation of the Marketing Strategic Plan, implementation of control of the strategy and interpretation or marketing information, and [2] Behavioral competencies: proactively push boundaries, dealing well with people and being business-minded. This process shows the importance that strategy has in management today.

Francés (2006) divides and defines strategy in two ways, broad and restricted. Broad, as the definition of objectives, actions, and resources that guide the development of an organization, and Restricted, as the action plan to reach the goals in an uncertain environment. According to Pérez-Uribe, Ocampo-Guzman, Ospina, Cifuentes, and Cubillos (2016), strategy takes elements that revitalize enterprises internally and externally, currently and in the future. Mintzberg (1987) considers strategy as being composed of 5 Ps: plan, play, pattern, position, and perspective.

Corporate strategic management is the process to formulate, implement, evaluate, and provide feedback on the functional and comprehensive decisions that allow an organization to reach its organizational objectives. Among its advantages, Pérez-Uribe (2018) affirms that it [1] provides a framework for action in the minds of employees and the organization; [2] allows organizational leaders to move the firm towards a shared vision; [3] increases the organizational capability to implement a strategic plan; [4] helps the organization to develop, organize and use tools to understand the environment better; [5] provides a basis to adjust actions from competitors; and [6] allows the organization to anticipate to activities made by competitors.

AVAILABLE TOOLS TO PERFORM THE ANALYSIS

There are some tools available to researchers to evaluate firms selected. Both PESTEL and Porter's Five Forces models help understand the different external and internal factors that influence the organizational management process. The PESTEL method is the starting point to understand the industry in which an enterprise operates by providing managers an easy understanding of the key factors that boost change and the differential impact of external influences in industries, markets, and organizations. (Johnson, Scholes, & Whittington, 2006). Porter's Five Forces model was initially developed to evaluate industries' appealing. It permits the understanding of sources of competition in an industry; the five forces are the threat of new entrants, bargaining power of suppliers, the risk of substitutes, the bargaining power of buyers, and industry rivalry.

According to Johnson, Scholes, and Whittington (2006), the threat of new entrants refers to the entry barriers that new entrants must overcome to be competitive. The risk of substitutes refers to the demand for a specific type of product. The bargaining power of buyers and suppliers occurs when at least one of these conditions is present: high concentration or buyers or suppliers, the cost of changing a supplier, the supplier is taken over by the buyer, and/or the buyer creates a business for competing against the suppliers. The industry rivalry happens when the enterprise and its closest competitors have similar products and want to reach the same market segments.

The following matrices are tools used to determine the current situation of enterprises.

a) *Trend Analysis Matrix*. Based on the PESTEL model, it includes a list of trends, where the degree of impact over the sector ranks on a scale from low to high.
b) The *Competitive Analysis Matrix* was developed under a similar scale to identify the factors that have an influence on the enterprise, based on the Porter Model (Rugman and D'Cruz, 1993). It includes a list of behaviors based on such a model (competitors, suppliers, buyers, new entrants, and substitutes) to analyze the strength of each variable compared to other players.
c) The *Competitive Profile Matrix* identifies the position of competitors in the market according to the key factors of success, which arise from the correlation between trends and behaviors, considering that the lower the number of competitors with the same essential element, the stronger the player. According to David (2013), this matrix is complemented with the PESTEL analysis is a model of strategic management, which includes political, economic, social, technological, ecological, and legal factors; this tool is useful to analyze the market in which an enterprise operates.
d) The *EFE Evaluation Matrix* is a way to organize the external factors into categories to analyze the response of an enterprise's management to these factors according to how important they are considered by firms (Wheelen, & Hunger, 2013). Managers use this tool to evaluate external key aspects, from which opportunities and threats are identified regarding geographic, economic, political, social, technological, and competitive topics. Then, value and grade were assigned to calculate a final result to determine the most and least important factors for the organization. Internal key factors were analyzed using the EFI. This matrix considers the managerial, financial, technological, competitive, and human capabilities of the organization in terms of strengths and weaknesses (Forero, & Gaona, 2019).

The SWOT analysis helps to analyze the relationship between the influence of the environment and the strategic capabilities of an organization regarding its competitors (Johnson, Scholes, & Whittington, 2006). The SWOT analysis performs from the results obtained with the EFE and EFI Matrices, by evaluating the situation of the firm regarding its strengths, weaknesses, and capabilities to take advantage of opportunities for mitigating threats coming from the external environment. The SWOT Matrix shows the opportunities, threats, strengths, and weaknesses faced by firms to propose four strategic alternatives. Firms use this tool to create corporate and business strategies (Wheelen, & Hunger, 2013).

The Strategic Map, which is a simplified graphical representation or the strategy of an organization, by which it is possible to determine its currents situation and a future line of action (Kaplan, & Norton, 2004), was developed based on the SWOT Matrix. The Balanced Scorecard is considered a tool useful for top management to lead the organization with strategies to achieve long term success, providing a structure for strategic management to organize topics, information, and critical processes (Kaplan, & Norton, 2002). Firms use both methodologies to develop competitive and corporate strategies to establish a management model of the organization.

METHODOLOGY

These tools were developed along with CVR staff, most of them engineers, in four working sessions, using open interviews to identify each of the factors described in the matrices. For this assessment, different models and tools were used to get information from, analyze, and identify the organization´s situation to propose actions to improve organizational growth. The diagnosis was performed using the guidelines presented according to theoretical models.

In the first stage, the researchers collected the necessary information about the firm, performing interviews with the CEO and key professionals of CVR. Based on such interviews, researchers assessed the organization and proposed meeting twice per month with technical and administrative staff to develop the activities planned for this consulting process. Researchers conducted four interviews, each lasting 50 minutes, to the CVR technical and organizational team members, who added new information that was analyzed.

The first meeting occurred in March 2017; with such information, and using the PESTEL model, the researchers identified the critical external factors for the enterprise, considering the five analysis areas (political, legal, economic, social, and technological environments), as stated by Johnson, Scholes, and Whittington (2006). Then, such factors were evaluated to prioritize those that affect the organization the most, being them those related to legal and political trends and social trends that go along technological tendencies. This fact occurred because of the development of ICTs had allowed the implementation of technical strategies to innovate.

The analysis of internal capabilities was performed during the second meeting, using Porter's Model. The results showed that providers have a bargaining power since they provide inputs necessary to fulfill contractual terms and conditions previously agreed by the organization. Following the same methodology to obtain information, the EFE Evaluation Matrix was applied to evaluate critical external factors. Information about the macro environment was collected through secondary sources, gathering data from public and private organizations to identify the most relevant elements influencing SME's management. Such information was analyzed using the trend matrix and the EFE matrix to prioritize the information found. Results were validated with the CVR working team.

Such a tool allowed us to identify geographical, economic, political, social, technological, and competitive opportunities and threats. Then, information published in the CVR website and brochure was reviewed, as well as other online communication that is necessary for microenvironment analysis and the internal organizational assessment, following Porter's model. For this, the behavior, competitive profile, and EFI Matrices were used, validated, and evaluated by the researchers and the CVR working team. The application of the EFI Evaluation Matrix allowed identifying critical internal factors, considering organizational strengths and weaknesses in managerial, financial, technological, competitive, and human capabilities.

Once all matrices were filled, and the compiled information validated and evaluated, the SWOT Analysis was performed to analyze the relationship between the environment and the strategic capabilities of the organization (Johnson, Scholes, and Whittington, 2006). The results of the analysis were used to develop the SWOT Matrix and the Strategic Map to propose corporate and strategic strategies to design a management model suitable to the needs of the organization from four perspectives: financing, customers, internal processes, and organizational learning. Some of the strategies proposed were: a model of management by competencies, the standardization of missional processes, the implementation of a coaching program for organizational leaders, and the design of processes of resource management.

PESTEL RESULTS. EXTERNAL ANALYSIS

After thoughtful consideration of the categories defined by the PESTEL to identify the influences of the macro environment, the researchers verified the information collected to perform the external analysis of the most critical trends in the model of management of enterprises of services of training and consulting in the agricultural and livestock industry as follows:

Political and Legal Trends

The directions found for this category complied with Colombian regulations, as follows

a) Law 905, issued in 2004 to stimulate the development of MSMEs as well as the promotion of highly competitive markets through the constant creation and operation of MSMEs (Congreso de la República de Colombia, 2004)
b) Law 1429, issued in 2010, aimed at 1) formalizing enterprises by providing incentives during their first years of operation, simplifying paperwork and reducing formalization costs, and 2) create jobs (Congreso de la República de Colombia, 2010)
c) Law 1314, issued in 2009, to 1) regulate accounting as well as financial information and assurance principles and regulations, and 2) appoint competent authorities and institutions to assure the compliance with the Law (Congreso de la República de Colombia, 2009).
d) Law 80 issued in 1993 that published the Statute of Public Procurement, which regulates public procurement and applies to every person or entity that enters into a contract with the State (Congreso de la República de Colombia, 1993)
e) Law 23, issued in 1982 that regulates copyrights and specifies some topics related to it (Congreso de la República de Colombia, 1982). There are other legal regulations on copyrights such as Law 44 issued in 1993, which modified some provisions contained in Law 23 published in 1982; Decree 1474 issued in 2002, which accepted the World Copyright Treaty; Statutory Law 1581 issued in 2012, which regulated specific issues about protection of personal information (Ministerio de las Tecnologías de la Información y las Comunicaciones, 2012)
f) Regulating Decree 1072, issued in 2015, establishes guidelines to implement the System of Management of Safety and Health at the Workplace (Ministerio del Trabajo, 2016).

The System of Management of Safety and Health at the Workplace is about the development of a logic, stage by stage process, based on continuous improvement, which includes policies, organization, planning, application, evaluation, auditing, and improvement actions aimed at anticipating, recognizing, evaluating and controlling risks that may affect safety and health at workplaces (Velandia, 2013)

Compliance with the Labor Code was issued in 1951, which deals with regulations regarding hiring and human resource management processes, aimed to reach fairness in organizations (Ministerio de Protección Social, 2011). Therefore, concepts such as labor contract, its types, causes of termination, probationary and learning periods, salary determination, fringe benefits, safety at work, vacations, maternity leave, among others, are defined.

Considering the previous trends, CVR believes high impact: compliance with Law 905 issued in 2004 and Law 1429 issued in 2010, which define and classify enterprises, stimulate their growth, and generate formalization; Law 1314, published in 2009, is also considered of high impact. Plans for land use were classified as high impact trends when organizations develop their activities. Tax reforms were also classified as high impact trends since they follow economic interest and the interest of the people in charge of the government, which may significantly affect economic activities.

The Statute of Public Procurement was classified as medium impact since it applies only in contracts with the Government. Regulations regarding copyrights and the Labor Code were also classified as medium impact.

Economic Trends

GDP grew 3.3% in 2019. Wholesale and retail trade, automotive and motorcycle repair, transportation and storage, lodging and food services increased 4.9%. Public administration and defense, mandatory Social Security, education, health, and social services grew by 4.9%. Administrative services and support activities grew by 3.7% (Departamento Administrativo Nacional de Estadísticas –DANE, 2020).

Colombian GDP at current prices in its original series grew 2.7% in the third quarter of 2018 compared to the same period in 2017, with the following behavior by industry: mining grew 1%, public administration and defense, education, and health grew 4.5%; wholesale and retail trade 2.6%; manufacturing grew 2.9%; professional, scientific and technical activities grew 3.6%, and real estate grew 2.1%, artistic activities, recreation, and other services grew 1.0% (Departamento Administrativo Nacional de Estadísticas –DANE, 2018). Such results could bring more investment to the agricultural sector, therefore to the service industry, generating higher demand and supply for these and other industries. COVID-19 has ruined all these positive growth figures.

The fluctuation of the USD is another tendency related to the model of management of organizations since it impacts specific industries, significantly those indebted overseas and/or those that import raw materials since their production costs may increase (BBC, 2015). This trend is considered of high impact for CVR since it imports machinery and equipment, and an increase in the USD price increments its costs, which may cause a budget deficit, making it necessary to implement initiatives that may have an impact on organizational management.

Social Trends

A trend that has become important for organizations is sustainable development and green strategies, also called Green Marketing, as an alternative to traditional products that have polluting components not appealing to customers (Castellano, & Urdaneta, 2015).

Berrio (2006) states that the number of people who follow this lead, as well as the demand for environment-friendly products, has significantly increased. Therefore, it is higher the number of enterprises that allocate resources to research and create new technologies to obtain a competitive advantage and decrease acquisitions of raw materials used in their production processes.

Currently, trading is changing because customers use mobile devices to get information about products, search for coupons, discounts, buy, manage their finances, verify their banking products, transfer money, and access to products all over the world. Then, organizations get closer to their customers via web and mobile apps, and they can also close physical locations, therefore saving money in infrastructure (Nielsen, 2016). Thus, organizations have become more visible online and use new technologies to optimize resources and increase efficiency levels. Another critical trend is organizational innovation, which must be understood as a strategy that goes along the management process to answer timely and rightly to administrative procedures to increase competitiveness (Villamil, 2017).

Regarding these trends, CVR considers Green Marketing as a tendency of high impact, since many of its products are oriented to the use of environment-friendly strategies, and they focus their processes of training and consulting from such perspective. CVR considers that promoting strategies and environment-friendly products requires constant innovation to guarantee the efficiency and effectiveness of services offered and its management process. Organizational innovation is also thought of high impact since, at CVR, they are continually creating new ideas and strategies focused on improving their services and value chain.

Technological Trends

Organizations tend to implement digital strategies to organize information better, aimed at having a more efficient implementation of new technologies and available resources. Some methods are remote working, cloud computing management of human resources, SaaS, and financial management using mobile solutions (Santana, 2014).

A trend that has gained importance is developing new mobile apps or collaborative apps, which work as a tool to integrate knowledge and data to make them available quickly. Given the importance of ICT use, SMEs must dispose of technological tools to be closer to their customers to offer customized services in real-time (Rojas, n.d; Corso, Martini, Pellegrini, & Paolucci, 2003).

Technologies such as Big Data goes beyond a standard software analysis. Such data is processed using different techniques to change data into relevant information about the relationship between customer and organization. Thus, Big Data becomes an excellent business opportunity since it enables decision making in firms (Nuñez, 2015).

CVR considered trends regarding the implementation of digital strategies and the development of mobile apps to increase the availability of its products and services to the market.

Environmental Trends

CVR develops processes of identification to obtain, store, and treat water for agriculture, based on a design that determines the total amount of rain during the cropping process. According to Critchel and Siegert (1996), the amount of precipitation over the obtaining area will provide the surface overflow necessary to satisfy the crops' water needs (FAO, 2013).

Basins keep the balance between social and economic uses of the soil, water, flora, and fauna to keep the physical biotic structure of the basins and mitigate the environmental decline and the impact on natural resources (Ministerio de Ambiente y Desarrollo Sostenible, n.d.). It was evidenced that CVR is at the forefronts to take care of the environment (Table 1).

INTERNAL ANALYSIS – MICROENVIRONMENT

It is necessary to understand its environment and the power it has over the organization to analyze an enterprise and its strategies. So, Porter's Model was used, as according to Johnson, Scholes, and Whittington (2006), it allows the understanding of the sources of competition in an industry. By the use of this model, it was found that CVR leading suppliers are: 1) IDECO, an enterprise that supplies technical support and communication strategies to position the brand and gets loyalty by its stakeholders; this supplier is strong since its activity contributes to growth, productivity improvement, customer satisfaction, reaching new markets and access to stakeholders; 2) Proplanta, with whom CVR has a strategic alliance to acquire agricultural products demanded by buyers and to exchange knowledge. Colposoz, Tradecorp, and AGQ. have joined this Alliance to form Alenza, which is created from the need of the allied enterprises to supply Colombian produces with a new alternative to optimize the genetic potential of crops in terms of quantity and quality, based on the model agreed by the producer and the market (CVR Ingenieria del Conocimiento, n.d.). Finally, CAFAM, which provides outsourced staff for administrative and missional activities, is classified as a weak supplier.

CVR's size, structure, customers, and services were considered to classify competitors. No enterprises with similar characteristics to become competitors were found. Therefore, CVR deems to be unique in the market, integrating into its value chain those supporting activities that contribute to improving efficacy and efficiency to the organization to add value. Besides, no substitutes were found since the service provided by CVR focuses on the use of new technologies to optimize environmental and entrepreneurial resources in the context of the development of an efficient working plan. The Bogota Chamber of Commerce and the Calima Mall are buyers of CVR services, having no power or strength.

Finally, stakeholders worth mentioning are the Ministry of Finance and Economics, Ministry of Labor, Ministry of Industry and Trade, and some Major offices. They all play some roles in regulating macroeconomic, fiscal, trade, labor, and local policies.

Through their regulations, these players influence organizations that have to comply with the law to operate, so they have some power over the enterprise; failure to fulfill the law may result in monetary or legal sanctions.

COMPETITIVE PROFILE ANALYSIS

Once tendencies and behaviors by players were analyzed, it was determined that CVR is an organization with specific characteristics created exclusively for the development of its mission.

The methodology used to perform mutual learning and training processes has been decisive to position itself in the market; prove of this are the strategic alliances created to answer adequately to the needs of customers and to reach new markets. This fact is part of the key factors that have made the organization successful so far, along with the strategy of continuous improvement and the capability of integrating activities that add value to its value chain.

Table 1. Trend Analysis Matrix

TRENDS	TREND ANALYSIS MATRIX (PRIORITIZATION BY IMPACT)	*IMPACT*		
	Trend Description	Low	Medium	High
		1	3	5
POLITICAL & LEGAL	Compliance of Law 905 issued in 2004 (to promote the development of MSMEs in Colombia)			*
	Compliance of Law 1429 issued in 2010 (to formalize enterprises and create jobs)			*
	Compliance of Law 1314, issued in 2009 (to regulate principles and norms of accounting, financial information, and information safety accepted in Colombia)			*
	Compliance of Law 80, issued in 1993 (creation of the Statute of Public procurement)		*	
	Compliance of Law 23, issued in 1982 (which established norms related to Copyright and enacted the Treaty of the World Intellectual Property Organization).		*	
	Compliance of Law 1581, issued in 2012 (which established general norms to protect personal information).	*		
	Compliance of Decree 1072, issued in 2015 (which enacts mandatory norms to implement the System of Management of Safety and Health at the workplace).	*		
	Compliance of the Trade Code.		*	
	Compliance of the Labor Code.		*	
	Compliance of Land Use Plans.			*
	Tax Reforms impact different sectors of the industry.			*
ECONOMIC	Fluctuations of the USD price impact specific sectors of the industry.			*
	GDP behavior increases or reduces investment in a specific industry.	*		
SOCIAL	Enterprises implement sustainable development and Green strategies.			*
	Enterprises go online		*	
	Enterprises implement innovation in their products.			*
TECHNOLOGICAL	Enterprises implement digital strategies.			*
	Enterprises implement mobile apps.			*
	New technology tools (Big Data) facilitate data analysis and interpretation.		*	
ENVIRONMENTAL	Enterprises identify areas to get, store, and purify water.			*
	Enterprises properly handle river basins.			*

Source: The authors based on the PESTEL Model

Table 2. Competitive Analysis Matrix

COMPETITIVE ANALYSIS MATRIX						
STRENGTHS	**Behavioral Description**	*IMPACT OF BEHAVIOR CONCERNING THE POWER BASED ON STRENGHT*				
		Low	**Lower Middle**	**Middle**	**Upper Middle**	**High**
		1	**2**	**3**	**4**	**5**
INTENSITY COMPETITION (POWER OF COMPETITORS) N/A						
POWER OF BUYERS Bogota Chamber of Commerce Calima Mall						
	Customers demand punctuality from service providers.	*				
	Customers require to get what was agreed.	*				
POWER OF SUPPLIERS ALENZA IDECO CAFAM						
	Suppliers establish strategic alliances.				*	
	Suppliers develop profitable agro-industrial business models.				*	
	Suppliers fulfill CVR's requirements				*	
	Suppliers advise CVR in marketing				*	
	Suppliers provide human resources according to CVR's requirements.		*			
SUBSTITUTE PRODUCTS N/A						
(STAKEHOLDERS) **Ministry of Economics** **Ministry of Labor** **Ministry of Industry and Trade** **Mayors' Offices**						
	Defines, formulates, and executes the country's tax policy				*	
	Coordinates Colombian macroeconomic policy				*	
	Regulates labor matters			*		
	Protects customers' rights				*	
	Promotes free competition				*	
	Regulate policies established by Land use plans.				*	

Source: the Authors based on Porter's Model

EXTERNAL ANALYSIS

In the last years, the industry of professional, scientific, and technical activities in Colombia has been continuously growing: according to DANE (2020), this industry grew significantly during the first three quarters of 2019, considering that it has a high possibility to grow, benefiting the country's economy.

This fact will be possible as long as enterprises can identify external opportunities and threats to take actions that favor their growth and performance.

The External Factors Evaluation Matrix EFE was elaborated to assess the situation; the matrix correlates the information compiled about opportunities and threats, classifies according to geographic, economic, political, social, technological, and competitive factors that could affect the enterprise's performance. A value in percentage is assigned to each opportunity and threat (the sum of all values assigned should equal 100). Then, a score (on a scale of 1 to 4 with 1 being the lowest and 4 being the highest) was assigned according to the CVR's ability to take advantage of opportunities or mitigate threats.

Table 3. EFE Evaluation Matrix

EFE EVALUATION MATRIX				
KEY EXTERNAL FACTORS		Value	Classification	Weighted Value
OPPORTUNITIES		(A)	(B)	(A*B)
GEOGRAPHICAL	N/A			
ECONOMIC	N/A			
POLITICAL	N/A			
SOCIAL	The use of new technologies aids and boosts the work methodology.	25	3	75
TECHNOLOGICAL	Taking advantage of new technologies favors the enterprise's digital marketing.	25	3	75
	The implementation of technological resources helps the management of the organization	25	3	75
COMPETITIVE	Lack of strong competitors	25	4	100
SUBTOTAL		100		325
THREATS		(A)	(B)	(A*B)
GEOGRAPHIC	The absence of financial institutions in the area limits access to banking operations.	30	3	90
	The enterprise's location does not increase workers' performance.	30	3	90
ECONOMIC	Tax reforms that tend to increase taxes affect operating costs in the industry.	10	1	10
POLITICAL	The promotion of post-conflict policies limits the enterprise's management.	30	3	90
SOCIAL	N/A			
TECHNOLOGICAL	N/A			
COMPETITIVE	N/A			
	SUBTOTAL	100		280

Source: Wheelen and Hunger (2013)

After having analyzed the information, the researchers concluded that taking advantage of technological tools to aid internal and external management is an opportunity for CVR. Through them, CVR can grow more, have a better position in the market, promote its brand, segment the market, and apply more dynamic methodologies, increasing its competitiveness.

The researchers identified threats that need to be addressed to avoid brain drain. Also, the lack of financial institutions close to CVR facilities limits the ability to perform banking transactions and does not favor a worker's performance. CVR's location in the northern outskirts of Bogota ease the access to customers (since most of them located in the north area of the city) but negatively affect operational processes related to financing and worker's welfare.

INTERNAL ANALYSIS

The Matrix of Evaluation of Internal Factors (EFI) was used to analyze strengths and weaknesses related to management, financing, technology, and human talent. Besides, the relation between different areas or processes of the enterprise was assessed.

A value in percentage is assigned to each strength and weakness (the sum of all values assigned should equal 100). Then a score (on a scale of 1 (lowest) to 4 (highest)) was set according to the CVR's gap and the aspect evaluated. Interviews with CVR staff were performed to elaborate on the matrix. Through those interviews, the researchers identified opportunities, strengths, threats, and weaknesses, from which critical factors of each one of them were established.

Qualified and motivated staff, people-oriented policies, the process of qualification in audiovisual topics, the motivation of staff from a moral responsibility perspective, and a constant self-learning and innovation process were identified as strengths based on the results obtained. The analysis also identified the following weaknesses: inadequate organization of functions, high operational costs, inadequate control of expenses, insufficient staff, lack of human resource management, and insufficient use of communication channels.

SWOT ANALYSIS

The SWOT analysis was performed based on compiled information and having the EFE and EFI Matrices as references to identify CVR's main opportunities, threats, strengths, and weaknesses. The SWOT Analysis associates internal and external factors to generate strategies to take advantage of opportunities and strengths and to mitigate threats and weaknesses, aimed at obtaining a competitive advantage in the market (Universidad de Cantabria, 2014). The analysis showed that CVR has a highly qualified staff, motivated and responsible, motivated from a moral perspective, which guarantees the successful fulfillment of assignments. This fact also allows having dynamic training methodologies, generating higher customer satisfaction levels. Besides, this improves business links, creating more mature self-learning and innovation processes, keeping in mind that the latter is one of the main characteristics of CVR's people-oriented policy.

The researchers identified weaknesses that could cause a crisis due to inadequate organization of processes, and lack of planning, forecasts, and expenses control. Besides, CVR does not have enough staff to adequately deal with all management areas, leading to inefficient use of resources.

As of opportunities, CVR is a unique enterprise, a circumstance that has allowed it to have a good position in the market and to answer adequately to customer's needs. Besides, CVR has no strong competitors. CVR can take advantage of technological tools to increase its digital marketing, boost its working methodology, and improve management, given the high levels of digital use in Colombia.

Table 4. EFI. Evaluation Matrix

EFI EVALUATION MATRIX				
KEY INTERNAL FACTORS		EVALUATION		
		Value	Classification	Weighted Value
STRENGTHS		(A)	(B)	(A*B)
MANAGEMENT	The team is motivated from a perspective of moral responsibility	15	4	60
FINANCING	Strategic alliances contribute to cost reductions	10	3	30
HUMAN RESOURCES	Staff is qualified and motivated	15	4	60
	Work policies are people-oriented	10	4	40
	Outsourcing of the hiring process improves HR management efficiency	10	2	20
TECHNOLOGY	Qualification in audiovisual topics is adequate	10	4	40
COMPETITIVENESS	There are constant processes of self-learning and innovation	15	4	60
	Its location provides recognition and status	5	4	20
	It is easy for a customer to access organizational facilities	10	3	30
TOTAL		100		360
WEAKNESSES		(A)	(B)	(A*B)
MANAGEMENT	Organization of processes is inadequate	20	1	20
	There are no defined policies for organizational management	10	1	10
	There are no organizational planning processes.	10	2	20
FINANCING	There are no controls to verify forecasts	10	2	20
	There are high operating costs and lack of adequate control of expenses	10	2	20
HUMAN RESOURCES	Staff is not enough for organizational needs	10	3	30
	There are no policies of Safety and health at the workplace.	5	2	10
	There is no H.R. management	10	2	20
TECHNOLOGY	Communication channels are not adequately used	10	2	20
COMPETITIVENESS	Process standardization is low	5	1	5
	TOTAL	100		175

Source: Wheelen and Hunger (2013)

As of threats, CVR's location does not favor worker's performance, since they have to commute long distances from their places of residence to CVR facilities. The absence of financial institutions in the area makes it challenging to conduct specific paperwork procedures. Another threat was the promotion of post-conflict policies since they pose challenges for SMEs and big enterprises in Colombia, limiting the impact on CVR's room for action and management.

Table 5. SWOT Analysis

STRENGTHS **1. The team is motivated by a moral responsibility perspective.** **2. The staff is qualified and motivated.** **3. Work policies are people-oriented.** **4. Qualification in audiovisual topics is adequate.** **5. There are constant processes of self-learning and innovation.**	**WEAKNESSES** **1. The organization of processes is inadequate.** **2. There are no organizational planning processes.** **3. There are no controls to verify forecasts.** **4. There are high operating costs and a lack of adequate supervision of expenses.** **5. Staff is not enough for organizational needs.** **6. There is no HR management.** **7. Communication channels are not adequately used.**
OPPORTUNITIES **1. Taking advantage of new technologies favors the enterprise's digital marketing.** **2. The use of new technologies favors and boost the work methodology,** **3. The implementation of technological resources helps the management of the organization.** **4. Lack of strong competitors.**	THREATS 1. The absence of financial institutions in the area limits access to banking operations. 2. The promotion of post-conflict policies specifies the enterprise's management. 3. The enterprise's location does not increase workers' performance.

Source: Johnson, Scholes, and Whittington (2006)

STRATEGIC FORMULATION – SWOT MATRIX

Once the information obtained was analyzed, and CVR's resources and capabilities were considered, the most critical factors were included in the SWOT Matrix proposed by Wheelen and Hunger (2013). As a result, the authors crossed information to suggest SO, ST, WO, and WT strategies. The factors identified were the following:

ü *STRENGTHS*
S1. The team is motivated by a moral responsibility perspective.
S2. The staff is qualified and motivated.
S3. Work policies are people-oriented.
S4. Qualification in the audiovisual topic is adequate.
S5. There are constant processes of self-learning and innovation.
ü *OPPORTUNITIES*
O1. Taking advantage of new technologies favors the enterprise's digital marketing.
O2. The use of new technologies aids and boosts the work methodology.
O3. The implementation of technological resources helps the management of the organization
O4. Lack of strong competitors
ü *WEAKNESSES*
W1. The organization of processes is inadequate.
W2. There are no organizational planning processes.
W3. There are no controls to verify forecasts.
W4. There are high operating costs and a lack of adequate control of expenses.
W5. Staff is not enough for the organization's needs.
W6. There is no HR management.
W7. Communication channels are not adequately used.
ü *THREATS*

T1. The absence of financial institutions in the area limits access to banking operations.
T2. The promotion of post-conflict policies limits the enterprise's management.
T3. The enterprise's location does not increase the worker's performance.

SO (Strengths/Opportunities) Strategies are oriented towards providing tools so the enterprise can take advantage of its environment. The researchers propose creating a model of competencies to evaluate specific competencies for each position and identify those needed for the professional and personal growth of the enterprise's workers. Another SO Strategy is the standardization of missional processes to place in a single operation all those procedures conducted heterogeneously. This fact will allow having more effective control and evaluation mechanisms for the continuous improvement of organizational dynamics.

ST (Strengths/Threats) Strategies are aimed at reducing the impact caused by external threats. Such strategies are oriented to adopt a differential organizational policy so the organization can adequately face challenges posed by post-conflict policies, answering timely and efficiently to any matter caused by them. Another strategy is implementing a coaching program for managers to train them in topics related to the importance of strategic management, starting from proper planning to manage all the resources of the enterprise adequately.

WO (Weaknesses/Opportunities) Strategies try to eliminate, mitigate, or transform weaknesses into strengths to take advantage of the environment. Such strategies were designed to define a model of strategic orientation that facilitates internal reengineering of processes to rethink the organization and direct it towards continuous improvement cycles. So, the researchers proposed implementing policies of human resources to increase personal satisfaction levels, avoid brain drain, and provide higher value-added to workers through the management of internal and external resources. Besides, the authors propose implementing programs and strategies of promotion and internal communication to socialize policies, plans, and objectives, establishing efficient interaction channels to guarantee to pass on relevant information to all workers.

WT (Weaknesses/Threats) Strategies are: to establish processes to strengthen the organization's capability to have elements that enable it to transform, increase, or diversify the enterprise to boost its growth. Also, it was proposed to implement processes of resource management to have better control of expenses and to optimize those elements available to the organization to fulfill its mission.

PLAN FOR IMPLEMENTATION OF STRATEGIES

The next step was to design the corporate strategies, keeping in mind finances, customers, internal processes, and organizational learning to propose solutions coherent with organizational objectives, mission, and vision. Consequently, the financial strategy deals with full control of the cost structure, strengthening the process of corporate planning and management to optimize the use of resources to increase income and managing cash flow at 90% at least. Once the financial component is organized, the cash flow must be planed yearly and financial resources distributed to fulfill organizational goals- previous review and authorization from top management.

Regarding customers, the strategy is the increase in staff efficiency and efficacy, getting them to become goal-oriented. To do so, researchers propose standardization and interaction of all organizational processes to clarify the origin and use of resources to take the most advantage of them.

To improve internal processes, the researchers propose implementing policies of management of human resources, for which it is necessary to have an appropriate team of professionals in charge of designing such policies and managing human resources. The researchers also recommend creating a training program suitable for organizational needs, for which it is necessary to have the appropriate financial resources.

Another strategy proposed is the promotion of an organizational culture oriented towards the continuous improvement of internal processes. Therefore, it is necessary to implement the PDCA (plan, do, check, act) methodology to implement self-assessment methods to achieve constant improvement of daily procedures and activities (Departamento Administrativo de la Función Pública, 2009). Besides, the researchers propose the development of internal and external communication processes that contribute to strengthen organizational management by developing the following activities: a selection of suitable personnel for the design and development of communication strategies, the definition of protocols, and improvement of communication and information organizational channels such as magazines, newspapers, memos, intranet, webs, news bulletin, e-mail, etc.

Researchers propose creating a working schedule to include all organizational areas or teams by promoting acceptable communication practices to spread information at all hierarchical levels, and the proper use of communication channels such as boards, social networks, chats, etc.

Finally, from the organizational learning perspective, the strategy proposed is to establish a management model to guide CVT; such a model must consider this analysis and the mission, vision, and goals. Hence, researchers also proposed the definition of processes needed for proper management. Therefore, it is necessary to be clear about the enterprise's structure and comprehensive objectives since those are essential to organize and direct tasks, to define functions, and to develop activities effectively to achieve successful results. Another strategy deals with the administration of processes of organizational transformation from top management by incorporating coaching programs to train managers biannually. Another is using outdoor training in topics related to strategic leadership, teamwork, management focused on processes, effective communication, and the use of symbols and language.

CONCLUSIONS AND RECOMMENDATIONS

Based on documents consulted at the Bogota Chamber of Commerce and several digital sources, we conclude that CVR is a firm with unique characteristics that helped it to achieve leadership positions in the agricultural and livestock industry, to expand its activities to other sectors. Its experience has allowed the firm to create strategic alliances to gain specialized knowledge and boost business growth.

The use of new technologies was identified as an opportunity. If properly taken advantage of them, they can favor organizational management; their use could improve positioning, growth, and brand promotion as well as helping with the process of market segmentation and with the dynamics of working methodologies.

The absence of financial institutions near CVR facilities was identified as a threat that needs to be addressed to reduce the risk of brain drain, low workers' performance, and its impact on internal financial operations and human resources processes.

The following strengths, essential for the development and efficiency of an organization, were identified: people-oriented working policies, qualification processes in audiovisual topics, qualified and motivated staff, constant self-learning and innovation processes, and motivation of staff from a moral responsibility perspective. However, weaknesses found include lack of control of expenses, lack of planning and organization of operations, lack of rules for forecast verification, high operating costs, inefficient use of communication channels, and low levels of human resources management. Therefore, the researchers recommend the implementation of an improvement plan to perform a structural intervention of the organization to increase efficacy and efficiency levels, increase customer satisfaction, encourage continuous organizational growth, and to organize and standardize internal processes and procedures. The implementation of the plan will provide managers with a corporate structure following the characteristics of CVR, which facilitates the determination of a strategic management style suitable to manage the organization.

Such a plan must be implemented together with a process or managerial and strategic reengineering, oriented towards redefining the enterprises' vision and aligning the new organizational structure, processes, procedures, and corporate policies.

CVR has broad expertise in providing comprehensive solutions –by applying knowledge management- for the agricultural and livestock industry. Through the years, it has gained recognition in the market and has formed strategic alliances to structure, promote, and follow high impact business initiatives; this has brought economic growth. However, some internal situations are risky and threaten the enterprise's development. Regardless of its expertise in its training methodology, CVR presents difficulties in its organizational structure because roles are not defined. Besides, there is no organization, neither standardization of operating processes since there is no unified criterion to perform certain activities. This fact increases the risk of resource flight, affects transparency, and makes it challenging to develop an organizational culture based on acceptable working practices and continuous improvement.

Moreover, CVR presents weaknesses in the development of financial activities, since there are no mechanisms to control costs and cash flow, which could result in inefficient use of resources and the detriment of the capital available for the operation of the organization. Hence, the enterprise could incur unnecessary expenses due to the lack of control and process planning. This fact is worthy of performing a detailed review of financial statements with its resulting high costs to identify shortcomings. Also, CVR must address those threats such as barriers of entry for customers, which could have a significant impact on operational processes related to finances and workers' welfare.

Besides, there is not enough staff specialized in management to optimize the enterprise's administration. This fact is visible in terms of a lack of human resources management, which is required to assign roles and functions adequately and manage the qualifications and recruitment of specialized professionals. This situation is also reflected in the inadequate use of communication channels, since CVR's online channels' information is not updated, neither available for internal and external customers, affecting the few digital marketing actions performed by the enterprise.

Another dimension of the organization requiring attention is strategic management, as there is a lack of strategies for the orientation of the firm. Therefore, CVR faces an uncertain future in regards to its growth and development. Thus, it is necessary to implement management policies that define and bring together all components required to reach the proposed goals and objectives, achieving adequate management of the organization. Hence, reengineering is necessary to have a broader and more competitive vision about the use of resources.

The findings previously described helped to identify variables that have an impact on the problems of the organization; most of them relate to strategic management and management of the organization due to lack of managerial training and low levels of commitment with the development and improvement of the organization. Such situations harm the firm since the shortcomings of management can affect the future such as money flight, lower profits, lack of motivation of workers, low productivity, brain drain, loss of competitive advantage, and any others that could take CVR out of business.

That is why the researchers recommend the organization to implement a process of organizational transformation from top management, which leads to defining a model of strategic management oriented towards the orientation of the organization and then express those processes necessary to optimize its administration.

REFERENCES

BBC. (2015). *¿Quién gana y quién pierde con el alza del dólar en América Latina?* Retrieved from: https://www.bbc.com/mundo/noticias/2015/08/150819_economia_america_latina_dolar_alza_egn

Berrio, S. K. (2006). *Mercadeo verde: Otra Forma de Ayudar al Mundo.* Retrieved from: https://www.dinero.com/columna-del-lector/opinion/articulo/mercadeo-verde-otra-forma-ayudar-mundo/33121

Camara de Comercio de Medellín. (2015). *Informativo Camara.* Retrieved from: http://www.camara-medellin.com.co/site/Portals/0/Documentos/Informativo%20Camara%202015.pdf

Castellano, S., & Urdaneta, G. J. A. (2015). Estrategias de Mercadeo Verde Utilizadas por Empresas a Nivel Mundial. *Telos*, *17*(3), 476–494.

Corso, M., Martini, A., Pellegrini, L., & Paolucci, E. (2003). Technological and organizational tools for knowledge management: In search of configurations. *Small Business Economics*, *21*(4), 397–408. doi:10.1023/A:1026123322900

David, F. R. (2013). *Administración Estratégica.* Mexico: Pearson.

de la República de ColombiaC. (1982). Ley 23. Retrieved from: https://www.revistapym.com.co/noticias/derechos-autor/ley-que-reglamenta-derechos-autor-colombia

de la República de ColombiaC. (1993). Ley 80. Retrieved from: http://www.secretariasenado.gov.co/senado/basedoc/ley_0080_1993.html

de la República de ColombiaC. (2004). Ley 905. Retrieved from: http://www.secretariasenado.gov.co/senado/basedoc/ley_0905_2004.html

de la República de Colombia, C. (2009). Ley 1314. Bogotá, Colombia.

de la República de Colombia, C. (2010). Ley 1429. Retrieved from: http://www.secretariasenado.gov.co/senado/basedoc/ley_1429_2010.html

Departamento Administrativo Nacional de Estadisticas DANE. (2018). Boletín Técnico. Cuentas Trimestrales - Colombia, Producto Interno Bruto (PIB) Tercer Trimestre 2018. Retrieved from: https://www.dane.gov.co/files/investigaciones/boletines/pib/bol_PIB_IIItrim18_producion_y_gasto.pdf

Education Departamento Administrativo de la Función Pública. (2009). Decreto 4485. Norma Técnica de Calidad en la Gestión Pública - NTCGP 1000. Retrieved from: https://www.alcaldiabogota.gov.co/sisjurMantenimiento/normas/Norma1.jsp?i=37853

FAO (Food and Agriculture Organization of the United Nations). (2013). *Capacitación y Almacenamiento de Agua de Lluvia. Opciones técnicas para la agricultura familiar en América latina y el Caribe*. FAO.

Forero Herrera, A. J., & Gaona Guevara, J. (2019). *Propuesta de planeación estratégica para la empresa Angora Confecciones* (B.Sc. Dissertation). Universidad de La Salle, Bogota Colombia.

Francés, A. (2006). *Estrategia y planes para la empresa con el Cuadro de mando integral*. Ciudad de Mexico: Pearson Educación de México.

García, J. A. (2017). *Direccionamiento Estratégico en las PYMEs* (B.Sc. Dissertation). Universidad Militar de Nueva Granada, Colombia.

Ingeniería del ConocimientoC. V. R. (n.d.). Retrieved from: https://www.lasempresas.com.co/bogota/cvr-ingenieria-del-conocimiento-sas/

Johnson, G., Scholes, K., & Whittington, R. (2006). *Dirección Estratégica*. Pearson.

Kaplan, R., & Norton, D. (2002). *El Cuadro de Mando Integral. Gestion.*

Kaplan, R., & Norton, D. (2004). *Mapas Estratégicos. Gestion.*

Kotler, P. (1999). *Marketing Management*. Prentice-Hall.

Kotler, P., & Keller, L. (2006). *Dirección de Marketing*. Ciudad de Mexico: Pearson Educación.

Marketing Science Institute (MSI). (2006). *Research Priorities - A Guide to MSI research programmes and procedures 2006-2008*. Cambridge, MA: Marketing Science Institute.

Ministerio de Ambiente y Desarrollo Sostenible. (n.d.). *Planes de Ordenación y Manejo de Cuencas Hidrográficas (POMCA)*. Ministry of Environment and Sustainable Development.

Ministerio de las Tecnologías de la Información y las Comunicaciones. (2012). Ley Estratutaria 1581. Retrieved from: http://www.secretariasenado.gov.co/senado/basedoc/ley_1581_2012.html

Ministerio de Protección Social. (2011). *Código Sustantivo del Trabajo*. Retrieved from: https://www.ilo.org/dyn/travail/docs/1539/CodigoSustantivodelTrabajoColombia.pdf

Ministerio del Trabajo. (2016). *Decreto Unico Reglamentario 1072*. Retrieved from: https://www.mintrabajo.gov.co/documents/20147/0/DUR+Sector+Trabajo+Actualizado+a+15+de+abril++de+2016.pdf/a32b1dcf-7a4e-8a37-ac16-c121928719c8

Ministerio del Trabajo. (n.d.). *Sistema de Gestión de Seguridad y Salud en el Trabajo*. Retrieved from: https://www.mintrabajo.gov.co/relaciones-laborales/riesgos-laborales/sistema-de-gestion-de-seguridad-y-salud-en-el-trabajo

Mintzberg, H. (1987). The Strategy Concept I: Five Ps for Strategy. *California Management Review*, *30*(1), 11–24. doi:10.2307/41165263

Nielsen. (2016). *Dinero Movil*. Santiago de Chile: Nielsen.

Pérez-Uribe, R. (2018). *Gerencia estratégica corporativa*. Ecoe Ediciones.

Pérez-Uribe, R., Ocampo-Guzman, D., Ospina, J., Cifuentes, J., & Cubillos, C. (2016). *MIIGO Modelo de intervención e innovación para el direccionamiento estratégico*. Ediciones EAN. doi:10.21158/9789587564143

Richardson, M. (2018). *Identification and analysis of marketing manager competencies that determine marketing department capabilities and the underlying importance of courage traits* (Ph.D. Dissertation). Aston University.

Rojas, A. (n.d.). *Tendencias en Aplicaciones Móviles para Pymes*. IT Now.

Rugman, A. M., & D'Cruz, J. R. (1993). The "double diamond" model of international competitiveness: The Canadian experience. *MIR. Management International Review*, *34*, 17–39.

Santana, C. (2014). *Cloud Computing y SaaS serán las estrellas en 2016*. Retrieved from: https://blog.acsendo.com/saas-y-cloud-computing-seran-las-estrellas-en-2016/

Universidad de Cantabria. (2014). *Definición de Alternativas Estratégicas*. University of Cantabria. Retrieved from: https://web.unican.es/unidades/serviciopdiretribuciones/Gestionporprocesos/PDIP-LA-03%20DEFINICI%C3%93N%20DE%20ALTERNATIVAS%20ESTRAT%C3%89GICAS.pdf

Velandia, J. H. M., & Pinilla, N. A. (2013). De la salud ocupacional a la gestión de la seguridad y salud en el trabajo: Más que semántica, una transformación del sistema general de riesgos laborales. *INNOVAR. Revista de Ciencias Administrativas y Sociales*, *23*(48), 21–31.

Villamil, A. M. (2017). *La Planeación Estratégica y la Gestión por Resultados* (B.Sc. Dissertation). Universidad Militar de Nueva Granada, Colombia. Retrieved from: https://repository.unimilitar.edu.co/bitstream/handle/10654/16974/TabordaVillamilAlvaroMiguel.pdf?sequence=3

Wheelen, T. L., & Hunger, J. D. (2013). *Administración Estratégica y Política de Negocios*. Pearson Educación de Colombia.

KEY TERMS AND DEFINITIONS

Balance ScoreCard: A strategic management tool used to identify and improve organizational strategy.

CVR Ingeniería del Conocimiento: It is a Colombian enterprise, subject of this study, founded in 2011, which provides solutions for the agriculture and livestock industry by applying knowledge management.

Economic Trends: The overall tendency of a country's economy.

Latin America: A region in the Americas composed by countries where Romance languages are predominant.

Organizational Management: The process to structure, plan, and direct corporate resources to achieve the organization's objectives.

SMEs: For the service industry in Colombia, SMEs are those enterprises with an annual income of 483.034 Tax Value Units or less.

Strategic Map: A visual representation of the objectives of an organization.

SWOT Analysis: A strategic planning tool used to identify strengths, weaknesses, opportunities, and threats.

Chapter 13
Shopping for an English Language Tutor:
Factors Affecting Chinese College Student Selection of English Tutoring Institutions

Hao Zheng
Wenzhou-Kean University, China

Rob Kim Marjerison
https://orcid.org/0000-0003-1181-8695
Wenzhou-Kean University, China

Oliver R. Keels
Wenzhou-Kean University, China

ABSTRACT

English is often considered to be the international language of commerce and, more recently, e-commerce. English is also the predominant language of the internet, science, and many, the language of higher education. As a result, English tutoring institutions are thriving in the Chinese Mainland in recent years in a substantial and competitive market. The objective of this chapter is to reveal what are the factors that affect Chinese college students' selection of English tutoring institutions in China so that tutoring institution managers may focus on the most important criteria for their prospective customers. In this chapter, 212 Chinese college students participated in the online survey. The authors analyzed the correlation between purchase intention and price, brand image, service variety, and customer relationship. Through data analysis, they show that price, brand image, service variety, and customer relationships are all positively associated with Chinese college students' purchase intention of English tutoring institutions.

DOI: 10.4018/978-1-7998-5036-6.ch013

INTRODUCTION

As in other parts of the world, the number of private tutoring institutions has expanded significantly in mainland China during the past decade (W. Zhang, 2014). Among those students who attend English tutoring institutions, many of them are studying TOEFL, SAT, GMAT, GRE, and so on, for further undergraduate and graduate at academic institutions in the US and abroad (Y. Zhang, 2013). The possibility of studying abroad has been growing in popularity in China (Henze & Zhu, 2012). There are a number of motivators that attract students to study abroad. One of these motivators is program feature. Program feature is supported to be one of clear attractions for students to study abroad (Bodycott, 2009). To conclude, the market of English tutoring institutions in China is growing in a very fast speed (Mazzarol & Soutar, 2002) (Brannen et al., 2017) (Nickerson, 2005) (Mamiseishvili, 2012) (Freihat & Al-Machzoomi, 2012).

Within this wider market, the private tutoring industry has become an increasingly important and diverse segment, though growth has been neither straightforward nor steady (Bai et al., 2019). In addition, with a clear division of labor among tutoring instructors, technical support teams, and teaching research teams; the English tutoring market has gradually developed a more comprehensive tutoring research system in continuous search for the balance between criteria for quality control and diverse options for individuals' learning demands (Bai et al., 2019). It conveys that many of English tutoring institutions in China have already developed systematic approaches to teaching. The purpose of this paper is to find some of crucial factors that affect Chinese college student's selection of English tutoring institutions. In this paper, it focuses on price, brand image, service variety, and customer relationship factors.

LITERATURE REVIEW - BACKGROUND

Purchase Intention

Purchase intention is defined as the possibility that consumers will purchase the product or service (Sam & Tahir, 2009). Information quality, perceived price, brand image and trust factors are considered to be crucial and influential factors toward purchase intention (Bonsón Ponte et al., 2015; Erdil, 2015; D. J. Kim et al., 2008; J. N. K. Liu & Zhang, 2014).

Product Price

Price, as an attribute of a product, plays an important role in a product. Price in the marketplace is determined by the interaction between the force of supply and the force of demand (Dodds et al., 1991). In particular, many online products/services are intangible (Alkibsi & Lind, 2011). Given a product/service, consumers evaluate the appropriateness of the price based on its quality, and this perceived price is also directly related to consumers value and purchase intentions (Chiang & Jang, 2007). Previous research on tutoring has suggested that tutoring in Malaysia (Wan & Weerasena, 2017), and Cambodia (Bray et al., 2018) is seen as an inevitable component of education, but has not explored the impact of price on consumer choice. Similarly, geography and the urban/rural divide has been shown to influence price for tutoring, but has not explored the impact of pricing on demand (Kobakhidze, 2018). Liu and Bray (2020) have found that parents in Myanmar associated lower prices for tutoring with lower quality.

Brand Image

Brand image is an intangible asset, which can generate value for shareholders (Nandan, 2005). Customers who have awareness of one brand tend to choose the known brand instead of choosing other brands that they do not know, often preferring a known brand over a higher quality alternative (Hoyer & Brown, 1990). A company brand can significantly influence customers' perceived quality and loyalty (Binninger, 2008; Chiang & Jang, 2007; M. T. Liu et al., 2017; Yu et al., 2005), whether tutoring company brand image could bring tutoring institutions businesses is not clear, though there is some research on the phenomenon of celebrity tutors in Hong Kong (Bray, 2013) and the ubiquity of tutorial center advertisements in Hong Kong (Koh, 2016).

Service Variety

Product/service variety is defined as a consumer evaluation of the variety of product/service types in stores (Wu et al., 2011). The term "variety" is frequently used to indicate consumers' choices. Educational institutions are defined by the services they offer and face pressure to expand the number and quality of services they offer to consumers (Saiz-Alvarez, 2020). Consumers are often satisfied with having variety of choices from which to choose (Paul & Rana, 2012). English tutoring firms offer several approaches to tutoring students, from offline, one-on-one tutoring, to online lectures. (Bray et al., 2014; Byun & Baker, 2015; Y. C. Kim & Jung, 2019).

Customer Relationship

Brand loyalty offers firms protection from competitors in the field. Companies need to build strong customer relationships with their existing customers so than they can keep them as long as possible (A. J. Kim & Ko, 2010). Loyalty and customer relationship have significant positive effects on consumers' repurchase intentions (Chiu et al., 2009; Lin et al., 2009; Lu et al., 2019; Pizzutti dos Santos & Basso, 2012). Aurini and Davies (2004) have demonstrated that tutoring services rely heavily on referrals for increasing business over advertising, suggesting the emphasis placed on brand loyalty will determine success.

STATEMENT OF HYPOTHESIS

As a major consideration in making purchase decisions, perceived price will be evaluated by a majority of customers in purchase decisions (Chiang & Jang, 2007). Price usually acts as an indicator of product quality, meaning that consumers expect high quality when the price is high (Chiang & Jang, 2007). If the price is relatively low, consumers will feel that it is a fair price, indicating that they are willing to pay it for a relatively low quality good or service. Moreover, perception of quality increases with the price (Dodds et al., 1991; Konuk, 2019), illustrating a strong relationship for consumers between the price of a good and the quality of a good. For education quality, the authors assume that students will prioritize considerations of quality over price. Thus, perceived price is hypothesized to be positively associated with purchase intention.

Strong brand image can add value to consumer purchase evaluations (Khodabandeh & Lindh, 2020; Wolfe, 1993). If a company has a good brand image, the authors assume that company will benefit from an advantage over comparable competitors within the field (H. Kim & Kim, 2005; Zameer et al., 2020). Thus, company brand of selection of English tutoring institutions is hypothesized to be positively associated with purchase intention.

Product/service variety is defined as a consumer evaluation of the variety of product/service types in stores (Wu et al., 2011). It might influence consumers' purchase intentions since it influences consumers' evaluations of this brand. As in other industries, service variety may also influence consumers purchase intentions with regards to selecting tutoring services. English tutoring institutions in China have a variety of services, such as one-to-one tutoring, fundamental course, small size class, online class, and so on. Thus, service variety of selection of English tutoring institutions is hypothesized to be positively associated with purchase intention.

Customer relationship has a significant positive effect on consumers' repurchase intentions (Chiu et al., 2009). Thus, customer relationship is hypothesized to be positively associated with purchase intention.

Based on the existing body of knowledge reported above, the following hypotheses are derived.

Research Question (RQ): What are the factors affecting Chinese college student's selection of English tutoring institutions?

Hypothesis 1: Perceived price of selection of English tutoring institutions is positively associated with consumer's purchase intention.

Hypothesis 2: Company brand of selection of English tutoring institutions is positively associated with consumer's purchase intention.

Hypothesis 3: Service variety of selection of English tutoring institutions is positively associated with consumer's purchase intention.

Hypothesis 4: Customer relationship of selection of English tutoring institutions is positively associated with consumer's purchase intention.

METHODOLOGY

Instrumentation Design (Quantitative Method)

In order to test these hypotheses, students were asked through a WJX online survey to respond to a series of questions. The online survey consists of three parts: Part I seeks students' personal information, such as gender, age, year level in college year, and personal or family income. Part II seeks students' attitudes towards selecting English tutoring company with considering several factors, which are perceived price, brand image, service variety, and customer relationship. These factors might influence their purchase intentions. Part III seeks students' purchase intentions by giving different situations. The online survey will be shown in the appendix.

Sampling

As a major part of customers of English tutoring institutions, Chinese college students who have experienced English tutoring service will be the target population. The sample size should be 100 or larger for factor analysis. Thus, in this research, the online survey has collected 212 Chinese college students' responses. The reason why this research does not use a simple random sampling is that a simple random sampling has some limitations in terms of time and expense, particularly with a large population. One considerable limitation is that researchers may choose those groups who can provide the data he/she prefers. Thus, the simple random sampling is not appropriate for every research program (Kadilar & Cingi, 2006). In this research, College students self-selected to answer this online survey. While this presents the risk of self-selection bias in answers, this approach provides an efficient way to target students who would be most likely to find and use English tutoring services.

1. Survey Question on personal information

Several options were presented as possible responses for each question.

Gender
Year level in college year
Personal or family income per month

For the demographic questions, four options were presented as possible responses. Setting demographic questions is crucial. To know who are these people answering this online survey is very important because it might directly influence the data that gathered from these participants (Huff & Tingley, 2015).

2. Survey Question on the four factors that consumers might consider as important of selecting English tutoring institutions.

A Likert Scale (scaled from one to seven) contains four items that were provided to measure the factors:

Perceived price
Brand image
Service variety
Customer relationship

As the literature review and statement of hypothesis discussed above, perceived price, brand image, service variety, and customer relationship are the four factors that have high possibility in influencing consumers purchase intentions. There are four questions on each four items asking for college students' perceived price, brand image, service variety, and customer relationship of selecting English tutoring institutions.

3. Survey Question on purchase intention based on giving one scenario of each four factors

A Likert Scale (scaled from one to seven) contains four items each with its scenario was provided to measure purchase intentions of consumers. There are four questions asked for college students' purchase intentions.

RESULTS

Demographic Characteristics

Table 1. Demographic Characteristics

		Gender	Age	YearL	Income
N	Valid	212	212	212	212
	Missing	0	0	0	0
Mean		1.57	1.82	3.45	2.75
Std. Error of Mean		.034	.030	.062	.078
Std. Deviation		.496	.431	.909	1.134
Variance		.246	.186	.827	1.286
Skewness		-.288	-.939	-1.557	-.254
Std. Error of Skewness		.167	.167	.167	.167
Kurtosis		-1.935	.769	1.274	-1.375
Std. Error of Kurtosis		.333	.333	.333	.333

The online survey has collected 212 college students in total, and the valid data are 212, which contain 91 males, and 121 females. Table 1 illustrates demographic characteristics for the sample of college students surveyed. The skewness of all four attributes are negative, indicating that in normal distribution curve, the four curves are inclining on the right, and showing that the age of participants is around 20, that the college year level of participants is around senior, and that the income of participants is around 15,000 per month based on the survey questions.

Table 2. Descriptive Statistics of Variables

	N	Minimum	Maximum	Mean		Std. Deviation	Skewness		Kurtosis	
	Statistic	Statistic	Statistic	Statistic	Std. Error	Statistic	Statistic	Std. Error	Statistic	Std. Error
QPrice	212	1.50	7.00	5.1144	.08654	1.26010	-1.125	.167	.911	.333
QBrand	212	1.50	7.00	5.0531	.08875	1.29223	-.801	.167	-.013	.333
QService	212	2.00	7.00	5.1297	.08018	1.16740	-.806	.167	.048	.333
QRelationship	212	1.50	7.00	4.9988	.08601	1.25237	-1.085	.167	.564	.333
MeanPI	212	1.50	7.00	4.9965	.09567	1.39300	-1.020	.167	.140	.333
Valid N (listwise)	212									

Table 2 describes the mean, std. deviation, skewness, and kurtosis of the mean of four questions for perceived price, the mean of four questions for brand image, the mean of four questions for service variety, the mean of four questions for customer relationship, and the mean of the four questions for purchase intention.

ANALYSIS

Reliability Analysis

Table 3. Reliability Statistics

Constructs	Cronbach's alpha	No. of items
Price	0.843	4
Brand	0.867	4
Service Variety	0.822	4
Customer Relationship	0.814	4
Purchase Intention	0.864	4

The reliability analysis reveals that whether a scale can consistently reflect the construct it measured or not (Hinton et al., 2014). In order to get scales to consistently reflect the constructs, a high reliability or a high Cronbach's alpha is required in research. Typically, a Cronbach's alpha is supposed to be greater than 0.7, which can support the data that gathered from participants are reliable (Weaver & Maxwell, 2014).

In Table 3, it shows that the Cronbach's alpha of Price containing four items is 0.843, that the Cronbach's alpha of Brand containing four items is 0.867, that the Cronbach's alpha of Service Variety containing four items is 0.822, that the Cronbach's alpha of Customer Relationship containing four items is 0.814, and that the Cronbach's alpha of Purchase Intention containing four items is 0.864. Based on the reliability analysis mentioned above, all of these five constructs' Cronbach's alpha are greater than 0.7, meaning all of these five constructs are reliable.

Correlation Analysis

Table 4. Correlation Between the Four Factors and Their Purchase Intentions

		QPrice	QBrand	QService	QRelationship	MeanPI
QPrice	Pearson Correlation	1	.376**	.357**	.335**	.533**
	Sig. (2-tailed)		.000	.000	.000	.000
	N	212	212	212	212	212
QBrand	Pearson Correlation	.376**	1	.374**	.303**	.521**
	Sig. (2-tailed)	.000		.000	.000	.000
	N	212	212	212	212	212
QService	Pearson Correlation	.357**	.374**	1	.340**	.480**
	Sig. (2-tailed)	.000	.000		.000	.000
	N	212	212	212	212	212
QRelationship	Pearson Correlation	.335**	.303**	.340**	1	.473**
	Sig. (2-tailed)	.000	.000	.000		.000
	N	212	212	212	212	212
MeanPI	Pearson Correlation	.533**	.521**	.480**	.473**	1
	Sig. (2-tailed)	.000	.000	.000	.000	
	N	212	212	212	212	212

**. Correlation is significant at the 0.01 level (2-tailed).

The correlation analysis method is widely used in marketing research area. The correlation analysis method refers to a study method used in exploring or determining the statistical relationship between two quantitatively measured variables (Ezekiel, 1930). For using correlation analysis method, given that at 0.01 level and 2 -tailed, the value is found can be positive and negative. If the value is positive, it means that if one variable increases, the other variable will increase simultaneously. On the contrary, if the value is negative, it indicates that if one variable increases, the other one will decrease simultaneously (Hardoon et al., 2004).

In Table 4, the five constructs are all the mean of their items. Using the mean to calculate the correlations between each other. Initially, the value of the correlation between QPrice and MeanPI is equal to .533**, which means that the correlation between QPrice and MeanPI is positive and significant at 0.01 level (2-tailed). Thus, Hypothesis 1, which states that perceived price of selection of English tutoring institutions is positively associated with consumer's purchase intention, can be supported. Second, the value of the correlation between QBrand and MeanPI is equal to .521**, which indicates that the correlation between QPrice and MeanPI is positive and significant. Thus, Hypothesis 2, which states that company brand of selection of English tutoring institutions is positively associated with consumer's purchase intention, can be supported. Third, the value of the correlation between QService and MeanPI is equal to .480**, which reveals that the correlation between QService and MeanPI is positive and significant. Hence, Hypothesis 3, which hypothesized that service variety of selection of English tutoring institutions is positively associated with consumer's purchase intention, can be supported. Fourth, the value of the correlation between QRelationship and MeanPI is equal to .473**, which conveys that the correlation between QRelationship and MeanPI is positive and significant. Hence, Hypothesis 4, which states that customer relationship of selection of English tutoring institutions is positively associated with consumer's purchase intention can be supported.

CONCLUSIONS AND PRACTICAL IMPLICATIONS

In conclusion, as mentioned in the analysis section, all four hypotheses are supported by results. For the Hypothesis 1, which states that perceived price of selection of English tutoring institutions is positively associated with consumer's purchase intention, managers of Chinese English tutoring institutions can balance the demand and the price that they charged from consumers in order to maximize their profits. The results show that consumers are inclined to choose the provider whose price is higher with the assumption that the quality will be higher, ensuring the best value for their investment of time and money into outside tutoring services. There are two ways to increase profits, which are reducing the cost and increasing the revenue (Lieberman, 2003). Consumers are more sensitive to some goods or services than others. Consumers may refrain from purchasing non-essential items if their prices rise. Consumers may not buy them from that company anymore. Nevertheless, English tutoring education appears to be different. Consumers may consider that higher price represents high quality. Rather than helping sales, managers may find that lowering prices may harm their brand and therefore their sales. This finding is in line with research from Myanmar (Liu & Bray, 2020) where discounts were associated with lower quality tutoring. For managers, higher prices may be a good way to protect brand identity, as well as maximize profits.

Hypothesis 2 hypothesizes that company brand of selection of English tutoring institutions is positively associated with consumer's purchase intention. It means that the higher brand image an institution has, the stronger competitive advantage it has. College students believe that institutions who have high brand equity have high education quality. In this case, managers should try their best to build high brand image value. This is even more important considering the limitations in lowering the price for services. They may do more advertisements that highlight the effectiveness of tutoring services such as customer testimonials, guarantees for improvement in English proficiency scores, or highlight the English language credentials of their tutors. Managers may also consider promoting activities outside of service quality that can increase their brand image through greater corporate social responsibility practices (Tkalac Verčič & Sinčić Ćorić, 2018). For instance, some institutions donate money to Red Cross to help poor children or by making commitments to sustainability that can help create a positive association with their brand and offer a distinct advantage over competitors.

Hypothesis 3 states that service variety of selection of English tutoring institutions is positively associated with consumer's purchase intention. It conveys that increasing the service variety can strengthen institutions' competitive advantage. As Aurini and Davies (2004) discussed, tutoring services in Canada broadened services provided to customers to develop long-term relationships. Managers in southern China may consider employing a similar strategy to expand beyond one-off English proficiency tests to more specialized curriculum. Managers should consider "niche" language courses for specific technical and business fields, academic English for students preparing to study abroad, and language tutoring for differing age ranges to not only expand to new customers, but also create more opportunities for existing customers to continue receiving tutoring services. Managers can also innovate more ways of delivering their courses (academic knowledge) to students. For instance, some English institutions have a variety courses, such as one-to-one course, fundamental knowledge course, and deep-thinking course. Different approaches to language learning and different platforms for learning language would help appeal to different learner types who may otherwise be hesitant to pay for formal tutoring.

Hypothesis 4 assumes that customer relationship of selection of English tutoring institutions is positively associated with consumer's purchase intention. It expresses that institutions which have stronger customer relationships have a stronger competitive advantage. As tutoring services moves toward a diversified model, referrals and positive customer reviews become central for maintaining a strong brand identity and an expanded customer base. For this point, managers can use several strategies to build strong customer relationships. English tutoring services present a unique environment where customers have different reasons for pursuing tutoring. Managers can tailor curriculum in small-group and one-on-one sessions based on customer expectations, needs, and feedback. This would impose higher costs on managers in terms of teaching materials and tutoring time but would offer a more responsive model of tutoring as a distinct competitive advantage. Outside of service content, managers may consider improving the tutoring environment for customers. For example, they can build a passionate and enthusiastic image to their consumers. They may hold some activities and encourage students to engage through social media platforms to foster greater brand loyalty and seek feedback in real time.

LIMITATIONS AND FUTURE RESEARCH

According to the results and the analysis, there are still some limitations within this research. The participants cannot represent the whole China English tutoring market. Moreover, many of participants are only from one part of China - southern China. Thus, strictly speaking, this study findings can only be used to exhibit or explain the situation in southern China. For future research, researchers should be more concentrated on data collecting. Researchers may distribute their online survey to participants all around China, including northern China, middle China, and western China.

REFERENCES

Alkibsi, S., & Lind, M. (2011). Service Quality Dimensions Within Technology-Based Banking Services. *International Journal of Strategic Information Technology and Applications*, *2*(3), 36–83. doi:10.4018/jsita.2011070104

Aurini, J., & Davies, S. (2004). The Transformation of Private Tutoring: Education in a Franchise Form. *Canadian Journal of Sociology*, *29*(3), 419–438. doi:10.2307/3654674

Bai, Y., Tang, X., Li, X., & Fan, S. (2019). Explorations in Teaching Research by a Tutoring Institution in China. *ECNU Review of Education*, *2*(1), 87–94. doi:10.1177/2096531119840866

Binninger, A. (2008). Exploring the relationships between retail brands and consumer store loyalty. *International Journal of Retail & Distribution Management*, *36*(2), 94–110. doi:10.1108/09590550810853057

Bodycott, P. (2009). Choosing a higher education study abroad destination: What mainland Chinese parents and students rate as important. *Journal of Research in International Education*, *8*(3), 349–373. doi:10.1177/1475240909345818

Bonsón Ponte, E., Carvajal-Trujillo, E., & Escobar-Rodríguez, T. (2015). Influence of trust and perceived value on the intention to purchase travel online: Integrating the effects of assurance on trust antecedents. *Tourism Management*, *47*, 286–302. doi:10.1016/j.tourman.2014.10.009

Brannen, M. Y., Piekkari, R., & Tietze, S. (2017). The Multifaceted Role of Language in International Business: Unpacking the Forms, Functions and Features of a Critical Challenge to MNC Theory and Performance. In M. Y. Brannen & T. Mughan (Eds.), *Language in International Business: Developing a Field* (pp. 139–162). Springer International Publishing. doi:10.1007/978-3-319-42745-4_6

Bray, M. (2013). Benefits and Tensions of Shadow Education: Comparative Perspectives on the Roles and Impact of Private Supplementary Tutoring in the Lives of Hong Kong Students. *Journal of International and Comparative Education*, *2*(1), 18–30. doi:10.14425/00.45.72

Bray, M., Kobakhidze, M. N., Zhang, W., & Liu, J. (2018). The hidden curriculum in a hidden marketplace: Relationships and values in Cambodia's shadow education system. *Journal of Curriculum Studies*, *50*(4), 435–455. doi:10.1080/00220272.2018.1461932

Bray, M., Zhan, S., Lykins, C., Wang, D., & Kwo, O. (2014). Differentiated demand for private supplementary tutoring: Patterns and implications in Hong Kong secondary education. *Economics of Education Review*, *38*, 24–37. doi:10.1016/j.econedurev.2013.10.002

Byun, S.-Y., & Baker, D. P. (2015). Shadow Education. In *Emerging Trends in the Social and Behavioral Sciences* (pp. 1–9). American Cancer Society. doi:10.1002/9781118900772.etrds0301

Chiang, C.-F., & Jang, S. S. (2007). The Effects of Perceived Price and Brand Image on Value and Purchase Intention: Leisure Travelers' Attitudes Toward Online Hotel Booking. *Journal of Hospitality & Leisure Marketing*, *15*(3), 49–69. doi:10.1300/J150v15n03_04

Chiu, C., Chang, C., Cheng, H., & Fang, Y. (2009). Determinants of customer repurchase intention in online shopping. *Online Information Review*, *33*(4), 761–784. doi:10.1108/14684520910985710

Dodds, W. B., Monroe, K. B., & Grewal, D. (1991). *Effects of Price, Brand, and Store Information on Buyers' Product Evaluations*. Academic Press.

Erdil, T. S. (2015). Effects of Customer Brand Perceptions on Store Image and Purchase Intention: An Application in Apparel Clothing. *Procedia: Social and Behavioral Sciences*, *207*, 196–205. doi:10.1016/j.sbspro.2015.10.088

Ezekiel, M. (1930). *Methods of correlation analysis*. Wiley.

Freihat, S., & Al-Machzoomi, K. (2012). The picture of workplace oral communication skills for ESP Jordanian business graduate employees. *International Journal of Business. Human Technology*, *2*(1), 159–173.

Hardoon, D. R., Szedmak, S., & Shawe-Taylor, J. (2004). Canonical Correlation Analysis: An Overview with Application to Learning Methods. *Neural Computation*, *16*(12), 2639–2664. doi:10.1162/0899766042321814 PMID:15516276

Henze, J., & Zhu, J. (2012). Current Research on Chinese Students Studying Abroad. *Research in Comparative and International Education*, *7*(1), 90–104. doi:10.2304/rcie.2012.7.1.90

Hinton, P. R., McMurray, I., & Brownlow, C. (2014). SPSS explained (2nd ed.). Routledge, Taylor & Francis Group. doi:10.4324/9781315797298

Hoyer, W. D., & Brown, S. P. (1990). Effects of Brand Awareness on Choice for a Common, Repeat-Purchase Product. *The Journal of Consumer Research*, *17*(2), 141. doi:10.1086/208544

Huff, C., & Tingley, D. (2015). "Who are these people?" Evaluating the demographic characteristics and political preferences of MTurk survey respondents. *Research & Politics*, *2*(3), 205316801560464. doi:10.1177/2053168015604648

Kadilar, C., & Cingi, H. (2006). Improvement in estimating the population mean in simple random sampling. *Applied Mathematics Letters*, *19*(1), 5. doi:10.1016/j.aml.2005.02.039

Khodabandeh, A., & Lindh, C. (2020). The importance of brands, commitment, and influencers on purchase intent in the context of online relationships. *Australasian Marketing Journal*. Advance online publication. doi:10.1016/j.ausmj.2020.03.003

Kim, A. J., & Ko, E. (2010). Impacts of Luxury Fashion Brand's Social Media Marketing on Customer Relationship and Purchase Intention. *Journal of Global Fashion Marketing*, *1*(3), 164–171. doi:10.1080/20932685.2010.10593068

Kim, D. J., Ferrin, D. L., & Rao, H. R. (2008). A trust-based consumer decision-making model in electronic commerce: The role of trust, perceived risk, and their antecedents. *Decision Support Systems*, *44*(2), 544–564. doi:10.1016/j.dss.2007.07.001

Kim, H., & Kim, W. G. (2005). The relationship between brand equity and firms' performance in luxury hotels and chain restaurants$. *Tourism Management*, *26*(4), 12. doi:10.1016/j.tourman.2004.03.010

Kim, Y. C., & Jung, J.-H. (2019). Five Forms of Shadow Education Practices. In Y. C. Kim & J.-H. Jung (Eds.), *Shadow Education as Worldwide Curriculum Studies* (pp. 61–88). Springer International Publishing., doi:10.1007/978-3-030-03982-0_3

Kobakhidze, M. N. (2018). Economic Sociology of the Shadow Education Market. In M. N. Kobakhidze (Ed.), *Teachers as Tutors: Shadow Education Market Dynamics in Georgia* (pp. 164–202). Springer International Publishing., doi:10.1007/978-3-319-95915-3_7

Koh, A. (2016). On 'Gods' and 'Kings' in the Tutorial Industry: A 'Media Spectacle' Analysis of the Shadow Education in Hong Kong. In J. Moss & B. Pini (Eds.), *Visual Research Methods in Educational Research* (pp. 189–208). doi:10.1057/9781137447357_11

Konuk, F. A. (2019). The influence of perceived food quality, price fairness, perceived value and satisfaction on customers' revisit and word-of-mouth intentions towards organic food restaurants. *Journal of Retailing and Consumer Services*, *50*, 103–110. doi:10.1016/j.jretconser.2019.05.005

Lieberman, W. H. (2003). Getting the most from revenue management. *Journal of Revenue and Pricing Management*, *2*(2), 103–115. doi:10.1057/palgrave.rpm.5170055

Lin, N.-H., Tseng, W.-C., Hung, Y.-C., & Yen, D. C. (2009). Making customer relationship management work: Evidence from the banking industry in Taiwan. *Service Industries Journal*, *29*(9), 1183–1197. doi:10.1080/02642060701846788

Liu, J., & Bray, M. (2020). Private Subtractory Tutoring: The Negative Impact of Shadow Education on Public Schooling in Myanmar. *International Journal of Educational Development*, *76*, 102213. doi:10.1016/j.ijedudev.2020.102213

Liu, J. N. K., & Zhang, E. Y. (2014). An investigation of factors affecting customer selection of online hotel booking channels. *International Journal of Hospitality Management*, *39*, 71–83. doi:10.1016/j.ijhm.2014.01.011

Liu, M. T., Wong, I. A., Tseng, T.-H., Chang, A. W.-Y., & Phau, I. (2017). Applying consumer-based brand equity in luxury hotel branding. *Journal of Business Research*, *81*, 192–202. doi:10.1016/j.jbusres.2017.06.014

Lu, C.-C., Wu, I.-L., & Hsiao, W.-H. (2019). Developing customer product loyalty through mobile advertising: Affective and cognitive perspectives. *International Journal of Information Management*, *47*, 101–111. doi:10.1016/j.ijinfomgt.2018.12.020

Mamiseishvili, K. (2012). International student persistence in U.S. postsecondary institutions. *Higher Education*, *64*(1), 1–17. doi:10.100710734-011-9477-0

Mazzarol, T., & Soutar, G. N. (2002). "Push-pull" factors influencing international student destination choice. *International Journal of Educational Management*, *16*(2), 82–90. doi:10.1108/09513540210418403

Nandan, S. (2005). *An exploration of the brand identity–brand image linkage: A communications perspective*. Academic Press.

Nickerson, C. (2005). English as a lingua franca in international business contexts. *English for Specific Purposes*, *24*(4), 367–380. doi:10.1016/j.esp.2005.02.001

Paul, J., & Rana, J. (2012). Consumer behavior and purchase intention for organic food. *Journal of Consumer Marketing*, *29*(6), 11. doi:10.1108/07363761211259223

Pizzutti dos Santos, C., & Basso, K. (2012). Do ongoing relationships buffer the effects of service recovery on customers' trust and loyalty? *International Journal of Bank Marketing*, *30*(3), 168–192. doi:10.1108/02652321211222540

Saiz-Alvarez, J. M. (2020). Quality Management Principles Application to Higher Educational Institutions. In *Quality Management Principles and Policies in Higher Education*. IGI Global; doi:10.4018/978-1-7998-1017-9.ch001

Sam, M. F. M., & Tahir, N. H. (2009). *Website Quality And Consumer Online Purchase Intention Of Air Ticket*. Academic Press.

Tkalac Verčič, A., & Sinčić Ćorić, D. (2018). The relationship between reputation, employer branding and corporate social responsibility. *Public Relations Review*, *44*(4), 444–452. doi:10.1016/j.pubrev.2018.06.005

Wan, C. D., & Weerasena, B. (2017). Shadow Education in Malaysia: Identifying the Determinants of Spending and Amount of Time Attending Private Supplementary Tutoring of Upper Secondary School Students. Journal of International and Comparative Education, 91–103. doi:10.14425/jice.2017.6.2.91

Weaver, B., & Maxwell, H. (2014). Exploratory factor analysis and reliability analysis with missing data: A simple method for SPSS users. *The Quantitative Methods for Psychology*, *10*(2), 143–152. doi:10.20982/tqmp.10.2.p143

Wolfe, A. (1993). *Profit from strategic marketing: How to succeed in business markets*. Financial Times, Pitman Pub.

Wu, P. C. S., Yeh, G. Y.-Y., & Hsiao, C.-R. (2011). The effect of store image and service quality on brand image and purchase intention for private label brands. *Australasian Marketing Journal*, *19*(1), 30–39. doi:10.1016/j.ausmj.2010.11.001

Yu, C. J., Wu, L., Chiao, Y., & Tai, H. (2005). Perceived quality, customer satisfaction, and customer loyalty: The case of lexus in Taiwan. *Total Quality Management & Business Excellence*, *16*(6), 707–719. doi:10.1080/14783360500077393

Zameer, H., Wang, Y., & Yasmeen, H. (2020). Reinforcing green competitive advantage through green production, creativity and green brand image: Implications for cleaner production in China. *Journal of Cleaner Production*, *247*, 119119. doi:10.1016/j.jclepro.2019.119119

Zhang, W. (2014). The demand for shadow education in China: Mainstream teachers and power relations. *Asia Pacific Journal of Education*, *34*(4), 436–454. doi:10.1080/02188791.2014.960798

Zhang, Y. (2013). Does private tutoring improve students' National College Entrance Exam performance?—A case study from Jinan, China. *Economics of Education Review*, *32*, 1–28. doi:10.1016/j.econedurev.2012.09.008

KEY TERMS AND DEFINITIONS

Brand Image: An intangible asset that may influence costumer perceptions of quality and loyalty.

Customer Relationship: The interaction between firms and their customers that can influence customer repurchase intention, perception of brand, and offer firms protection from competitors.

English Tutoring Institutions: The tutoring industry, sometimes referred to as "shadow education," that provides private education services for consumers interested in learning English.

Perceived Quality: Customer perceptions of excellence in a product or service.

Price: An attribute of a product determined by the forces of supply and demand.

Purchase Intention: The possibility that a customer will purchase a product or service.

Service Variety: The consumer evaluation of the service variety offered by firms.

Southern China: The region of China south of the Yangtze River.

APPENDIX

An Investigation of Factors Affecting Chinese College Student Selection of English Tutoring Institutions

In this section, I will ask you some questions about your personal information. Your response will help me figure out your gender, age and some other personal information. **Again, I ensure you of the complete anonymity of your response.**

Direction:

Please indicate your personal information by placing a tick in the appropriate category.

1. What is your gender?
   Male
   Female
2. What is your age group?
   younger than 21
   21-25 years old
   26-30 years old
   older than 30
3. What is your year level in college year?
   Freshman
   Sophomore
   Junior
   Senior
4. What is your/your family monthly income?(RMB)
   <¥10000
   ¥10001-15000
   ¥15001-20000
   >¥20001

Now, I want to investigate what is your attitude to choose different English tutoring Companies considering price, company brand, service variety, website quality, and customer relationship. **I can ensure that your responses will be completely anonymous.**

Take XDF English tutoring institution as an example, please answer the following questions based on given 1 to 7 score to each item.

Perceived Price: IF “x_+3” “<INERABLOB[REMOVED IF FIELD]>” “” @003@004@005

Table 5. IF "x_+3"

	strongly disagree 1	**2**	**3**	**Neutral 4**	**5**	**6**	**strongly agree 7**
I think that for buying the same course, price in XDF is relatively reasonable.							
I think that the price of XDF is stable and not fluctuate significantly.							
I think that XDF has a large promotion.							
I am very satisfied with the payment of purchasing the course of XDF.							
IF "x_-3" "</INERABLOB>" "" @003@005	strongly disagree 1	2	3	Neutral 4	5	6	strongly agree 7
XDF has a high reputation in the market.							
XDF has a long English tutoring history.							
XDF has a good reputation and no bad news reported.							
The tutoring institution is a leader in the English training industry.							

Table 6. Brand Image: Service Variety:

	strongly disagree 1	**2**	**3**	**Neutral 4**	**5**	**6**	**strongly agree 7**
This institution can meet the reasonable service needs of the students in a timely manner.							
I am satisfied with the service provided by XDF.							
The service provided by XDF is well regulated.							
The institution provides students with a personalized tutoring program.							

Table 7.

	strongly disagree 1	2	3	Neutral 4	5	6	strongly agree 7
XDF provides special treatment for students who regularly purchase their courses, making me feel that I am important and valuable to them.							
XDF will take the initiative to communicate with me and inform me of the latest course information.							
The way XDF communicates with me is very close and personal.							
When the representative of XDF communicated with me, he showed great respect for me.							

Table 8. Customer Relationship: Purchase Intention:

	strongly disagree 1	2	3	Neutral 4	5	6	strongly agree 7
I am willing to buy the latest course that XDF promoted.							
I will insist to buy XDF's English tutoring course.							
If there are relatives and friends who want to choose an English tutoring institution, I will recommend XDF.							
If I re-select the English tutoring institution, I will choose it again.							

Compilation of References

Aaker, J. L. (1997). Dimensions of Brand Personality. *Journal of Marketing*, *3*(3), 347–355. doi:10.1177/002224379703400304

Aba, E. K., Badar, M. A., & Hayden, M. A. (2016). Impact of ISO 9001 certification on firms' financial operating performance. *International Journal of Quality & Reliability Management*, *33*(1), 78–89. doi:10.1108/IJQRM-02-2014-0021

Abdallah, A. B., Dahiyat, S. E., & Matsui, Y. (2019). Lean management and innovation performance: Evidence from international manufacturing companies. *Management Research Review*, *42*(2), 239–262. doi:10.1108/MRR-10-2017-0363

Acemoglu, D. (2003). Root Causes. A historical approach to assessing the role of institutions in economic development. *Finance & Development*, *40*(2), 27–30.

Acemoglu, D., Johnson, S., & Robinson, J. A. (2001). The colonial origins of comparative development: An empirical investigation. *The American Economic Review*, *91*(5), 1369–1401. doi:10.1257/aer.91.5.1369

Acemoglu, D., Johnson, S., & Robinson, J. A. (2005). Institutions as a fundamental cause of long-run growth. In P. Aghion & S. Durlauf (Eds.), *Handbook of Economic Growth* (pp. 385–472). Elsevier.

Acheampong, P., Zhiwen, L., Abubakar, R., Antwi, H. A., & Akomeah, M. O. (2016a). Stimulants of Online Shopping Behaviour among Chinese Millenials in China. *International Journal of Academic Research in Business and Social Sciences*, *6*(5), 331–349. doi:10.6007/IJARBSS/v6-i5/2152

Achrol, R. S., & Kotler, P. (1999). Marketing in the network economy. *Journal of Marketing*, *63*(4_suppl1), 146–163. doi:10.1177/00222429990634s114

Acs, Z. J., Audretsch, D. B., Braunerhjelm, P., & Carlsson, B. (2012). Growth and entrepreneurship. *Small Business Economics*, *39*(2), 289–300. doi:10.100711187-010-9307-2

Acs, Z. J., Braunerhjelm, P., Audretsch, D. B., & Carlsson, B. (2009). The knowledge spillover theory of entrepreneurship. *Small Business Economics*, *32*(1), 15–30. doi:10.100711187-008-9157-3

Acs, Z. J., Estrin, S., Mickiewicz, T., & Szerb, L. (2018). Entrepreneurship, institutional economics, and economic growth: An ecosystem perspective. *Small Business Economics*, *51*(2), 501–514. doi:10.100711187-018-0013-9

Adachi, T., & Hisada, T. (2017). Gender differences in entrepreneurship and intrapreneurship: An empirical analysis. *Small Business Economics*, *48*(3), 447–486. doi:10.100711187-016-9793-y

Adam, E. E. Jr, Flores, B. E., & Macias, A. (2001). Quality improvement practices and the effect on manufacturing firm performance: Evidence from Mexico and the USA. *International Journal of Production Research*, *39*(1), 43–63. doi:10.1080/00207540150208853

Adams, D. (2018). Quality improvement; part 1: Introduction and overview. *BJA Education*, *18*(3), 89–94. doi:10.1016/j.bjae.2017.12.002

Addey, J. (2004). The modern quality manager. *Total Quality Management & Business Excellence*, *15*(5-6), 879–889. doi:10.1080/14783360410001680314

Aft, L. S. (2018). *Fundamentals of industrial quality control*. CRC Press.

Agarwal, A., & Sharma, M. K. (2016). Lean management–a step towards a sustainable green supply chain. *Competitiveness Review*, *26*(3), 311–331. doi:10.1108/CR-05-2015-0040

Aggogeri, F., & Gentili, E. (2008). Six Sigma methodology: An effective tool for quality management. *International Journal of Manufacturing Technology and Management*, *14*(3-4), 289–298. doi:10.1504/IJMTM.2008.017728

Aghdaie, S. F. A., Piraman, A., & Fathi, S. (2011). An analysis of factors affecting the consumer's attitude of trust and their impact on internet purchasing behavior. *International Journal of Business and Social Science*, *2*(23).

Agwu, E., & Afieroho, E. (2016). Impact of Product Quality Management on the Growth of Small and Medium-Sized Enterprises. *European Journal of Soil Science*, *52*(2), 175–190.

Ahire, S. L., & Golhar, D. Y. (1996). Quality management in large vs. small firms. *Journal of Small Business Management*, *34*(2), 1–11.

Ajzen, I. (1988). *Attitudes, personality, and behavior*. Dorsey Press.

Ajzen, I. (1991). The theory of planned behavior. *Organizational Behavior and Human Decision Processes*, *50*(2), 179–211. doi:10.1016/0749-5978(91)90020-T

Ajzen, I. (2001). Nature and operation of attitudes. *Annual Review of Psychology*, *52*(1), 27–58. doi:10.1146/annurev.psych.52.1.27 PMID:11148298

Ajzen, I. (2002). Residual effects of past on later behavior: Habituation and reasoned action perspective. *Personality and Social Psychology Review*, *6*(2), 107–122. doi:10.1207/S15327957PSPR0602_02

Ajzen, I., Czasch, C., & Flood, M. G. (2009). From intentions to behavior: Implementation intention, commitment, and conscientiousness. *Journal of Applied Social Psychology*, *39*(6), 1356–1372. doi:10.1111/j.1559-1816.2009.00485.x

Akpolat, H. (2017). *Six sigma in transactional and service environments*. Routledge. doi:10.4324/9781315243030

Alam, A., Uddin, M., & Yazdifar, H. (2019). Institutional determinants of R&D investment: Evidence from emerging markets. *Technological Forecasting and Social Change*, *138*(1), 34–44. doi:10.1016/j.techfore.2018.08.007

Alba, Y., & Olarte, S. (2020). *Economía colaborativa: análisis de literatura un enfoque hacia el desarrollo local y sus limitantes en la innovación de América Latina*. Universidad Cooperativa de Colombia.

Alcivar, T. (2015). *La compensación Comercial. Tesis de doctorado en Empresa*. Universidad Antonio de Nebrija.

Aldrich, H. E., & Zimmer, C. (1986). Entrepreneurship through social networks. In D. Sexton & R. Smilor (Eds.), *The Art and Science of Entrepreneurship* (pp. 3–23). Ballinger.

Ali, S. I., & Khatoon, S. U. E. B. H. A. (2016). Implementation of total quality management. *International Journal of Emerging Trends in Engineering and Development*, *6*(6), 114–119.

Alkibsi, S., & Lind, M. (2011). Service Quality Dimensions Within Technology-Based Banking Services. *International Journal of Strategic Information Technology and Applications*, *2*(3), 36–83. doi:10.4018/jsita.2011070104

Alpkan, L., Bulut, C., Gundy, G., Ulusoy, G., & Kilic, K. (2010). Organizational support for intrapreneurship and its interaction with human capital to enhance innovative performance. *Management Decision*, *48*(5), 732–755. doi:10.1108/00251741011043902

Alvarez, S., & Busenitz, L. (2001). The entrepreneurship of resource-based theory. *Journal of Management, 27*(6), 755–775. doi:10.1177/014920630102700609

Amaratunga, D., Baldry, D., & Sarshar, M. (2001). Process improvement through performance measurement: The balanced scorecard methodology. *Work Study, 50*(5), 179–189. doi:10.1108/EUM0000000005677

América-Economía. (2018, July). *Tres razones por las que el idioma inglés es fundamental para el ámbito laboral*. Retrieved from https://mba.americaeconomia.com/articulos/notas/3-razones-por-las-que-el-idioma-ingles-es-fundamental-para-el-ambito-laboral

Andaleeb, S. (1988). Determinants of customer satisfaction with hospitals: A managerial model. *International Journal of Health Care Quality Assurance, 11*(6), 181–187. doi:10.1108/09526869810231541 PMID:10339090

Anderson, E. W., & Mittal, V. (2000). Strengthening the Satisfaction-Profit Chain. *Journal of Service Research, 3*(2), 107–120. doi:10.1177/109467050032001

Anderson, J. C., Rungtusanatham, M., & Schroeder, R. G. (1994). A theory of quality management underlying the Deming management method. *Academy of Management Review, 19*(3), 472–509. doi:10.5465/amr.1994.9412271808

Anil, A. P., & Satish, K. P. (2019). Enhancing customer satisfaction through total quality management practices–an empirical examination. *Total Quality Management & Business Excellence, 30*(13-14), 1528–1548. doi:10.1080/14783363.2017.1378572

Antony, J. (2014). *Design of experiments for engineers and scientists*. Elsevier.

Antony, J., & Bhaiji, M. (2003). *Key ingredients for a successful six sigma program*. Warwick Manufacturing Group School of Engineering, University of Warwick.

Antony, J., Krishan, N., Cullen, D., & Kumar, M. (2012). Lean Six Sigma for higher education institutions (HEIs) Challenges, barriers, success factors, tools/techniques. *International Journal of Productivity and Performance Management, 61*(8), 940–948. doi:10.1108/17410401211277165

Aparicio, S., Urbano, D., & Audretsch, D. (2016). Institutional factors, opportunity entrepreneurship and economic growth: Panel data evidence. *Technological Forecasting and Social Change, 102*, 45–61. doi:10.1016/j.techfore.2015.04.006

Aparicio, S., Urbano, D., & Stenholm, P. (2019). Institutions in Attracting the Entrepreneurial Potential: A Multilevel Approach. *Academy of Management Proceedings, 2019*(1), 15408. doi:10.5465/AMBPP.2019.15408abstract

Ardichvili, A., Cardozo, R., & Ray, S. (2003). A theory of entrepreneurial opportunity identification and development. *Journal of Business Venturing, 18*(1), 105–123. doi:10.1016/S0883-9026(01)00068-4

Arifeen, N., Hussain, M., Kazmi, S., Mubin, M., Mughal, S. L., & Qadri, W. (2014). Measuring Business Performance: Comparison of Financial, Non-Financial and Qualitative Indicators. *European Journal of Business and Management, 6*(4), 38–45.

Armitage, C. J., & Conner, M. (2001). Efficacy of the theory of planned behavior: A meta-analytic review. *British Journal of Social Psychology, 40*(4), 471–499. doi:10.1348/014466601164939 PMID:11795063

Arnheiter, E. D., & Maleyeff, J. (2005). The integration of lean management and Six Sigma. *The TQM Magazine, 17*(1), 5–18. doi:10.1108/09544780510573020

Asante, E. A., & Affum-Osei, E. (2019). Entrepreneurship as a career choice: The impact of locus of control on aspiring entrepreneurs' opportunity recognition. *Journal of Business Research, 98*, 227–235. doi:10.1016/j.jbusres.2019.02.006

Ashley, C., & Tuten, T. (2015). Creative strategies in social media marketing: An exploratory study of branded social content and consumer engagement. *Psychology and Marketing*, *33*(1), 15–27. doi:10.1002/mar.20761

Asian Development Bank. (2017). *Promoting Logistics Development in Rural Areas*. Mandaluyong.

Asimakopulos, A. (1988). *Theories of Income Distribution*. Springer Netherlands. doi:10.1007/978-94-009-2661-5

Ateljevic, I., & Doorne, S. (2000). Staying within the fence': Lifestyle entrepreneurship in tourism. *Journal of Sustainable Tourism*, *8*(5), 378–392. doi:10.1080/09669580008667374

Ateş, M. (2012). *Sağlık Hizmetleri ile İlgili Genel Bilgiler. In Sağlık İşletmeciliği*. Beta Yayınclık.

Atkinson, R. (1999). Project management: Cost, time and quality, two best guesses and a phenomenon, it's time to accept other success criteria. *International Journal of Project Management*, *17*(6), 337–342. doi:10.1016/S0263-7863(98)00069-6

Audretsch, D. B. (2005). The knowledge spillover theory of entrepreneurship and economic growth. In G. T. Vinig & R. C. W. Van Der Voort (Eds.), *The Emergence of Entrepreneurial Economics* (pp. 37–54). Emerald Group Publishing. doi:10.1016/S0737-1071(05)09003-7

Audretsch, D. B. (2014). From the entrepreneurial university to the university for the entrepreneurial society. *The Journal of Technology Transfer*, *39*(3), 313–321. doi:10.100710961-012-9288-1

Audretsch, D. B., & Keilbach, M. (2004a). Does entrepreneurship capital matter? *Entrepreneurship Theory and Practice*, *2*(5), 419–429. doi:10.1111/j.1540-6520.2004.00055.x

Audretsch, D. B., & Keilbach, M. (2004b). Entrepreneurship capital and economic performance. *Regional Studies*, *38*(8), 949–959. doi:10.1080/0034340042000280956

Audretsch, D., & Fritsch, M. (2003). Linking entrepreneurship to growth: The case of West Germany. *Industry and Innovation*, *10*(1), 65–73. doi:10.1080/1366271032000068104

Aurini, J., & Davies, S. (2004). The Transformation of Private Tutoring: Education in a Franchise Form. *Canadian Journal of Sociology*, *29*(3), 419–438. doi:10.2307/3654674

Autio, E., Kenney, M., Mustar, P., Siegel, D., & Wright, M. (2014). Entrepreneurial innovation: The importance of context. *Research Policy*, *43*(7), 1097–1108. doi:10.1016/j.respol.2014.01.015

Autio, E., Pathak, S., & Wennberg, K. (2013). Consequences of cultural practices for entrepreneurial behaviors. *Journal of International Business Studies*, *44*(4), 334–362. doi:10.1057/jibs.2013.15

Ayala, E., & Gonzales, S. (2015). *Tecnologías de la Información y la Comunicación*. Universidad Inca Garcilaso de la Vega.

Bai, Y., Tang, X., Li, X., & Fan, S. (2019). Explorations in Teaching Research by a Tutoring Institution in China. *ECNU Review of Education*, *2*(1), 87–94. doi:10.1177/2096531119840866

Baltaş, Z. (2013). *Memnuniyet Çalışmaları. In Hastane Yönetimi*. Nobel Tıp Kitabevleri.

Bandura, A. (2006). Guide for constructing self-efficacy scales. *Self-Efficacy Beliefs of Adolescents, 5*(1), 307-337.

Bandura, A. (1977). Self-efficacy: Toward a unifying theory of behavioral change. *Psychological Review*, *84*(2), 191–215. doi:10.1037/0033-295X.84.2.191 PMID:847061

Bandura, A. (1989). Human agency in social-cognitive theory. *The American Psychologist*, *44*(9), 1175–1184. doi:10.1037/0003-066X.44.9.1175 PMID:2782727

Bandura, A. (1997). *Self-efðcacy: The Exercise of Control*. Freeman.

Baporikar, N. (2016). Corporate Governance and Value Creation: Indian Experience. *International Journal of Asian Business and Information Management, 7*(2), 51–61. doi:10.4018/IJABIM.2016040104

Baporikar, N. (2017). Imperatives in Leading Institutions of Higher Learning: Focus B School. *International Journal of Technology and Educational Marketing, 7*(1), 38–51. doi:10.4018/IJTEM.2017010104

Baporikar, N. (2018). *Knowledge Integration Strategies for Entrepreneurship and Sustainability.* IGI Global. doi:10.4018/978-1-5225-5115-7

Baporikar, N. (2019). Preventing Academic Misconduct: Student-Centered Teaching Strategies. In D. Velliaris (Ed.), *Prevention and Detection of Academic Misconduct in Higher Education* (pp. 98–115). IGI Global. doi:10.4018/978-1-5225-7531-3.ch005

Baporikar, N. (2019). Significance and Role of Entrepreneurial University in Emerging Economies. *International Journal of Applied Management Sciences and Engineering, 6*(1), 46–61. doi:10.4018/IJAMSE.2019010104

Baporikar, N. (2020b). Understanding Entrepreneurial University: A Framework for Emerging Economies. In A. Daniel, A. Teixeira, & M. Preto (Eds.), *Examining the Role of Entrepreneurial Universities in Regional Development* (pp. 93–112). IGI Global. doi:10.4018/978-1-7998-0174-0.ch005

Baporikar, N., & Sony, M. (2020a). *Quality Management Principles and Policies in Higher Education.* IGI Global. doi:10.4018/978-1-7998-1017-9

Baregheh, A., Rowley, J., & Sambrook, S. (2009). Towards a multidisciplinary definition of innovation. *Management Decision, 47*(8), 1323–1339. doi:10.1108/00251740910984578

Bari, A. (2017). Our Oceans and the Blue Economy: Opportunities and Challenges. *Procedia Engineering Procedia Engineering, 194*, 5–11. doi:10.1016/j.proeng.2017.08.109

Baron, R., & Shane, S. (2007). *Entrepreneurship: A Process Perspective.* Cengage Learning.

Batini, C., Cappiello, C., Francalanci, C., & Maurino, A. (2009). Methodologies for data quality assessment and improvement. *ACM Computing Surveys, 41*(3), 16. doi:10.1145/1541880.1541883

Bazazo, I., Alansari, I., Alquraan, H., Alzgaybh, Y., & Masa'deh, R. E. (2017). The influence of total quality management, market orientation and e-marketing on hotel performance. *International Journal of Business Administration, 8*(4), 79. doi:10.5430/ijba.v8n4p79

BBC. (2015). *¿Quién gana y quién pierde con el alza del dólar en América Latina?* Retrieved from: https://www.bbc.com/mundo/noticias/2015/08/150819_economia_america_latina_dolar_alza_egn

Beck, R., Avital, M., Rossi, M., & Thatcher, J. B. (2017). *Blockchain technology in business and information systems research.* Academic Press.

Becket, N., & Brookes, M. (2005). Analysing quality audits in higher education. *Brookes Ejournal of Learning and Teaching, 1*(2), 1-12.

Beckford, J. (2016). *Quality: a critical introduction.* Routledge. doi:10.4324/9781315644028

Belin, J., Horbach, J., & Oltra, V. (2011). *Determinants and specificities of eco-innovations–An econometric analysis for the French and German industry based on the Community Innovation Survey* (No. 2011-17). Groupe de Recherche en Economie Théorique et Appliquée.

Beltrán, M. (2017). El Aprendizaje del Idioma Inglés como Lengua Extranjera. *Boletin Virtual, 6*(4), 91–98. doi:10.36260/rbr.v6i4.227

Bergman, B., & Klefsjö, B. (2010). *Quality from customer needs to customer satisfaction*. Studentlitteratur AB.

Berg-Schlosser, D., De Meur, G., Rihoux, B., & Ragin, C. C. (2009). Qualitative comparative analysis (QCA) as an approach. *Configurational comparative methods: Qualitative comparative analysis (QCA) and related techniques*, 1-18.

Berrio, S. K. (2006). *Mercadeo verde: Otra Forma de Ayudar al Mundo*. Retrieved from: https://www.dinero.com/columna-del-lector/opinion/articulo/mercadeo-verde-otra-forma-ayudar-mundo/33121

Bhasin, S. (2015). *Lean management beyond manufacturing*. Springer. doi:10.1007/978-3-319-17410-5

Bigne-Alcaniz, E., Ruiz-Mafé, C., Aldás-Manzano, J., & Sanz-Blas, S. (2008). Influence of online shopping information dependency and innovativeness on internet shopping adoption. *Online Information Review*, *32*(5), 648–667. doi:10.1108/14684520810914025

Binninger, A. (2008). Exploring the relationships between retail brands and consumer store loyalty. *International Journal of Retail & Distribution Management*, *36*(2), 94–110. doi:10.1108/09590550810853057

Bird, B. (1988). Implementing entrepreneurial ideas: The case for intention. *Academy of Management Review*, *13*(3), 442–453. doi:10.5465/amr.1988.4306970

Bjørnskov, C., & Foss, N. J. (2016). Institutions, entrepreneurship, and economic growth: What do we know and what do we still need to know? *The Academy of Management Perspectives*, *30*(3), 292–315. doi:10.5465/amp.2015.0135

Black, N., & Gruen, R. (2005). *Understanding Health Services*. Open University Press.

Bleich, S. N., Özaltin, E., & Murray, C. J. (2009). How does satisfaction with the healthcare system relate to patient experience? *Bulletin of the World Health Organization*, *87*(4), 271–278. doi:10.2471/BLT.07.050401 PMID:19551235

Blosch, M. (2019). *2019 Hype Cycles: 5 Priorities Shape the Further Evolution of Digital Innovation: A Gartner Trend Insight Report*. Gartner.

Bodycott, P. (2009). Choosing a higher education study abroad destination: What mainland Chinese parents and students rate as important. *Journal of Research in International Education*, *8*(3), 349–373. doi:10.1177/1475240909345818

Bolatan, G. I. S., Gozlu, S., Alpkan, L., & Zaim, S. (2016). The impact of technology transfer performance on total quality management and quality performance. *Procedia: Social and Behavioral Sciences*, *235*, 746–755. doi:10.1016/j.sbspro.2016.11.076

Bolter, J. (1984). Artificial Intelligence. *Daedalus*, *113*(3), 1–18. www.jstor.org/stable/20024925

Bonilla Priego, M. J., Najera, J. J., & Font, X. (2011). Environmental management decision-making in certified hotels. *Journal of Sustainable Tourism*, *19*(3), 361–381. doi:10.1080/09669582.2010.530350

Bonilla, A., & Rojas, R. (2012). El aprendizaje de lenguas extranjeras como herramienta para el desarrollo humano. *Congreso Iberoamericano de Lenguas En La Educacion y En La Cultura*, 11.

Bonsón Ponte, E., Carvajal-Trujillo, E., & Escobar-Rodríguez, T. (2015). Influence of trust and perceived value on the intention to purchase travel online: Integrating the effects of assurance on trust antecedents. *Tourism Management*, *47*, 286–302. doi:10.1016/j.tourman.2014.10.009

Bosma, N. (2013). The Global Entrepreneurship Monitor (GEM) and its impact on entrepreneurship research. *Foundations and Trends in Entrepreneurship*, *9*(2), 143–248. doi:10.1561/0300000033

Bosma, N., Content, J., Sanders, M., & Stam, E. (2018). Institutions, entrepreneurship, and economic growth in Europe. *Small Business Economics*, *51*(2), 483–499. doi:10.100711187-018-0012-x

Boudreaux, C. J., Nikolaev, B. N., & Klein, P. (2019). Socio-cognitive traits and entrepreneurship: The moderating role of economic institutions. *Journal of Business Venturing*, *34*(1), 178–196. doi:10.1016/j.jbusvent.2018.08.003

Bourke, J., & Roper, S. (2017). Innovation, quality management, and learning: Short-term and longer-term effects. *Research Policy*, *46*(8), 1505–1518. doi:10.1016/j.respol.2017.07.005

Brand, KW, & Jochum, G. (2000). The German Discourse on Sustainable Development. *MPS Texts, 1*, 2000.

Brannen, M. Y., Piekkari, R., & Tietze, S. (2017). The Multifaceted Role of Language in International Business: Unpacking the Forms, Functions and Features of a Critical Challenge to MNC Theory and Performance. In M. Y. Brannen & T. Mughan (Eds.), *Language in International Business: Developing a Field* (pp. 139–162). Springer International Publishing. doi:10.1007/978-3-319-42745-4_6

Bray, M. (2013). Benefits and Tensions of Shadow Education: Comparative Perspectives on the Roles and Impact of Private Supplementary Tutoring in the Lives of Hong Kong Students. *Journal of International and Comparative Education*, *2*(1), 18–30. doi:10.14425/00.45.72

Bray, M., Kobakhidze, M. N., Zhang, W., & Liu, J. (2018). The hidden curriculum in a hidden marketplace: Relationships and values in Cambodia's shadow education system. *Journal of Curriculum Studies*, *50*(4), 435–455. doi:10.1080/00220272.2018.1461932

Bray, M., Zhan, S., Lykins, C., Wang, D., & Kwo, O. (2014). Differentiated demand for private supplementary tutoring: Patterns and implications in Hong Kong secondary education. *Economics of Education Review*, *38*, 24–37. doi:10.1016/j.econedurev.2013.10.002

Brieger, S. A., Bäro, A., Criaco, G., & Terjesen, S. A. (2020). (in press). Entrepreneurs' age, institutions, and social value creation goals: A multi-country study. *Small Business Economics*. Advance online publication. doi:10.100711187-020-00317-z

Brigham, E. F., & Houston, J. F. (2012). *Fundamentals of financial management*. Cengage Learning.

Brønn, P. S., & Vidaver-Cohen, D. (2009). Corporate motives for social initiative: Legitimacy, sustainability, or the bottom line? *Journal of Business Ethics*, *87*(1), 91–109. doi:10.100710551-008-9795-z

Brown, A. (2019). The Real Robotics Revolution Arrives as a Service. *Interesting Engineering*. Retrieved from https://interestingengineering.com/

Bruton, A., Conway, J. H., & Holgate, S. T. (2000). Reliability: What is it, and how is it measured? *Physiotherapy*, *86*(2), 94–99. doi:10.1016/S0031-9406(05)61211-4

Bruton, G. D., Ahlstrom, D., & Li, H. L. (2010). Institutional theory and entrepreneurship: Where are we now, and where do we need to move in the future? *Entrepreneurship Theory and Practice*, *34*(3), 421–440. doi:10.1111/j.1540-6520.2010.00390.x

Buil, I., Martínez, E., & De Chernatony, L. (2010). Medición del valor de marca desde un enfoque formativo. In Cuadernos de Gestion (Vol. 10). doi:10.5295/cdg.100204ib

Bulchand, J., & Melián, S. (2019). *Trabajo y plataformas de servicios en la economia colaborativa: una oportunidad para emprendedores*. Academic Press.

Busenitz, L. W., Gomez, C., & Spencer, J. W. (2000). Country institutional profiles: Unlocking entrepreneurial phenomena. *Academy of Management Journal*, *43*(5), 994–1003.

Butler, R. W. (1980). The concept of a tourist area cycle of evolution: Implications for management of resources. *The Canadian Geographer. Geographe Canadien*, *24*(1), 5–12. doi:10.1111/j.1541-0064.1980.tb00970.x

Buttle, F. (1997). ISO 9000: Marketing motivations and benefits. *International Journal of Quality & Reliability Management*, *14*(9), 936–947. doi:10.1108/02656719710186867

Byun, S.-Y., & Baker, D. P. (2015). Shadow Education. In *Emerging Trends in the Social and Behavioral Sciences* (pp. 1–9). American Cancer Society. doi:10.1002/9781118900772.etrds0301

Camara de Comercio de Medellín. (2015). *Informativo Camara*. Retrieved from: http://www.camaramedellin.com.co/site/Portals/0/Documentos/Informativo%20Camara%202015.pdf

Cantalapiedra, B. (2019). Crowdfunding y audiovisual de proximidad. La economía colaborativa como instrumento de desarrollo sectorial. *CIRIEC-España, Revista de Economía Pública. Social y Cooperativa*, *95*, 257–288.

Cárdenas, J., & Vallejo, L. (2016). Agricultura y desarrollo rural en Colombia 2011-2013: Una aproximación. *Apuntes del Cenes*, *35*(62), 87–123. doi:10.19053/22565779.4411

Carnerud, D., Jaca, C., & Bäckström, I. (2018). Kaizen and continuous improvement–trends and patterns over 30 years. *The TQM Journal*, *30*(4), 371–390. doi:10.1108/TQM-03-2018-0037

Carr-Hill, R. A. (1992). The measurement of patient satisfaction. *Journal of Public Health Medicine*, *14*(3), 236–249. PMID:1419201

Carroll, A. B. (1991). The pyramid of corporate social responsibility: Toward the moral management of organizational stakeholders. *Business Horizons*, *34*(4), 39–48. doi:10.1016/0007-6813(91)90005-G

Carroll, A. B., & Shabana, K. M. (2010). The business case for corporate social responsibility: A review of concepts, research and practice. *International Journal of Management Reviews*, *12*(1), 85–105. doi:10.1111/j.1468-2370.2009.00275.x

Carsrud, A., & Brännback, M. (2011). Entrepreneurial motivations: What do we still need to know? *Journal of Small Business Management*, *49*(1), 9–26. doi:10.1111/j.1540-627X.2010.00312.x

Casadesus, M., Giménez, G., & Heras, I. (2001). Benefits of ISO 9000 implementation in the Spanish industry. *European Business Review*, *13*(6), 327–336. doi:10.1108/EUM0000000006195

Casillas, J. C., Barbero, J. L., & Sapienza, H. J. (2015). Knowledge acquisition, learning, and the initial pace of internationalization. *International Business Review*, *24*(1), 102–114. doi:10.1016/j.ibusrev.2014.06.005

Casson, M. (1982). *The Entrepreneur: An Economic Theory*. Martin Robertson.

Castaño, M. S., Méndez, M. T., & Galindo, M. A. (2016). Innovation, internationalization, and business-growth expectations among entrepreneurs in the services sector. *Journal of Business Research*, *69*(5), 1690–1695. doi:10.1016/j.jbusres.2015.10.039

Castellano, S., & Urdaneta, G. J. A. (2015). Estrategias de Mercadeo Verde Utilizadas por Empresas a Nivel Mundial. *Telos*, *17*(3), 476–494.

Chandra, D. G., & Malaya, D. B. (April 2011). Role of e-Agriculture in Rural Development in Indian Context. In *Proceedings of 2011 International Conference on Emerging Trends in Networks and Computer Communications (ETNCC)*. The Institution of Engineers. 10.1109/ETNCC.2011.6255913

Chang, T.-Z., & Wildt, A. R. (1994). Price, product information, and purchase intention: An empirical study. *Journal of the Academy of Marketing Science*, *22*(1), 16–27. doi:10.1177/0092070394221002

Chan, K. (2006). *Advertising and Hong Kong Society*. Chinese University Press.

Chan, L. K., & Wu, M. L. (2002). Quality function deployment: A literature review. *European Journal of Operational Research*, *143*(3), 463–497. doi:10.1016/S0377-2217(02)00178-9

Chávez, J., Castillo, U., & Alcívar, T. (2017). *La naturaleza del desvalor productivo*. UCSG.

Chen, Y.-H., & Barnes, S. (2007). Initial trust and online buyer behaviour. *Industrial Management & Data Systems*, *107*(1), 21–36. Advance online publication. doi:10.1108/02635570710719034

Chiang, C.-F., & Jang, S. S. (2007). The Effects of Perceived Price and Brand Image on Value and Purchase Intention: Leisure Travelers' Attitudes Toward Online Hotel Booking. *Journal of Hospitality & Leisure Marketing*, *15*(3), 49–69. doi:10.1300/J150v15n03_04

Chiu, C., Chang, C., Cheng, H., & Fang, Y. (2009). Determinants of customer repurchase intention in online shopping. *Online Information Review*, *33*(4), 761–784. doi:10.1108/14684520910985710

Cho, Y. C., & Sagynov, E. (2015). Exploring Factors That Affect Usefulness, Ease Of Use, Trust, And Purchase Intention In The Online Environment. *International Journal of Management & Information Systems*, *19*(1), 21–36. doi:10.19030/ijmis.v19i1.9086

Christensen, C. M., Raynor, M. E., & McDonald, R. (2015). What is disruptive innovation? *Harvard Business Review*, *93*(12), 44–53. PMID:17183796

Cieślik, J., Kaciak, E., & van Stel, A. (2018). Country-level determinants and consequences of overconfidence in the ambitious entrepreneurship segment. *International Small Business Journal*, *36*(5), 473–499. doi:10.1177/0266242617748201

Cifu, D. X., & Stewart, D. G. (1999). Factors affecting functional outcome after stroke: A critical review of rehabilitation interventions. *Archives of Physical Medicine and Rehabilitation*, *80*(5), S-35–S39. doi:10.1016/S0003-9993(99)90101-6 PMID:10326901

Claver, E., Tari, J. J., & Molina, J. F. (2003). Critical Factors And Results Of Quality Management: An Empirical Study. *Total Quality Management*, *14*(1), 91–118. doi:10.1080/14783360309709

Coad, A., Frankish, J. S., Roberts, R. G., & Storey, D. J. (2016). Why should banks provide entrepreneurship training seminars? *International Small Business Journal*, *34*(6), 733–759. doi:10.1177/0266242615593138

Coca-Carasila, A. M. (2010). Neuromarketing: Las Emociones Y El Comportamiento De Compra. *Perspectivas*, (25), 9–24. http://2011.www.redalyc.org/articulo.oa?id=425942454003

Contreras, J., Paredes, M., & Turbay, S. (2017). Circuitos cortos de comercialización agroecológica en el Ecuador. *Idesia*, *35*(3), 71–80. doi:10.4067/S0718-34292017005000302

Cooper, A. C., & Dunkelberg, W. C. (1987). Entrepreneurial Research: Old questions, new answers, and methodological issues. *American Journal of Small Business*, *11*(3), 11–24. doi:10.1177/104225878701100301

Cooper, A. C., Woo, C. Y., & Dunkelberg, W. C. (1988). Entrepreneurs' perceived chances for success. *Journal of Business Venturing*, *3*(2), 97–108. doi:10.1016/0883-9026(88)90020-1

Corbitt, B., Thanasankit, T., & Yi, H. (2003). Trust and E-commerce: A study of consumer perceptions. *Electronic Commerce Research and Applications*, *2*(3), 203–215. doi:10.1016/S1567-4223(03)00024-3

Corral, C. M. (2003). Sustainable production and consumption systems—cooperation for change: Assessing and simulating the willingness of the firm to adopt/develop cleaner technologies. The case of the In-Bond industry in northern Mexico. *Journal of Cleaner Production*, *11*(4), 411–426. doi:10.1016/S0959-6526(02)00063-X

Correa, G., Carrillo, V., Corona, A., Cruz, R., Ramírez, Y., & Ramírez, M. (2016). Tecnologías de Información y Comunicación en las Organizaciones. Universidad Nacional Autónoma de México.

Corso, M., Martini, A., Pellegrini, L., & Paolucci, E. (2003). Technological and organizational tools for knowledge management: In search of configurations. *Small Business Economics*, *21*(4), 397–408. doi:10.1023/A:1026123322900

Cortes-Jimenez, I. (2008). Which type of tourism matters to regional economic growth? The cases of Spain and Italy. *International Journal of Tourism Research*, *10*(2), 127–139. doi:10.1002/jtr.646

Craviotti, C., & Palacios, P. (2013). La diversificación de los mercados como estrategia de la agricultura familiar. *Revista de Economia e Sociologia Rural*, *51*(Suppl. 1), s063–s078. doi:10.1590/S0103-20032013000600004

Craviotti, C., & Soleno Wilches, R. (2015). Circuitos cortos de comercialización agroalimentaria: Un acercamiento desde la agricultura familiar diversificada en Argentina. *Mundo Agrario*, *16*(33), 1–19.

Cromarty, I. (1996). What do Patients Think About During Their Consultation? *The British Journal of General Practice*, *46*, 525–528. PMID:8917871

Cubillos Rodríguez, M. C., & Rozo Rodríguez, D. (2009). El concepto de calidad: Historia, evolución e importancia para la competitividad. *Revista de la Universidad de la Salle*, *2009*(48), 80–99.

D'Andrea, M., Garré, A., & Rodríguez, M. (2012). Una Lengua extranjera, ¿sólo una herramienta para la comunicación? *Invenio: Revista de Investigación Académica*, *15*(28), 11–17.

Dahlgaard-Park, S. M., Reyes, L., & Chen, C. K. (2018). The evolution and convergence of total quality management and management theories. *Total Quality Management & Business Excellence*, *29*(9-10), 1108–1128. doi:10.1080/14783363.2018.1486556

Davenport, T. H., & Prusak, L. (1997). *Information ecology: Mastering the information and knowledge environment.* Oxford University Press on Demand.

David, F. R. (2013). *Administración Estratégica*. Mexico: Pearson.

Davidson, J. (1999). Transforming the value of company reports through marketing measurement. *Journal of Marketing Management*, *15*(8), 757–777. doi:10.1362/026725799784772657

Davis, F. D. (1989). Perceived usefulness, perceived ease of use, and user acceptance of information technology. *Management Information Systems Quarterly*, *13*(3), 319–340. doi:10.2307/249008

Davvetas, V., & Diamantopoulos, A. (2018). "Should I Have Bought the Other One?" Experiencing Regret in Global Versus Local Brand Purchase Decisions. *Journal of International Marketing*, *26*(2), 1–21. doi:10.1509/jim.17.0040

De Carolis, D. M., & Saparito, P. (2006). Social capital, cognition, and entrepreneurial opportunities: A theoretical framework. *Entrepreneurship Theory and Practice*, *30*(1), 41–56. doi:10.1111/j.1540-6520.2006.00109.x

De Clercq, D., Danis, W. M., & Dakhli, M. (2010). The moderating effect of institutional context on the relationship between associational activity and new business activity in emerging economies. *International Business Review*, *19*(1), 85–101. doi:10.1016/j.ibusrev.2009.09.002

De Clercq, D., Lim, D. S., & Oh, C. H. (2013). Individual-Level Resources and New Business Activity: The Contingent Role of Institutional Context. *Entrepreneurship Theory and Practice*, *37*(2), 303–330. doi:10.1111/j.1540-6520.2011.00470.x

De Cleyn, S. H., & Braet, J. (2012). Do board composition and investor type influence innovativeness in SMEs? *The International Entrepreneurship and Management Journal*, *8*(3), 285–308. doi:10.100711365-010-0168-6

De Feo, A., & Barnard, W. (2004). *Juran Institute's Six Sigma*. McGraw-Hill.

de la República de Colombia, C. (2009). Ley 1314. Bogotá, Colombia.

de la República de Colombia, C. (2010). Ley 1429. Retrieved from: http://www.secretariasenado.gov.co/senado/basedoc/ley_1429_2010.html

de la República de ColombiaC. (1982). Ley 23. Retrieved from: https://www.revistapym.com.co/noticias/derechos-autor/ley-que-reglamenta-derechos-autor-colombia

de la República de ColombiaC. (1993). Ley 80. Retrieved from: http://www.secretariasenado.gov.co/senado/basedoc/ley_0080_1993.html

de la República de ColombiaC. (2004). Ley 905. Retrieved from: http://www.secretariasenado.gov.co/senado/basedoc/ley_0905_2004.html

De Marchi, V. (2012). Environmental innovation and R&D cooperation: Empirical evidence from Spanish manufacturing firms. *Research Policy*, *41*(3), 614–623. doi:10.1016/j.respol.2011.10.002

De Ruyter, K., Wetzels, M., & Bloemer, J. (1998). On the relationship between perceived service quality, service loyalty, and switching costs. *International Journal of Service Industry Management*, *9*(5), 436–453. doi:10.1108/09564239810238848

De Velasco, J. A. P. F. (2012). *Gestión Por Procesos*. 5a Edicion. ESIC editorial.

DeAngelo, L. E. (1981). Auditor size and audit quality. *Journal of Accounting and Economics*, *3*(3), 183–199. doi:10.1016/0165-4101(81)90002-1

Deis, D. R. Jr, & Giroux, G. A. (1992). Determinants of audit quality in the public sector. *The Accounting Review*, 462–479.

Departamento Administrativo Nacional de Estadisticas DANE. (2018). Boletín Técnico. Cuentas Trimestrales - Colombia, Producto Interno Bruto (PIB) Tercer Trimestre 2018. Retrieved from: https://www.dane.gov.co/files/investigaciones/boletines/pib/bol_PIB_IIItrim18_producion_y_gasto.pdf

DeTienne, D. R., & Chandler, G. N. (2007). The role of gender in opportunity identification. *Entrepreneurship Theory and Practice*, *31*(3), 365–386. doi:10.1111/j.1540-6520.2007.00178.x

Dilli, S., Elert, N., & Herrmann, A. M. (2018). Varieties of entrepreneurship: Exploring the institutional foundations of different entrepreneurship types through 'Varieties-of-Capitalism' arguments. *Small Business Economics*, *51*(2), 293–320. doi:10.100711187-018-0002-z

Ditto, P. H., Moore, K. A., Hilton, J. L., & Kalish, J. R. (1995). Beliefs About Physicians: Their Role in Health Care Utilization, Satisfaction, and Compliance. *Basic and Applied Social Psychology*, *17*(1), 23–48. doi:10.120715324834basp1701&2_2

Dodds, W. B., Monroe, K. B., & Grewal, D. (1991). *Effects of Price, Brand, and Store Information on Buyers' Product Evaluations*. Academic Press.

Doleski, O. D. (2015). *Integrated business model: applying the St. Gallen management concept to business models*. Springer Gabler. doi:10.1007/978-3-658-09698-4

Dooley, K. (2000). The paradigms of quality: evolution and revolution in the history of the discipline. *Advances in the Management of Organizational Quality*, *5*(1), 1-28.

Doolin, B., Dillon, S., Thompson, F., & Corner, J. L. (2005). Perceived Risk, the Internet Shopping Experience and Online Purchasing Behavior: A New Zealand Perspective. *Journal of Global Information Management*, *13*(2), 66–88. doi:10.4018/jgim.2005040104

Drucker, P. F. (1998). The discipline of innovation. *Harvard Business Review, 76*(6), 149–157. PMID:10187245

Dubé, L., Trudeau, E., & Bélanger, M. C. (1994). Determining the complexity of patient satisfaction with food services. *Journal of the American Dietetic Association, 94*(4), 394–401. doi:10.1016/0002-8223(94)90093-0 PMID:8144806

Dünhaupt, P. (2013). *Determinants of functional income distribution - Theory and empirical evidence.* Working Paper 18. Berlin, Germany: Global Labour University.

Duque Oliva, E. J., & Gómez, Y. D. (2014). Evolución conceptual de los modelos de medición de la percepción de calidad del servicio: Una mirada desde la educación superior. *Suma de Negocios, 5*(12), 180–191. doi:10.1016/S2215-910X(14)70040-0

Duque-Oliva. (2005). Revisión del concepto de calidad del servicio y sus modelos de medicioón. *Revista Innovar, 15*(25), 64–80. Retrieved from https://www.redalyc.org/articulo.oa?id=81802505

Duran, C., Çetindere, A., & Şahan, Ö. (2014). An analysis of the relationship between total quality management practices and knowledge management: The case of Eskişehir. *Procedia: Social and Behavioral Sciences, 109*, 65–77. doi:10.1016/j.sbspro.2013.12.422

Duyne, D. K. V., Landay, J., & Hong, J. I. (2002). *The design of sites: Patterns, principles, and processes for crafting a customer-centered Web experience.* Addison-Wesley Longman Publishing Co., Inc.

Dyason, M. D., & Kaye, M. M. (1995). Achieving a competitive edge through continuous quality improvement. In *Total Quality Management* (pp. 517–520). Springer. doi:10.1007/978-94-011-0539-2_92

Education Departamento Administrativo de la Función Pública. (2009). Decreto 4485. Norma Técnica de Calidad en la Gestión Pública - NTCGP 1000. Retrieved from: https://www.alcaldiabogota.gov.co/sisjurMantenimiento/normas/Norma1.jsp?i=37853

Ekos. (2018, August). *Guayaquil, capital comercial del Ecuador.* Retrieved from https://www.ekosnegocios.com/articulo/guayaquil-capital-comercial-del-ecuador

El Comercio. (2014, March 27). *Las academias privadas amplían la oferta de clases de inglés.* Retrieved from https://www.elcomercio.com/tendencias/academias-privadas-amplian-oferta-de.html

El Universo. (2013, October 6). *Estudiar idiomas en otro país, opción para jóvenes.* Retrieved from https://www.eluniverso.com/vida-estilo/2013/10/06/nota/1542306/estudiar-idiomas-otro-pais-opcion-jovenes

El Universo. (2015, February 11). *Ecuador tiene "nivel bajo de inglés", según informe de Education First.* Retrieved from https://www.eluniverso.com/noticias/2015/02/11/nota/4547176/ecuador-tiene-nivel-bajo-ingles-segun-informe-education-first

El Universo. (2019, March 26). *Inglés, cuando un idioma cambia vidas.* Retrieved from https://www.eluniverso.com/guayaquil/2019/03/26/nota/7252358/ingles

Elert, N., & Henrekson, M. (2017). Entrepreneurship and institutions: A bidirectional relationship. *Foundations and Trends in Entrepreneurship, 13*(3), 191–263. doi:10.1561/0300000073

Enciso, M., Mugarra, A., Muñecas, I., & Ruíz, A. (2019). Collaborative Economy vs Platform Economy: The Fairbnb Case and its Inspiring Principles Based on Cooperative Economy. *Boletín de Estudios Económicos, 74*(227), 259–283.

Eppler, M. J., & Muenzenmayer, P. (2002, November). Measuring Information Quality in the Web Context: A Survey of State-of-the-Art Instruments and an Application Methodology. In ICIQ (pp. 187-196). Academic Press.

Eppler, M., & Helfert, M. (2004, November). A classification and analysis of data quality costs. In *International Conference on Information Quality* (pp. 311-325). Academic Press.

Erdil, T. S. (2015). Effects of Customer Brand Perceptions on Store Image and Purchase Intention: An Application in Apparel Clothing. *Procedia: Social and Behavioral Sciences, 207*, 196–205. doi:10.1016/j.sbspro.2015.10.088

Evans, J.R., & Lindsay, W.M. (2015). *Administración y control de la calidad.* Cengage Learning Editors.

Evans, R. L., Connis, R. T., Hendricks, R. D., & Haselkorn, J. K. (1995). Multidisciplinary rehabilitation versus medical care: A meta-analysis. *Social Science & Medicine, 40*(12), 1699–1706. doi:10.1016/0277-9536(94)00286-3 PMID:7660183

Ezekiel, M. (1930). *Methods of correlation analysis.* Wiley.

Fahud, D. D. (2015). Impact of Lifestyle on Health. *Iranian Journal of Public Health, 44*(11), 1442–1444. PMID:26744700

Fan, Z., & Jarinto, K. (2018). Taobao, the marketing problem and recommendations for improving customer satisfaction. *RMUTT Global Business Accounting and Finance Review, 2*(1). Retrieved from http://www.profile.rmutt.ac.th/index.php/gbafr/article/view/1102

FAO (Food and Agriculture Organization of the United Nations). (2013). *Capacitación y Almacenamiento de Agua de Lluvia. Opciones técnicas para la agricultura familiar en América latina y el Caribe.* FAO.

Farris, P. W., Bendle, N., Pfeifer, P., & Reibstein, D. (2010). *Marketing metrics: The definitive guide to measuring marketing performance.* Pearson Education.

Fayolle, A., & Liñán, F. (2014). The future of research on entrepreneurial intentions. *Journal of Business Research, 67*(5), 663–666. doi:10.1016/j.jbusres.2013.11.024

Fayolle, A., Liñán, F., & Moriano, J. A. (2014). Beyond entrepreneurial intentions: Values and motivations in entrepreneurship. *The International Entrepreneurship and Management Journal, 10*(4), 679–689. doi:10.100711365-014-0306-7

Ferrer, M., & Maudes, A. (2019). Un futuro para la economía colaborativa y los nuevos modelos de negocio en las plataformas digitales. *Cuadernos Económicos de ICE, 97*(97), 155–185. doi:10.32796/cice.2019.97.6801

Fishbein, M., & Ajzen, I. (1975). *Belief, attitude, intention and behavior: An introduction to theory and research.* Addison-Wesley.

Fishbein, M., & Ajzen, I. (2011). *Predicting and changing behavior: The reasoned action approach.* Psychology Press. doi:10.4324/9780203838020

Fisher, N. I., & Nair, V. N. (2009). Quality management and quality practice: Perspectives on their history and their future. *Applied Stochastic Models in Business and Industry, 25*(1), 1–28. doi:10.1002/asmb.756

Fiss, P. C. (2007). A set-theoretic approach to organizational configurations. *Academy of Management Review, 32*(4), 1180–1198. doi:10.5465/amr.2007.26586092

Food and Agriculture Organization (FAO) of the United Nations. (2016). *E-agriculture Strategy Guide.* FAO.

Forero Herrera, A. J., & Gaona Guevara, J. (2019). *Propuesta de planeación estratégica para la empresa Angora Confecciones* (B.Sc. Dissertation). Universidad de La Salle, Bogota Colombia.

Forero, M., & Duque, E. (2014). Evolución y caracterización de los modelos de Brand Equity. *Suma de Negocios, 5*(12), 158–168. doi:10.1016/S2215-910X(14)70038-2

Forster, N. S., & Rockart, J. F. (1989). *Critical success factors: an annotated bibliography.* Academic Press.

Fournier, S. (1998). Consumers and Their Brands: Developing Relationship Theory in Consumer Research. *Chicago Journals, Journal of Consumer Research Inc.*, *24*(4), 343–353. doi:10.1086/209515

Francés, A. (2006). *Estrategia y planes para la empresa con el Cuadro de mando integral*. Ciudad de Mexico: Pearson Educación de México.

Francis, J., Huang, A. H., Rajgopal, S., & Zang, A. Y. (2008). CEO reputation and earnings quality. *Contemporary Accounting Research*, *25*(1), 109–147. doi:10.1506/car.25.1.4

Freihat, S., & Al-Machzoomi, K. (2012). The picture of workplace oral communication skills for ESP Jordanian business graduate employees. *International Journal of Business. Human Technology*, *2*(1), 159–173.

Frolova, I., & Lapina, I. (2014). Corporate social responsibility in the framework of quality management. *Procedia: Social and Behavioral Sciences*, *156*, 178–182. doi:10.1016/j.sbspro.2014.11.166

Fullerton, R. R., & McWatters, C. S. (2001). The production performance benefits from JIT implementation. *Journal of Operations Management*, *19*(1), 81–96. doi:10.1016/S0272-6963(00)00051-6

Furterer, S. L. (2016). *Lean Six Sigma in service: applications and case studies*. CRC Press. doi:10.1201/9781420079104

Gaglio, C. M., & Katz, J. A. (2001). The Psychological Basis of Opportunity Identification: Entrepreneurial Alertness. *Small Business Economics*, *16*(2), 95–111. doi:10.1023/A:1011132102464

Galindo, M. A., & Méndez, M. T. (2014). Entrepreneurship, economic growth, and innovation: Are feedback effects at work? *Journal of Business Research*, *67*(5), 825–829. doi:10.1016/j.jbusres.2013.11.052

Galindo, M. A., & Méndez-Picazo, M. T. (2013). Innovation, entrepreneurship and economic growth. *Management Decision*, *51*(3), 501–514. doi:10.1108/00251741311309625

Galindo-Martín, M. A., Méndez-Picazo, M. T., & Castaño-Martinez, M. S. (2019). The role of innovation and institutions in entrepreneurship and economic growth in two groups of countries. *International Journal of Entrepreneurial Behaviour & Research*, *26*(3), 485–502. doi:10.1108/IJEBR-06-2019-0336

Garay, L., & Font, X. (2012). Doing good to do well? Corporate social responsibility reasons, practices and impacts in small and medium accommodation enterprises. *International Journal of Hospitality Management*, *31*(2), 329–337. doi:10.1016/j.ijhm.2011.04.013

García, J. A. (2017). *Direccionamiento Estratégico en las PYMEs* (B.Sc. Dissertation). Universidad Militar de Nueva Granada, Colombia.

García-Cabrera, A. M., & García-Soto, M. G. (2008). Cultural differences and entrepreneurial behavior: An intra-country cross-cultural analysis in Cape Verde. *Entrepreneurship and Regional Development*, *20*(5), 451–483. doi:10.1080/08985620801912608

García, M. J. (2000). La valoración financiera de las marcas: Una revisión de los principales métodos utilizados. *Investigaciones Europeas de Dirección y Economía de la Empresa*, *6*(1), 31–52.

García-Rodríguez, F. J., Gutiérrez-Taño, D., & Ruiz-Rosa, I. (2019). Analysis of the Potential of Entrepreneurship Education in Young Children. *Entrepreneurship Research Journal*, *9*(1), 1–9. doi:10.1515/erj-2017-0064

Garland, M., Axon, S., Graziano, M., Morrissey, J., & Heidkamp, C. P. (2019). The blue economy: Identifying geographic concepts and sensitivities. *GEC3. Geography Compass*, *13*(7). Advance online publication. doi:10.1111/gec3.12445

Garza-Reyes, J. A., Rocha-Lona, L., & Kumar, V. (2015). A conceptual framework for the implementation of quality management systems. *Total Quality Management & Business Excellence*, *26*(11-12), 1298–1310. doi:10.1080/14783363.2014.929254

Ghobadian, A., Speller, S., & Matthew, J. (1994). Service Quality: Concepts and Models. *International Journal of Quality & Reliability Management*, *11*(9), 43–66. doi:10.1108/02656719410074297

Ghosh, M. (2012). Lean manufacturing performance in Indian manufacturing plants. *Journal of Manufacturing Technology Management*, *24*(1), 113–122. doi:10.1108/17410381311287517

Gielnik, M. M., Barabas, S., Frese, M., Namatovu-Dawa, R., Scholz, F. A., Metzger, J. R., & Walter, T. (2014). A temporal analysis of how entrepreneurial goal intentions, positive fantasies, and action planning affect starting a new venture and when the effects wear off. *Journal of Business Venturing*, *29*(6), 755–772. doi:10.1016/j.jbusvent.2013.09.002

Global Entrepreneurship Monitor Project (GEM). (2019). *APS-Global data 2014-2016*. https://www.gemconsortium.org/data/sets

Gnyawali, D. R., & Fogel, D. S. (1994). Environments for entrepreneurship development: Key dimensions and research implications. *Entrepreneurship Theory and Practice*, *18*(4), 43–62. doi:10.1177/104225879401800403

Gobierno Autónomo Descentralizado de la Provincia de Chimborazo. (2015). *Plan de desarrollo y ordenamiento territorial de Chimborazo*. Riobamba.

Gobierno Autónomo Descentralizado de la Provincia de Chimborazo. (2016). *Cantón Alausí*. Riobamba.

Goethner, M., Obschonka, M., Silbereisen, R. K., & Cantner, U. (2012). Scientists' transition to academic entrepreneurship: Economic and psychological determinants. *Journal of Economic Psychology*, *33*(3), 628–641. doi:10.1016/j.joep.2011.12.002

Goetsch, D. L., & Davis, S. B. (2014). *Quality management for organizational excellence*. Pearson.

Gökdemir, K., & Ali, T. (2017). The Examination and Comparison of Recreational Sports Centers With Regard to Quality of Service. *International Journal of Applied Exercise Physiology*, *6*(4), 26–36. doi:10.22631/ijaep.v6i4.195

Goleman, D. (2007). La Práctica de la Inteligencia Emocional. Editorial Kairós. S.A, Ed.

Gomez-Haro, S., Aragon-Correa, J. A., & Cordon-Pozo, E. (2011). Differentiating the effects of the institutional environment on corporate entrepreneurship. *Management Decision*, *49*(9-10), 1677–1693. doi:10.1108/00251741111183825

González López, I. (2004). Modelos de evaluación de la calidad orientados a la mejora de las instituciones educativas. XXI. *Review of Education*, *6*, 155–169.

Gonzalez-Alvarez, N., & Solis-Rodriguez, V. (2011). Discovery of entrepreneurial opportunities: A gender perspective. *Industrial Management & Data Systems*, *111*(5-6), 755–775. doi:10.1108/02635571111137296

Goolsby, D. (2018). *Critical Challenges faced by Quality Departments and Recommended Actions*. Quality Magazine.

Granovetter, M. (1985). Economic action and social structure: The problem of embeddedness. *American Journal of Sociology*, *91*(3), 481–510. doi:10.1086/228311

Grave, L. (2010). The "Sustainability Project". The limits of the sustainability concept from a cultural perspective. *Cultura21 eBooks Series on Culture and Sustainability, 1*.

Greenwald, H. P. (2010). *Health Care in The United States: Organization, Management, and Policy*. Jossey-Bass.

Grimaldi, D., & Fernandez, V. (2017). The alignment of University curricula with the building of a Smart City: A case study from Barcelona. *Technological Forecasting and Social Change*, *123*, 298–306. doi:10.1016/j.techfore.2016.03.011

Guadarrama, E. G., & Rosales, E. M. (2015). Marketing relacional: Valor, satisfacción, lealtad y retención del cliente. In Ciencia y Sociedad (Vol. 40). doi:10.1017/CBO9781107415324.004

Gu, M., & Wong, P. P. (2008). Coastal zone management focusing on coastal tourism in a transitional period of China. *Ocean & Coastal Management Ocean & Coastal Management*, *51*(1), 1–24. doi:10.1016/j.ocecoaman.2007.05.008

Hackman, J. R., & Wageman, R. (1995). Total quality management: Empirical, conceptual, and practical issues. *Administrative Science Quarterly*, *40*(2), 309–342. doi:10.2307/2393640

Hall, M. A. (2005). The importance of trust for ethics, law, and public policy. *Cambridge Quarterly of Healthcare Ethics*, *14*(2), 156–197. doi:10.1017/S096318010505019X PMID:15887807

Hardoon, D. R., Szedmak, S., & Shawe-Taylor, J. (2004). Canonical Correlation Analysis: An Overview with Application to Learning Methods. *Neural Computation*, *16*(12), 2639–2664. doi:10.1162/0899766042321814 PMID:15516276

Harvey, L., & Stensaker, B. (2008). Quality culture: Understandings, boundaries, and linkages. *European Journal of Education*, *43*(4), 427–442. doi:10.1111/j.1465-3435.2008.00367.x

Hassanein, K., & Head, M. (2007). Manipulating perceived social presence through the web interface and its impact on attitude towards online shopping. *International Journal of Human-Computer Studies*, *65*(8), 689–708. doi:10.1016/j.ijhcs.2006.11.018

Haug, A., Zachariassen, F., & Van Liempd, D. (2011). The costs of poor data quality. *Journal of Industrial Engineering and Management*, *4*(2), 168–193. doi:10.3926/jiem.2011.v4n2.p168-193

Haumann, T., Quaiser, B., Wieseke, J., & Rese, M. (2014). Footprints in the Sands of Time: A Comparative Analysis of the Effectiveness of Customer Satisfaction and Customer–Company Identification over Time. *Journal of Marketing*, *78*(6), 78–102. doi:10.1509/jm.13.0509

Hawkins, D. I. (1993). New business entrepreneurship in the Japanese economy. *Journal of Business Venturing*, *8*(2), 137–151. doi:10.1016/0883-9026(93)90016-X

Hayran, O. (2013). *Sağlık ve Hastalık. In Hastane Yönetimi.* Nobel Tıp Kitabevleri.

Hayton, J. C., George, G., & Zahra, S. A. (2002). National culture and entrepreneurship: A review of behavioral research. *Entrepreneurship Theory and Practice*, *26*(4), 33–52. doi:10.1177/104225870202600403

He, F., & Mykytyn, P. (2007). Decision Factors for the Adoption of an Online Payment System by Customers. *International Journal of E-Business Research*, *3*(4), 1–32. doi:10.4018/jebr.2007100101

Hellman, P., & Liu, Y. (2013). Development of quality management systems: How have disruptive technological innovations in quality management affected organizations? *Quality Innovation Prosperity*, *17*(1), 104–119. doi:10.12776/qip.v17i1.154

Henik, E. (2015). Understanding whistle-blowing: A set-theoretic approach. *Journal of Business Research*, *68*(2), 442–450. doi:10.1016/j.jbusres.2014.06.004

Henze, J., & Zhu, J. (2012). Current Research on Chinese Students Studying Abroad. *Research in Comparative and International Education*, *7*(1), 90–104. doi:10.2304/rcie.2012.7.1.90

Heritage Foundation. (2019). *Index of economic freedom.* Available at www.heritage.org/index/

Hernad, J. M. C., & Gaya, C. G. (2013). Methodology for implementing document management systems to support ISO 9001: 2008 quality management systems. *Procedia Engineering*, *63*, 29–35. doi:10.1016/j.proeng.2013.08.225

Hernández, B., Jiménez, J., & José Martín, M. (2011). Age, gender and income: Do they really moderate online shopping behaviour? *Online Information Review*, *35*(1), 113–133. doi:10.1108/14684521111113614

Hernandez, M. D., Wang, Y. J., Minor, M. S., & Liu, Q. (2008). Effects of superstitious beliefs on consumer novelty seeking and independent judgment making: Evidence from China. *Journal of Consumer Behaviour: An International Research Review*, *7*(6), 424–435. doi:10.1002/cb.261

Hess, T., Matt, C., Benlian, A., & Wiesböck, F. (2016). Options for formulating a digital transformation strategy. *MIS Quarterly Executive*, *15*(2), 103–119.

He, Z., & Ngee Goh, T. (2015). Enhancing the future impact of Six Sigma management. *Quality Technology & Quantitative Management*, *12*(1), 83–92. doi:10.1080/16843703.2015.11673368

Hinton, P. R., McMurray, I., & Brownlow, C. (2014). SPSS explained (2nd ed.). Routledge, Taylor & Francis Group. doi:10.4324/9781315797298

Hirt, S., & Limayem, M. (2000). Integrating three theoretical perspectives to explain internet-based technology usage by university students: A qualitative study. *ICIS 2000 Proceedings*, 47.

Hjalager, A.-M. (2010). A review of innovation research in tourism. *Tourism Management*, *48*(1), 1–12. doi:10.1016/j.tourman.2009.08.012

Hoetker, G. (2007). The use of logit and probit models in strategic management research: Critical issues. *Strategic Management Journal*, *28*(4), 331–343. doi:10.1002mj.582

Hofer, C., Eroglu, C., & Hofer, A. R. (2012). The effect of lean production on financial performance: The mediating role of inventory leanness. *International Journal of Production Economics*, *138*(2), 242–253. doi:10.1016/j.ijpe.2012.03.025

Hopwood, B., Mellor, M., & O'Brien, G. (2005). Sustainable development: Mapping different approaches. *Sustainable Development*, *13*(1), 38–52. doi:10.1002d.244

Horbach, J. (2008). Determinants of environmental innovation—New evidence from German panel data sources. *Research Policy*, *37*(1), 163–173. doi:10.1016/j.respol.2007.08.006

Hornsby, J. S., Kuratko, D. F., Shepherd, D. A., & Bott, J. P. (2009). Managers' corporate entrepreneurial actions: Examining perception and position. *Journal of Business Venturing*, *24*(3), 236–247. doi:10.1016/j.jbusvent.2008.03.002

Hoyer, W. D., & Brown, S. P. (1990). Effects of Brand Awareness on Choice for a Common, Repeat-Purchase Product. *The Journal of Consumer Research*, *17*(2), 141. doi:10.1086/208544

Hsin Chang, H., & Wen Chen, S. (2008a). The impact of online store environment cues on purchase intention: Trust and perceived risk as a mediator. *Online Information Review*, *32*(6), 818–841. doi:10.1108/14684520810923953

Huang, X., Jia, H., & Roiseux Racine, P. (2013). Urban and Rural Logistics and Distribution System Based on Supply and Marketing Cooperatives. *Applied Mechanics and Materials*, *253-255*, 1468–1471. doi:10.4028/www.scientific.net/AMM.253-255.1468

Huang, Y., Phau, I., & Lin, C. (2010). Consumer animosity, economic hardship, and normative influence: How do they affect consumers' purchase intention? *European Journal of Marketing*, *44*(7/8), 909–937. doi:10.1108/03090561011047463

Huff, C., & Tingley, D. (2015). "Who are these people?" Evaluating the demographic characteristics and political preferences of MTurk survey respondents. *Research & Politics*, *2*(3), 205316801560464. doi:10.1177/2053168015604648

Hwang, G. H., Lee, K. C., & Seo, Y. W. (2018). How does Six Sigma influence creativity and corporate performance through exploration and exploitation? *Total Quality Management & Business Excellence*, *29*(13-14), 1668–1684. doi:10.1080/14783363.2017.1297199

Iankova, S., Davies, I., Archer-Brown, C., Marder, B., & Yau, A. (2018). A comparison of social media marketing between B2B, B2C, and mixed business models. *Industrial Marketing Management*, *81*, 169–179. doi:10.1016/j.indmarman.2018.01.001

Ibrahim, O. (2013). Total Quality Management (TQM) and continuous improvement, as addressed by researchers. *International Journal of Scientific and Research Publications*, *3*(10), 1–4.

Ingason, H. Þ., & Jónsdóttir, E. R. (2017). The house of competence of the quality manager. *Cogent Business & Management*, *4*(1), 1345050. doi:10.1080/23311975.2017.1345050

Ingeniería del ConocimientoC. V. R. (n.d.). Retrieved from: https://www.lasempresas.com.co/bogota/cvr-ingenieria-del-conocimiento-sas/

Inove, K. (1985). *Education & Training of Industrial Manpower in Japan*. DIANE Publishing.

Instituto Nacional de Estadísticas y Censos. (2010). *Fascículo provincial Chimborazo*. Author.

Instituto Nacional de Estadísticas y Censos. (2016). *Encuesta de Superficie y Producción Agropecuaria Continua ESPAC 2016*. Quito, Ecuador: Author.

Iqbal, T., Huq, F., & Bhutta, M. K. S. (2018). Agile manufacturing relationship building with TQM, JIT, and firm performance: An exploratory study in the apparel export industry of Pakistan. *International Journal of Production Economics*, *203*, 24–37. doi:10.1016/j.ijpe.2018.05.033

Ireland, R. D., Hitt, M. A., & Simon, D. G. (2003). A model of strategic entrepreneurship: The construct and its dimensions. *Journal of Management*, *29*(6), 963–989. doi:10.1016/S0149-2063(03)00086-2

Ishikawa, K. (1989). *Introducción al Control de Calidad*. Díaz de Santos.

Jasti, N. V. K., & Kodali, R. (2015). Lean production: Literature review and trends. *International Journal of Production Research*, *53*(3), 867–885. doi:10.1080/00207543.2014.937508

Jenner, M. G. (1995). *Software quality management and ISO 9001: how to make them work for you*. John Wiley & Sons, Inc.

Jiang, L., Hoegg, J., Dahl, D. W., & Chattopadhyay, A. (2009). The persuasive role of incidental similarity on attitudes and purchase intentions in a sales context. *The Journal of Consumer Research*, *36*(5), 778–791. doi:10.1086/605364

Jiménez-Jiménez, D., Martinez-Costa, M., Martínez-Lorente, A. R., & Rabeh, H. A. D. (2015). Total quality management performance in multinational companies: A learning perspective. *The TQM Journal*, *27*(3), 328–340. doi:10.1108/TQM-01-2014-0002

Jimoh, R., Oyewobi, L., Isa, R., & Waziri, I. (2019). Total quality management practices and organizational performance: The mediating roles of strategies for continuous improvement. *International Journal of Construction Management*, *19*(2), 162–177. doi:10.1080/15623599.2017.1411456

Johnson, G., Scholes, K., & Whittington, R. (2006). *Dirección Estratégica*. Pearson.

Jones, M. A., Reynolds, K. E., & Arnold, M. J. (2006). Hedonic and utilitarian shopping value: Investigating differential effects on retail outcomes. *Journal of Business Research*, *59*(9), 974–981. doi:10.1016/j.jbusres.2006.03.006

Joshi, A., Kale, S., Chandel, S., & Pal, D. (2015). Likert scale: Explored and explained. *British Journal of Applied Science and Technology*, *7*(4), 396–403. doi:10.9734/BJAST/2015/14975

Juran, J., & Godfrey, A. B. (1999). *Quality handbook*. Republished McGraw-Hill.

Justesen, M. K., & Kurrild-Klitgaard, P. (2013). Institutional interactions and economic growth: The joint effects of property rights, veto players and democratic capital. *Public Choice*, *157*(3-4), 449–474. doi:10.100711127-013-0143-1

Kadilar, C., & Cingi, H. (2006). Improvement in estimating the population mean in simple random sampling. *Applied Mathematics Letters*, *19*(1), 5. doi:10.1016/j.aml.2005.02.039

Kafetzopoulos, D. P., Psomas, E. L., & Gotzamani, K. D. (2015). The impact of quality management systems on the performance of manufacturing firms. *International Journal of Quality & Reliability Management*, *32*(4), 381–399. doi:10.1108/IJQRM-11-2013-0186

Kamakura, W. A., & Russell, G. J. (1993). Measuring brand value with scanner data. *International Journal of Research in Marketing*, *10*(1), 9–22. doi:10.1016/0167-8116(93)90030-3

Kaplan, R. S., & Atkinson, A. A. (1998). *Advanced Management Accounting*. Prentice-Hall.

Kaplan, R., & Norton, D. (2002). *El Cuadro de Mando Integral. Gestion.*

Kaplan, R., & Norton, D. (2004). *Mapas Estratégicos. Gestion.*

Karimi, S., Biemans, H. J., Lans, T., Chizari, M., & Mulder, M. (2016). The impact of entrepreneurship education: A study of Iranian students' entrepreneurial intentions and opportunity identification. *Journal of Small Business Management*, *54*(1), 187–209. doi:10.1111/jsbm.12137

Kautonen, T., Tornikoski, E. T., & Kibler, E. (2011). Entrepreneurial intentions in the third age: The impact of perceived age norms. *Small Business Economics*, *37*(2), 219–234. doi:10.100711187-009-9238-y

Kautonen, T., van Gelderen, M., & Fink, M. (2015). Robustness of the Theory of Planned Behavior in Predicting Entrepreneurial Intentions and Actions. *Entrepreneurship Theory and Practice*, *39*(3), 655–674. doi:10.1111/etap.12056

Kautonen, T., Van Gelderen, M., & Tornikoski, E. T. (2013). Predicting entrepreneurial behavior: A test of the theory of planned behavior. *Applied Economics*, *45*(6), 697–707. doi:10.1080/00036846.2011.610750

Kavuncubaşı, Ş., & Yıldırım, S. (2018). Hastane ve Sağlık Kurumları Yönetimi (5. Baskı b.). Ankara, Turkey: Siyasal Kitabevi.

Keiningham, T., Gupta, S., Aksoy, L., & Buoye, A. (2014). The High Price of Customer Satisfaction. *Harvard Business Review*.

Keith, N. K., & Simmers, C. S. (2013). Adapting the marketing educational environment for multi-cultural millennials: The Chinese experience. *Academy of Educational Leadership Journal*, *17*(3), 83.

Kelchner, L. (2008). *Theories of Total Quality Management*. Academic Press.

Keller, K. L. (2013). *Strategic Brand Management Building, Measuring, and Managing Brand Equity*. Pearson; doi:10.2307/1252315

Kelley, D. J., Singer, S., & Herrington, M. (2012). *Global Entrepreneurship Monitor 2011 Global Report*. Global Entrepreneurship Research Association and London Business School.

Kemp, R. (2000). Technology and Environmental Policy—Innovation effects of past policies and suggestions for improvement. *Innovation and the Environment*, *1*, 35–61.

Kent, R., & Olsen, W. (2008). *Using fsQCA a brief guide and workshop for fuzzy-set qualitative comparative analysis.* Available at: http://www.cmist.manchester.ac.uk/medialibrary/archive-publications/working-papers/2008/2008-10-teaching-paper-fsqca.pdf

Kent, R. A. (2005). Cases as configurations: Using combinatorial and fuzzy logic to analyze marketing data. *International Journal of Market Research, 47*(2), 205–228. doi:10.1177/147078530504700202

Keshk, O. M., Pollins, B. M., & Reuveny, R. (2004). Trade still follows the flag: The primacy of politics in a simultaneous model of interdependence and armed conflict. *The Journal of Politics, 66*(4), 1155–1179. doi:10.1111/j.0022-3816.2004.00294.x

Khan, M. (2006). Consumer Behaviour and Advertising Management. New Age International Publishers.

Khanchanapong, T., Prajogo, D., Sohal, A. S., Cooper, B. K., Yeung, A. C., & Cheng, T. C. E. (2014). The unique and complementary effects of manufacturing technologies and lean practices on manufacturing operational performance. *International Journal of Production Economics, 153*, 191–203. doi:10.1016/j.ijpe.2014.02.021

Khodabandeh, A., & Lindh, C. (2020). The importance of brands, commitment, and influencers on purchase intent in the context of online relationships. *Australasian Marketing Journal.* Advance online publication. doi:10.1016/j.ausmj.2020.03.003

Kibler, E., Kautonen, T., & Fink, M. (2014). Regional social legitimacy of entrepreneurship: Implications for entrepreneurial intention and startup behavior. *Regional Studies, 48*(6), 995–1015. doi:10.1080/00343404.2013.851373

Kim, A. J., & Ko, E. (2010). Impacts of Luxury Fashion Brand's Social Media Marketing on Customer Relationship and Purchase Intention. *Journal of Global Fashion Marketing, 1*(3), 164–171. doi:10.1080/20932685.2010.10593068

Kim, D. J., Ferrin, D. L., & Rao, H. R. (2008). A trust-based consumer decision-making model in electronic commerce: The role of trust, perceived risk, and their antecedents. *Decision Support Systems, 44*(2), 544–564. doi:10.1016/j.dss.2007.07.001

Kim, D. Y., Kumar, V., & Kumar, U. (2012). Relationship between quality management practices and innovation. *Journal of Operations Management, 30*(4), 295–315. doi:10.1016/j.jom.2012.02.003

Kim, H., & Kim, W. G. (2005). The relationship between brand equity and firms' performance in luxury hotels and chain restaurants$. *Tourism Management, 26*(4), 12. doi:10.1016/j.tourman.2004.03.010

Kim, H., & Song, J. (2010). The quality of word-of-mouth in the online shopping mall. *Journal of Research in Interactive Marketing, 4*(4), 376–390. Advance online publication. doi:10.1108/17505931011092844

Kim, Y. C., & Jung, J.-H. (2019). Five Forms of Shadow Education Practices. In Y. C. Kim & J.-H. Jung (Eds.), *Shadow Education as Worldwide Curriculum Studies* (pp. 61–88). Springer International Publishing., doi:10.1007/978-3-030-03982-0_3

Kiran, D. R. (2016). *Total quality management: Key concepts and case studies.* Butterworth-Heinemann.

Kirzner, I. M. (1979). *Perception, Opportunity and Profit.* University of Chicago Press.

Klefsjö, B., Wiklund, H., & Edgeman, R. L. (2001). Six Sigma seen as a methodology for total quality management. *Measuring Business Excellence, 5*(1), 31–35. doi:10.1108/13683040110385809

Knight, G. A., & Cavusgil, S. T. (2004). Innovation, organizational capabilities, and the born-global firm. *Journal of International Business Studies, 35*(2), 124–141. doi:10.1057/palgrave.jibs.8400071

Kobakhidze, M. N. (2018). Economic Sociology of the Shadow Education Market. In M. N. Kobakhidze (Ed.), *Teachers as Tutors: Shadow Education Market Dynamics in Georgia* (pp. 164–202). Springer International Publishing., doi:10.1007/978-3-319-95915-3_7

Koh, A. (2016). On 'Gods' and 'Kings' in the Tutorial Industry: A 'Media Spectacle' Analysis of the Shadow Education in Hong Kong. In J. Moss & B. Pini (Eds.), *Visual Research Methods in Educational Research* (pp. 189–208). doi:10.1057/9781137447357_11

Konuk, F. A. (2019). The influence of perceived food quality, price fairness, perceived value and satisfaction on customers' revisit and word-of-mouth intentions towards organic food restaurants. *Journal of Retailing and Consumer Services, 50*, 103–110. doi:10.1016/j.jretconser.2019.05.005

Kostova, T., & Roth, K. (2002). Adoption of an organizational practice by subsidiaries of multinational corporations: Institutional and relational effects. *Academy of Management Journal, 45*(1), 215–233.

Kotler, P., & Keller, L. (2006). *Dirección de Marketing*. Ciudad de Mexico: Pearson Educación.

Kotler, P. (1999). *Marketing Management*. Prentice-Hall.

Kpakol, A., & Amah, E. (2014). Re-Engineering Corporate Culture for Organizational Receptivity to Change. *European Journal of Business and Management, 6*, 167–176.

Kraus, S., Ribeiro-Soriano, D., & Schüssler, M. (2018). Fuzzy-set qualitative comparative analysis (fsQCA) in entrepreneurship and innovation research–the rise of a method. *The International Entrepreneurship and Management Journal, 14*(1), 15–33. doi:10.100711365-017-0461-8

Krueger, N. F. (1993). The impact of prior entrepreneurial exposure on perceptions of new venture feasibility and desirability. *Entrepreneurship Theory and Practice, 18*(1), 5–21. doi:10.1177/104225879301800101

Krueger, N. F. Jr, & Brazeal, D. (1994). Entrepreneurial potential and potential entrepreneurs. *Entrepreneurship Theory and Practice, 18*(3), 91–104. doi:10.1177/104225879401800307

Krueger, N. F. Jr, Reilly, M. D., & Carsrud, A. L. (2000). Competing models of entrepreneurial intentions. *Journal of Business Venturing, 15*(5), 411 432. doi:10.1016/S0883 9026(98)00033 0

Kumar, P., Maiti, J., & Gunasekaran, A. (2018). Impact of quality management systems on firm performance. *International Journal of Quality & Reliability Management, 35*(5), 1034–1059. doi:10.1108/IJQRM-02-2017-0030

Kundu, S. C., & Rani, S. (2007). Human resources' self-esteem across gender and categories: A study. *Industrial Management & Data Systems, 107*(9), 1366–1390. doi:10.1108/02635570710834018

Kwahk, K.-Y., & Kim, B. (2017). Effects of social media on consumers' purchase decisions: Evidence from Taobao. *Service Business, 11*(4), 803–829. doi:10.100711628-016-0331-4

Kwak, Y. H., & Anbari, F. T. (2006). Benefits, obstacles, and future of six sigma approach. *Technovation, 26*(5-6), 708–715. doi:10.1016/j.technovation.2004.10.003

Lackey, R. M. (2000). *The role of the chief learning officer: Implications for theory and practice*. The University of New Mexico.

Lameijer, B. A., Antony, J., Chakraborty, A., Does, R. J. M. M., & Garza-Reyes, J. A. (2020). The role of organisational motivation and coordination in continuous improvement implementations: An empirical research of process improvement project success. *Total Quality Management & Business Excellence*, 1–17. doi:10.1080/14783363.2020.1757422

Lamine, K., & Lakhal, L. (2018). Impact of TQM/Six Sigma practices on the company's performance: Tunisian context. *International Journal of Quality & Reliability Management*, *35*(9), 1881–1906. doi:10.1108/IJQRM-05-2017-0097

Lam, M., O'Donnell, M., & Robertson, D. (2015). Achieving employee commitment for continuous improvement initiatives. *International Journal of Operations & Production Management*, *35*(2), 201–215. doi:10.1108/IJOPM-03-2013-0134

Laudon, K. C., & Traver, C. G. (2014). *E-commerce: business, technology, society* (10th ed.). Pearson.

Lee, K. (2010). The Green Purchase Behavior of Hong Kong Young Consumers: The Role of Peer Influence, Local Environmental Involvement, and Concrete Environmental Knowledge. *Journal of International Consumer Marketing*, *23*(1), 21–44. doi:10.1080/08961530.2011.524575

Lee, S. F., & Sai On Ko, A. (2000). Building Balanced Scorecard with SWOT Analysis, and implementing "Sun Tzu's The Art of Business Management Strategies" on QFD Methodology. *Managerial Auditing Journal*, *15*(1/2), 68–76. doi:10.1108/02686900010304669

Lee, Y. W., Strong, D. M., Kahn, B. K., & Wang, R. Y. (2002). AIMQ: A methodology for information quality assessment. *Information & Management*, *40*(2), 133–146. doi:10.1016/S0378-7206(02)00043-5

Leone, R. P., Rao, V. R., Keller, K. L., Luo, A. M., McAlister, L., & Srivastava, R. (2006). Linking brand equity to customer equity. *Journal of Service Research*, *9*(2), 125–138. doi:10.1177/1094670506293563

Lévesque, M., & Stephan, U. (2019). (in press). It's Time We Talk About Time in Entrepreneurship. *Entrepreneurship Theory and Practice*. Advance online publication. doi:10.1177/1042258719839711

Levinson, W. A., & Rerick, R. A. (2002). *Lean Enterprise: A Synergistic Approach to Minimizing Waste*. ASQ Quality Press.

Lewis, J. R. (1994). Patient views on quality care in general practice: A literature review. *Social Science & Medicine*, *39*(5), 655–670. doi:10.1016/0277-9536(94)90022-1 PMID:7973865

Li, Y-H., & Huang, J. (n.d.). *Applying Theory of Perceived Risk and Technology Acceptance Model in the Online Shopping Channel*. Academic Press.

Lieberman, W. H. (2003). Getting the most from revenue management. *Journal of Revenue and Pricing Management*, *2*(2), 103–115. doi:10.1057/palgrave.rpm.5170055

Lim, D. S. K., Oh, C. H., & De Clercq, D. (2016). Engagement in entrepreneurship in emerging economies: Interactive effects of individual-level factors and institutional conditions. *International Business Review*, *25*(4), 933–945. doi:10.1016/j.ibusrev.2015.12.001

Lim, Y. J., Osman, A., Salahuddin, S. N., Romle, A. R., & Abdullah, S. (2016). Factors Influencing Online Shopping Behavior: The Mediating Role of Purchase Intention. *Procedia Economics and Finance*, *35*, 401–410. doi:10.1016/S2212-5671(16)00050-2

Liñán, F., & Chen, Y. W. (2009). Development and Cross-Cultural Application of a Specific Instrument to Measure Entrepreneurial Intentions. *Entrepreneurship Theory and Practice*, *33*(3), 593–617. doi:10.1111/j.1540-6520.2009.00318.x

Liñán, F., & Fayolle, A. (2015). A systematic literature review on entrepreneurial intentions: Citation, thematic analyses, and research agenda. *The International Entrepreneurship and Management Journal*, *11*(4), 907–933. doi:10.100711365-015-0356-5

Liñán, F., Nabi, G., & Krueger, N. (2013). British and Spanish entrepreneurial intentions: A comparative study. *Revista de Economía Mundial*, *33*, 73–103.

Linden, G., Smith, B., & York, J. (2003). Amazon.com Recommendations: Item-to-Item Collaborative Filtering. *IEEE Internet Computing; Los Alamitos, 7*(1), 76–80. doi:10.1109/MIC.2003.1167344

Lin, N.-H., Tseng, W.-C., Hung, Y.-C., & Yen, D. C. (2009). Making customer relationship management work: Evidence from the banking industry in Taiwan. *Service Industries Journal, 29*(9), 1183–1197. doi:10.1080/02642060701846788

Lipman-Blumen, J. (2000). *Connective Leadership: Managing in a Changing World.* Oxford University Press.

Liu, S. (2014). *From the Marine Economy to Blue Economy.* Retrieved from https://wenku.baidu.com/view/4ef9de21767f5acfa0c7cd5a.html

Liu, J. N. K., & Zhang, E. Y. (2014). An investigation of factors affecting customer selection of online hotel booking channels. *International Journal of Hospitality Management, 39*, 71–83. doi:10.1016/j.ijhm.2014.01.011

Liu, J., & Bray, M. (2020). Private Subtractory Tutoring: The Negative Impact of Shadow Education on Public Schooling in Myanmar. *International Journal of Educational Development, 76*, 102213. doi:10.1016/j.ijedudev.2020.102213

Liu, M. T., Wong, I. A., Tseng, T.-H., Chang, A. W.-Y., & Phau, I. (2017). Applying consumer-based brand equity in luxury hotel branding. *Journal of Business Research, 81*, 192–202. doi:10.1016/j.jbusres.2017.06.014

Liu, S., Heilig, G. K., Chen, J., & Heino, M. (2007). Interactions between economic growth and environmental quality in Shenzhen, China's first special economic zone. *Ecological Economics, 62*(3-4), 559–570. doi:10.1016/j.ecolecon.2006.07.020

Li, Y., & Huang, J. (2009). Applying theory of perceived risk and technology acceptance model in the online shopping channel. *World Academy of Science, Engineering and Technology, 53*(1), 919–925.

Löfgren, M., & Witell, L. (2008). Two decades of using Kano's theory of attractive quality: A literature review. *The Quality Management Journal, 15*(1), 59–75. doi:10.1080/10686967.2008.11918056

López, P. (2016). *Herramientas para la mejora de la Calidad.* FC Editorial. Fundación Confemetal.

Lovelock, C., Patterson, P., & Wirtz, J. (2004). Services Marketing. Edinburgh Business School.

Lu, C.-C., Wu, I.-L., & Hsiao, W.-H. (2019). Developing customer product loyalty through mobile advertising: Affective and cognitive perspectives. *International Journal of Information Management, 47*, 101–111. doi:10.1016/j.ijinfomgt.2018.12.020

Lundberg, A., & Westerman, G. (2019). The Transformer CLO. *Harvard Business Review.* Retrieved from https://hbr.org/

Ma, Y. (2019). *2018 China Coastal Tourism Passenger Flow Big Data Report.* Retrieved from https://www.3mbang.com/p-1021774.html

Maderuelo Fernández, J. A. (2002). Gestión de la calidad total: El modelo EFQM de excelencia. *Medifam, 12*(10), 41–54. doi:10.4321/S1131-57682002001000004

Madu, C. N., & Kuei, C. H. (1993). Introducing strategic quality management. *Long Range Planning, 26*(6), 121–131. doi:10.1016/0024-6301(93)90214-Z

Makgosa, R., & Mohube, K. (2007). *Peer influence on young adults' products purchase decisions.* Academic Press.

Malhotra, N. K. (2008). *Investigación de mercados: un enfoque aplicado.* Prentice-Hall Hispanoamericana.

Mamiseishvili, K. (2012). International student persistence in U.S. postsecondary institutions. *Higher Education, 64*(1), 1–17. doi:10.100710734-011-9477-0

Mangleburg, T. F., Doney, P. M., & Bristol, T. (2004). Shopping with friends and teens' susceptibility to peer influence. *Journal of Retailing*, *80*(2), 101–116. doi:10.1016/j.jretai.2004.04.005

Mangstl, A. (2008). Emerging Issues, Priorities, and Commitments in e-agriculture. *Agricultural Information Worldwide*, *1*(1), 5–6.

Marketing Science Institute (MSI). (2006). *Research Priorities - A Guide to MSI research programmes and procedures 2006-2008*. Cambridge, MA: Marketing Science Institute.

Marr, B. (2012). Key Performance Indicators (KPI): The 75 measures every manager needs to know. Pearson UK.

Marsh, R. (2005). Drowning in dirty data? It's time to sink or swim: A four-stage methodology for total data quality management. *Journal of Database Marketing & Customer Strategy Management*, *12*(2), 105–112. doi:10.1057/palgrave.dbm.3240247

Martin, C. A., & Bush, A. J. (2000). Do role models influence teenagers' purchase intentions and behavior? *Journal of Consumer Marketing*, *17*(5), 441–453. Advance online publication. doi:10.1108/07363760010341081

Martínez Martínez, A. (2019). *El paradigma AIRBNB: cambios estructurales en el sector turístico con relación a la economia colaborativa* (B.Sc. Dissertation). Palma de Mallorca, Spain: Universidad de las Islas Baleares.

Martínez-Polo, J., & Navarro-Beltrá, M. (2020). Estudio bibliométrico sobre reputación digital y economía colaborativa (2004-2017). *Revista de Comunicación de la SEECI*, *51*, 83–107. doi:10.15198eeci.2020.51.83-107

Martin, R. D. (2013). Audit quality indicators: Audit practice meets audit research. *Current Issues in Auditing*, *7*(2), A17–A23. doi:10.2308/ciia-50581

Masayna, V., Koronios, A., Gao, J., & Gendron, M. (2007, June). Data quality and KPIs: a link to be established. In *The 2nd World Congress on Engineering Asset Management (EAM) and The 4th International Conference on Condition Monitoring* (pp. 1377-1386). Academic Press.

Masoud, E. Y. (2013). The Effect of Perceived Risk on Online Shopping in Jordan. *European Journal of Business and Management*, 13.

Mättö, T. (2019). Innovation through the implementation of a quality improvement method. *The TQM Journal*, *31*(6), 987–1002. doi:10.1108/TQM-12-2018-0193

Mauri, A. G., Minazzi, R., & Muccio, S. (2013). A Review of Literature on the Gaps Model on Service Quality: A 3-Decades Period: 1985–2013. *International Business Research*, *6*(12). Advance online publication. doi:10.5539/ibr.v6n12p134

Maxham Iii, J. G. (2001). Service recovery's influence on consumer satisfaction, positive word-of-mouth, and purchase intentions. *Journal of Business Research*, *54*(1), 11–24. doi:10.1016/S0148-2963(00)00114-4

Mazur, G. (2003, May). Voice of the customer (define): QFD to define value. In *Proceedings of the 57th American Quality Congress* (pp. 1-7). Academic Press.

Mazzarol, T., & Soutar, G. N. (2002). "Push-pull" factors influencing international student destination choice. *International Journal of Educational Management*, *16*(2), 82–90. doi:10.1108/09513540210418403

McClusky, R. (2000). The rise, fall, and revival of Six Sigma. *Measuring Business Excellence*, *4*(2), 6–17.

McGrath, R. G., Macmillan, I. C., Ai-Yuan Yang, E., & Tsai, W. (1992). Does culture endure or is it malleable? *Journal of Business Venturing*, *7*(6), 441–458. doi:10.1016/0883-9026(92)90019-N

Mejia, A. (2016). *La evaluación del idioma inglés en el Ecuador*. Retrieved from http://repositorio.uasb.edu.ec/bitstream/10644/5457/1/T2168-MINE-Mejia-La evaluacion.pdf

Méndez-Picazo, M. T., Galindo-Martín, M. A., & Ribeiro-Soriano, D. (2012). Governance, entrepreneurship and economic growth. *Entrepreneurship and Regional Development*, *24*(9-10), 865–877. doi:10.1080/08985626.2012.742323

Merton, R. C., & Bodie, Z. (1995). A conceptual framework for analyzing the financial system. *The global financial system: A functional perspective*, 3-31.

Michalska, J., & Szewieczek, D. (2007). The 5S methodology as a tool for improving the organization. *Journal of Achievements in Materials and Manufacturing Engineering*, *24*(2), 211–214.

Mikušová, M., & Janečková, V. (2010). Developing and implementing successful key performance indicators. *World Academy of Science, Engineering and Technology*, *42*, 969–981.

Ministerio de Agricultura, Ganadería, Acuacultura, Ganadería, Acuacultura y Pesca (2016). *La política agropecuaria ecuatoriana: hacia el desarrollo territorial rural sostenible: 2015-2025 II Parte*. Quito, Ecuador: Author.

Ministerio de Ambiente y Desarrollo Sostenible. (n.d.). *Planes de Ordenación y Manejo de Cuencas Hidrográficas (POMCA)*. Ministry of Environment and Sustainable Development.

Ministerio de las Tecnologías de la Información y las Comunicaciones. (2012). Ley Estratutaria 1581. Retrieved from: http://www.secretariasenado.gov.co/senado/basedoc/ley_1581_2012.html

Ministerio de Protección Social. (2011). *Código Sustantivo del Trabajo*. Retrieved from: https://www.ilo.org/dyn/travail/docs/1539/CodigoSustantivodelTrabajoColombia.pdf

Ministerio de Telecomunicaciones y de la Sociedad de la Información. (2014). *Penetración de Banda Ancha incide directamente en crecimiento del PIB*. Author.

Ministerio de Telecomunicaciones y de la Sociedad de la Información. (2015). Plan Nacional de Telecomunicaciones y Tecnologías de Información del Ecuador 2016-2021. Quito, Ecuador: Author.

Ministerio de Telecomunicaciones y de la Sociedad de la Información. (2017). *MINTEL inauguró los Infocentros de Joyagshí y Alausí*. Author.

Ministerio del Trabajo. (2016). *Decreto Unico Reglamentario 1072*. Retrieved from: https://www.mintrabajo.gov.co/documents/20147/0/DUR+Sector+Trabajo+Actualizado+a+15+de+abril++de+2016.pdf/a32b1dcf-7a4e-8a37-ac16-c121928719c8

Ministerio del Trabajo. (n.d.). *Sistema de Gestión de Seguridad y Salud en el Trabajo*. Retrieved from: https://www.mintrabajo.gov.co/relaciones-laborales/riesgos-laborales/sistema-de-gestion-de-seguridad-y-salud-en-el-trabajo

Mintzberg, H. (1987). The Strategy Concept I: Five Ps for Strategy. *California Management Review*, *30*(1), 11–24. doi:10.2307/41165263

Mittal, V., & Frennea, C. (2010). *Customer Satisfaction A Strategic Review and Guidelines for Managers*. The Marketing Science Institute.

Mittelmark, M. B., Kickbusch, I., Rootman, I., Scriven, A., & Tones, K. (2017). *Health Promotion. In International Encyclopedia of Public Health*. Elsevier Inc.

Modgil, S., & Sharma, S. (2016). Total productive maintenance, total quality management and operational performance: An empirical study of the Indian pharmaceutical industry. *Journal of Quality in Maintenance Engineering*, *22*(4), 353–377. doi:10.1108/JQME-10-2015-0048

Mokhlis, S. (2009). An Investigation of Consumer Decision-Making Styles of Young-Adults in Malaysia. *International Journal of Business and Management*, *4*(4), 140–148. doi:10.5539/ijbm.v4n4p140

Montgomery, D. C., & Borror, C. M. (2017). Systems for modern quality and business improvement. *Quality Technology & Quantitative Management*, *14*(4), 343–352. doi:10.1080/16843703.2017.1304032

Moon, S. J., Yuh, Y., & Hanna, S. D. (2002). Financial ratio analysis of Korean households. *Family and Consumer Sciences Research Journal*, *30*(4), 496–525. doi:10.1177/1077727X02030004004

Moore, J. N., Hopkins, C. D., & Raymond, M. A. (2013). Utilization of relationship-oriented social Media in the Selling Process: A comparison of consumer (B2C) and industrial (B2B) salespeople. *Journal of Internet Commerce*, *12*(1), 48–75. doi:10.1080/15332861.2013.763694

Mueller, S. L., & Thomas, A. S. (2000). Culture and entrepreneurial potential: A nine country study of locus of control and innovativeness. *Journal of Business Venturing*, *16*(1), 51–75. doi:10.1016/S0883-9026(99)00039-7

Munro, R. A., Ramu, G., & Zrymiak, D. J. (2015). *The certified Six Sigma green belt handbook*. ASQ Quality Press.

Muralidharan, K. (2015). Six Sigma for organizational excellence. *Springer Proceedings of the Institution of Mechanical Engineers, 203*, 43-50.

Mustafi, M. A., Islam, M., & Islam, M. J. (2015). Patients' Satisfaction in Healthcare Services: A Comparative Analysis on Public and Private Hospitals in Bangladesh. *Scholar Journal of Business and Social Science*, *1*(1), 14–24.

Naidu, A. (2009). Factors affecting patient satisfaction and healthcare quality. *International Journal of Health Care Quality Assurance*, *22*(4), 366–381. doi:10.1108/09526860910964834 PMID:19725209

Nalebuff, B., & Brandenburger, A. (2002). *Co-opetition*. Academic Press.

Nandan, S. (2005). *An exploration of the brand identity–brand image linkage: A communications perspective*. Academic Press.

Nanda, V. (2016). *Quality management system handbook for product development companies*. CRC Press.

Nepomuceno, M. V., Laroche, M., & Richard, M.-O. (2014). How to reduce perceived risk when buying online: The interactions between intangibility, product knowledge, brand familiarity, privacy and security concerns. *Journal of Retailing and Consumer Services*, *21*(4), 619–629. doi:10.1016/j.jretconser.2013.11.006

Neti, S. (2011). Social media and its role in marketing. *International Journal of Enterprise Computing and Business Systems*, *1*, 1–15.

Ng, E. S. W., Schweitzer, L., & Lyons, S. T. (2010). New Generation, Great Expectations: A Field Study of the Millennial Generation. *Journal of Business and Psychology*, *25*(2), 281–292. doi:10.100710869-010-9159-4

Nickerson, C. (2005). English as a lingua franca in international business contexts. *English for Specific Purposes*, *24*(4), 367–380. doi:10.1016/j.esp.2005.02.001

Nielsen. (2016). *Dinero Movil*. Santiago de Chile: Nielsen.

Nissan, E., Galindo Martín, M. A., & Méndez Picazo, M. T. (2011). Relationship between organizations, institutions, entrepreneurship and economic growth process. *The International Entrepreneurship and Management Journal*, *7*(3), 311–324. doi:10.100711365-011-0191-2

Noguera, M., Alvarez, C., & Urbano, D. (2013). Socio-cultural factors and female entrepreneurship. *The International Entrepreneurship and Management Journal*, *9*(2), 183–197. doi:10.100711365-013-0251-x

North, D. C. (1990). *Institutions, institutional change and economic performance*. Cambridge University Press. doi:10.1017/CBO9780511808678

North, D. C. (2005). *Understanding the process of economic change*. Princeton University Press. doi:10.1515/9781400829484

Nowiński, W., & Haddoud, M. Y. (2019). The role of inspiring role models in enhancing entrepreneurial intention. *Journal of Business Research*, *96*, 183–193. doi:10.1016/j.jbusres.2018.11.005

Oakland, J. S. (2014). *Total quality management and operational excellence: text with cases*. Routledge. doi:10.4324/9781315815725

Ohene-Djan, J. (2008). *Electronic commerce*. University of London.

Olalla, B. (2011). Costes asociados a la Calidad en los Servicios de Tecnologías de la Información. Congreso Académico itSMF España.

Olalla, B., San José, C., & Mata, M. (2012). Factor humano: un elemento clave en la búsqueda de la eficiencia de los proyectos. In *VII Congreso Nacional VISION12*. Madrid: itSMF Spain.

Olalla, B., & Mata, M. (2012). *Little Big Data*. ITSMF Service Talk.

Olalla, B., & Mata, M. (2016). Value Creation in a Network Economy. In J. M. Saiz-Alvarez (Ed.), *Handbook of Research on Social Entrepreneurship and Solidarity Economics* (pp. 93–110). IGI Global. doi:10.4018/978-1-5225-0097-1.ch006

Olivieri, J. (2010). *Comercialización*. Universidad de Belgrano.

Oliya, E., Saleh Owlia, M., Dehdashti Shahrokh, Z., & Olfat, L. (2012). Improving marketing process using Six Sigma techniques (case of Saman Bank). *International Journal of Lean Six Sigma*, *3*(1), 59–73. doi:10.1108/20401461211223731

Ormiston, J., & Seymour, R. (2011). Understanding value creation in social entrepreneurship: The importance of aligning mission, strategy and impact measurement. *Journal of Social Entrepreneurship*, *2*(2), 125–150. doi:10.1080/19420676.2011.606331

Ospina, L., Cifuentes, D., Gaitán, L., & Londoño-Cardozo, J. (2019). La RSO y la Economía Colaborativa: fundamentos para su análisis | The RSO and the collaborative Economy: foundations for its analysis. *Revista Argentina de Investigación y Negocios*, *5*(1), 13–25.

Osterwalder, A., Viki, T., & Pigneur, Y. (2019). Why Your Organization Needs an Innovation Ecosystem. *Harvard Business Review*. Retrieved from https://hbr.org/

Paap, J., & Katz, R. (2004). Anticipating disruptive innovation. *Research Technology Management*, *47*(5), 13–22. doi:10.1080/08956308.2004.11671647

Pahnke, A., & Welter, F. (2019). The German Mittelstand: Antithesis to Silicon Valley entrepreneurship? *Small Business Economics*, *52*(2), 345–358. doi:10.100711187-018-0095-4

Parasuraman, A., Zeithaml, V. A., & Berry, L. L. (1988). Servqual: A multiple-item scale for measuring consumer perc. *Journal of Retailing*, *64*(1), 12–40.

Parasuraman, A., Zeithaml, V. A., & Berry, L. L. (1988). SERVQUAL: A Multiple-Item Scale for Measuring Consumer Perceptions of Service Quality. *Journal of Retailing*, *64*(1), 12–40. doi:10.1016/S0148-2963(99)00084-3

Parasuraman, A., Zeithhaml, V. A., & Berry, L. L. (1988). SERVQUAL: A multiple-item scale for measuring consumer perceptions of service quality. *Journal of Retailing*, *64*(1), 12–40.

Pardo, A. (1984). *Third-world Lecture 1984-Ocean Space and Mankind*. Carfax.

Park, I., Sharman, R., & Rao, H. R. (2015). Disaster Experience and Hospital Information Systems: An Examination of Perceived Information Assurance, Risk, Resilience, and HIS Usefulness. *Management Information Systems Quarterly, 39*(2), 317–344. doi:10.25300/MISQ/2015/39.2.03

Patel, P. C. (2019). Opportunity related absorptive capacity and entrepreneurial alertness. *The International Entrepreneurship and Management Journal, 15*(1), 63–73. doi:10.100711365-018-0543-2

Patidar, L., Soni, V. K., & Soni, P. K. (2016). Continuous improvement philosophy for manufacturing productivity: A critical review. *Trends in Industrial and Mechanical Engineering, 30*, 34–45.

Paul, J., & Rana, J. (2012). Consumer behavior and purchase intention for organic food. *Journal of Consumer Marketing, 29*(6), 11. doi:10.1108/07363761211259223

Pavletić, D., Soković, M., & Paliska, M. S. G. (2008, January). Practical application of quality tools. *2nd International Quality Conference.*

Pearce, D., Markandya, A., & Barbier, E. (2013). *Blueprint 1: for a green economy.* Routledge. doi:10.4324/9781315070223

Perea y Monsuwé, T., Dellaert, B. G. C., & de Ruyter, K. (2004). What drives consumers to shop online? A literature review. *International Journal of Service Industry Management, 15*(1), 102–121. doi:10.1108/09564230410523358

Pérez-Uribe, R. (2018). *Gerencia estratégica corporativa.* Ecoe Ediciones.

Pérez-Uribe, R., Ocampo-Guzman, D., Ospina, J., Cifuentes, J., & Cubillos, C. (2016). *MIIGO Modelo de intervención e innovación para el direccionamiento estratégico.* Ediciones EAN. doi:10.21158/9789587564143

Peris-Ortiz, M., Álvarez-García, J., & Rueda-Armengot, C. (Eds.). (2015). Achieving competitive advantage through quality management. Cham, Switzerland: Springer.

Petrick, J. (2017). *Total quality in managing human resources.* Routledge. doi:10.1201/9780203735534

Phillips, A. (2003). *Healthcare Management Dictionary.* Radcliffe Medical Press.

Piperopoulos, P., & Dimov, D. (2015). Burst bubbles or builds steam? Entrepreneurship education, entrepreneurial self-efficacy, and entrepreneurial intentions. *Journal of Small Business Management, 53*(4), 970–985. doi:10.1111/jsbm.12116

Pitt, L. F., Watson, R. T., & Kavan, C. B. (1995). Service quality: A measure of information systems effectiveness. *Management Information Systems Quarterly, 19*(2), 173–187. doi:10.2307/249687

Pizzutti dos Santos, C., & Basso, K. (2012). Do ongoing relationships buffer the effects of service recovery on customers' trust and loyalty? *International Journal of Bank Marketing, 30*(3), 168–192. doi:10.1108/02652321211222540

Plaza-Angulo, J. (2019). La nueva organización empresarial: Capitalismo, digitalización y economía colaborativa. *Revista Internacional y Comparada de Relaciones Laborales y Derecho del Empleo, 7*(4), 353–384.

Popp, D., Hafner, T., & Johnstone, N. (2007). Policy vs. consumer pressure: Innovation and diffusion of alternative bleaching technologies in the pulp industry (No. w13439). National Bureau of Economic Research.

Porche, I., Wilson, B., Johnson, E., Tierney, S., & Saltzman, E. (2014). Big Data: Challenges and Opportunities. In Data Flood: Helping the Navy Address the Rising Tide of Sensor Information (pp. 1-6). RAND Corporation.

Powell, T. C. (1995). Total quality management as competitive advantage: A review and empirical study. *Strategic Management Journal, 16*(1), 15–37. doi:10.1002mj.4250160105

Prakash, B. (2010). Patient Satisfaction. *Journal of Cutaneous and Aesthetic Surgery, 3*(3), 151–155. doi:10.4103/0974-2077.74491 PMID:21430827

Preciado-Hoyos, A. (2020). Marco propositivo de relaciones entre innovación colaborativa abierta y comunicación estratégica: Aplicación a un grupo de empresas de origen antioqueño. *Palabra Clave (La Plata), 23*(2), e2326.

Prendergast, G., Ho, B., & Phau, I. (2002). A Hong Kong view of offensive advertising. *Journal of Marketing Communications, 8*(3), 165–177. doi:10.1080/13527260210147342

Priskin, J. (2003). Tourist perceptions of degradation caused by coastal nature-based recreation. *Environmental Management, 32*(2), 189–204. doi:10.100700267-002-2916-z

Przeworski, A., & Limongi, F. (1993). Political regimes and economic growth. *The Journal of Economic Perspectives, 7*(3), 51–69. doi:10.1257/jep.7.3.51

Psomas, E., Vouzas, F., Bouranta, N., & Tasiou, M. (2017). Effects of total quality management in local authorities. *International Journal of Quality and Service Sciences, 9*(1), 41–66. doi:10.1108/IJQSS-04-2016-0035

Psomas, E., Vouzas, F., & Kafetzopoulos, D. (2014). Quality management benefits through the "soft" and "hard" aspect of TQM in food companies. *The TQM Journal, 26*(5), 431–444. doi:10.1108/TQM-02-2013-0017

Ragin, C. C. (2008). *User's guide to fuzzy-set/qualitative comparative analysis.* Available at: http://www.u.arizona.edu/~cragin/fsQCA/download/fsQCAManual.pdf

Ragin, C. C. (1987). *The comparative method: Moving beyond qualitative and quantitative methods.* University of California.

Ragin, C. C. (2006). Set relations in social research: Evaluating their consistency and coverage. *Political Analysis, 14*(3), 291–310. doi:10.1093/pan/mpj019

Ragin, C. C., & Sonnett, J. (2005). Between complexity and parsimony: Limited diversity, counterfactual cases, and comparative analysis. In *Vergleichen in der Politikwissenschaft* (pp. 180–197). VS Verlag für Sozialwissenschaften. doi:10.1007/978-3-322-80441-9_9

Raja Sreedharan, V., Raju, R., & Srivatsa Srinivas, S. (2017). A review of the quality evolution in various organisations. *Total Quality Management & Business Excellence, 28*(3-4), 351–365. doi:10.1080/14783363.2015.1082421

Ralston, P. M., Blackhurst, J., Cantor, D. E., & Crum, M. R. (2015). A structure–conduct–performance perspective of how strategic supply chain integration affects firm performance. *The Journal of Supply Chain Management, 51*(2), 47–64. doi:10.1111/jscm.12064

Ramayah, T., & Ignatius, J. (2005). Impact of perceived usefulness, perceived ease of use and perceived enjoyment on intention to shop online. *ICFAI Journal of Systems Management, 3*(3), 36–51.

Ramos, V. (2002). Modelos multidimensionales para la medición del valor de marca. *Investigaciones Europeas de Dirección y Economía de la Empresa, 8*(3), 13–44.

Ramsaran, R. R. (2005). Identifying Health Care Quality Attributes. *Journal of Health and Human Services Administration, 27*(4), 428–443. PMID:16318013

Ramus, C. A., & Steger, U. (2000). The roles of supervisory support behaviors and environmental policy in employee "Ecoinitiatives" at leading-edge European companies. *Academy of Management Journal, 43*(4), 605–626.

Randall, D. M., & Fernandes, M. F. (2013). The social desirability response bias in ethics research. In *Citation classics from the Journal of Business Ethics* (pp. 173–190). Springer. doi:10.1007/978-94-007-4126-3_9

Rauch, A., & Frese, M. (2007). Let's put the person back into entrepreneurship research: A meta-analysis on the relationship between business owners' personality traits, business creation, and success. *European Journal of Work and Organizational Psychology, 16*(4), 353–385. doi:10.1080/13594320701595438

Redman, T. C. (1998). The impact of poor data quality on the typical enterprise. *Communications of the ACM, 41*(2), 79–82. doi:10.1145/269012.269025

Ren, J. (2017). Modelling quality dynamics, business value and firm performance in a big data analytics environment. *International Journal of Production Research, 55*(17), 5011–5026. doi:10.1080/00207543.2016.1154209

Renny, G., Guritno, S., & Siringoringo, H. (2013). Perceived Usefulness, Ease of Use, and Attitude Towards Online Shopping Usefulness Towards Online Airlines Ticket Purchase. *Procedia: Social and Behavioral Sciences, 81*, 212–216. doi:10.1016/j.sbspro.2013.06.415

Revell, A., & Blackburn, R. (2007). The business case for sustainability? An examination of small firms in the UK's construction and restaurant sectors. *Business Strategy and the Environment, 16*(6), 404–420. doi:10.1002/bse.499

Reynolds, P. D. (2007). New firm creation in the United States a PSED I overview. *Foundations and Trends in Entrepreneurship, 3*(1), 1–150. doi:10.1561/0300000010

Ricart, J. E. (2009). *Business Model: The Missing Link in Strategic Management*. Universia Business Review.

Richardson, M. (2018). *Identification and analysis of marketing manager competencies that determine marketing department capabilities and the underlying importance of courage traits* (Ph.D. Dissertation). Aston University.

Richins, M. L. (1994). Valuing Things: The Public and Private Meanings of Possessions. *The Journal of Consumer Research, 21*(3), 504–521. doi:10.1086/209414

Richmond, J. (2018). *What Does Modern Leadership Really Mean?* Retrieved from https://www.business.com/articles/leadership-styles-millennials/

Ritala, P., Olander, H., Michailova, S., & Husted, K. (2015). Knowledge sharing, knowledge leaking and relative innovation performance: An empirical study. *Technovation, 35*, 22–31. doi:10.1016/j.technovation.2014.07.011

Riviezzo, A., Santos, S. C., Liñán, F., Napolitano, M. R., & Fusco, F. (2019). European universities seeking entrepreneurial paths: The moderating effect of contextual variables on the entrepreneurial orientation-performance relationship. *Technological Forecasting and Social Change, 141*, 232–248. doi:10.1016/j.techfore.2018.10.011

Rodríguez, D., Cruz, C., & Lam, F. (2009). *Logística para la exportación de productos agrícolas, frescos y procesados*. IICA.

Rodríguez, M. (2019). El impacto y los efectos de la economía colaborativa y de plataformas en el empleo del sector turístico, *RIDETUR. Revista Internacional de Derecho del Turismo, 3*(1), 3–15. doi:10.21071/ridetur.v3i.12132

Rodríguez, R., & Pérez, M. (2017). Modelos de negocio en la economía colaborativa: Síntesis y sugerencias. *Market Economics and Business Journal., 48*(2), 255–274.

Rodrik, D. (2005). Growth strategies. In P. Aghion & S. Durlauf (Eds.), *Handbook of Economic Growth* (Vol. 1, pp. 967–1014). Elsevier.

Rojas, A. (n.d.). *Tendencias en Aplicaciones Móviles para Pymes*. IT Now.

Romero, M., & Ribadeneria, T. (2010). El comercio electrónico en Ecuador: Régimen jurídico y comentarios. *Iuris Dictio, 1*(2), 108–114.

Roodman, D. (2011). Fitting Fully Observed recursive Mixed-process Models with CMP. *The Stata Journal, 11*(2), 159–206. doi:10.1177/1536867X1101100202

Rosano, A. (2018). *Access to Primary Care and Preventative Health Services of Migrants*. Springer. doi:10.1007/978-3-319-73630-3

Ross, J. E. (2017). *Total quality management: Text, cases, and readings*. Routledge. doi:10.1201/9780203735466

Ross, S. A., Westerfield, R. W., Jaffe, J. F., & Jordan, B. D. (2011). *Core principles and applications of corporate finance*. McGraw-Hill/Irwin.

Rugman, A. M., & D'Cruz, J. R. (1993). The "double diamond" model of international competitiveness: The Canadian experience. *MIR. Management International Review*, *34*, 17–39.

Ruíz, S. (2016). El Sector Agroalimentario y su competitividad a partir de modelos asociativos. *Ingeniería Industrial*, *37*(3), 323–332.

Rumelt, R. P., & Lamb, R. (1984). Competitive strategic management. *Toward a Strategic Theory of the Firm*, *26*(1), 556-570.

Rusu, C. (2016). From quality management to managing quality. *Procedia: Social and Behavioral Sciences*, *221*, 287–293. doi:10.1016/j.sbspro.2016.05.117

Ruzevicius, J., Adomaitiene, R., & Sirvidaite, J. (2004). Motivation and efficiency of quality management systems implementation: A study of Lithuanian organizations. *Total Quality Management & Business Excellence*, *15*(2), 173–189. doi:10.1080/1478336032000149018

Saavedra, Y. A. M., Avila, E. O., & Mendívil, B. C. (2020). Una Reflexión Crítica de los Sistemas De Gestión de Calidad: Ventajas y Desventajas. *Revista En-contexto*, *8*(12).

Saavedra, J. L., Colmenares, O., & Pirela, J. L. (2007). Correlación entre dimensiones de personalidad de marca y la marca emocional. Estudio en Cadena de Farmacias. *Revista de Ciencias Sociales*, *10*(2), 9–20. doi:10.1111/j.1532-5415.2012.04166.x

Sadikoglu, E., & Olcay, H. (2014). The effects of total quality management practices on performance and the reasons of and the barriers to TQM practices in Turkey. *Advances in Decision Sciences*, *2014*(2), 1–17. doi:10.1155/2014/537605

Sadikoglu, E., & Zehir, C. (2010). Investigating the effects of innovation and employee performance on the relationship between total quality management practices and firm performance: An empirical study of Turkish firms. *International Journal of Production Economics*, *127*(1), 13–26. doi:10.1016/j.ijpe.2010.02.013

Saiz-Alvarez, J. M. (2020). Quality Management Principles Application to Higher Educational Institutions. In *Quality Management Principles and Policies in Higher Education*. IGI Global; doi:10.4018/978-1-7998-1017-9.ch001

Saiz-Alvarez, J. M., & Olalla, B. (2010). Gestión del conocimiento y sistemas de Calidad en los clusters de empresas familiares. *EAN Journal*, *68*, 70–85.

Saiz-Alvarez, J. M., & Olalla, B. (2013). Modelo EFQM y creación de valor: Una aproximación teórica. *The Anáhuac Journal: Business and Economics*, *13*(1), 31–54.

Salguero, J., Muñoz-Cauqui, M. C., Batista, M., Calvino, A., Aguayo, F., & Marcos, M. (2015). R&D&I management system in distributed manufacturing systems. *Procedia Engineering*, *132*, 54–61. doi:10.1016/j.proeng.2015.12.479

Salo, J. (2017). Social media research in the industrial marketing ðeld: Review of literature and future research directions. *Industrial Marketing Management*, *66*(August), 115–129. doi:10.1016/j.indmarman.2017.07.013

Sam, M. F. M., & Tahir, N. H. (2009). *Website Quality And Consumer Online Purchase Intention Of Air Ticket*. Academic Press.

Samuels. (2017). *Advice on exploratory factor analysis.* Academic Press.

Samuelson, P. A., Nordhaus, W. D., Blanco Huitrón, C., & Doras Quiñones, A. (2010). *Microeconomía con aplicaciones a Latinoamérica.* McGrawHill.

Sánchez, J., & Moreno, Y. (2019). Desarrollo de la economía colaborativa en Ecuador, *Espirales: Revista Multidisciplinaria de Investigación Científica, 3*(29), 1.10.

Sánchez, A. (2006). Peter Drucker, innovador maestro de la administración de empresas. *Cuadernos Latinoamericanos de Administración, 2*(2), 69–89. doi:10.1039/C1DT11184A

Sánchez, M. F., & Castro, J. G. (2005). *Calidad total: modelo EFQM de excelencia.* FC Editorial.

Santana, C. (2014). *Cloud Computing y SaaS serán las estrellas en 2016.* Retrieved from: https://blog.acsendo.com/saas-y-cloud-computing-seran-las-estrellas-en-2016/

Satyanarayanan, M. (2017). The emergence of edge computing. *Computer, 50*(1), 30–39. doi:10.1109/MC.2017.9

Saunila, M. (2017). Understanding innovation performance measurement in SMEs. *Measuring Business Excellence, 21*(1), 1–16. doi:10.1108/MBE-01-2016-0005

Schillo, R. S., Persaud, A., & Jin, M. (2016). Entrepreneurial readiness in the context of national systems of entrepreneurship. *Small Business Economics, 46*(4), 619–637. doi:10.100711187-016-9709-x

Schlaegel, C., & Koenig, M. (2014). Determinants of entrepreneurial intent: A meta-analytic test and integration of competing models. *Entrepreneurship Theory and Practice, 38*(2), 291–332. doi:10.1111/etap.12087

Schmutzler, J., Andonova, V., & Diaz-Serrano, L. (2019). How context shapes entrepreneurial self-efficacy as a driver of entrepreneurial intentions: A multilevel approach. *Entrepreneurship Theory and Practice, 43*(5), 880–920. doi:10.1177/1042258717753142

Schroeder, R. G., Linderman, K., & Zhang, D. (2005). Evolution of quality: First fifty issues of production and operations management. *Production and Operations Management, 14*(4), 468–481. doi:10.1111/j.1937-5956.2005.tb00234.x

Schulz, R., & Johnson, A. C. (2003). Management of Hospitals and Health Services: Strategic Issues and Performance. Washington, DC: Academic Press.

Schumpeter, J. A. (1911). *The Theory of Economic Development: An Inquiry into Profits, Capital, Credit, Interest and Business Cycle.* Harvard University Press.

Schumpeter, J. A. (1950). *Capitalism, Socialism, and Democracy.* Harper & Brother Publishers.

Schumpeter, J. A. (1968). *The theory of economic development: An inquiry into profits, capital, credit, interest, and the business cycle.* Harvard Univ. Pr.

Schuster, M. A., McGlynn, E. A., & Brook, R. H. (1998). How good is the quality of health care in the United States? *The Milbank Quarterly, 76*(4), 517–563. doi:10.1111/1468-0009.00105 PMID:9879302

Secretaría Nacional de Planificación y Desarrollo. (2017). Plan Nacional de Desarrollo 2017-2021. Quito, Ecuador: Author.

Sequeira, J., Mueller, S. L., & Mcgee, J. E. (2007). The iñuence of social ties and self-efficacy in forming entrepreneurial intentions and motivating nascent behavior. *Journal of Developmental Entrepreneurship, 12*(3), 275–293. doi:10.1142/S108494670700068X

Shane, S. (1992). Why do some societies invent more than others? *Journal of Business Venturing, 7*(1), 29–46. doi:10.1016/0883-9026(92)90033-N

Shane, S. (2012). Reflections on the 2010 AMR decade award: Delivering on the promise of entrepreneurship as a field of research. *Academy of Management Review*, *37*(1), 10–20. doi:10.5465/amr.2011.0078

Shane, S., & Venkataraman, S. (2000). The Promise of Entrepreneurship as a Field of Research. *Academy of Management Review*, *25*(1), 217–226. doi:10.5465/amr.2000.2791611

Shapero, A. (1975). The displaced, uncomfortable entrepreneur. *Psychology Today*, *9*, 83–88.

Shapero, A., & Sokol, L. (1982). Social dimensions of entrepreneurship. In C. A. Kent, D. L. Sexton, & K. H. Vesper (Eds.), *Encyclopedia of Entrepreneurship* (pp. 72–90). Prentice-Hall.

Sharifi, M., Ayat, M., Ibrahim, S., & Sahibuddin, S. (2009). The most applicable KPIs of problem management process in organizations. *International Journal of Simulation: Systems. Science & Technology*, *10*(3), 77–83.

Shawyun, T. (1998). Quality Assurance and Strategic Implementation in educational institutions: A Holistic Alliance? *International Journal of Quality & Reliability Management*, *15*(1), 1–15.

Shook, C. L., Priem, R. L., & McGee, J. E. (2003). Venture creation and the enterprising individual: A review and synthesis. *Journal of Management*, *29*(3), 379–399. doi:10.1016/S0149-2063(03)00016-3

Short, J. C., Ketchen, D. J. Jr, Combs, J. G., & Ireland, R. D. (2010). Research methods in entrepreneurship opportunities and challenges. *Organizational Research Methods*, *13*(1), 6–15. doi:10.1177/1094428109342448

Short, J. C., Ketchen, D. J. Jr, Shook, C. L., & Ireland, R. D. (2009). The concept of "opportunity" in entrepreneurship research: Past accomplishments and future challenges. *Journal of Management*, *36*(1), 40–65. doi:10.1177/0149206309342746

Sichtmann, C., Davvetas, V., & Diamantopoulos, A. (2018, October 16). The relational value of perceived brand globalness and localness. *Journal of Business Research*. Advance online publication. doi:10.1016/j.jbusres.2018.10.025

Siemieniako, D. (2018). Bibliometric Analysis of Scientific Research on Customer Loyalty in the Business-to-Business Context. *Handel Wewnętrzny*, *5*(376), 13–23.

Silvi, R., Bartolini, M., Raffoni, A., & Visani, F. (2015). The practice of strategic performance measurement systems: Models, drivers and information effectiveness. *International Journal of Productivity and Performance Management*, *64*(2), 194–227. doi:10.1108/IJPPM-01-2014-0010

Simon, C. J., & Sullivan, M. W. (1993). The Measurement and Determinants of Brand Equity: A Financial Approach. *Marketing Science*, *12*(1), 28–52. doi:10.1287/mksc.12.1.28

Simón-Moya, V., Revuelto-Taboada, L., & Guerrero, R. F. (2014). Institutional and economic drivers of entrepreneurship: An international perspective. *Journal of Business Research*, *67*(5), 715–721. doi:10.1016/j.jbusres.2013.11.033

Simons, H. (2013). *Getting to know schools in a democracy: The politics and process of evaluation*. Routledge. doi:10.4324/9780203064528

Sirdeshmukh, D., Singh, J., & Sabol, B. (2002). Consumer Trust, Value, and Loyalty in Relational Exchanges. *Journal of Marketing*, *66*(1), 15–37. doi:10.1509/jmkg.66.1.15.18449

Sirowy, L., & Inkeles, A. (1990). The effects of democracy on economic growth and inequality: A review. *Studies in Comparative International Development*, *25*(1), 126–157. doi:10.1007/BF02716908

Sistema Nacional de Información. (2015). *Actualización del Plan de Desarrollo y Ordenamiento Territorial del Cantón Alausí*. Author.

Smith, R. (2008, July 8). The end of disease and the beginning of health. *Richard Smith: The end of disease and the beginning of health.* Accessed July 22, 2019 https://blogs.bmj.com/bmj/2008/07/08/richard-smith-the-end-of-disease-and-the-beginning-of-health/

Smith, S. L. (1994). The tourism product. *Annals of Tourism Research, 21*(3), 582–595. doi:10.1016/0160-7383(94)90121-X

Sokovic, M., Pavletic, D., & Pipan, K.K. (2010). Quality improvement methodologies–PDCA cycle, RADAR matrix, DMAIC, and DFSS. *Journal of Achievements in Materials and Manufacturing Engineering, 43*(1), 476-483.

Spencer, J. W., & Gomez, C. (2004). The relationship among national institutional structures, economic factors, and domestic entrepreneurial activity: A multi-country study. *Journal of Business Research, 57*(10), 1098–1107. doi:10.1016/S0148-2963(03)00040-7

Sproles, G. B., & Kendall, E. (1986). A methodology for profiling consumers' decision-making. *A Methodology for Profiling Consumers'. Decision-Making Styles, 2*(20), 267–279.

Steenkamp, J.-B. E. M., & de Jong, M. G. (2010). A Global Investigation into the Constellation of Consumer Attitudes Toward Global and Local Products. *Journal of Marketing, 74*(6), 18–40. doi:10.1509/jmkg.74.6.18

Stephan, U., & Uhlaner, L. M. (2010). Performance-based vs. socially supportive culture: A cross-national study of descriptive norms and entrepreneurship. *Journal of International Business Studies, 41*(8), 1347–1364. doi:10.1057/jibs.2010.14

Stevenson, H. H., Roberts, M. J., & Grousbeck, H. I. (1985). *New Business Ventures and the Entrepreneur.* Irwin.

Steyaert, C. (2007). Entrepreneuring' as a conceptual attractor? A review of process theories in 20 years of entrepreneurship studies. *Entrepreneurship and Regional Development, 19*(6), 453–477. doi:10.1080/08985620701671759

Stokburger-Sauer, N., Ratneshwar, S., & Sen, S. (2012). Drivers of consumer-brand identification. *International Journal of Research in Marketing, 29*(4), 406–418. doi:10.1016/j.ijresmar.2012.06.001

Stroke Unit Trialists' Collaboration. (2002). Organised inpatient (stroke unit) care for stroke. *Cochrane Database of Systematic Reviews, 1*, CD000197. PMID:11869570

Stuetzer, M., Obschonka, M., Brixy, U., Sternberg, R., & Cantner, U. (2014). Regional characteristics, opportunity perception and entrepreneurial activities. *Small Business Economics, 42*(2), 221–244. doi:10.100711187-013-9488-6

Sukarma, L., & Azmi, H. (2015). The measures of performance for world-class manufacturing practices: A critical review. *Applied Mechanics and Materials, 761*, 545–549. doi:10.4028/www.scientific.net/AMM.761.545

Sullivan, P., & Heitmeyer, J. (2008). Looking at Gen Y shopping preferences and intentions: Exploring the role of experience and apparel involvement. *International Journal of Consumer Studies, 32*(3), 285–295. doi:10.1111/j.1470-6431.2008.00680.x

Sundbo, J., Orfila-Sintes, F., & Sorensen, F. (2007). The innovative behaviour of tourism firms. Comparative studies of Denmark and Spain. *Research Policy Research Policy, 36*(1), 88–106. doi:10.1016/j.respol.2006.08.004

Sunder, M. V. (2016). Lean Six Sigma project management–a stakeholder management perspective. *The TQM Journal, 28*(1), 132–150. doi:10.1108/TQM-09-2014-0070

Sung, Y., & Tinkham, S. F. (2005). Brand personality structures in the United States and Korea: Common and culture-specific factors. *Journal of Consumer Psychology, 15*(4), 334–350. doi:10.120715327663jcp1504_8

Sun, X., & Ansari, N. (2016). EdgeIoT: Mobile edge computing for the Internet of Things. *IEEE Communications Magazine, 54*(12), 22–29. doi:10.1109/MCOM.2016.1600492CM

Superintendencia de Control de Poder de Mercado. (2017). Supertienda Ecuador, alternativa para comercializar los productos de la EPS (406). Quito, Ecuador: Author.

Surange, V. G. (2015). Implementation of Six Sigma to reduce cost of quality: A case study of automobile sector. *Journal of Failure Analysis and Prevention*, *15*(2), 282–294. doi:10.100711668-015-9927-6

Suwandej, N. (2015). Factors influencing total quality management. *Procedia: Social and Behavioral Sciences*, *197*, 2215–2222. doi:10.1016/j.sbspro.2015.07.361

Svalastog, A. L., Donev, D., Kristoffersen, N. J., & Gajović, S. (2017). Concepts and definitions of health and health-related values in the knowledge landscapes of the digital society. *Croatian Medical Journal*, *58*(6), 431–435. doi:10.3325/cmj.2017.58.431 PMID:29308835

Swani, K., Milne, G. R., Brown, B. P., Assaf, A. G., & Donthu, N. (2017). What messages to post? Evaluating the popularity of social media communications in business versus consumer markets. *Industrial Marketing Management*, *62*, 77–87. doi:10.1016/j.indmarman.2016.07.006

Swan, J. E., Richardson, L. D., & Hutton, J. D. (2003). Do appealing hospital rooms increase patient evaluations of physicians, nurses, and hospital services? *Journal of Management Review*, *28*(3), 254–264. PMID:12940347

Swanson, D. L., Esposito, R. A., & Jester, J. (1999). Managing Quality for Information Technology. *Quality Digest*, *19*, 43–45.

Swarnakar, V., & Vinodh, S. (2016). Deploying Lean Six Sigma framework in an automotive component manufacturing organization. *International Journal of Lean Six Sigma*, *7*(3), 267–293. doi:10.1108/IJLSS-06-2015-0023

Szerb, L., & Vörös, Z. (2019). The changing form of overconfidence and its effect on growth expectations at the early stages of startups. *Small Business Economics*. Advance online publication. doi:10.100711187-019-00297-9

Tasci, A. D. A. (2016). Consumer Value and Brand Value: Rivals or Allies in Consumer-Based Brand Equity? *Tourism Analysis*, *21*(5), 481–496. doi:10.3727/108354216X14653218477561

Tengilimoğlu, D., Işık, O., & Akbolat, M. (2015). *Sağlık İşletmelerinde Yönetim*. Nobel Yayıncılık.

Tennant, G. (2017). *Six Sigma: SPC and TQM in manufacturing and services*. Routledge. doi:10.4324/9781315243023

Thakur, R., & Workman, L. (2016). Customer portfolio management (CPM) for improved customer relationship management (CRM): Are your customers platinum, gold, silver, or bronze? *Journal of Business Research*, *69*(10), 4095–4102. doi:10.1016/j.jbusres.2016.03.042

Thomas, R. K. (2010). Marketing Health Services (2nd ed.). Health Administration Press.

Thompson, C. J., Rindleisch, A., & Arsel, Z. (2006). Emotional branding and the strategic value of the Doppelganger brand image. *Journal of Marketing*, *70*(1), 50–64. doi:10.1509/jmkg.70.1.050.qxd

Thornton, P. H., Ribeiro-Soriano, D., & Urbano, D. (2011). Socio-cultural factors and entrepreneurial activity: An overview. *International Small Business Journal*, *29*(2), 105–118. doi:10.1177/0266242610391930

Tigani, D. (2006). Excelencia Excelencia en Servicio. Liderazgo 21.

Tkalac Verčič, A., & Sinčić Ćorić, D. (2018). The relationship between reputation, employer branding and corporate social responsibility. *Public Relations Review*, *44*(4), 444–452. doi:10.1016/j.pubrev.2018.06.005

Tomes, A. E., & Chee Peng Ng, S. (1995). Service quality in hospital care: The development of an inpatient questionnaire. *International Journal of Health Care Quality Assurance*, *8*(3), 25–33. doi:10.1108/09526869510089255 PMID:10143994

Topalović, S. (2015). The implementation of total quality management in order to improve production performance and enhancing the level of customer satisfaction. *Procedia Technology*, *19*, 1016–1022. doi:10.1016/j.protcy.2015.02.145

Torrent-Sellens, J. (2019). ¿Economía colaborativa o economía de plataforma? Más allá de un debate inacabable. *Harvard Deusto Business Review*, *289*, 58–69.

Torres, P., & Augusto, M. (2019). Cultural configurations and entrepreneurial realisation. *International Journal of Entrepreneurial Behaviour & Research*, *25*(1), 112–128. doi:10.1108/IJEBR-12-2017-0525

Tran, M. D., Khairi, K. F., & Laili, N. H. (2019). A longitudinal study of audit quality differences among independent auditors. *Journal of Economic Development*, *21*(2), 234–246. doi:10.1108/JED-10-2019-0040

Triguero, A., Moreno-Mondéjar, L., & Davia, M. A. (2013). Drivers of different types of eco-innovation in European SMEs. *Ecological Economics*, *92*, 25–33. doi:10.1016/j.ecolecon.2013.04.009

Tsai, K. H., Chang, H. C., & Peng, C. Y. (2016). Refining the linkage between perceived capability and entrepreneurial intention: Roles of perceived opportunity, fear of failure, and gender. *The International Entrepreneurship and Management Journal*, *12*(4), 1127–1145. doi:10.100711365-016-0383-x

Tucker, J. L. (2002). The moderators of patient satisfaction. *Journal of Management in Medicine*, *16*(1), 48–66. doi:10.1108/02689230210428625 PMID:12069351

Uhl, A., & Gollenia, L. A. (Eds.). (2016). *A handbook of business transformation management methodology*. Routledge. doi:10.4324/9781315570631

Uluskan, M., Godfrey, A. B., & Joines, J. A. (2017). Integration of Six Sigma to traditional quality management theory: An empirical study on organisational performance. *Total Quality Management & Business Excellence*, *28*(13-14), 1526–1543. doi:10.1080/14783363.2016.1150173

Ungaretti, J. (2013). Adaptación del Consumer Style Inventory (CSI) al contexto argentino. *Revista de Investigación En Psicología Social*, *1*(1), 25–34.

Universidad de Cantabria. (2014). *Definición de Alternativas Estratégicas*. University of Cantabria. Retrieved from: https://web.unican.es/unidades/serviciopdiretribuciones/Gestionporprocesos/PDIPLA-03%20DEFINICI%C3%93N%20DE%20ALTERNATIVAS%20ESTRAT%C3%89GICAS.pdf

Upton, D. M. (1994). The management of manufacturing flexibility. *California Management Review*, *36*(2), 72–89. doi:10.2307/41165745

Urbano, D. (2006). *New business creation in Catalonia: Support measures and attitudes towards entrepreneurship*. CIDEM.

Urbano, D., & Alvarez, C. (2014). Institutional dimensions and entrepreneurial activity: An international study. *Small Business Economics*, *42*(4), 703–716. doi:10.100711187-013-9523-7

Urbano, D., & Aparicio, S. (2016). Entrepreneurship capital types and economic growth: International evidence. *Technological Forecasting and Social Change*, *102*, 34–44. doi:10.1016/j.techfore.2015.02.018

Urbano, D., Aparicio, S., & Audretsch, D. (2019). Twenty-five years of research on institutions, entrepreneurship, and economic growth: What has been learned? *Small Business Economics*, *53*(1), 21–49. doi:10.100711187-018-0038-0

Urbano, D., Aparicio, S., Guerrero, M., Noguera, M., & Torrent-Sellens, J. (2017). Institutional determinants of student employer entrepreneurs at Catalan universities. *Technological Forecasting and Social Change*, *123*, 271–282. doi:10.1016/j.techfore.2016.06.021

Urbano, D., Audretsch, D., Aparicio, S., & Noguera, M. (2019). (in press). Does entrepreneurial activity matter for economic growth in developing countries? The role of the institutional environment. *The International Entrepreneurship and Management Journal*. Advance online publication. doi:10.100711365-019-00621-5

Urbano, D., Toledano, N., & Ribeiro-Soriano, D. (2011). Socio-cultural factors and transnational entrepreneurship: A multiple case study in Spain. *International Small Business Journal*, *29*(2), 119–134. doi:10.1177/0266242610391934

Urbano, D., Turro, A., & Aparicio, S. (2019). (in press). Innovation through R&D activities in the European context: Antecedents and consequences. *The Journal of Technology Transfer*. Advance online publication. doi:10.100710961-019-09752-x

Valmohammadi, C., & Roshanzamir, S. (2015). The guidelines of improvement: Relations among organizational culture, TQM and performance. *International Journal of Production Economics*, *164*, 167–178. doi:10.1016/j.ijpe.2014.12.028

Van Gelderen, M., Kautonen, T., & Fink, M. (2015). From entrepreneurial intentions to actions: Self-control and action-related doubt, fear, and aversion. *Journal of Business Venturing*, *30*(5), 655–673. doi:10.1016/j.jbusvent.2015.01.003

Van Hoose, D. D. (2011). *E.commerce economics* (2nd ed.). Routledge.

Vazques, R., Roríguez, I., & Díaz, A. (1996). Estructura multimensional de la calidad de servicio en cadenas ve supermercdos: desarrollo y validación de la escala CALSUPER. In *Documentos de trabajo (Universidad de Oviedo. Facultad de Ciencias Económicas)* (Vol. 119). Retrieved from https://www.ncbi.nlm.nih.gov/pubmed/17295951

Velandia, J. H. M., & Pinilla, N. A. (2013). De la salud ocupacional a la gestión de la seguridad y salud en el trabajo: Más que semántica, una transformación del sistema general de riesgos laborales. *INNOVAR. Revista de Ciencias Administrativas y Sociales*, *23*(48), 21–31.

Venkataraman, S. (1997). The distinctive domain of entrepreneurship research: an editor's perspective. In J. Katz & R. Brockhaus (Eds.), *Advances in Entrepreneurship* (Vol. 3, pp. 119–138). Firm Emergence, and Growth.

Verbano, C., & Venturini, K. (2012). Technology transfer in the Italian space industry: Organizational issues and determinants. *Management Research Review*, *35*(3/4), 272–288. doi:10.1108/01409171211210163

Vergés, J. M. V., Tarrés, C. S., Obra, A. R. del Á., & Meléndez, A. P. (2001). La economía digital y su impacto en la empresa: Bases teóricas y situación en España. *Boletín económico de ICE. Información Comercial Española*, *2705*, 7–24.

Verheul, I., Block, J., Burmeister-Lamp, K., Thurik, R., Tiemeier, H., & Turturea, R. (2015). ADHD-like behavior and entrepreneurial intentions. *Small Business Economics*, *45*(1), 85–101. doi:10.100711187-015-9642-4

Vij, S., & Bedi, H. S. (2016). Are subjective business performance measures justified? *International Journal of Productivity and Performance Management*, *65*(5), 603–621. doi:10.1108/IJPPM-12-2014-0196

Villamil, A. M. (2017). *La Planeación Estratégica y la Gestión por Resultados* (B.Sc. Dissertation). Universidad Militar de Nueva Granada, Colombia. Retrieved from: https://repository.unimilitar.edu.co/bitstream/handle/10654/16974/TabordaVillamilAlvaroMiguel.pdf?sequence=3

Viscomi, C. (2017). *7 New Types of Leadership Models for Innovative Thinkers*. Retrieved from https://alistemarketing.com/blog/types-of-leadership-models/

Wahab, S., & Cooper, C. (2014). *Tourism in the age of globalisation*. Routledge.

Wan, C. D., & Weerasena, B. (2017). Shadow Education in Malaysia: Identifying the Determinants of Spending and Amount of Time Attending Private Supplementary Tutoring of Upper Secondary School Students. Journal of International and Comparative Education, 91–103. doi:10.14425/jice.2017.6.2.91

Weaver, B., & Maxwell, H. (2014). Exploratory factor analysis and reliability analysis with missing data: A simple method for SPSS users. *The Quantitative Methods for Psychology*, *10*(2), 143–152. doi:10.20982/tqmp.10.2.p143

Weinhardt, C., & Holtmann, C. (Eds.). (2002). *E-Commerce*. Physica-Verlag. doi:10.1007/978-3-642-57487-0

Wennekers, S., van Stel, A., Thurik, R., & Reynolds, P. (2005). Nascent entrepreneurship and the level of economic development. *Small Business Economics*, *24*(3), 293–309. doi:10.100711187-005-1994-8

Wheelen, T. L., & Hunger, J. D. (2013). *Administración Estratégica y Política de Negocios*. Pearson Educación de Colombia.

Whitehurst, J. (2016). Leaders Can Shape Company Culture Through Their Behaviors. *Harvard Business Review*. Retrieved from https://hbr.org/

Whiteley, R., & Hessan, D. (1996). *Customer centred growth: Five strategies for building competitive advantage*. Academic Press.

Wiersema, F. (2013). The B2B agenda: The current state of B2B marketing and a look ahead. *Industrial Marketing Management*, *42*(4), 470–488. doi:10.1016/j.indmarman.2013.02.015

Wiersema, M. F., & Bowen, H. P. (2009). The use of limited dependent variable techniques in strategy research: Issues and methods. *Strategic Management Journal*, *30*(6), 679–692. doi:10.1002mj.758

Williams, A. M., & Shaw, G. (2011). Internationalization and innovation in tourism. *Annals of Tourism Research*, *38*(1), 27–51. doi:10.1016/j.annals.2010.09.006

Wilson, F., Kickul, J., & Marlino, D. (2007). Gender, entrepreneurial self-efficacy, and entrepreneurial career intentions: Implications for entrepreneurship education. *Entrepreneurship Theory and Practice*, *31*(3), 387–406. doi:10.1111/j.1540-6520.2007.00179.x

Wilson, F., Marlino, D., & Kickul, J. (2004). Our entrepreneurial future: Examining the diverse attitudes and motivations of teens across gender and ethnic identity. *Journal of Developmental Entrepreneurship*, *9*(3), 177–197.

Wolfe, A. (1993). *Profit from strategic marketing: How to succeed in business markets*. Financial Times, Pitman Pub.

Womack, J. P., & Jones, D. T. (2003). *Lean Thinking: Banish Waste and Create Wealth in Your Corporation*. Free Press.

Wongrassamee, S., Simmons, J. E., & Gardiner, P. D. (2003). Performance measurement tools: The Balanced Scorecard and the EFQM Excellence Model. *Measuring Business Excellence*, *7*(1), 14–29. doi:10.1108/13683040310466690

Wood, R., & Bandura, A. (1989). Social cognitive theory of organizational management. *Academy of Management Review*, *14*(3), 361–384. doi:10.5465/amr.1989.4279067

Wood, R., Hull, F., & Azumi, K. (1983). Evaluating quality circles: *The American application. California Management Review*, *26*(1), 37–53. doi:10.2307/41165049

Woodside, A. G. (2013). Moving beyond multiple regression analysis to algorithms: Calling for adoption of a paradigm shift from symmetric to asymmetric thinking in data analysis and crafting theory. *Journal of Business Research*, *66*(4), 463–472. doi:10.1016/j.jbusres.2012.12.021

Woodside, A. G., Frey, L. L., & Daly, R. T. (1989). Linking service quality, customer satisfaction. *Journal of Health Care Marketing and Behavior Intention*, *9*(4), 5–17. PMID:10304174

World Bank. (2019). *World development indicators*. Available at http://datatopics.worldbank.org/world-development-indicators/

World Health Organisation (WHO). (1992). *Our Planet, Our Health: Report of the WHO Commission on Health and Environment*. World Health Organisation.

World Health Organization (WHO). (2006, October). *Constitution of The World Health Organisation.* Accessed July 22, 2019. https://www.who.int/governance/eb/who_constitution_en.pdf

World Health Organization (WHO). (2019). *World Health Organization.* https://www.who.int/healthinfo/systems/WHO_MBHSS_2010_section1_web.pdf

Worster, D. (1993). *The wealth of nature: environmental history and the ecological imagination.* Oxford University Press on Demand.

Wright. (2005). Researching Internet-based populations: Advantages and disadvantages of online survey research, online questionnaire authoring software packages, and web survey services. *Journal of Computer-Mediated Communication, 10*(3).

Wright, F., Filatotchev, I., Hoskisson, R. E., & Peng, M. W. (2005). Strategy research in emerging economies: Challenging the conventional wisdom. *Journal of Management Studies, 42*(1), 1–33. doi:10.1111/j.1467-6486.2005.00487.x

Wu, H. C., Ai, C. H., & Cheng, C. C. (2019). Experiential quality, experiential psychological states and experiential outcomes in an unmanned convenience store. *Journal of Retailing and Consumer Services, 51*, 409–420. doi:10.1016/j.jretconser.2019.07.003

Wu, P. C. S., Yeh, G. Y.-Y., & Hsiao, C.-R. (2011). The effect of store image and service quality on brand image and purchase intention for private label brands. *Australasian Marketing Journal, 19*(1), 30–39. doi:10.1016/j.ausmj.2010.11.001

Xie, G., Zhu, J., Lu, Q., & Xu, S. (2011). Influencing factors of consumer intention towards web group buying. *2011 IEEE International Conference on Industrial Engineering and Engineering Management*, 1397–1401. 10.1109/IEEM.2011.6118146

Yang, M. G. M., Hong, P., & Modi, S. B. (2011). Impact of lean manufacturing and environmental management on business performance: An empirical study of manufacturing firms. *International Journal of Production Economics, 129*(2), 251–261. doi:10.1016/j.ijpe.2010.10.017

Yu, C. J., Wu, L., Chiao, Y., & Tai, H. (2005). Perceived quality, customer satisfaction, and customer loyalty: The case of lexus in Taiwan. *Total Quality Management & Business Excellence, 16*(6), 707–719. doi:10.1080/14783360500077393

Zairi, M. (1997). Business process management: A boundaryless approach to modern competitiveness. *Business Process Management Journal, 3*(1), 64–80. doi:10.1108/14637159710161585

Zameer, H., Wang, Y., & Yasmeen, H. (2020). Reinforcing green competitive advantage through green production, creativity and green brand image: Implications for cleaner production in China. *Journal of Cleaner Production, 247*, 119119. doi:10.1016/j.jclepro.2019.119119

Zangwill, W. I., & Kantor, P. B. (1998). Toward a theory of continuous improvement and the learning curve. *Management Science, 44*(7), 910–920. doi:10.1287/mnsc.44.7.910

Zeithaml, V., & Bitner, M. (2000). *Services Marketing: Integrating Customer Focus across the Firm.* McGraw-Hill.

Zeng, J., Phan, C. A., & Matsui, Y. (2015). The impact of hard and soft quality management on quality and innovation performance: An empirical study. *International Journal of Production Economics, 162*, 216–226. doi:10.1016/j.ijpe.2014.07.006

Zhang, W. (2014). The demand for shadow education in China: Mainstream teachers and power relations. *Asia Pacific Journal of Education, 34*(4), 436–454. doi:10.1080/02188791.2014.960798

Zhang, Y. (2013). Does private tutoring improve students' National College Entrance Exam performance?—A case study from Jinan, China. *Economics of Education Review*, *32*, 1–28. doi:10.1016/j.econedurev.2012.09.008

Zhao, F., & Bryar, P. (2001, April). Integrating knowledge management and total quality: A complementary process. *6th International Conference on ISO, 9000, 17-19.*

Zhao, H., Seibert, S. E., & Hills, G. E. (2005). The mediating role of self-efficacy in the development of entrepreneurial intentions. *The Journal of Applied Psychology*, *90*(6), 1265–1272. doi:10.1037/0021-9010.90.6.1265 PMID:16316279

Zhao, L., & Guo, S. (2012). The Value Creation of B2B2C E-Business Mode based on SaaS. *Journal of Electronic Commerce in Organizations*, *10*(3), 1–12. doi:10.4018/jeco.2012070101

Zhou, R., Hentschel, J., & Kumar, N. (2017). *Goodbye text, hello emoji: Mobile communication on wechat in China.* ACM. doi:10.1145/3025453.3025800

Zhu, Z., Wang, J., Wang, X., & Wan, X. (2016, August 9). *Exploring factors of users peer-influence behavior in social media on purchase intention: Evidence from QQ.* Retrieved November 16, 2019, from Computers in Human Behavior website: https://eurekamag.com/research/064/849/064849121.php

Ziglio, E., Currie, C., & Rasmussen, V. B. (2004). The WHO cross-national study of health behavior in school-aged children from 35 countries: Findings from 2001-2002. *The Journal of School Health*, *76*, 204–206. PMID:15468523

Zortea-Johnston, E., Darroch, J., & Matear, S. (2012). Business orientations and innovation in small and medium-sized enterprises. *The International Entrepreneurship and Management Journal*, *8*(2), 145–164. doi:10.100711365-011-0170-7

About the Contributors

José Manuel Saiz-Alvarez has a Ph.D. in Economic and Business Sciences, Universidad Autónoma de Madrid, Spain. Ph.D. in Political Sciences and Sociology, Universidad Pontificia de Salamanca, Spain. Visiting professor, Universidad Católica de Santiago de Guayaquil, Ecuador, and Universidad Autónoma de Manizales, Colombia. International researcher, CEIEF-Universidad de Santiago de Chile. Officially accredited in Spain by ANECA. Regular member, Mexican Academy of Sciences and Accademia Tiberina già Pontificia, Italy. GEM Jalisco member and Business Controller accredited by the College of Economists of Madrid, Spain. He was a research professor, Tecnológico de Monterrey, Mexico, and member of the National System of Researchers of Mexico. Director for BA Doctoral Studies, Universidad Nebrija, Spain. Professor, Universidad Pontificia de Salamanca, Spain, and Universidad Alfonso X El Sabio, Spain. Academic leader, Tecnológico de Monterrey, Mexico. Diploma of Recognition, The House of Representatives from the Capitol of Puerto Rico. Honor Diploma, Universitatea Valahia din Targoviste, Romania. Honorary Professor, Universidad Autónoma de Madrid, Spain. Who's Who in the World since 2011.

* * *

María Teresa Alcívar-Avilés has a B.Sc. in Economics, University of Guayaquil, Ecuador. Specialization in International Negotiations, The Catholic University of Santiago de Guayaquil, Ecuador. M.Sc. in Territorial Development and Business Creation, Complutense University of Madrid, Spain. She has a Ph. D. in Business Sciences from Nebrija University, Spain. She is a lecturer and the director of the M.Sc.in Finance and Business Economics and the M.Sc. in International Business, Catholic University of Santiago de Guayaquil, Ecuador.

Sebastian Aparicio is an Assistant Professor in Entrepreneurship at Durham University Business School. In addition, He is affiliated as a Research Fellow in the Centre for University Entrepreneurship (CIEU-UAB–); as a Research Fellow at the Centre for Entrepreneurship and Social Innovation Research (CREIS) at Universitat Autònoma de Barcelona (UAB); as a Junior Research Fellow in the Institute for Development Strategies at the School of Public and Environmental Affairs (IDS-SPEA, Indiana University); as well as External Researcher at Fundación ECSIM (Medellin, Colombia). He focuses on the relationship between entrepreneurship and economic development under the institutional lenses.

Özgür Atılgan is Ph.D. in Management and Organizations and M.Sc. in Economics, both at Istanbul University, Turkey. B.Sc. in Business, Istanbul Bilgi University, Turkey. He holds a Minor in International Relations at German High School in Turkey. He works as Research Assistant at Istanbul Kultur University, Turkey.

Neeta Baporikar is currently Professor (Management) at Harold Pupkewitz Graduate School of Business (HP-GSB), Namibia University of Science and Technology, Namibia. Prior to this, she was Head-Scientific Research, with Ministry of Higher Education CAS-Salalah, Sultanate of Oman, Professor (Strategic Management and Entrepreneurship) at IIIT Pune and BITS India. With more than a decade of experience in the industry, consultancy, and training, she made a lateral switch to research and academics in 1995. Prof Baporikar holds D.Sc. (Management Studies) USA, Ph.D. in Management, the University of Pune INDIA with MBA (Distinction) and Law (Hons.) degrees. Apart from this, she is also an external reviewer, Oman Academic Accreditation Authority, Accredited Management Teacher, Qualified Trainer, Doctoral Guide and Board Member of Academics and Advisory Committee in accredited B-Schools. She has to her credit many conferred doctorates, is international and editorial advisory board member and reviewer for Emerald, IGI, Inderscience refereed journals, published numerous refereed research papers, and authored books in the area of entrepreneurship, strategy, management, and higher education.

Danny C. Barbery Montoya is an economist in Business Management specializing in Marketing at the Escuela Superior Politécnica del Litoral (ESPOL, Ecuador); Master in Business Administration from ESPAE (Ecuador); Master in Management and Strategic Marketing of Escuela de Organización Industrial E.O.I. (Spain); Master in Creation and Business Management of Nebrija University (Spain) and Doctor Cum Laude in Administrative Sciences specialized in Family Business of Nebrjia University (Spain). In his professional career, he has worked in national and internacional institutions such as IPG-Mediabrands, Industria Conservera del Guayas, Salud Corp., Marketing & Research Consultants, Junta de Beneficencia de Guayaquil, Servicio de Rentas Internas and MasterCard of Ecuador, merging administrative, commercial and financial roles in his professional experience. With 18 years of experience in his teaching career, he hasparticiped as a visiting professor in public and private universities in Ecuador. At present, he is the Academic Director to the Communication School of the Espíritu Santo University and professor in ESAI Business School.

Carlos Bautista-Nuques is a graduate in graphic and advertising design at the Escuela Superior Politécnica del Litoral (ESPOL); later he obtained his master's degree in brand management at the same university. Carlos has worked as a designer in important companies within Guayaquil, working as a designer, supervisor, and art director. Currently, he is art director for the multinational advertising agency Ogilvy, in Ecuador.

María-Soledad Castaño Martínez is PhD in Economics and Associate Professor of Applied Economics at the University of Castilla-La Mancha (Spain) where she teaches courses of Fiscal and Monetary Policy and International Economic Policy. Her research areas are Economic Growth, Economic Policy, Entrepreneurship and Innovation. She has published several articles in international specialised journals and books. She is also reviewer and Editorial Board Member of international journals.

Uriel Hitamar Castillo-Nazareno is a B.Sc. in Economics, Catholic University of Guayaquil, Ecuador. Specialization in International Negotiations, Catholic University of Santiago de Guayaquil, Ecuador, and has an M.Sc. in Territorial Development and Business Creation, Complutense University of Madrid, Spain. He is a Ph. D. in Business Sciences from Nebrija University, Spain, and a researcher and lecturer at the Catholic University of Santiago de Guayaquil, Ecuador.

Miguel-Ángel Galindo-Martín is Professor of Applied Economics at University of Castilla-La Mancha (Spain). His research areas are Economic Growth, Fiscal and Monetary Policies, Entrepreneurship and Ethics. He has published several articles on these topics in international specialised journals. He has edited books for several publishers such as Springer and Nova Press.

Yiqi Hu is pursuing a graduate degree at University College London, U.K..in the field of Organizational Change and Development. Her research topics include Peer Influence and Online Commerce.

Oliver Keels is a lecturer of political science at Wenzhou-Kean University, China. He is a Ph.D. (c) in International and Comparative Education at the University of Minnesota, USA, and has an M.Sc. in Diplomacy and International Commerce, University of Kentucky, USA. He has a B.A. in German and Classical Civilizations, Berea College, USA.

Rob Kim Marjerison is Asst Professor of Global Business at Wenzhou-Kean University in Wenzhou, China. His previous affiliations include; Royal University of Bhutan, Royal Thimphu College, Endiccott College of International Studies - Woosong University, Universidad Tecnologico de Monterrey. Dr. Marjerison has a PhD in International Business from the International School of Management in Paris France, a Master of Science in Information Systems from Louisiana State University, and a Masters in Public Administration from California State University. His research interests include Sino-US Trade, Sustainable Economic Development, Organizational and New venture Assessment and Social Entrepreneurship.

Montserrat Mata Fernández has a degree in Computer Science with a Master in Business Management and several certifications as PMP Certification and ITIL v3 Foundation among others. Collaborator in articles and papers. Wide experience as Project Manager, dealing with national and international projects.

Jessica Silvana Matute-Petroche is a B.Ing. in Administration with an M.Sc. in Business Administration, University of Guayaquil, Ecuador. Ph. D. candidate in Business Administration, Catholic University of Buenos Aires, Argentina. Professor at the Catholic University of Santiago de Guayaquil, Ecuador. Expert in University Institutional Budgets and the Management of University Treasury.

María-Teresa Méndez Picazo is Associate Professor of Financial Economy and Accounting at the University Complutense of Madrid (Spain). Her research areas are Entrepreneurship, International Accounting, Financial Analysis and Accounting Statements. She has published several articles on these topics in international specialised journals and books. She is editor and member of Editorial Review Board of different international journals. She is also reviewer of various international journals.

Anlly Luz Mosquera is a psychologist. Magister in Organization Management. Specialist in Assessment of Damage in Mental Health with knowledge of Public Policies. Nine years of professional experience in training and social inclusion processes for vulnerable populations. Assessment of Damage in people victims of a traumatic event, and Management of human talent.

Maria Noguera is Head and Professor of Tourism and Hotel Management School and scientific committee member of the Centre for University Entrepreneurship (CIEU-UAB) at Universitat Autònoma de

Barcelona (UAB). She received a PhD (International Doctorate in Entrepreneurship and Management) from UAB. Her research areas are focused on institutions and female entrepreneurship.

Beatriz Olalla-Caballero has a Ph.D. in Computer Science, Information Technologies and Knowledge Society, Pontifical University of Salamanca (Spain). M.Sc. in Quality Engineer, American Society for Quality. B.Sc. in Telecommunication Engineer, University of Valladolid (Spain). Project Management Professional, and ITIL Expert. Several years working in Information Technologies services and Quality and Projects Management. Author of papers and articles about quality, projects, and Information Technologies.

Omar Ovalle has a Ph.D. in Business Administration, Master in Organization Management, Maitrise in Sciences, MSc, Master in Business Management and Creation, Specialist in Personnel Administration, Practicing Lawyer, Comprehensive Internal Auditor, Internal Auditor in ISO 27001-2013 Standards Management System Information Security (ISMS), ISO 2600–2010 Corporate Social Responsibility, Certificate in competition standards in consulting, with extensive experience in the fields of law. He has twenty-five years of professional experience in business consulting and university teaching in face-to-face and virtual methodology (undergraduate and postgraduate) in areas of Business Law, Human Management, Strategic Planning, Legal and Fiscal Environment of the Company, Management and Development of Organizational Competences, Organization Business and Human Resources Management, Leadership, Entrepreneurship, and Research seminars.

María del Pilar Ramírez-Salazar has a Ph.D. in Business Sciences, Universidad Antonio de Nebrija, Spain. Ph.D. in Management, Universidad EAN, Colombia. Master in Management, Universidad EAN, Colombia. Maître es Sciences Université du Québec a Chicoutimi, Canada. Specialist in management and evaluation indicators for Higher Education Institutions. Business Administrator, Universidad EAN, Colombia. Education Professional, Universidad Pedagógica Nacional, Colombia. Professor at the School of Administration, Finance and Economic Science, Universidad EAN, Colombia. Senior researcher of the G3Pymes Research Group in Innovation, Entrepreneurship, Management, and Sustainability. Author of research articles indexed in international and national journals, book chapters and book editor with Springer, and IGI-Global. Her main research topics are Innovation, Management, Sustainability, Entrepreneurship.

Carlos Salcedo-Perez has a PhD. in Business Sciences. Master of Science in Economic Development, Bachelor of Science in Business Administration. Professor and researcher at Universidad EAN, Colombia.

Andreu Turro is Serra-Hunter fellow at the Universitat Autònoma de Barcelona (UAB) Department of Business and member of the Centre for Entrepreneurship and Social Innovation Research (CREIS). Previously, he worked as an assistant professor at the Utrecht University School of Economics (the Netherlands). He received a Ph.D. (International Doctorate in Entrepreneurship and Management -IDEM) from UAB. He has a double degree in Business Administration and Market Research by the UAB and a Master in Marketing Management by ESADE Business School. His research is focused on conditioning factors for corporate entrepreneurship from a quantitative analysis. He published several academic papers in this research field. Currently he is participating in various Spanish and international projects on this topic.

David Urbano is professor of entrepreneurship at the Department of Business and deputy director at the Centre for Entrepreneurship and Social Innovation Research -CREIS- (Universitat Autònoma de Barcelona), and ICREA-Academia Research Fellow. His research focuses on the analysis of factors affecting entrepreneurship in different contexts, using institutional economics as a theoretical framework, and combining quantitative and qualitative methodologies. He participates in several international research projects (e.g. GEM, PSED, GUESSS) and also regularly visits Haas School of Business (University of California, Berkeley).

Yuxi Zhao is a Lecturer of Economics at Wenzhou-Kean University. She received her PhD from the Ohio State University. Her research interests include entrepreneurship, sustainability, commercialization of natural resources, and connecting landscape pixels with the market to create new ventures.

Index

V

www.ingramcontent.com/pod-product-compliance
Lightning Source LLC
LaVergne TN
LVHW060425300926
849162LV00006B/1527